JESSICA JONES: ALIAS

Brian Michael Bendis
WRITER

Michael Gaydos
ARTIST

Matt Hollingsworth
COLORIST

Mark Bagley, Art Thibert & Dean White
JEWEL SEQUENCES

Rick Mays & Dean White
JEAN GREY FLASHBACK

Cory Petit
LETTERER

David Mack
COVER ART

Marc Sumerak & Stephanie Moore
ASSISTANT EDITORS

C.B. Cebulski, Tom Brevoort & Andy Schmidt
EDITORS

ALIaS CREATED BY BRIAN MICHAEL BENDIS & MICHAEL GAYDOS

Collection Editor: Jennifer Grünwald
Assistant Editor: Sarah Brunstad
Associate Managing Editor: Alex Starbuck
Editor, Special Projects: Mark D. Beazley
Senior Editor, Special Projects: Jeff Youngquist
SVP Print, Sales & Marketing: David Gabriel
Book Designer: Jay Bowen

Editor in Chief: Axel Alonso
Chief Creative Officer: Joe Quesada
Publisher: Dan Buckley
Executive Producer: Alan Fine

JESSICA JONES: ALIAS VOL. 4. Contains material originally published in magazine form as ALIAS #22-28. First printing 2015. ISBN# 978-0-7851-9858-1. Published by MARVEL WORLDWIDE, INC., a subsidiary of MARVEL ENTERTAINMENT, LLC. OFFICE OF PUBLICATION: 135 West 50th Street, New York, NY 10020. **Printed in the U.S.A.** ALAN FINE, President, Marvel Entertainment; DAN BUCKLEY, President, TV, Publishing and Brand Management; JOE QUESADA, Chief Creative Officer; TOM BREVOORT, SVP of Publishing; DAVID BOGART, SVP of Operations & Procurement, Publishing; C.B. CEBULSKI, VP of International Development & Brand Management; DAVID GABRIEL, SVP Print, Sales & Marketing; JIM O'KEEFE, VP of Operations & Logistics; DAN CARR, Executive Director of Publishing Technology; SUSAN CRESPI, Editorial Operations Manager; ALEX MORALES, Publishing Operations Manager; STAN LEE, Chairman Emeritus. For information regarding advertising in Marvel Comics or on Marvel.com, please contact Jonathan Rheingold, VP of Custom Solutions & Ad Sales, at jrheingold@marvel.com. For Marvel subscription inquiries, please call 800-217-9158. **Manufactured between 11/6/2015 and 12/14/2015 by R.R. DONNELLEY, INC., SALEM, VA, USA.**

10 9 8 7 6 5 4 3 2 1

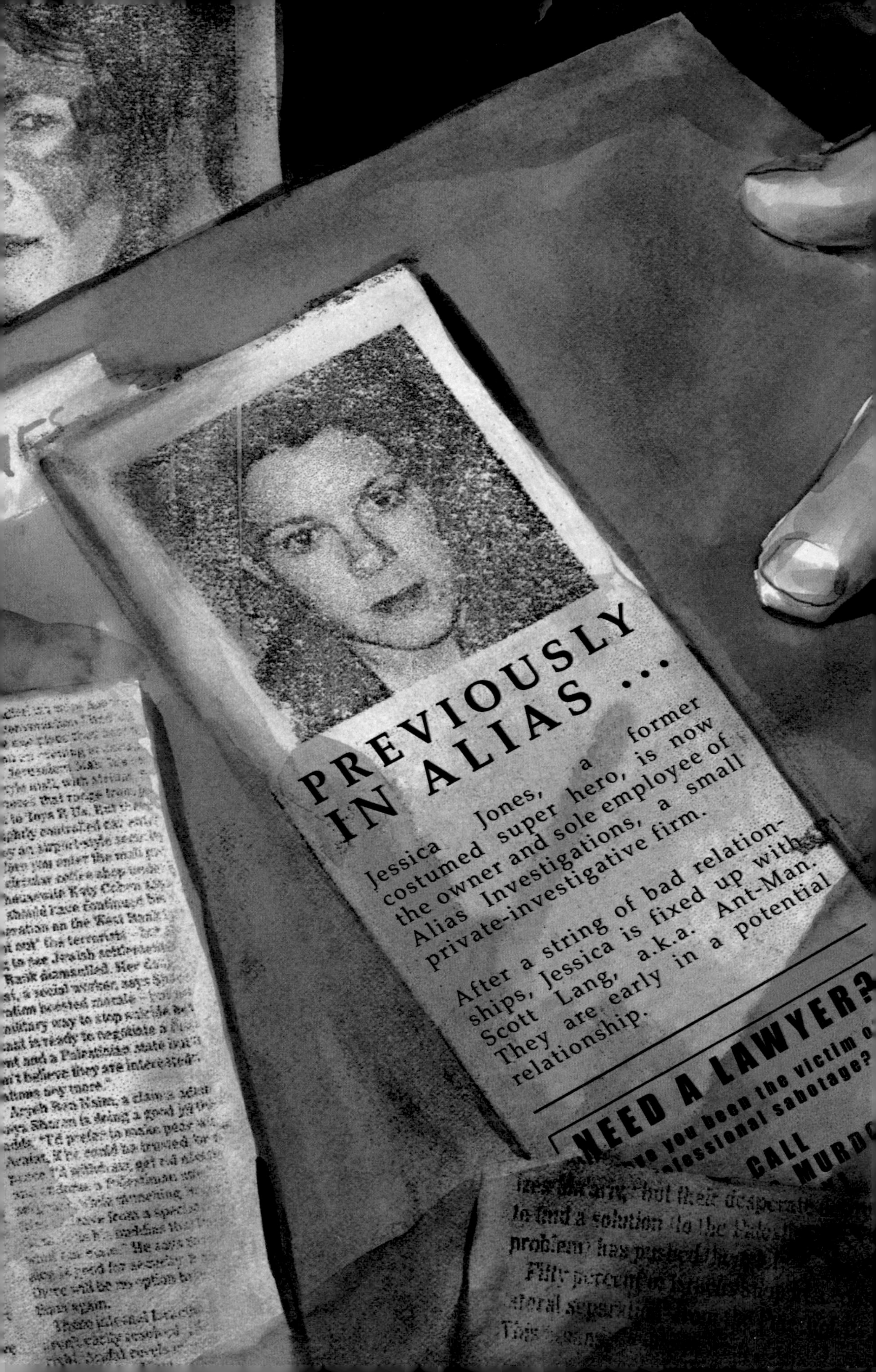
PREVIOUSLY IN ALIAS ...
Jessica Jones, a former costumed super hero, is now the owner and sole employee of Alias Investigations, a small private-investigative firm.
After a string of bad relationships, Jessica is fixed up with Scott Lang, a.k.a. Ant-Man. They are early in a potential relationship.
NEED A LAWYER?
CALL

M[redacted]HIGH

ISSUE #22

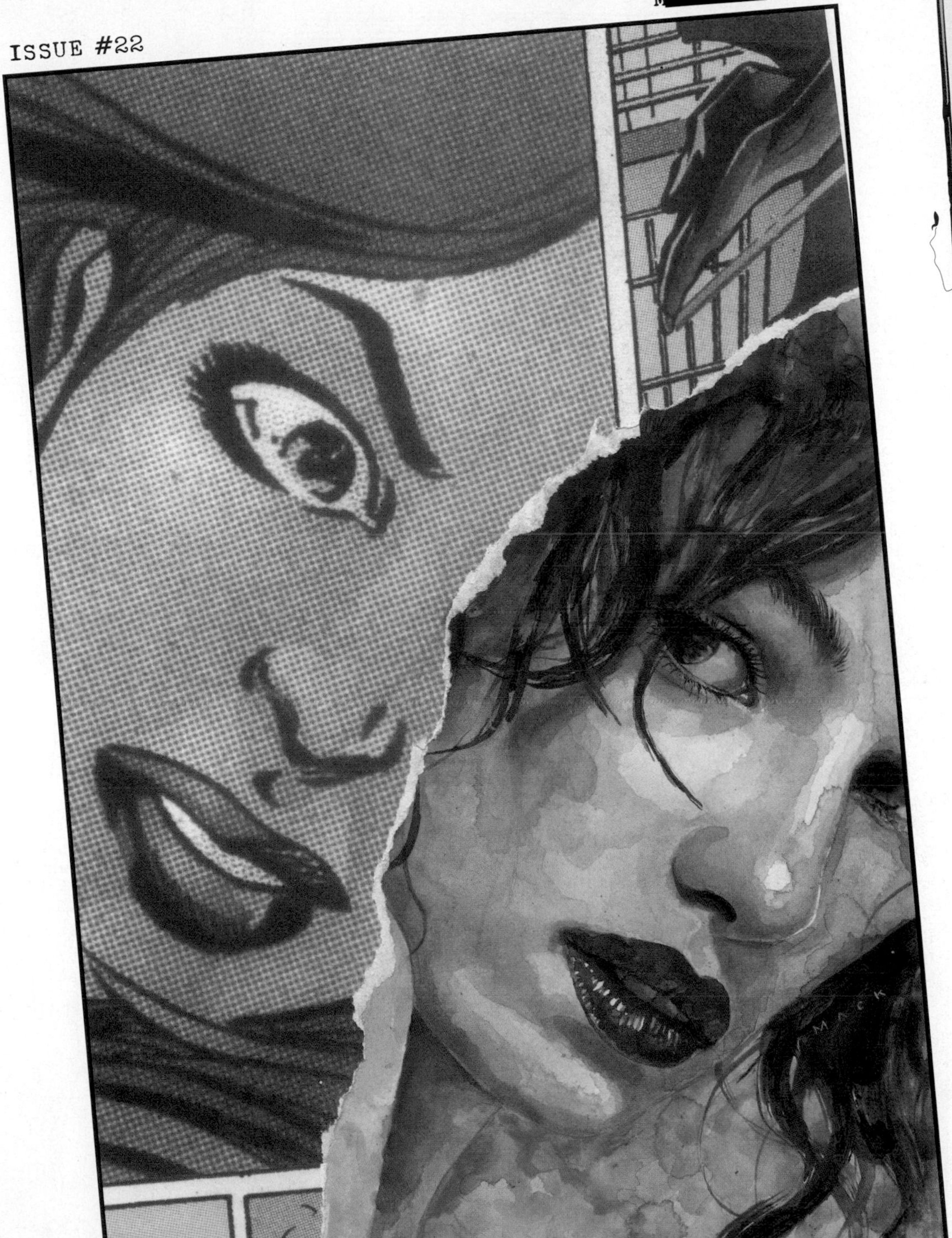

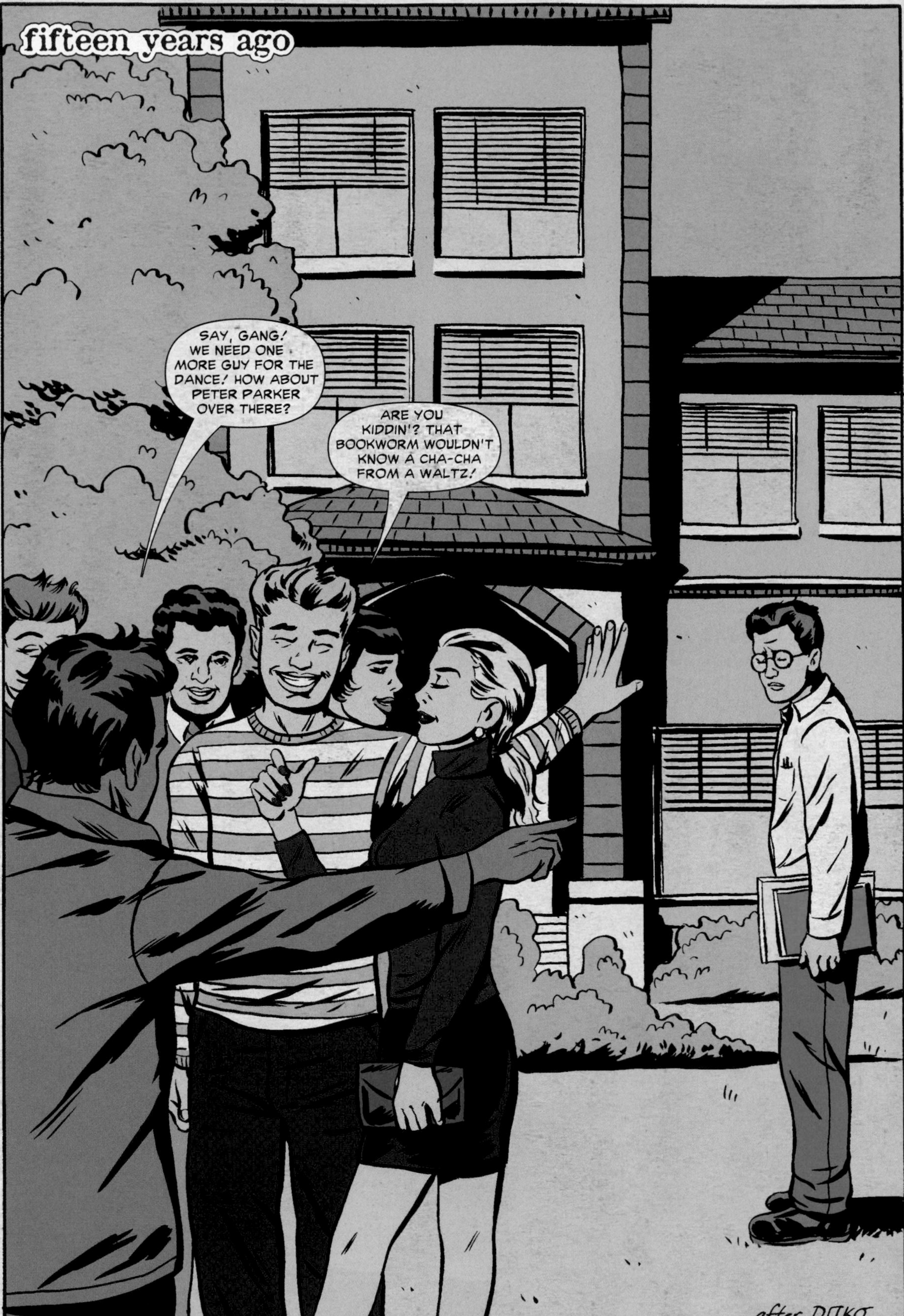
fifteen years ago
SAY, GANG! WE NEED ONE MORE GUY FOR THE DANCE! HOW ABOUT PETER PARKER OVER THERE?
ARE YOU KIDDIN'? THAT BOOKWORM WOULDN'T KNOW A CHA-CHA FROM A WALTZ!
after DITKO

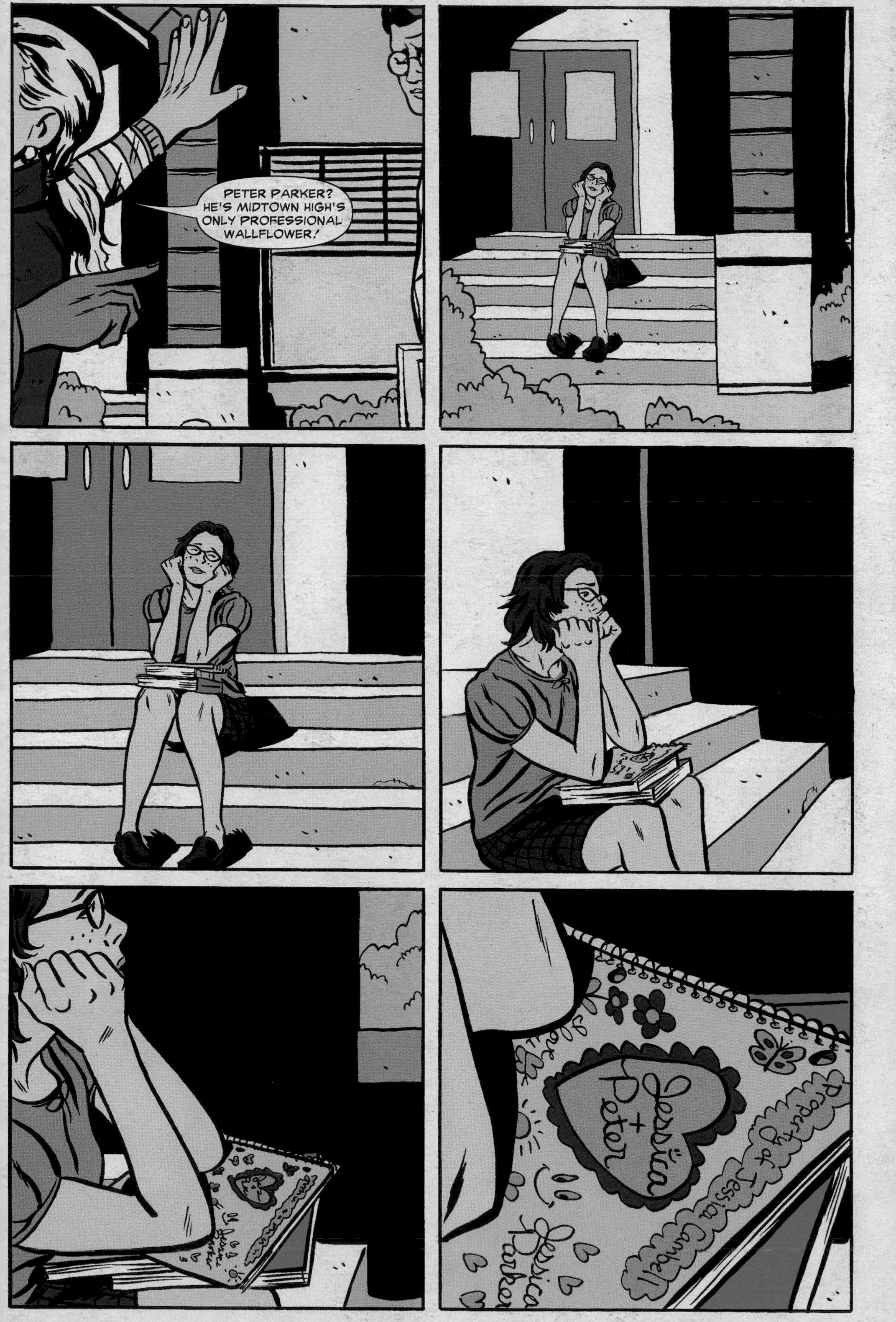
PETER PARKER? HE'S MIDTOWN HIGH'S ONLY PROFESSIONAL WALLFLOWER!
Jessica + Peter
Property of Jessica Campbell
Jessica Parker

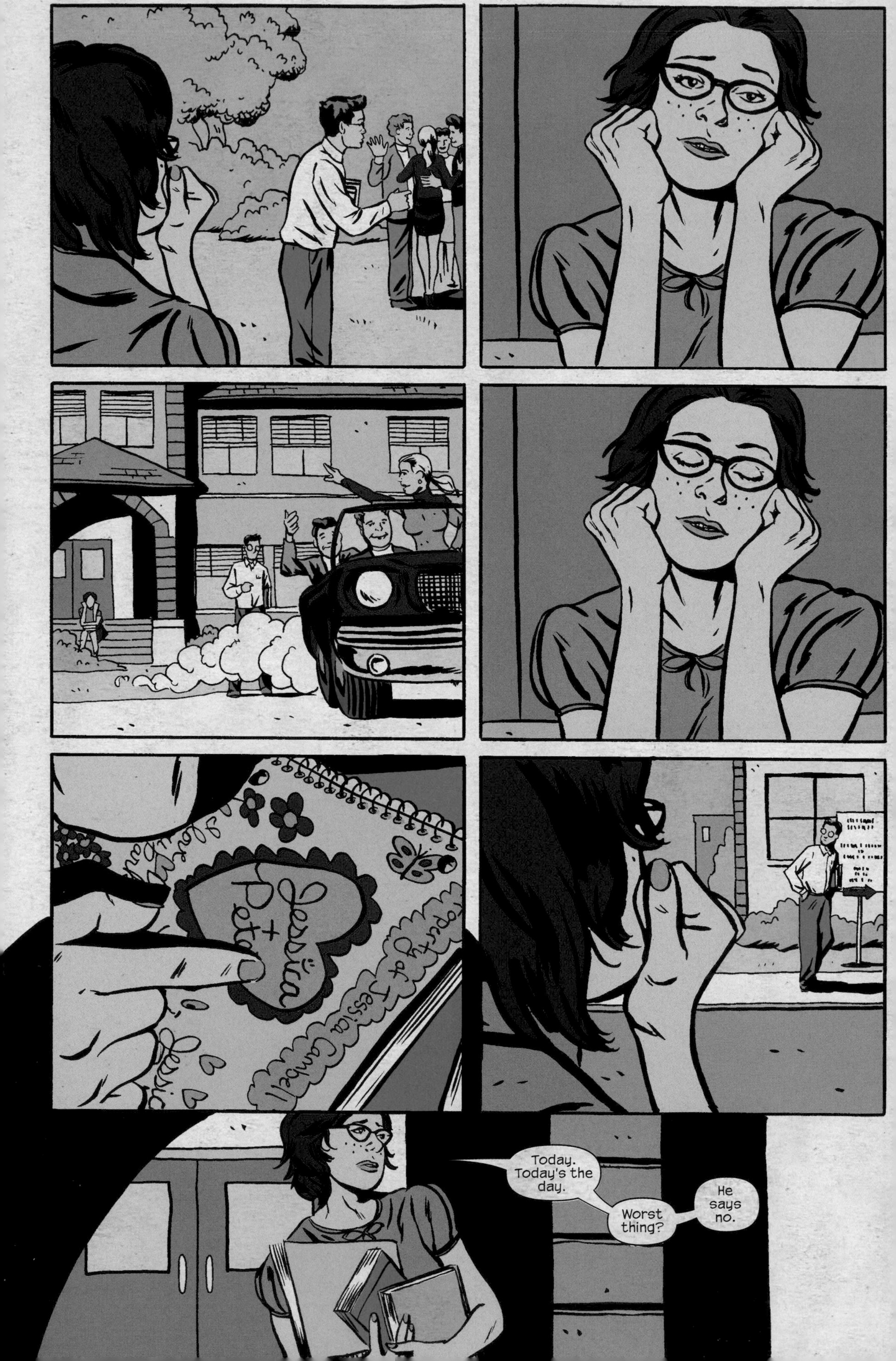
Today. Today's the day.
Worst thing?
He says no.

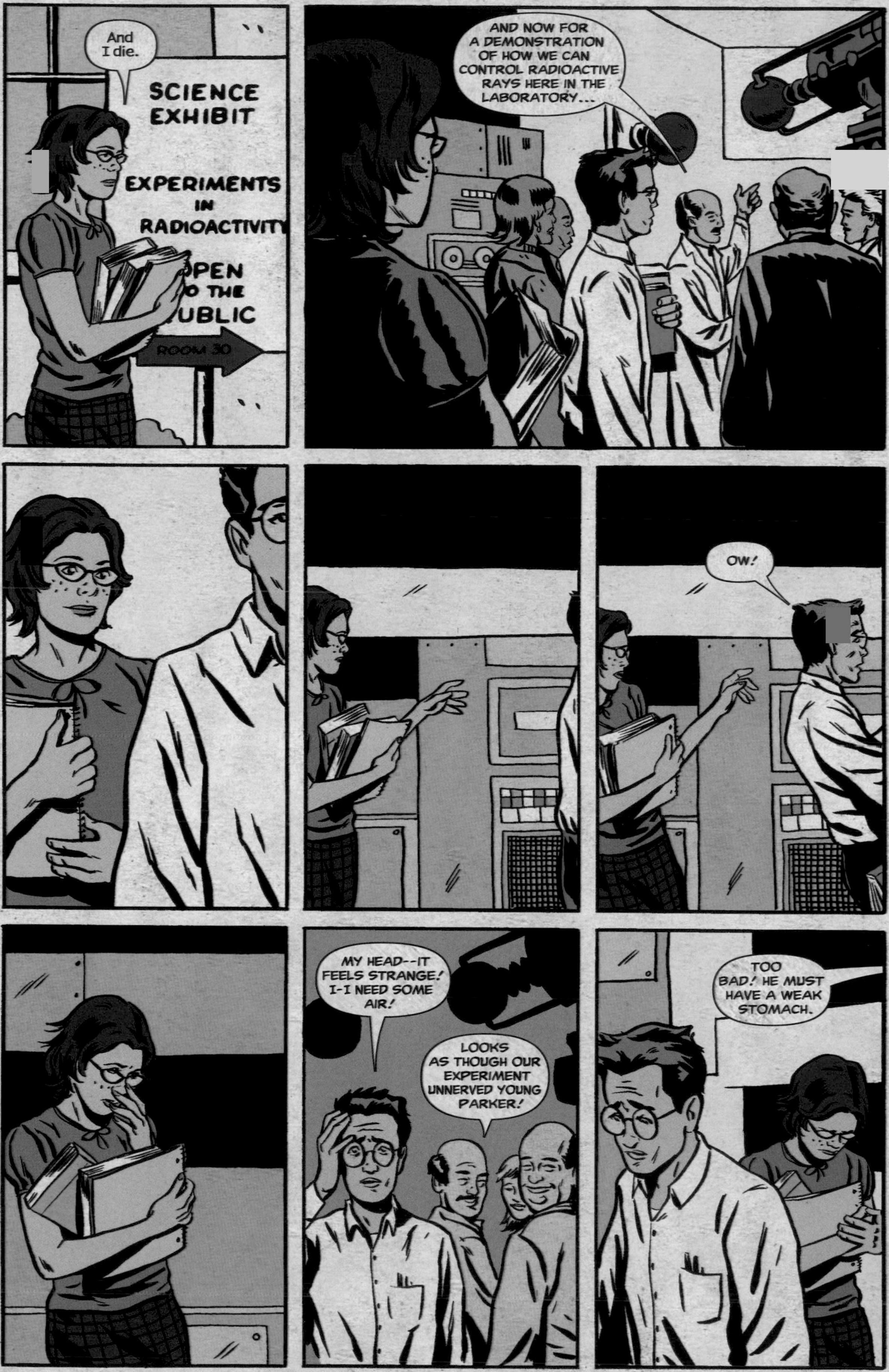
And I die.
SCIENCE EXHIBIT
EXPERIMENTS IN RADIOACTIVITY
OPEN TO THE PUBLIC
ROOM 30
AND NOW FOR A DEMONSTRATION OF HOW WE CAN CONTROL RADIOACTIVE RAYS HERE IN THE LABORATORY...
OW!
MY HEAD--IT FEELS STRANGE! I-I NEED SOME AIR!
LOOKS AS THOUGH OUR EXPERIMENT UNNERVED YOUNG PARKER!
TOO BAD! HE MUST HAVE A WEAK STOMACH.

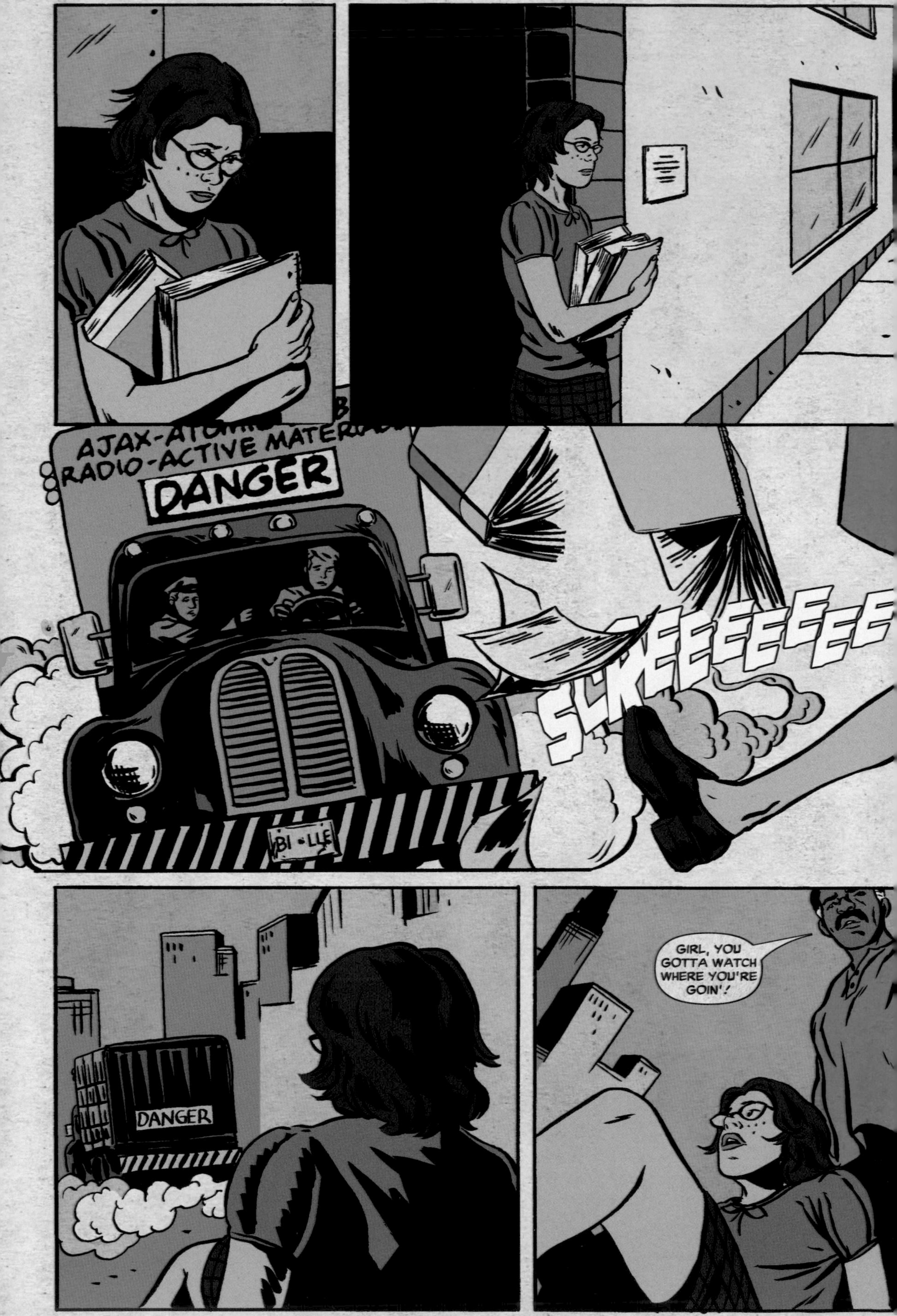
AJAX-ATOMIC
RADIO-ACTIVE MATER
DANGER
SCREEEEEEEEE
DANGER
GIRL, YOU GOTTA WATCH WHERE YOU'RE GOIN'!

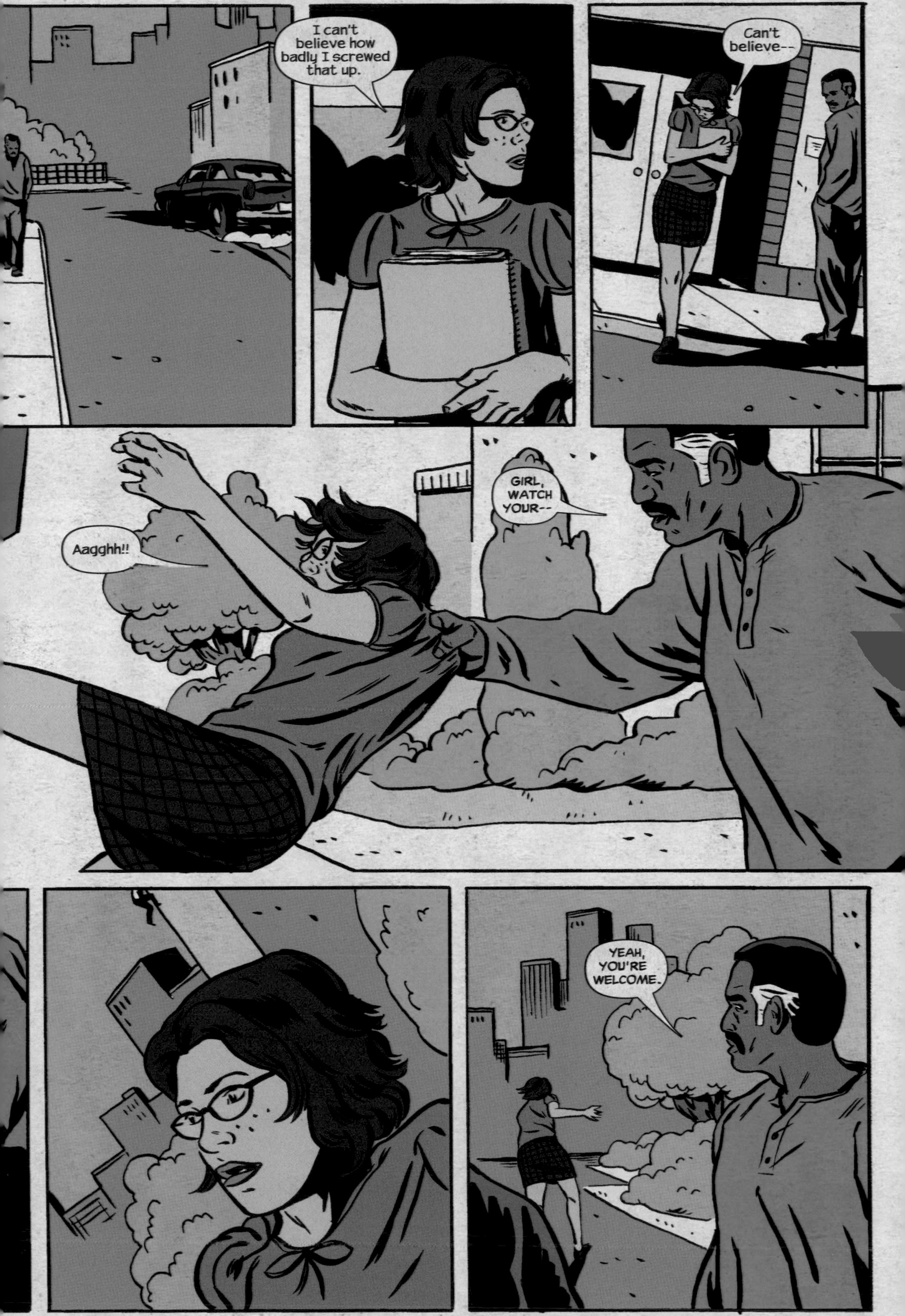
I can't believe how badly I screwed that up.
Can't believe--
Aagghh!!
GIRL, WATCH YOUR--
YEAH, YOU'RE WELCOME.

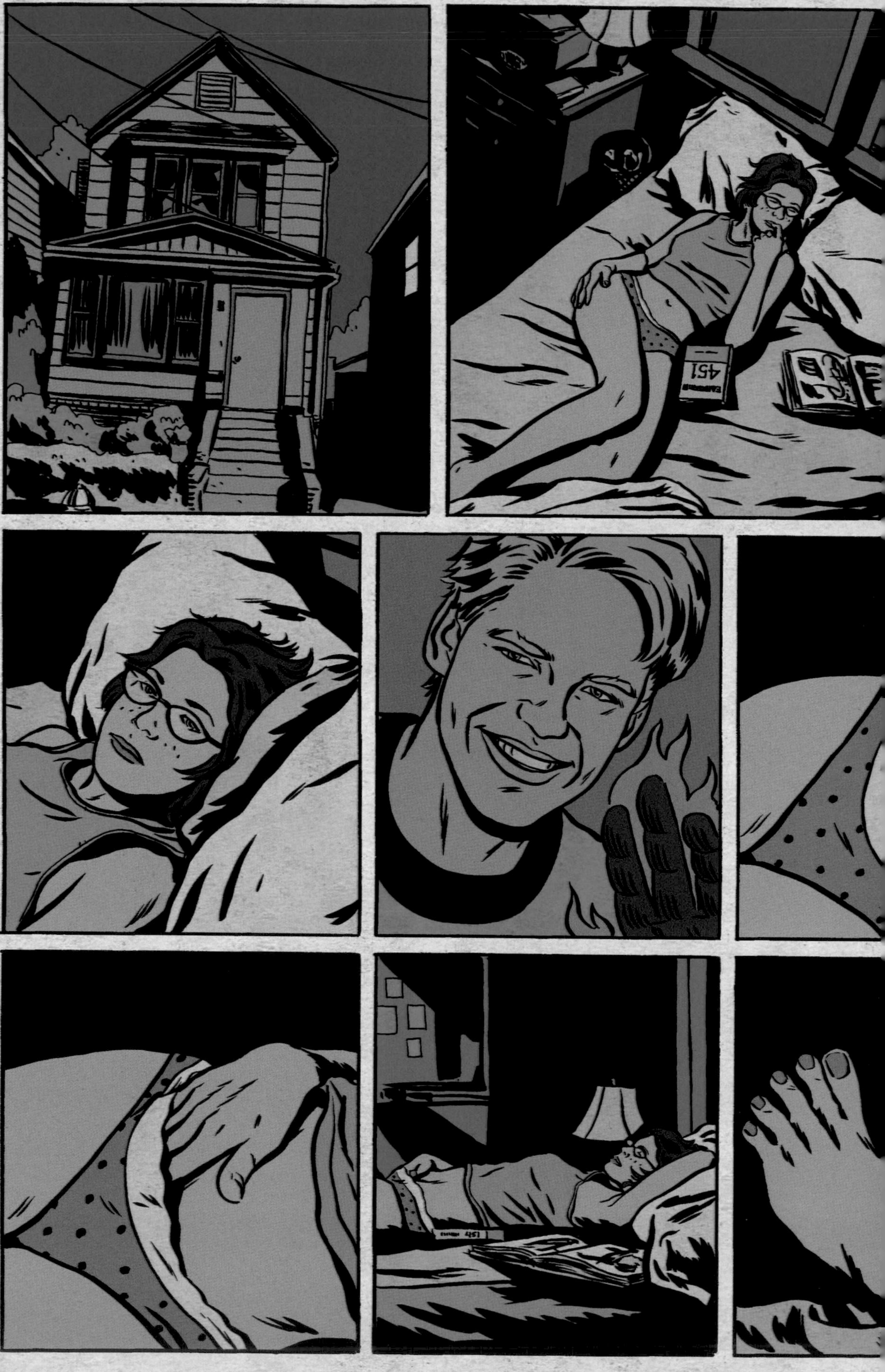
451

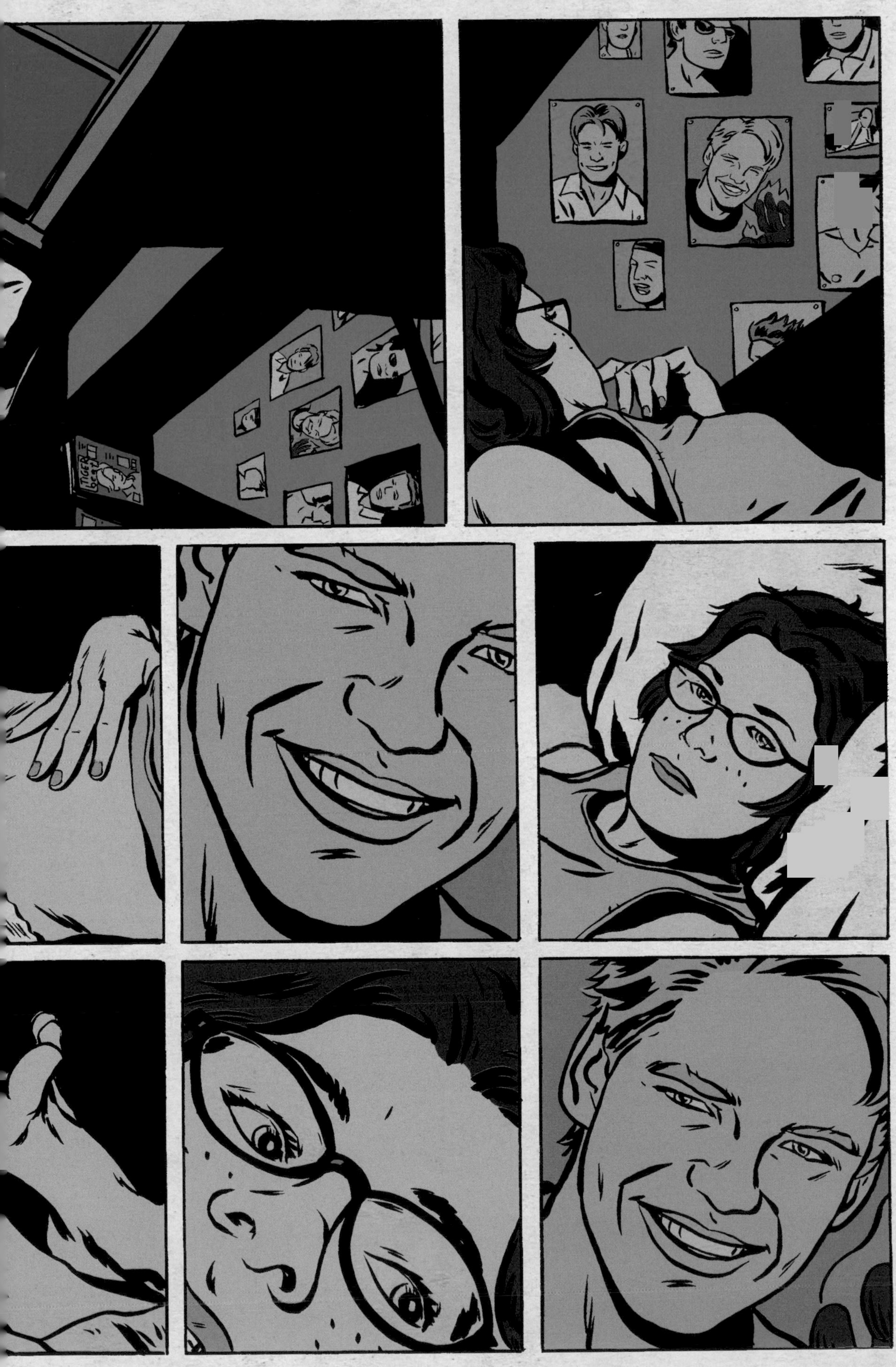
TIGER beat

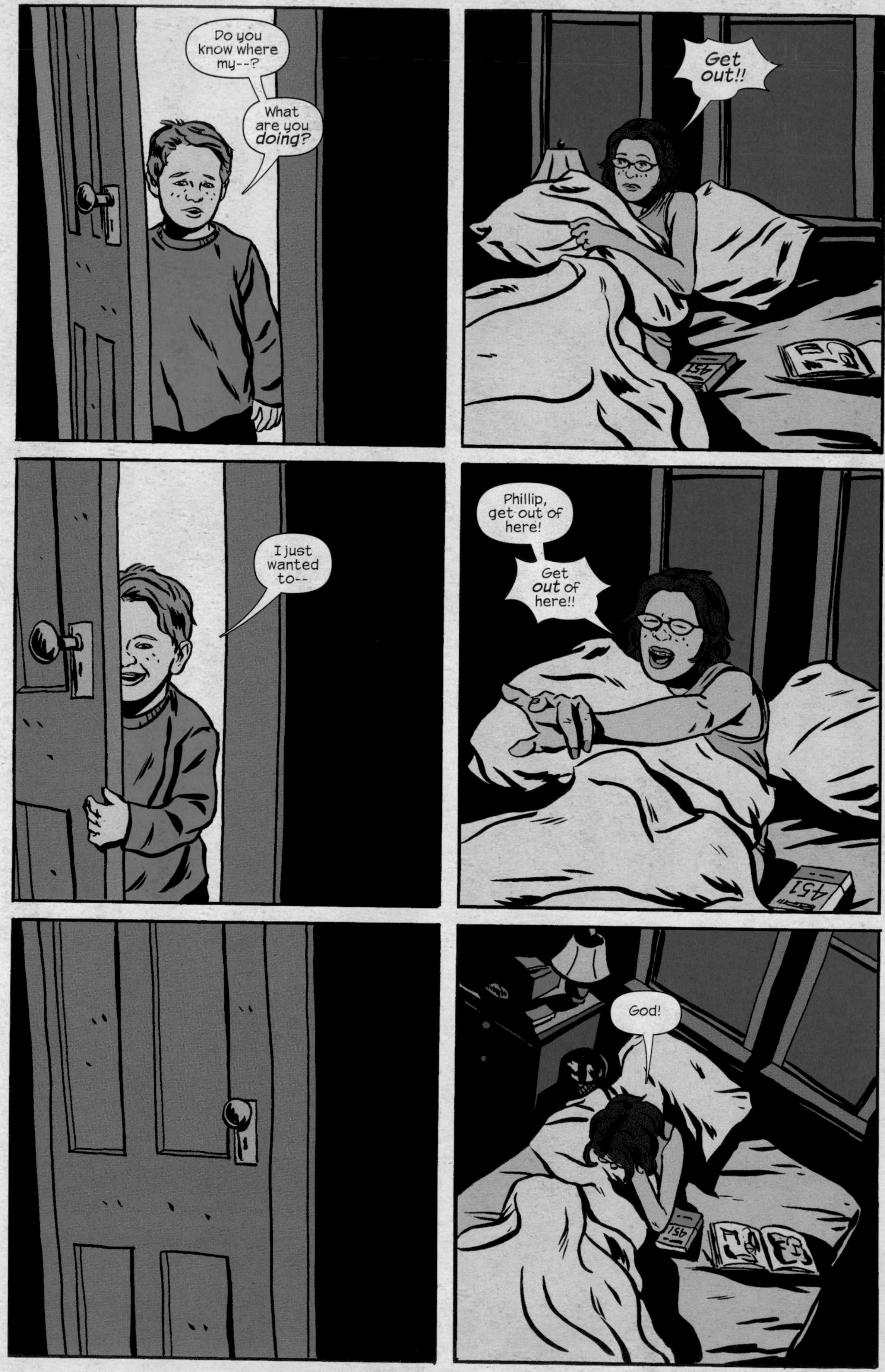

Do you know where my--?
What are you doing?
Get out!!
I just wanted to--
Phillip, get out of here!
Get out of here!!
God!

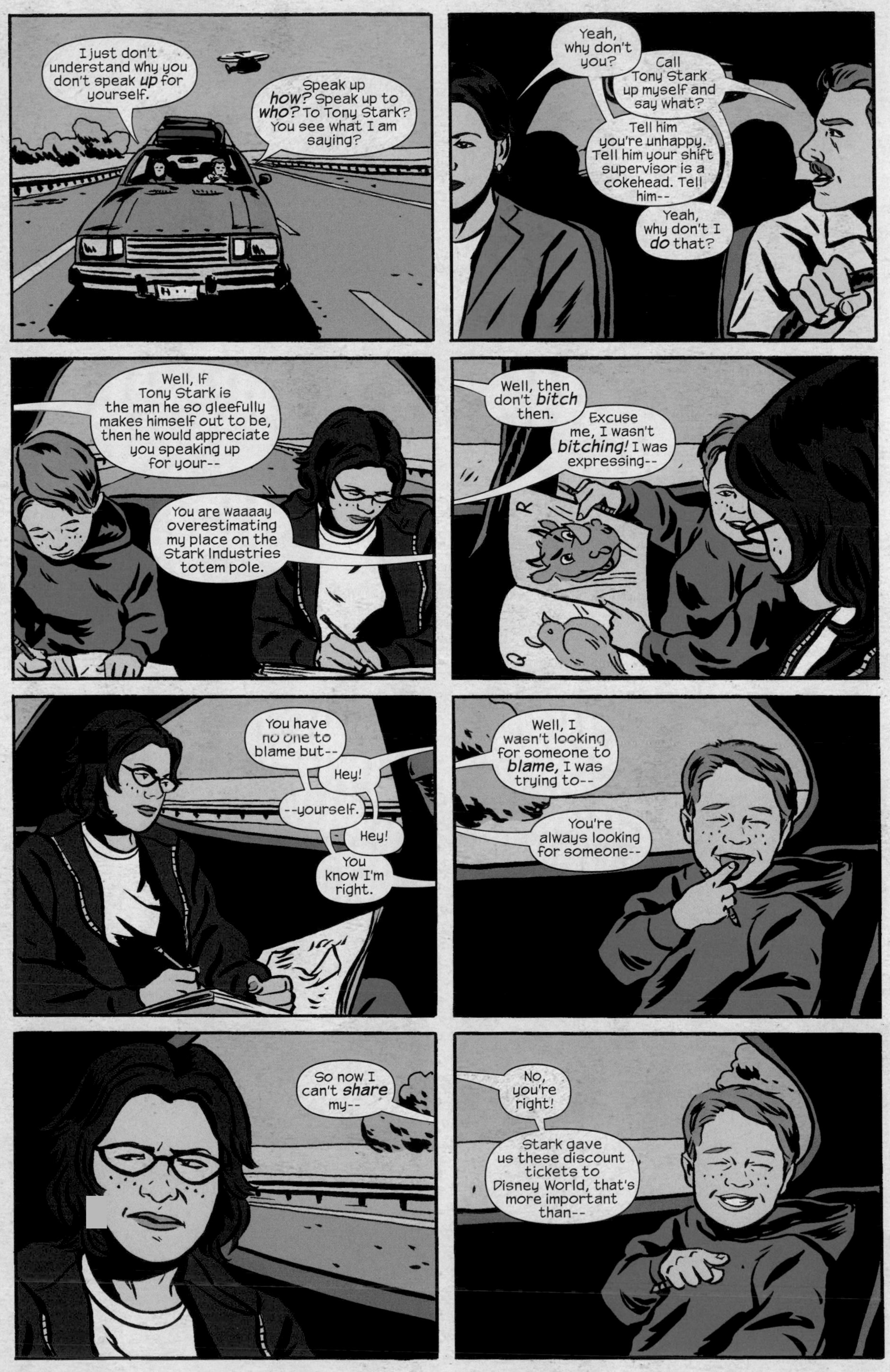
I just don't understand why you don't speak *up* for yourself.
Speak up *how?* Speak up to *who?* To Tony Stark? You see what I am saying?
Yeah, why don't you?
Call Tony Stark up myself and say what?
Tell him you're unhappy. Tell him your shift supervisor is a cokehead. Tell him--
Yeah, why don't I *do* that?
Well, If Tony Stark is the man he so gleefully makes himself out to be, then he would appreciate you speaking up for your--
You are waaaay overestimating my place on the Stark Industries totem pole.
Well, then don't *bitch* then.
Excuse me, I wasn't *bitching!* I was expressing--
You have no one to blame but--
Hey!
--yourself.
Hey!
You know I'm right.
Well, I wasn't looking for someone to *blame,* I was trying to--
You're always looking for someone--
So now I can't *share* my--
No, you're right!
Stark gave us these discount tickets to Disney World, that's more important than--

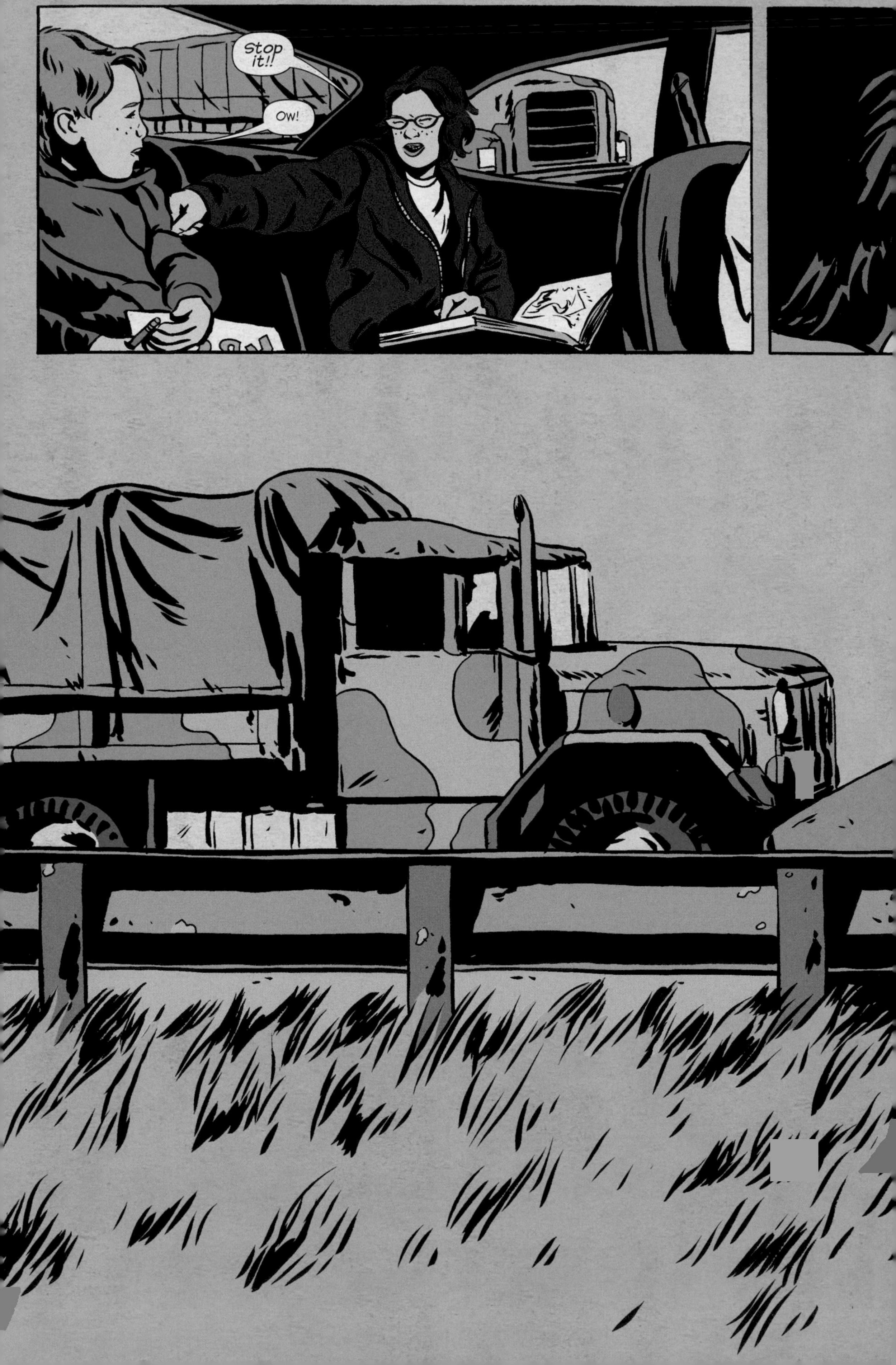
Stop it!!
OW!

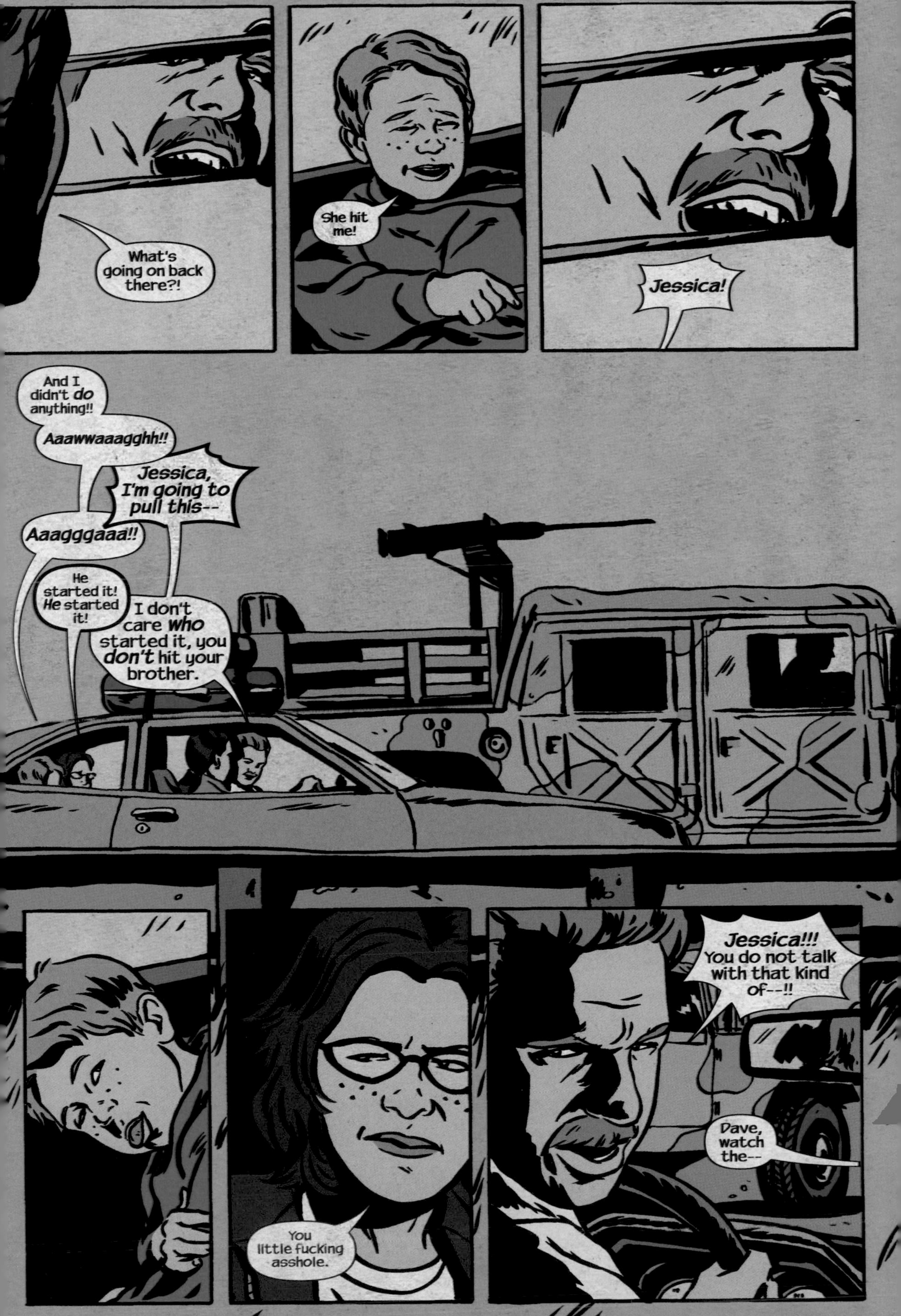
What's going on back there?!
She hit me!
Jessica!
And I didn't do anything!!
Aaawwaaagghh!!
Jessica, I'm going to pull this--
Aaagggaaa!!
He started it! He started it!
I don't care who started it, you don't hit your brother.
You little fucking asshole.
Jessica!!! You do not talk with that kind of--!!
Dave, watch the--

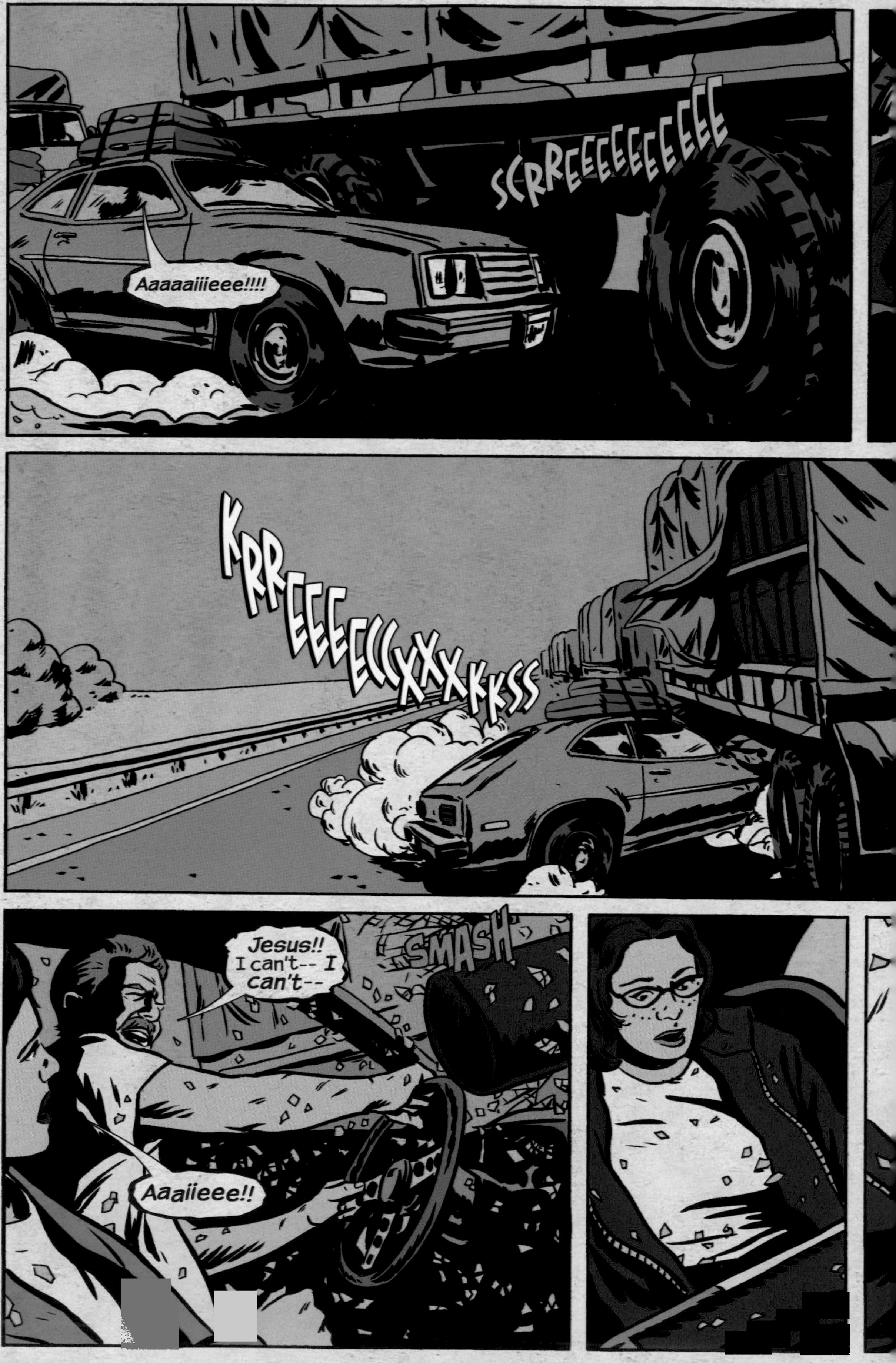

SCRREEEEEEEEEE
Aaaaaiiieee!!!!
KRREEEECCXXXKKSS
Jesus!! I can't-- I can't--
SMASH
Aaaiieee!!

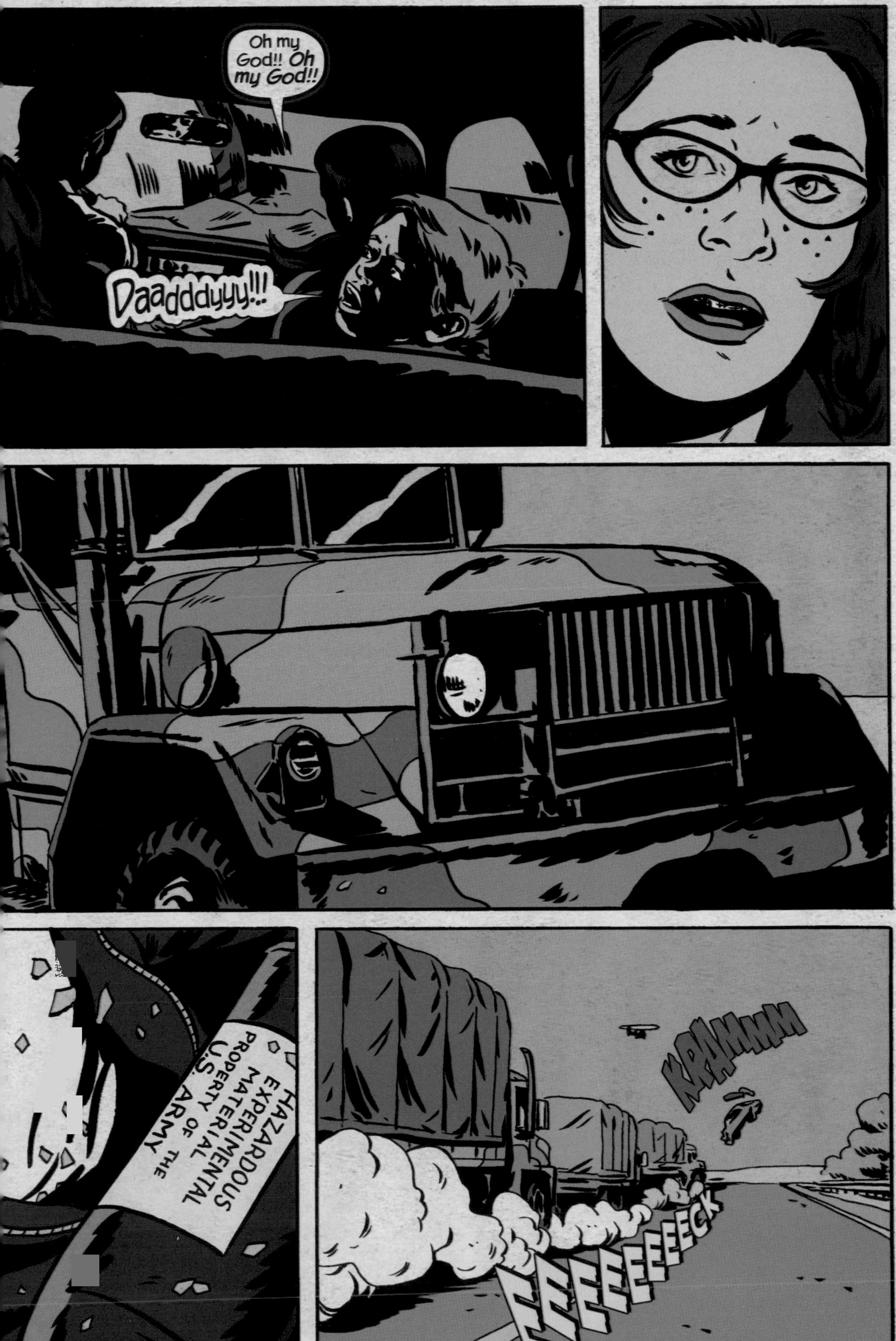
Oh my God!! Oh my God!!
Daaddddyyy!!!
HAZARDOUS EXPERIMENTAL MATERIAL PROPERTY OF THE U.S. ARMY
KRAMMM
EEEEEEEEECK

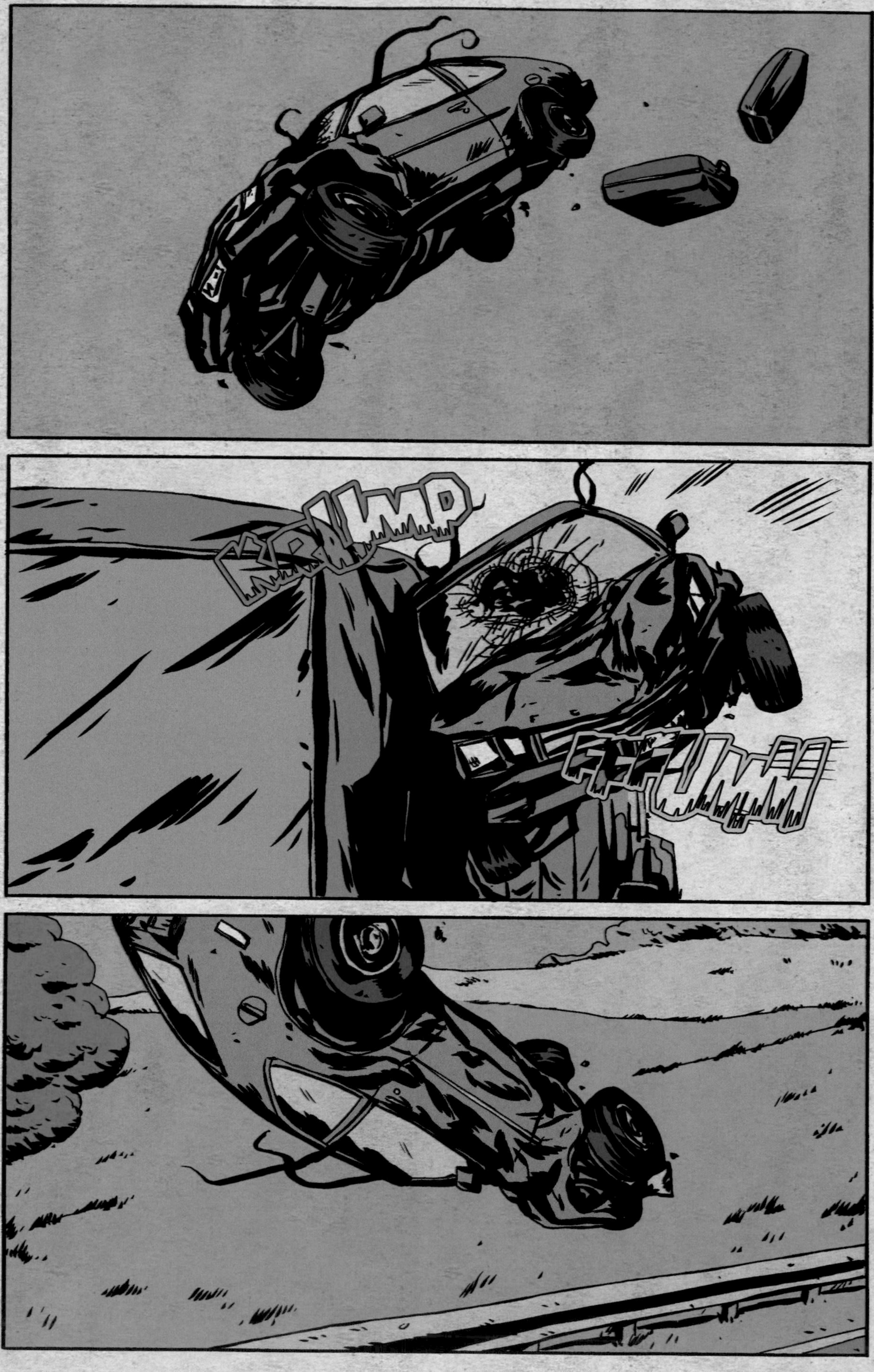
KRUMP
FFFUMM

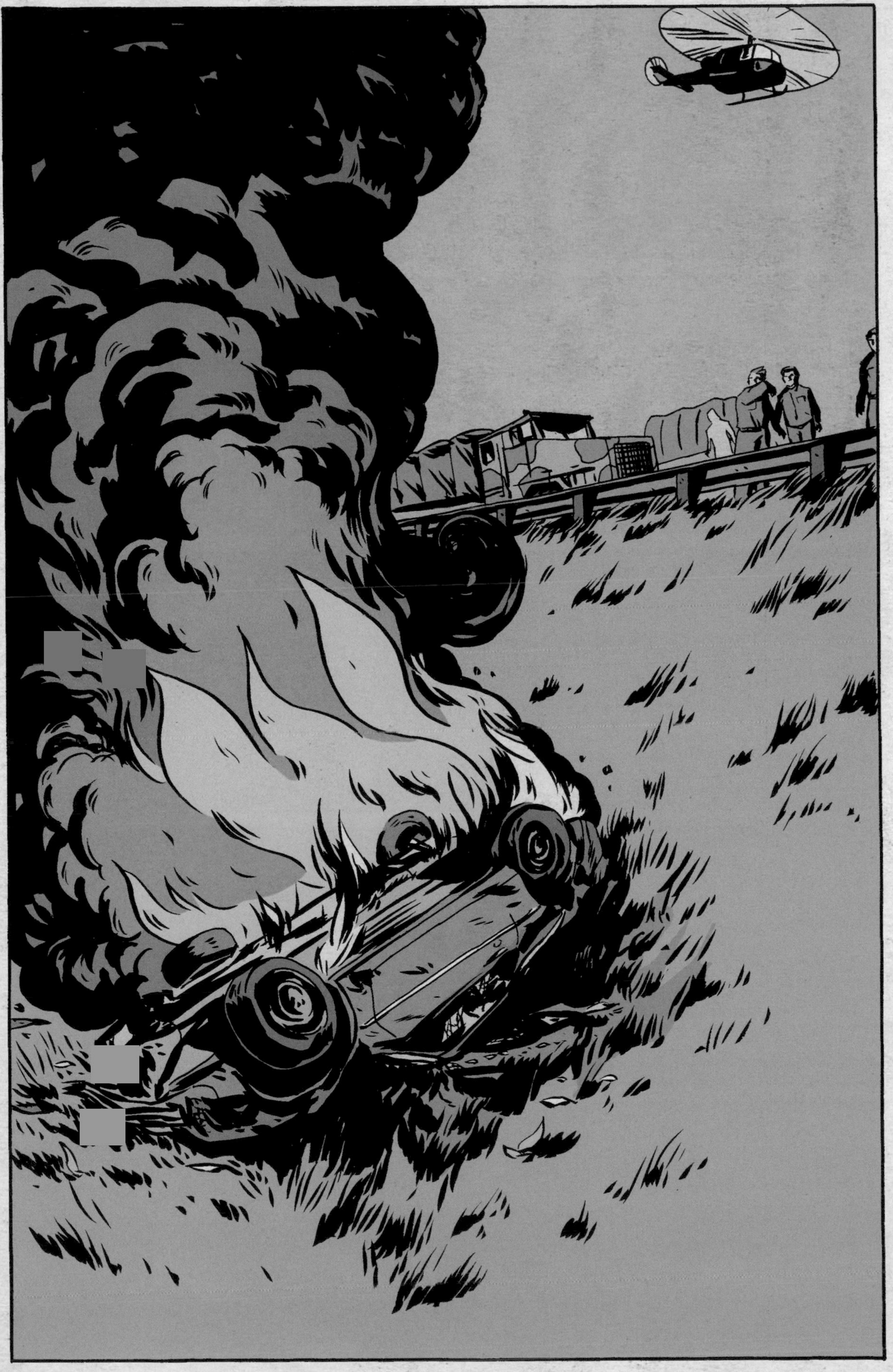

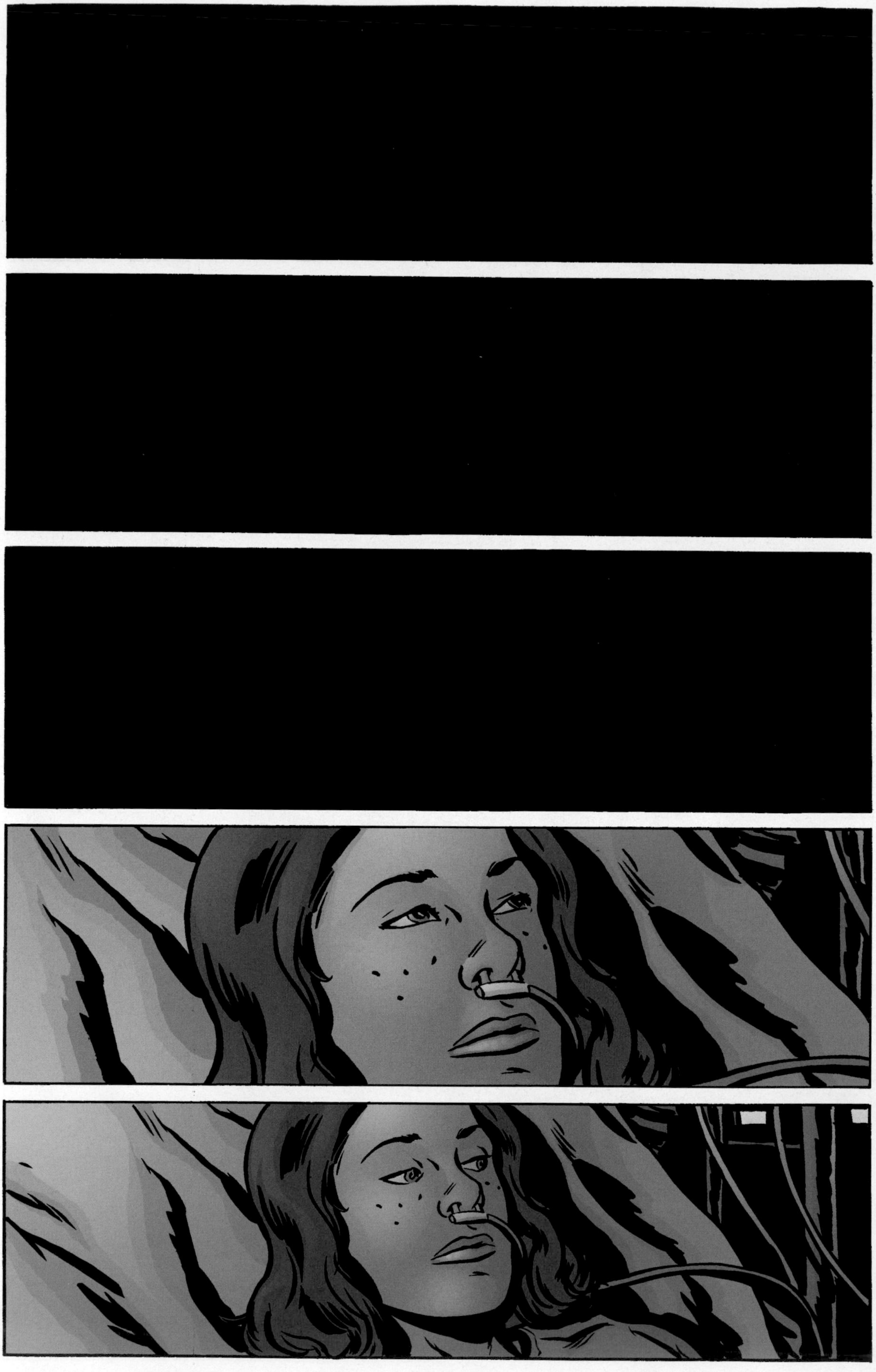

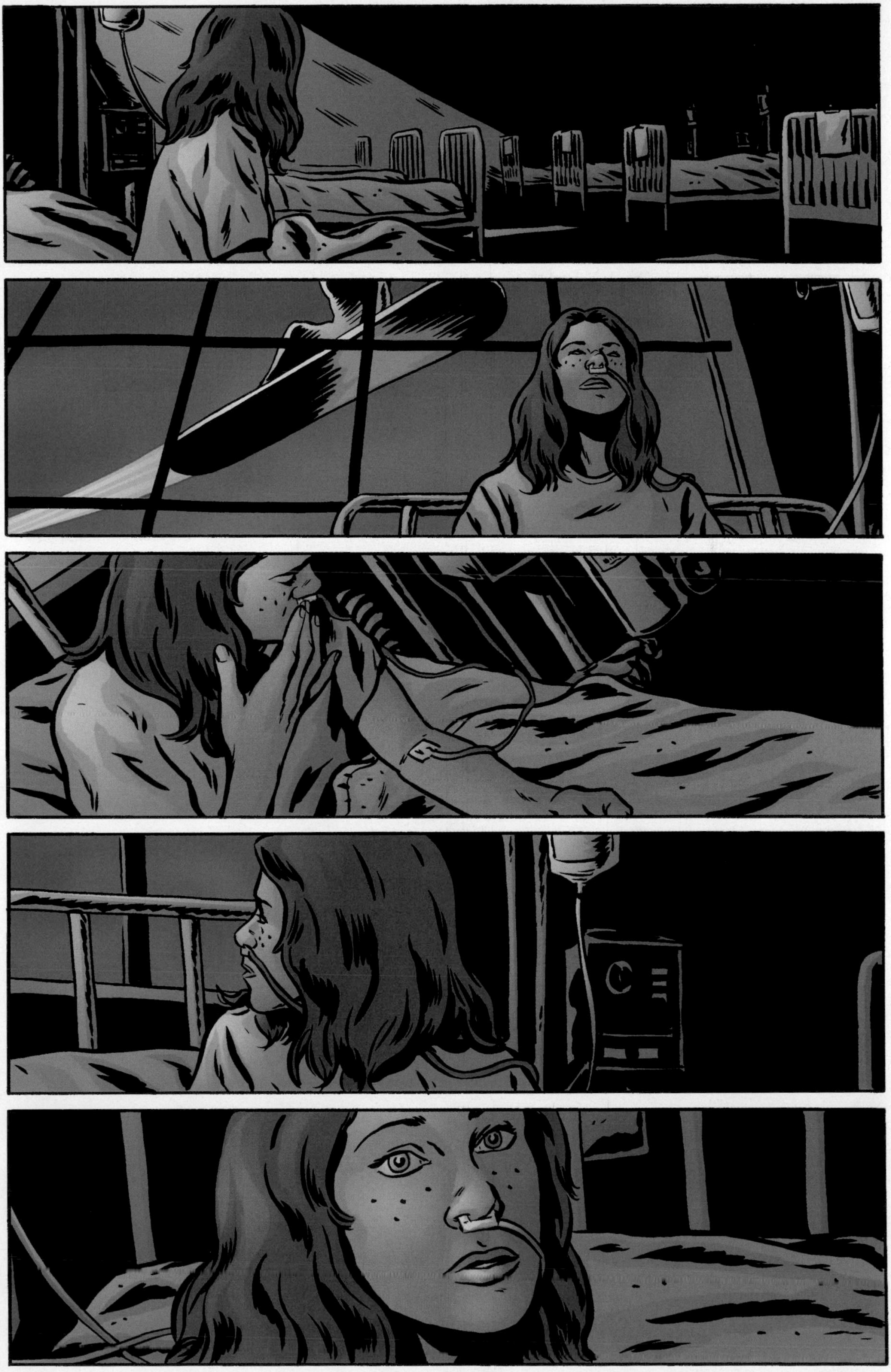

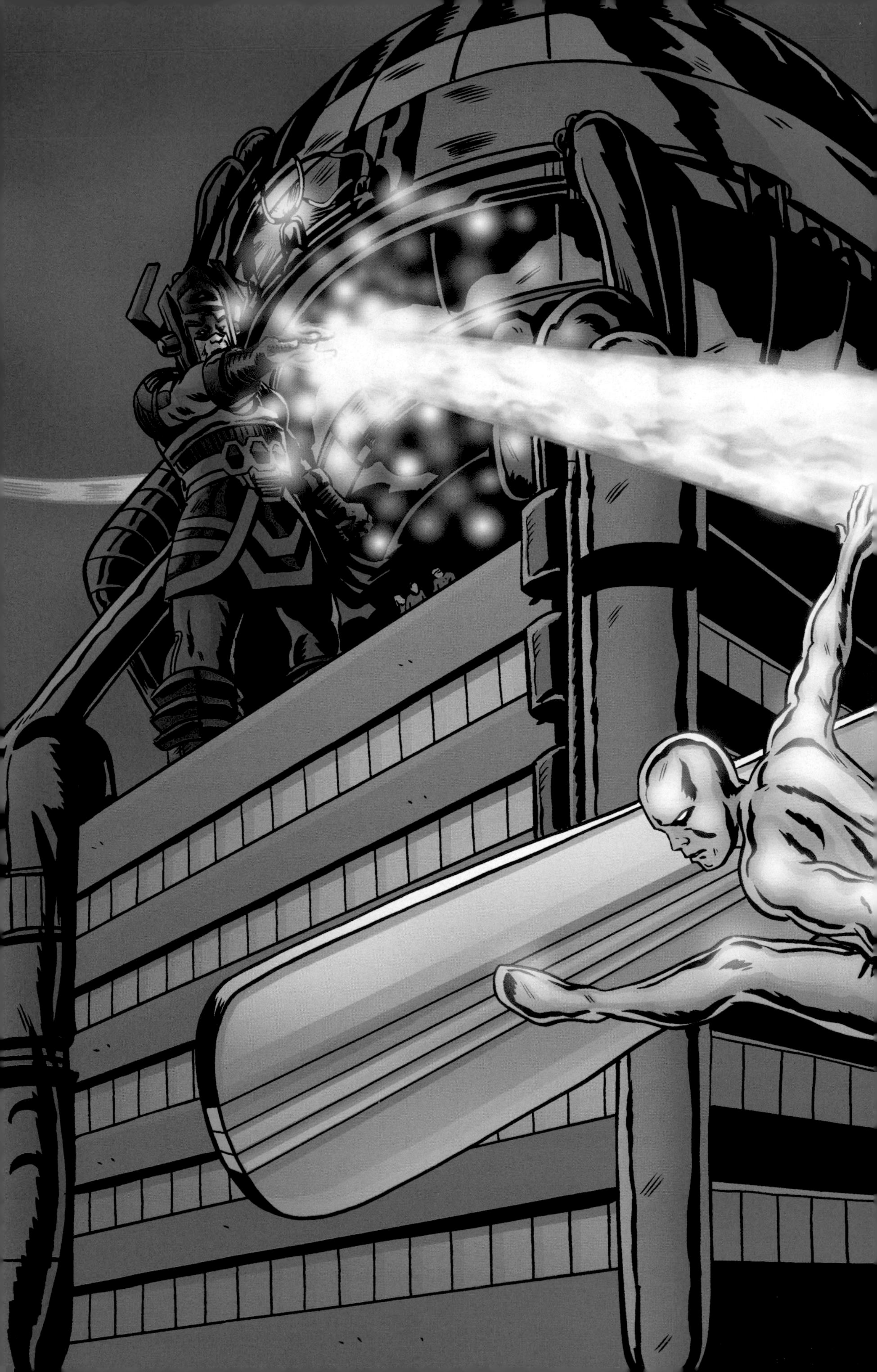

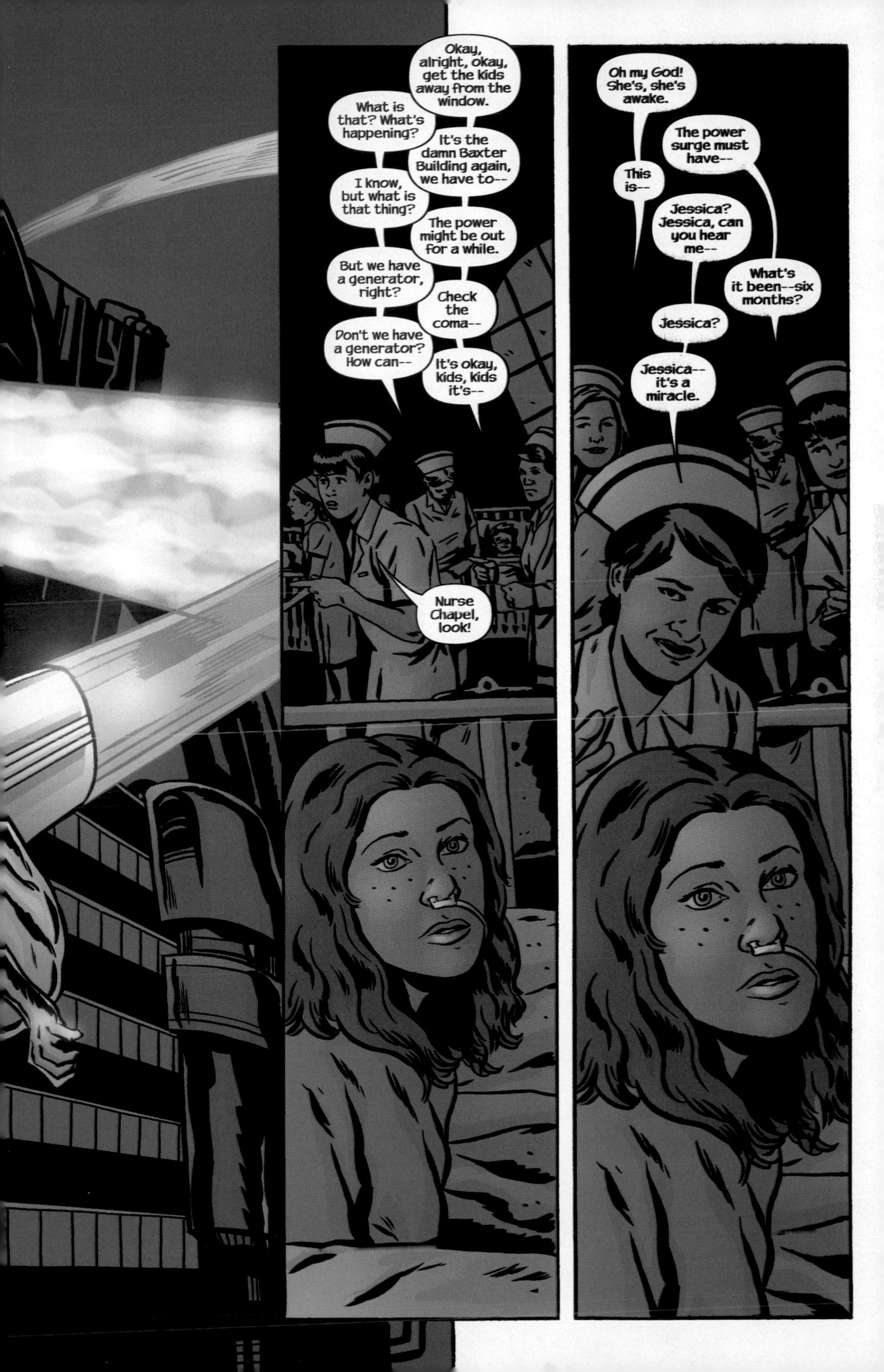

Okay, alright, okay, get the kids away from the window.
What is that? What's happening?
It's the damn Baxter Building again, we have to--
I know, but what is that thing?
The power might be out for a while.
But we have a generator, right?
Check the coma--
Don't we have a generator? How can--
It's okay, kids, kids it's--
Nurse Chapel, look!
Oh my God! She's, she's awake.
The power surge must have--
This is--
Jessica? Jessica, can you hear me--
What's it been--six months?
Jessica?
Jessica--it's a miracle.

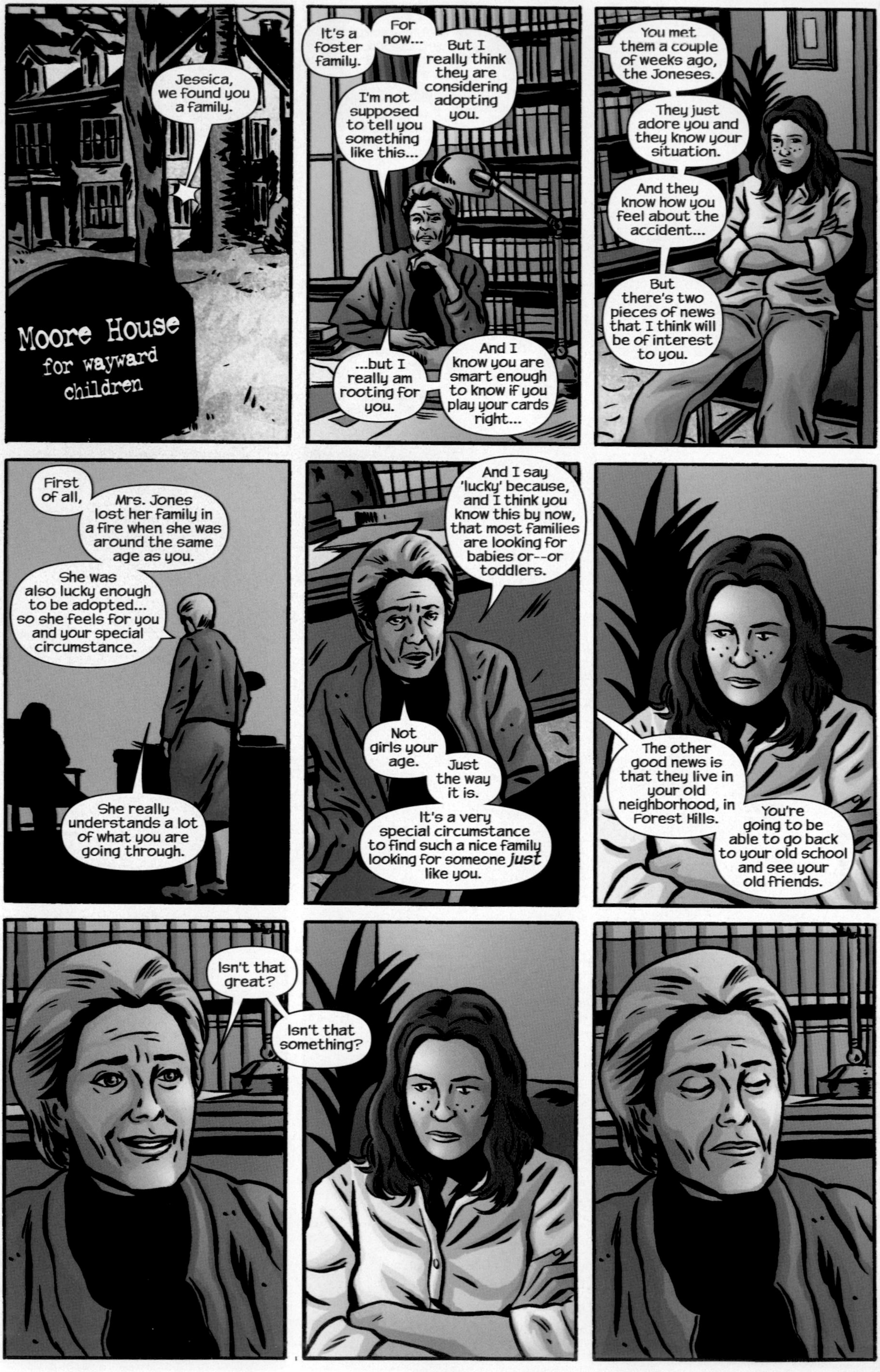
Jessica, we found you a family.
Moore House for wayward children
It's a foster family.
For now...
But I really think they are considering adopting you.
I'm not supposed to tell you something like this...
...but I really am rooting for you.
And I know you are smart enough to know if you play your cards right...
You met them a couple of weeks ago, the Joneses.
They just adore you and they know your situation.
And they know how you feel about the accident...
But there's two pieces of news that I think will be of interest to you.
First of all,
Mrs. Jones lost her family in a fire when she was around the same age as you.
She was also lucky enough to be adopted... so she feels for you and your special circumstance.
She really understands a lot of what you are going through.
And I say 'lucky' because, and I think you know this by now, that most families are looking for babies or--or toddlers.
Not girls your age.
Just the way it is.
It's a very special circumstance to find such a nice family looking for someone *just* like you.
The other good news is that they live in your old neighborhood, in Forest Hills.
You're going to be able to go back to your old school and see your old friends.
Isn't that great?
Isn't that something?

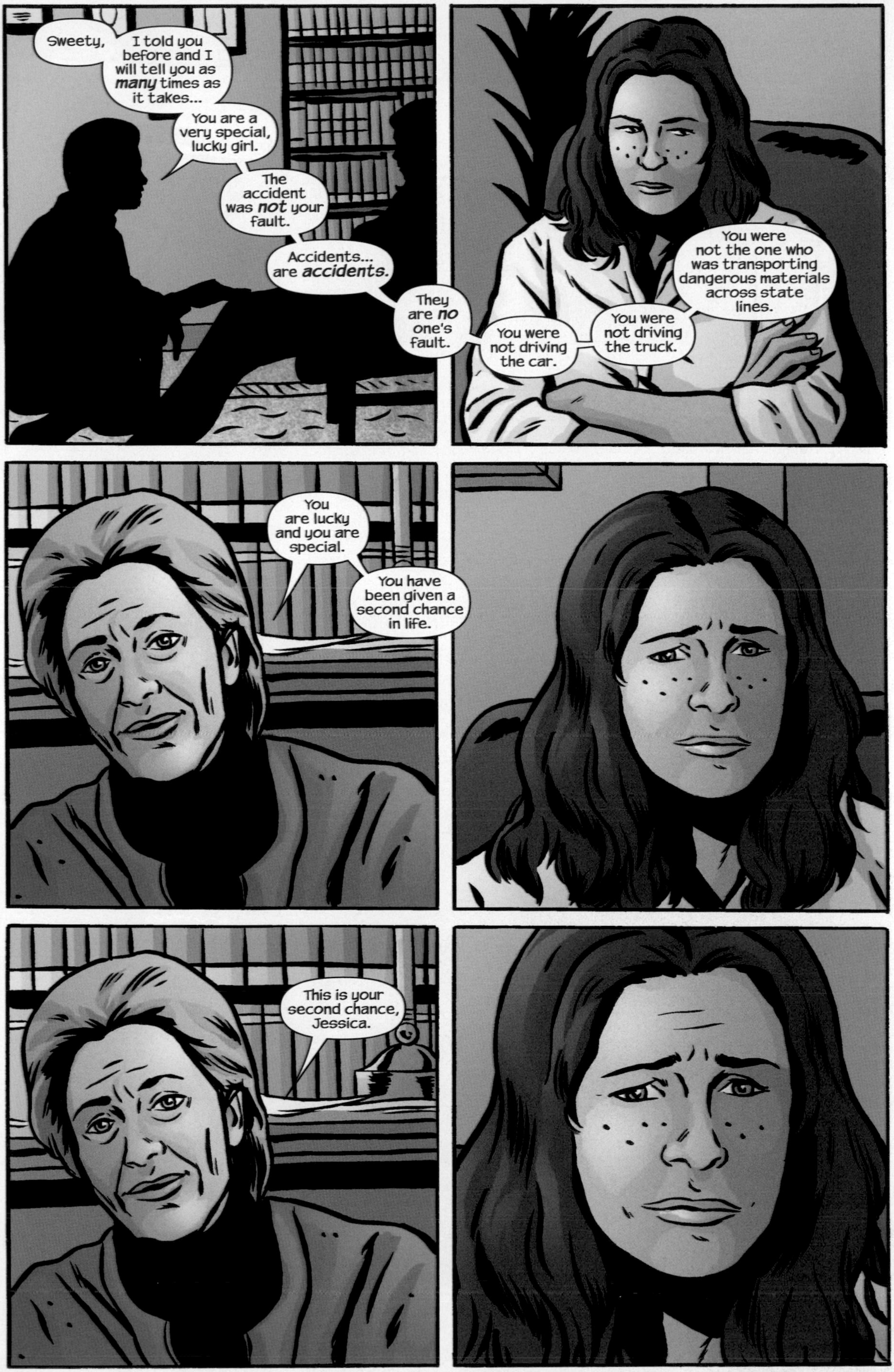
Sweety,
I told you before and I will tell you as *many* times as it takes...
You are a very special, lucky girl.
The accident was *not* your fault.
Accidents... are *accidents.*
They are *no* one's fault.
You were not driving the car.
You were not driving the truck.
You were not the one who was transporting dangerous materials across state lines.
You are lucky and you are special.
You have been given a second chance in life.
This is your second chance, Jessica.

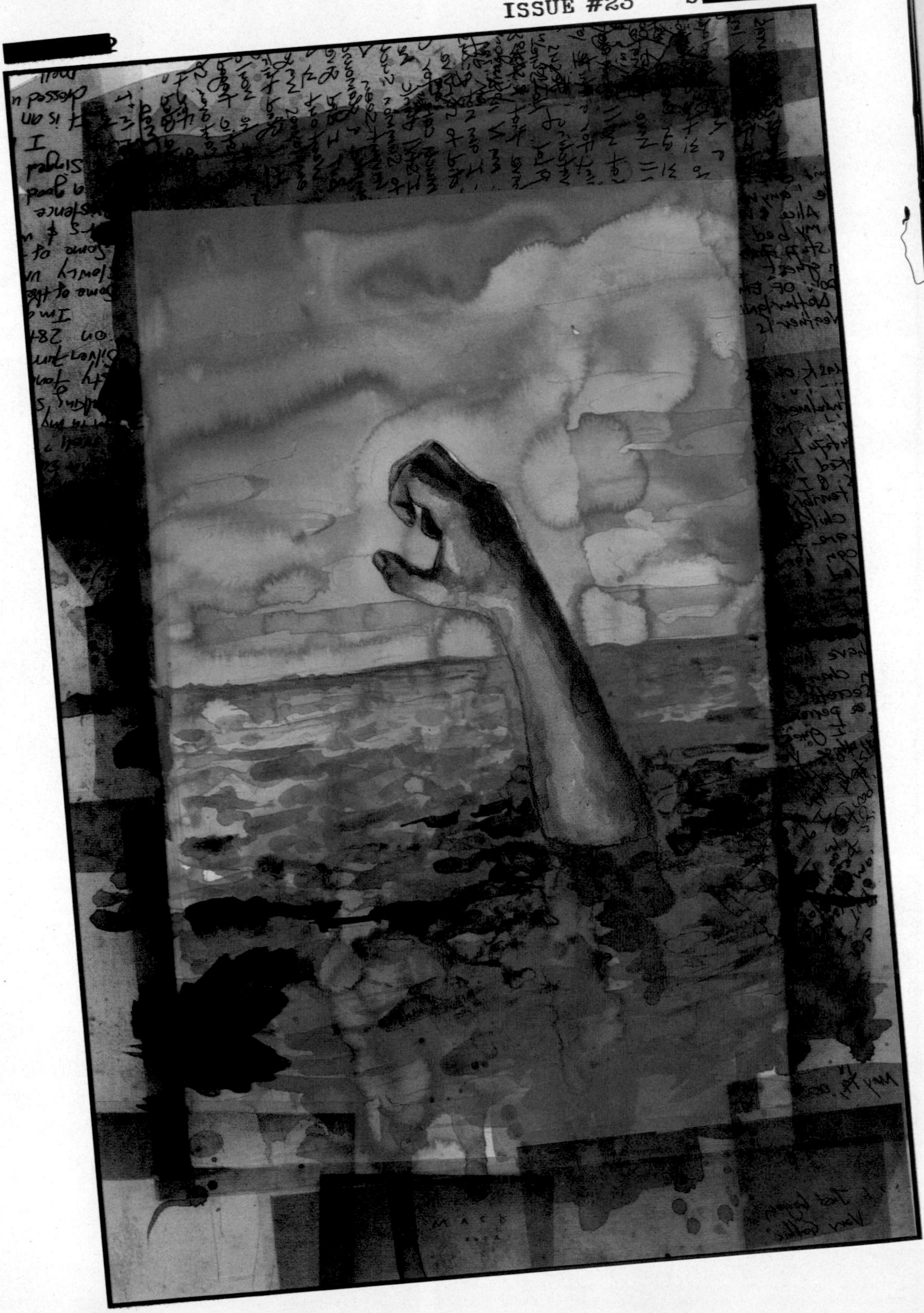

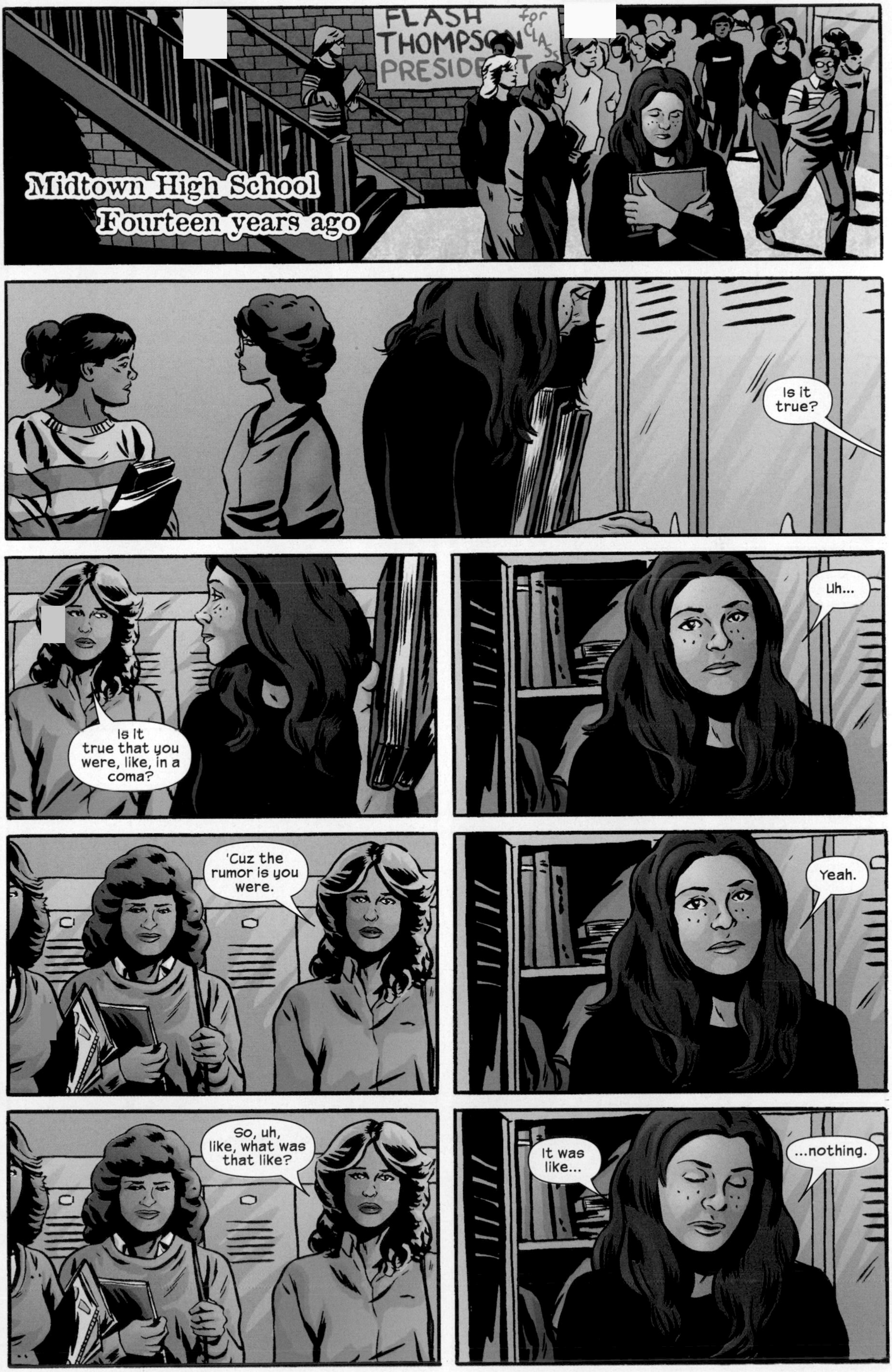
FLASH THOMPSON for CLASS PRESIDENT
Midtown High School
Fourteen years ago
Is it true?
Is it true that you were, like, in a coma?
Uh...
'Cuz the rumor is you were.
Yeah.
So, uh, like, what was that like?
It was like...
...nothing.

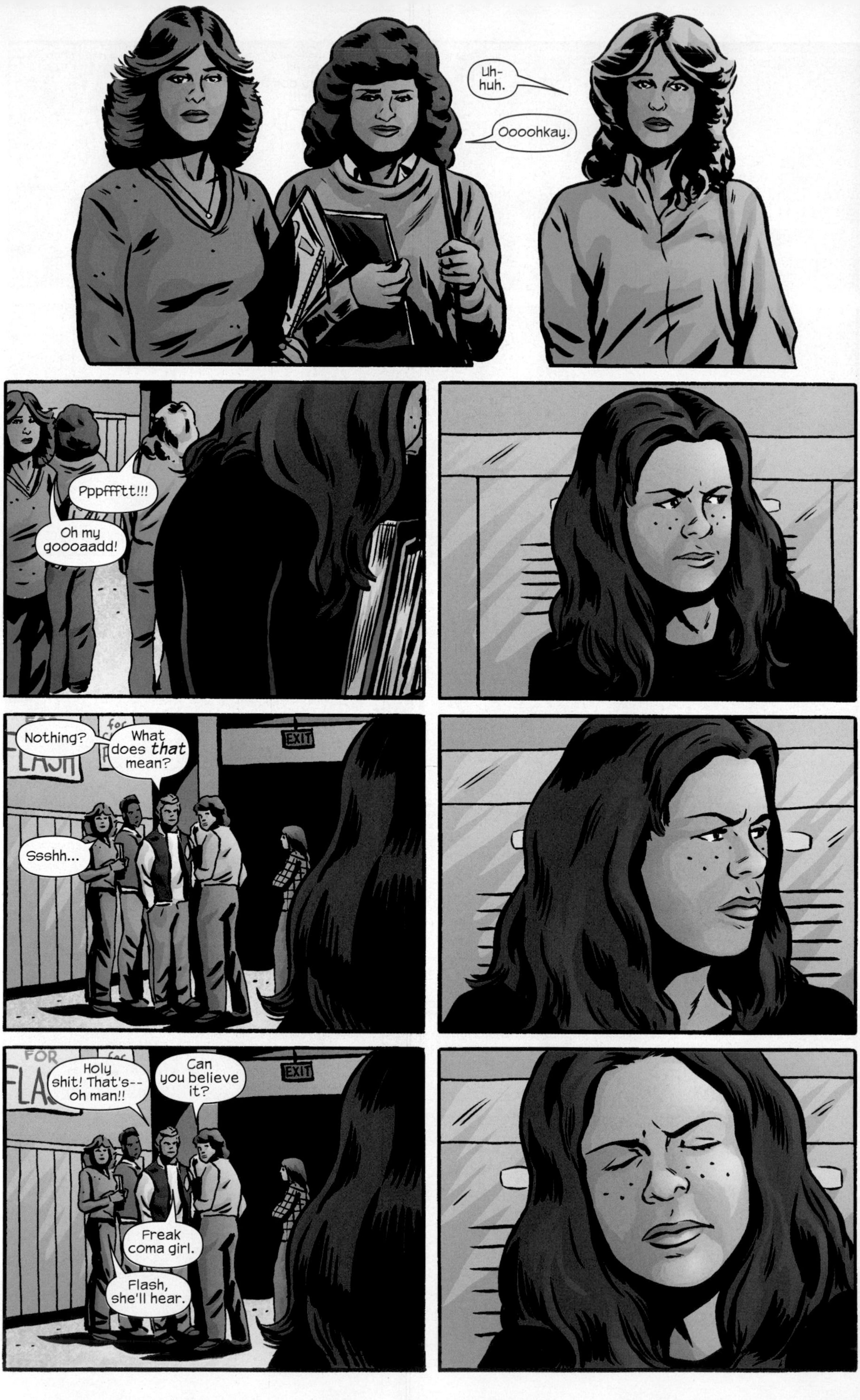
Uh-huh.
Oooohkay.
Pppffftt!!!
Oh my goooaadd!
EXIT
Nothing?
What does *that* mean?
Ssshh...
Holy shit! That's--oh man!!
Can you believe it?
EXIT
Freak coma girl.
Flash, she'll hear.

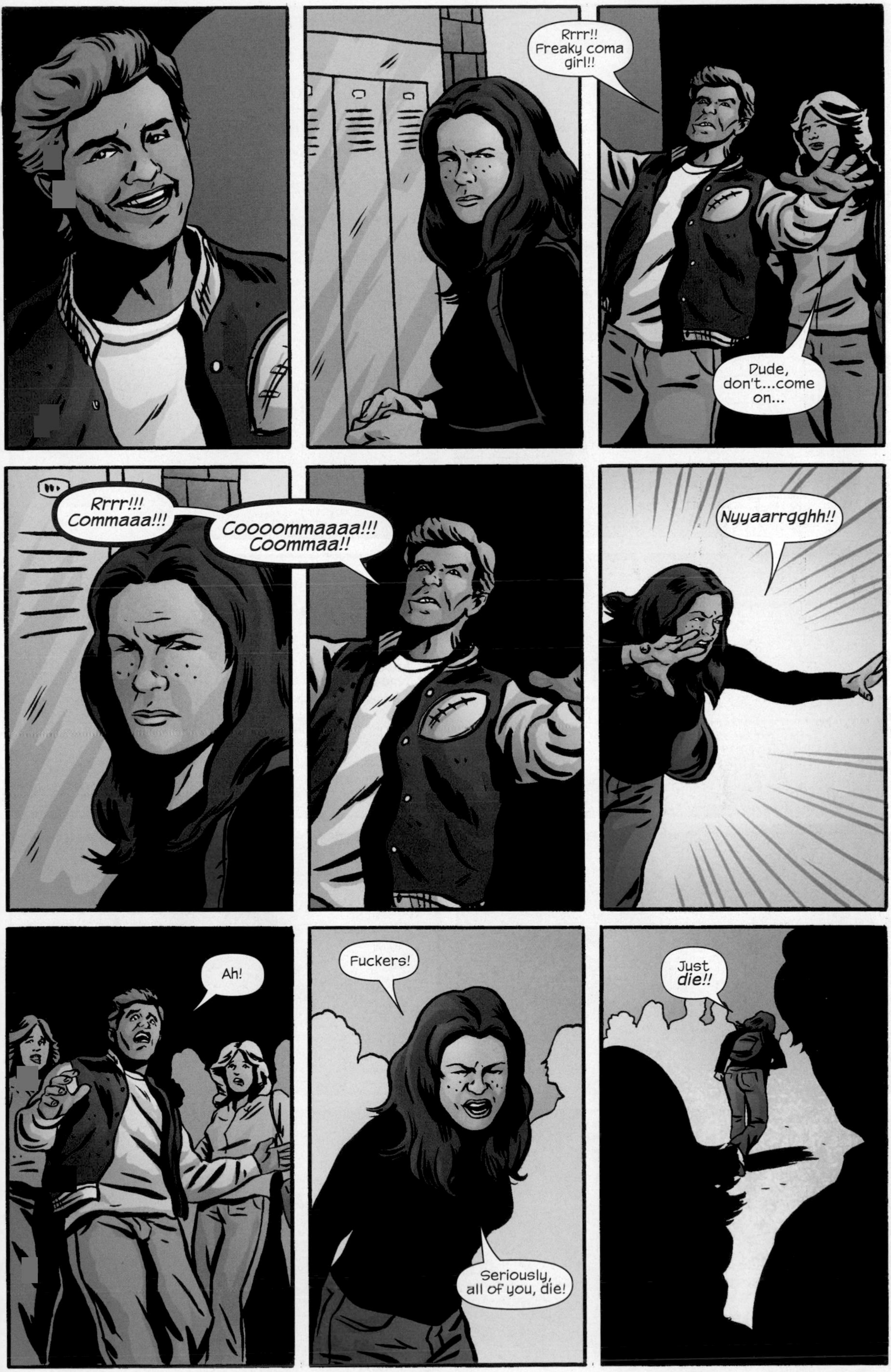
Rrrr!!
Freaky coma girl!!
Dude, don't...come on...
Rrrr!!!
Commaaa!!!
Coooommaaaa!!!
Coommaa!!
Nyyaarrgghh!!
Ah!
Fuckers!
Seriously, all of you, die!
Just die!!

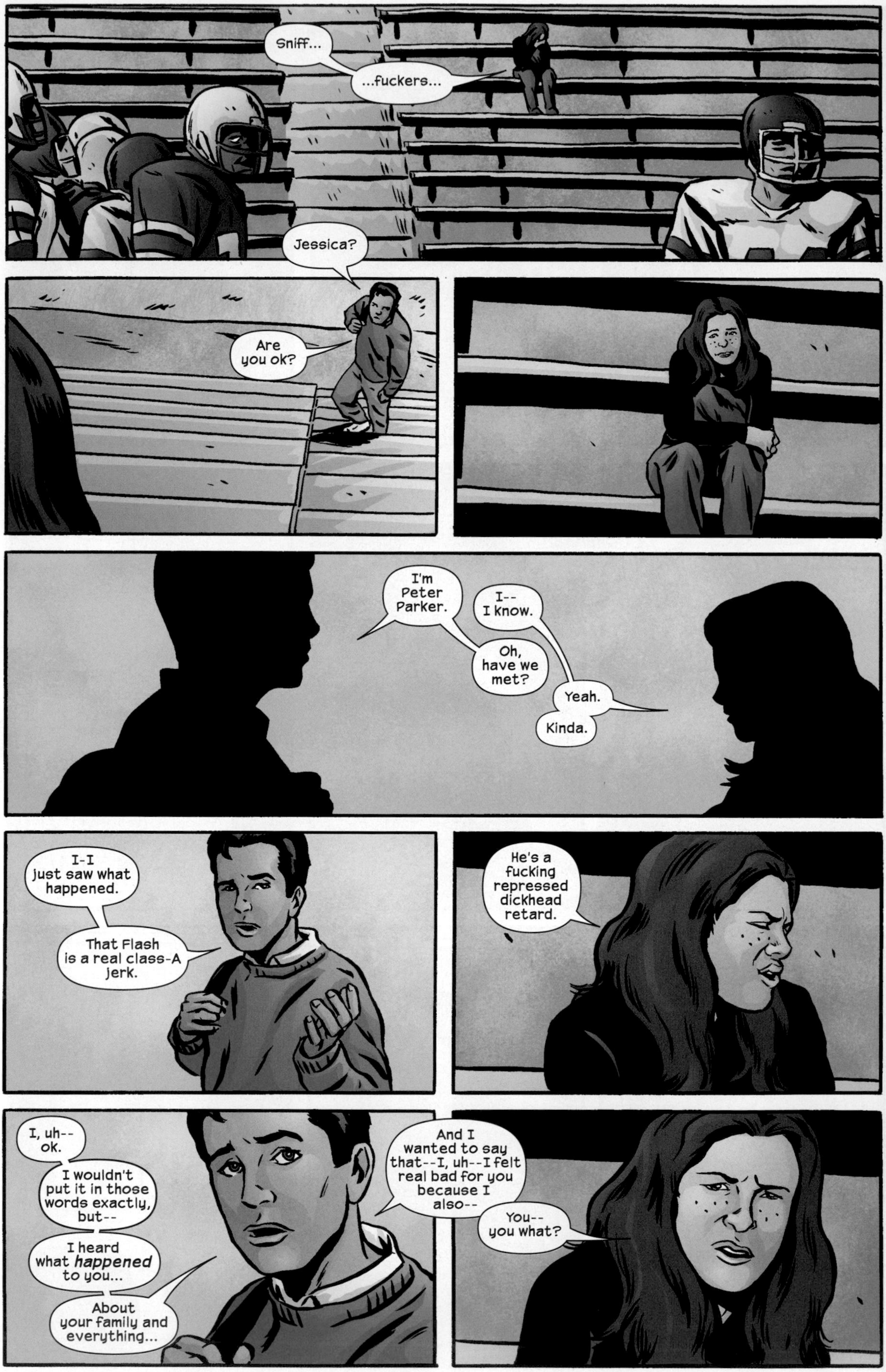
Sniff...
...fuckers...
Jessica?
Are you ok?
I'm Peter Parker.
I-- I know.
Oh, have we met?
Yeah.
Kinda.
I-I just saw what happened.
That Flash is a real class-A jerk.
He's a fucking repressed dickhead retard.
I, uh-- ok.
I wouldn't put it in those words exactly, but--
I heard what *happened* to you...
About your family and everything...
And I wanted to say that--I, uh--I felt real bad for you because I also--
You-- you what?

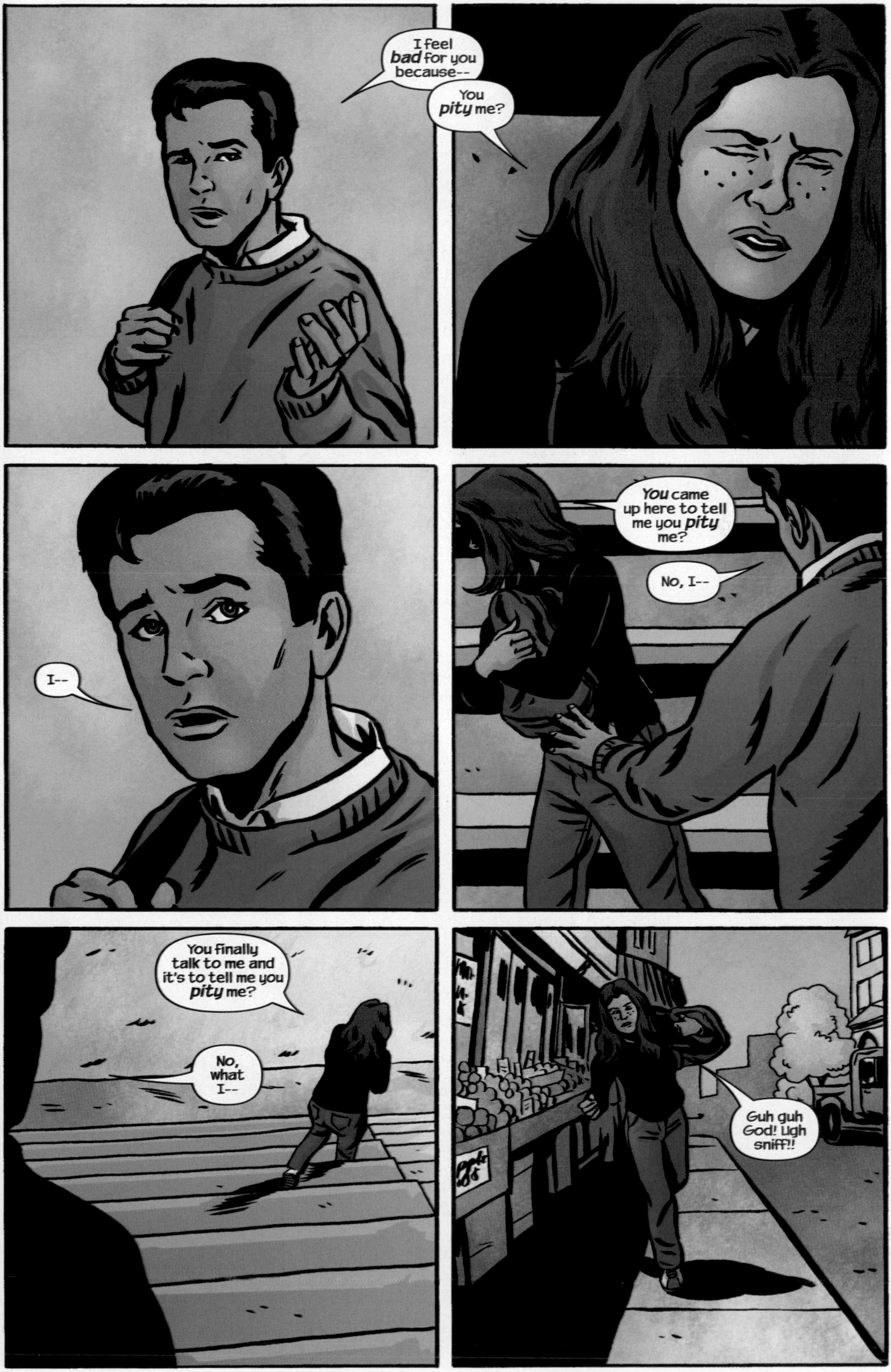
I feel **bad** for you because--
You *pity* me?
I--
You came up here to tell me you *pity* me?
No, I--
You finally talk to me and it's to tell me you *pity* me?
No, what I--
Guh guh God! Ugh sniff!!

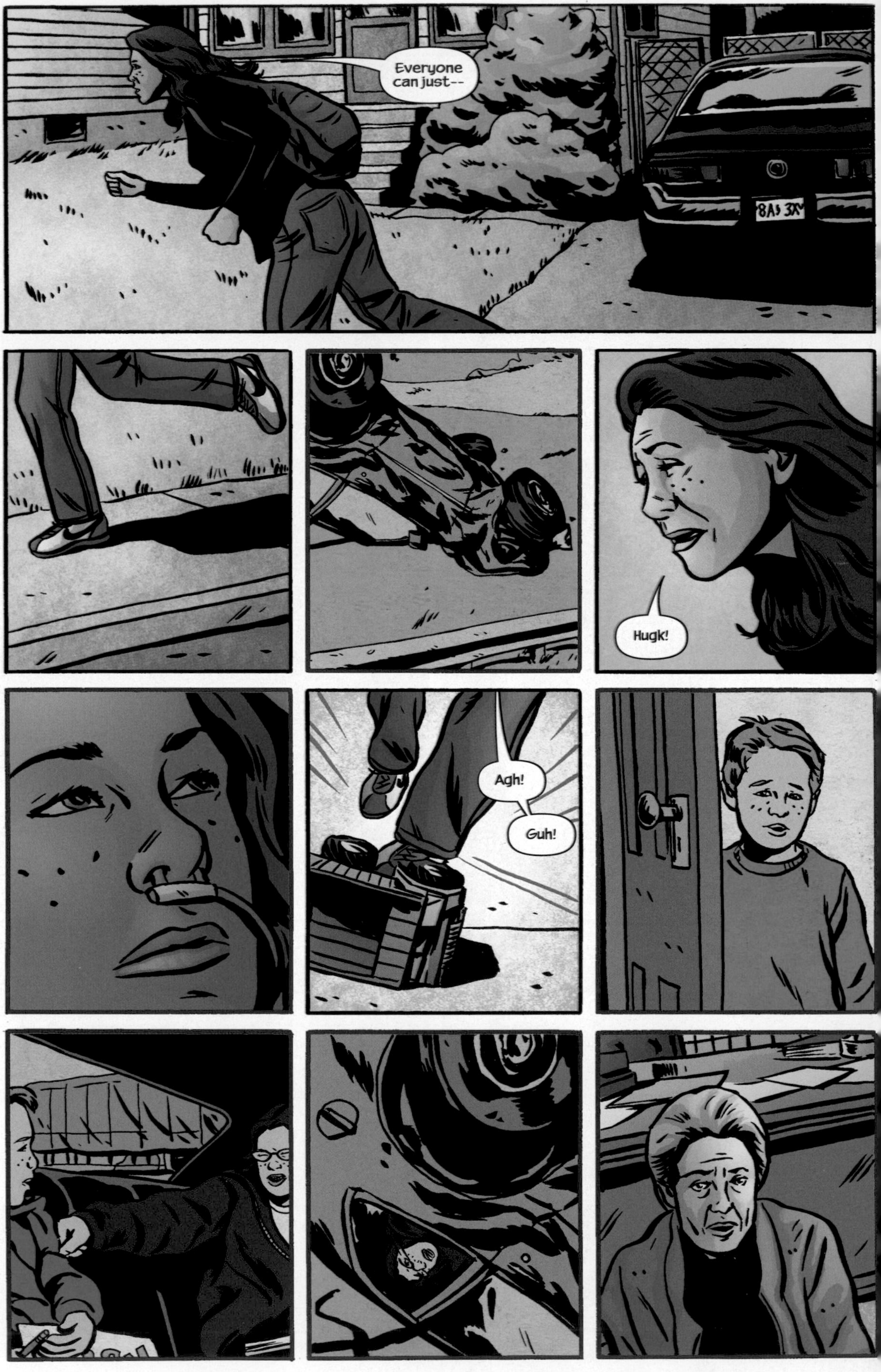
Everyone can just--
Hugk!
Agh!
Guh!

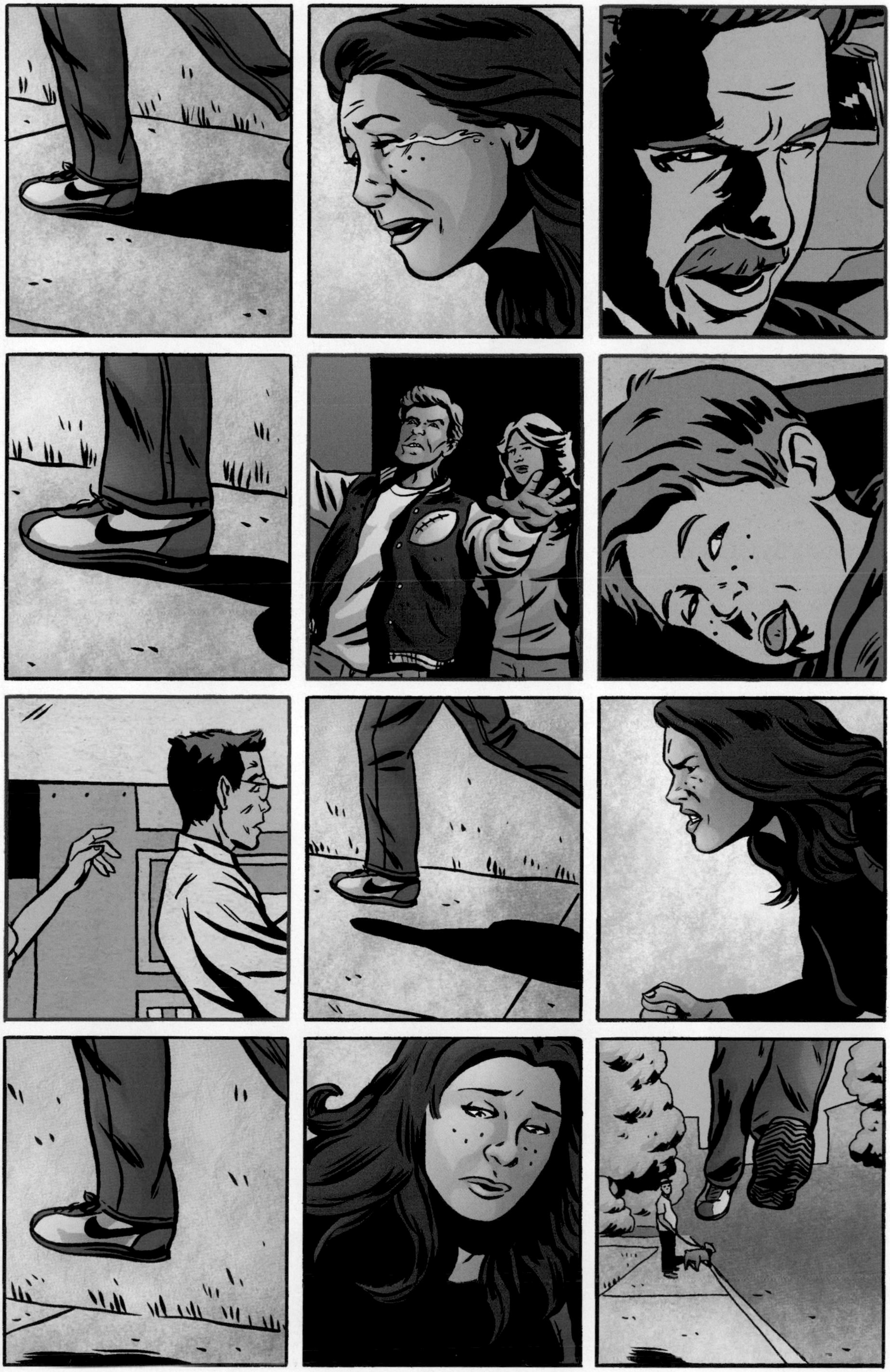

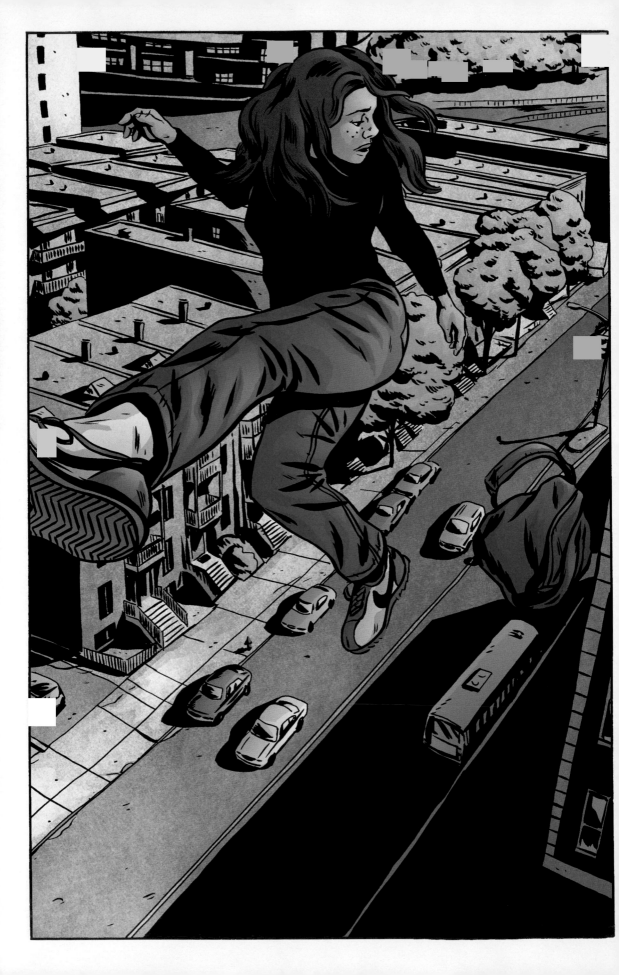

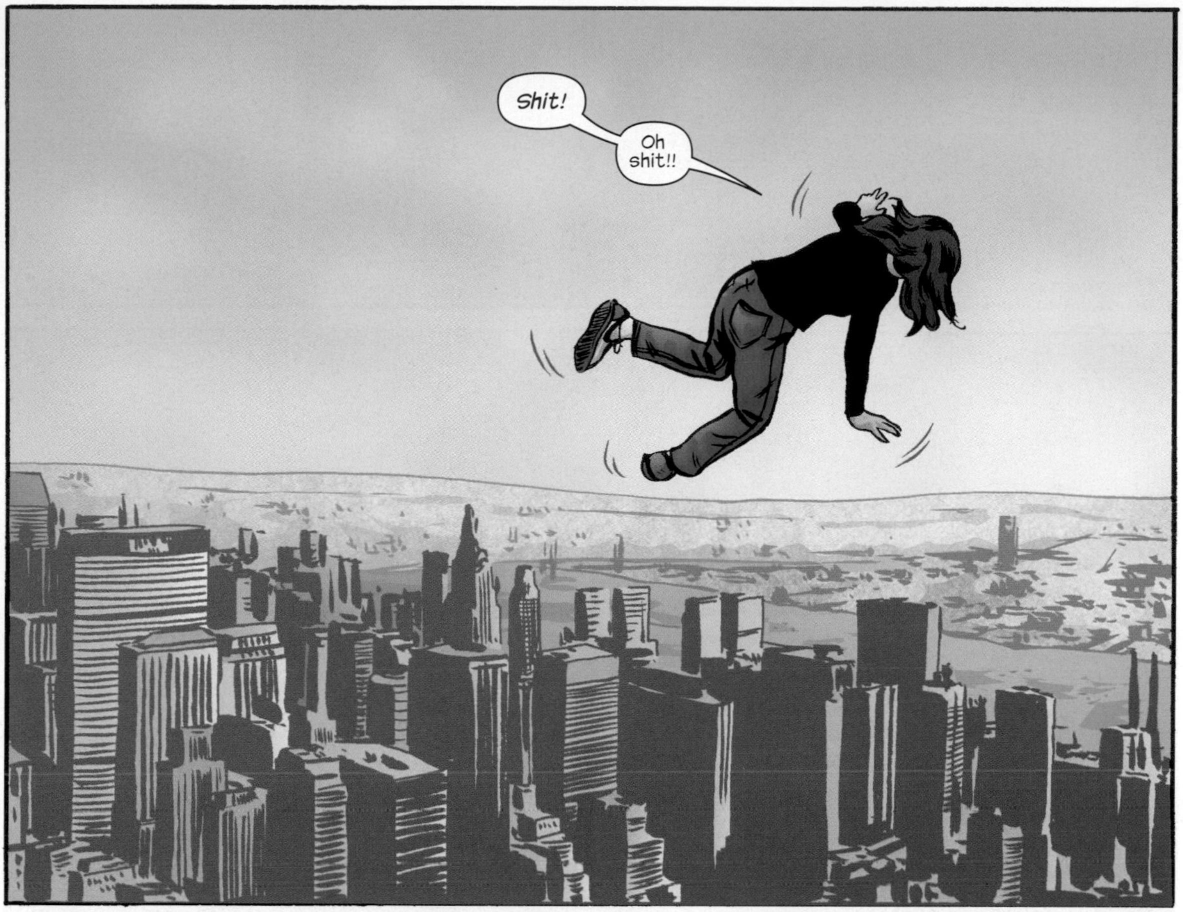
Shit!
Oh shit!!

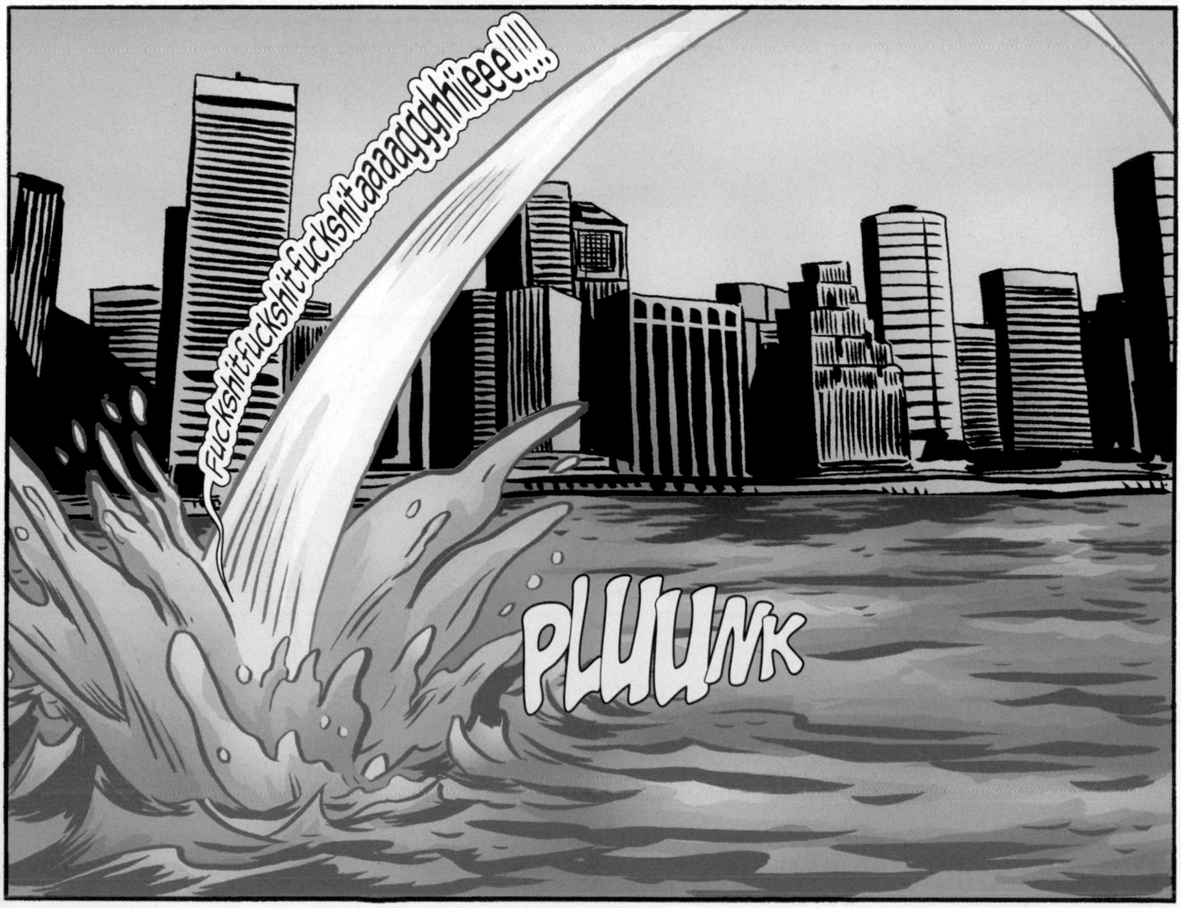
Fuckshitfuckshitfuckshitaaaagggghiieee!!!!
PLUUNK

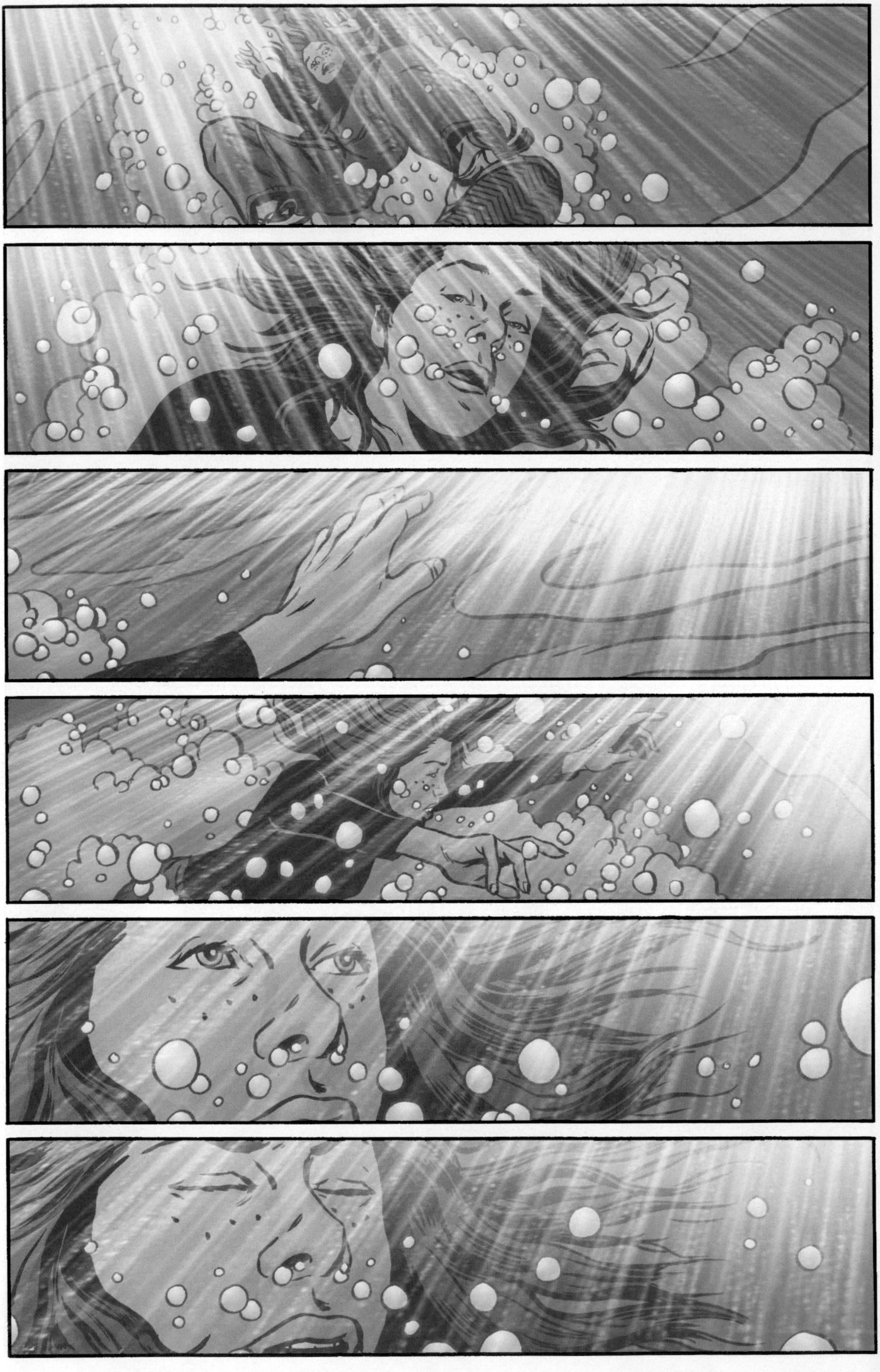

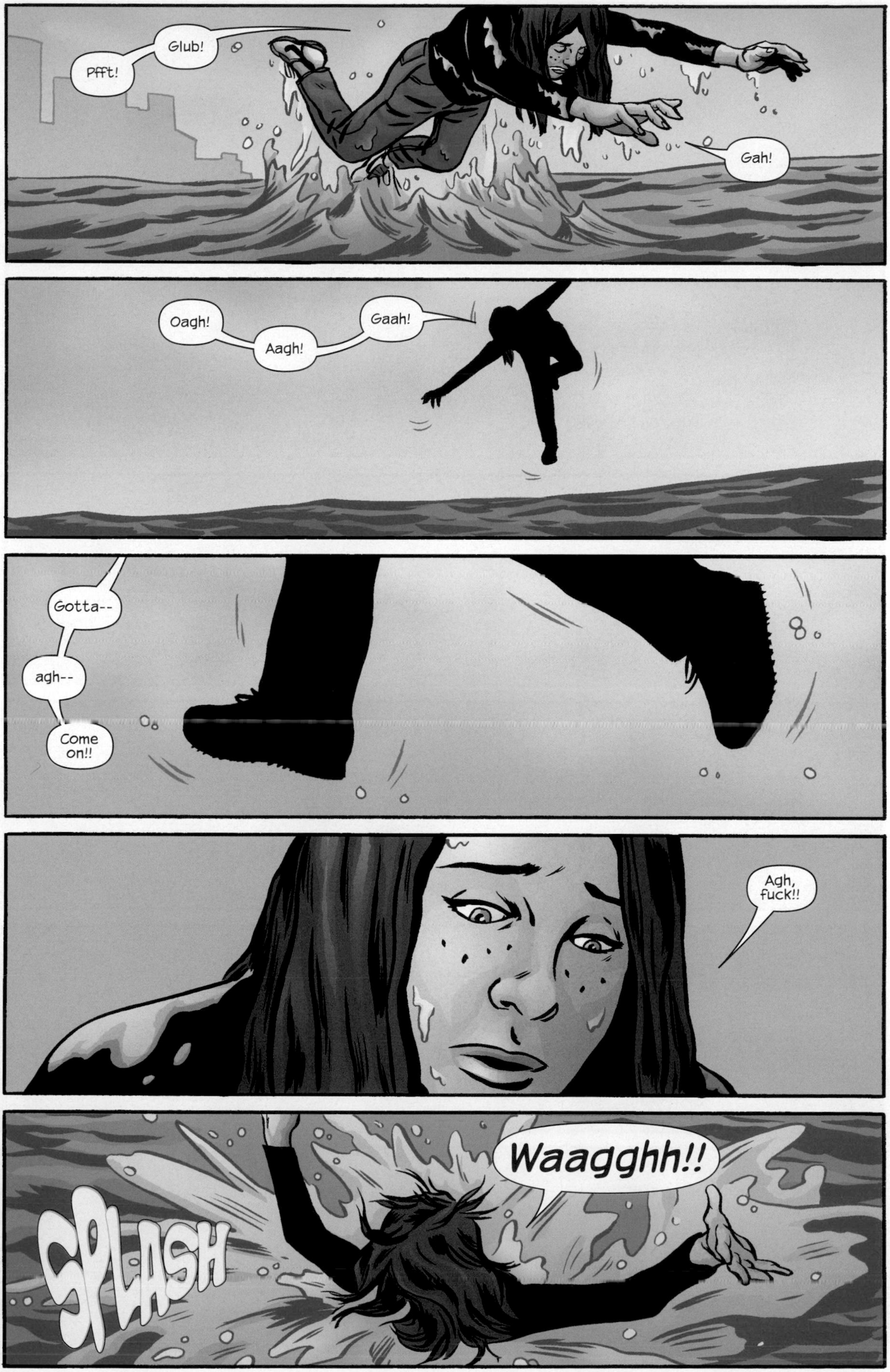
Pfft!
Glub!
Gah!
Oagh!
Aagh!
Gaah!
Gotta--
agh--
Come on!!
Agh, fuck!!
SPLASH
Waagghh!!

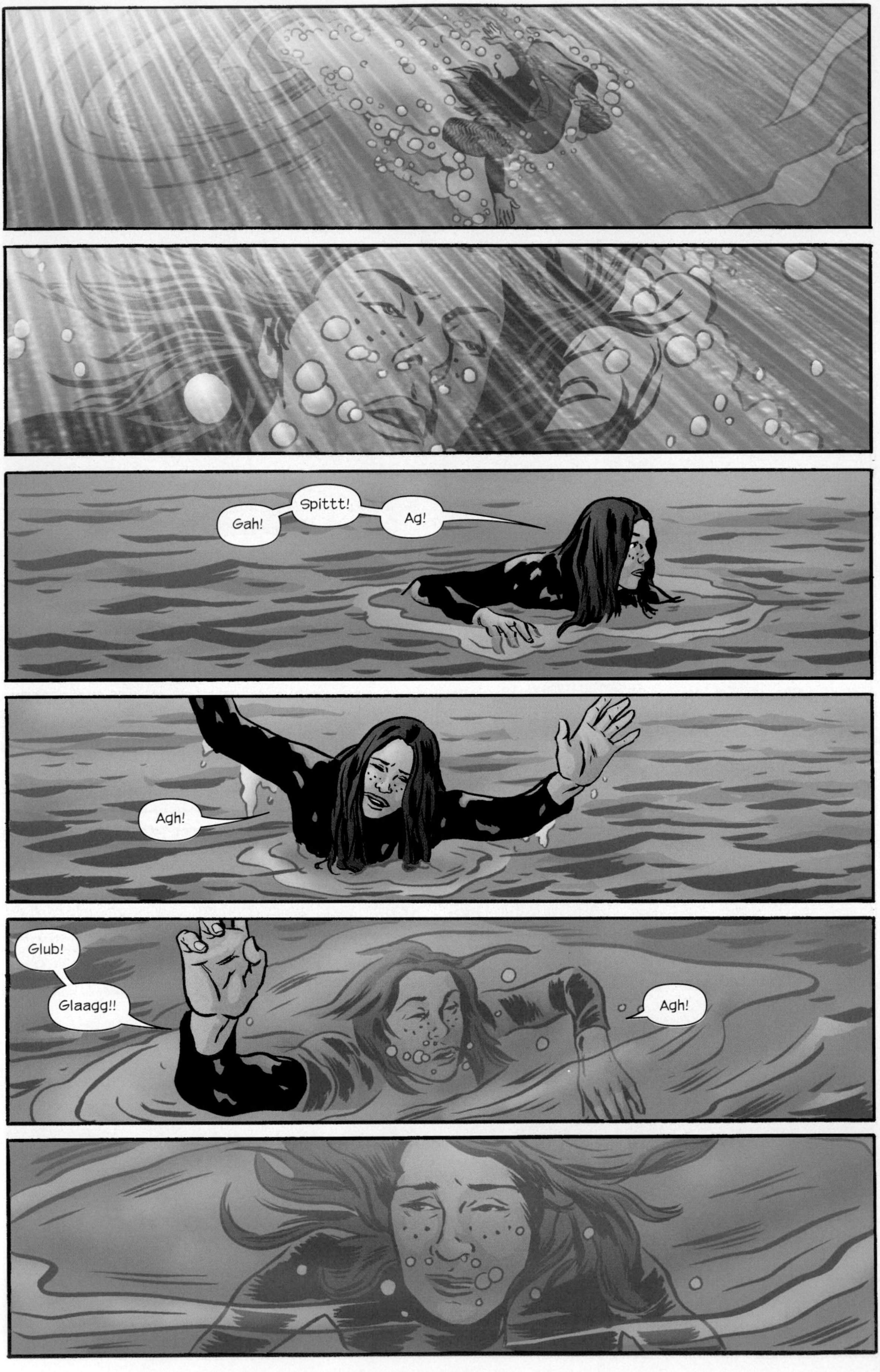

Gah!
Spittt!
Ag!
Agh!
Glub!
Glaagg!!
Agh!

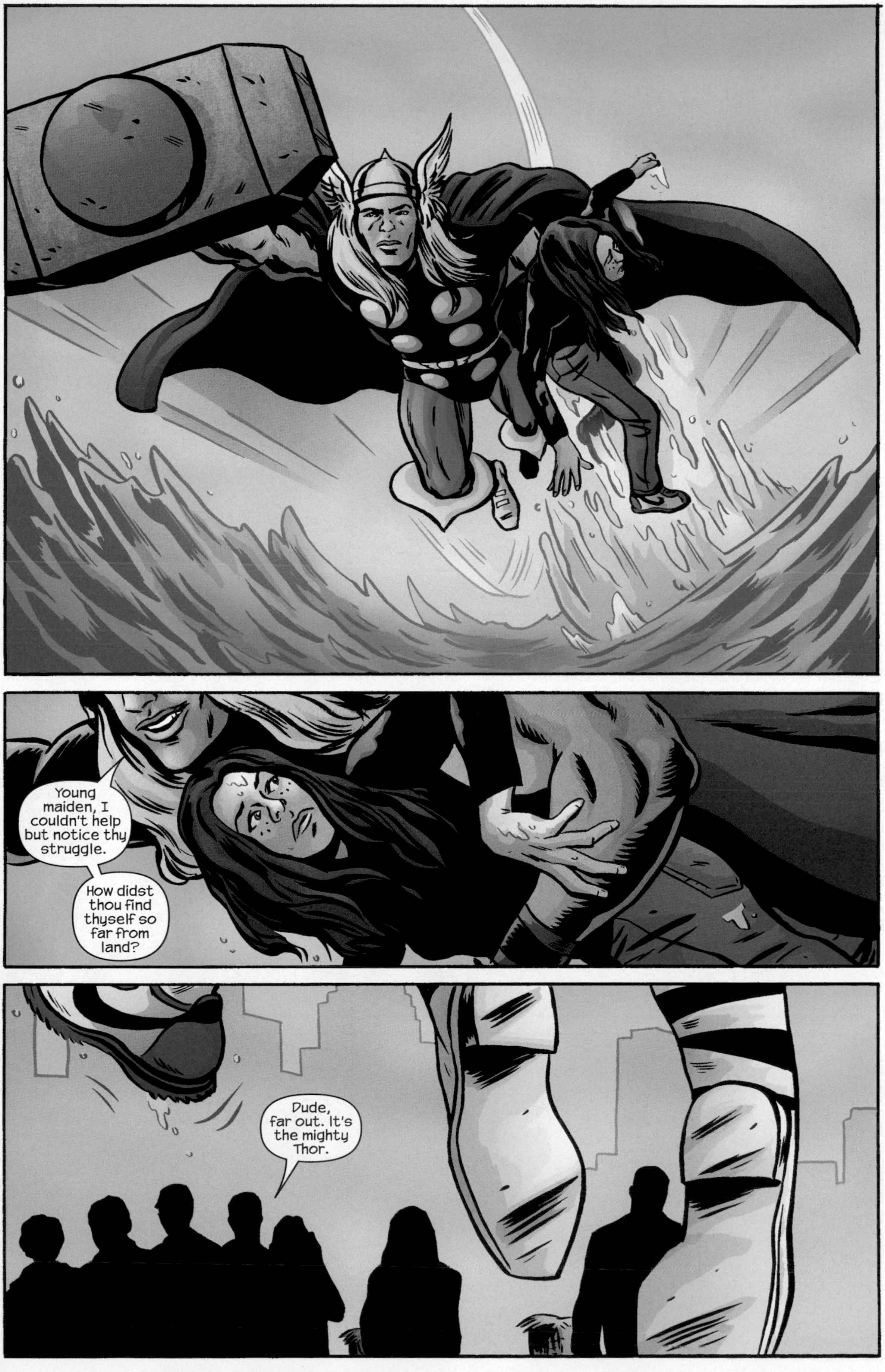
Young maiden, I couldn't help but notice thy struggle.
How didst thou find thyself so far from land?
Dude, far out. It's the mighty Thor.

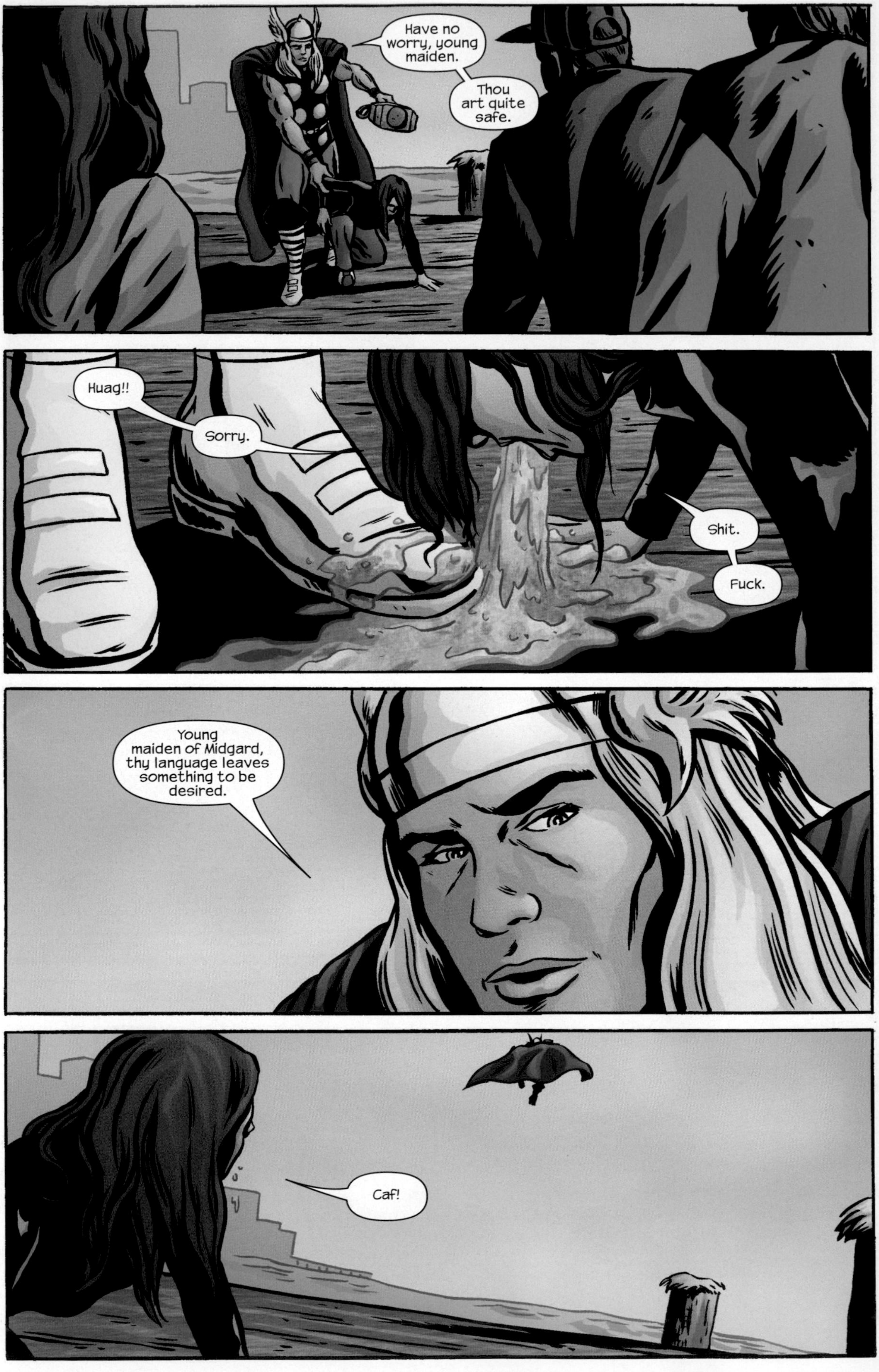
Have no worry, young maiden.
Thou art quite safe.
Huag!!
Sorry.
Shit.
Fuck.
Young maiden of Midgard, thy language leaves something to be desired.
Caf!

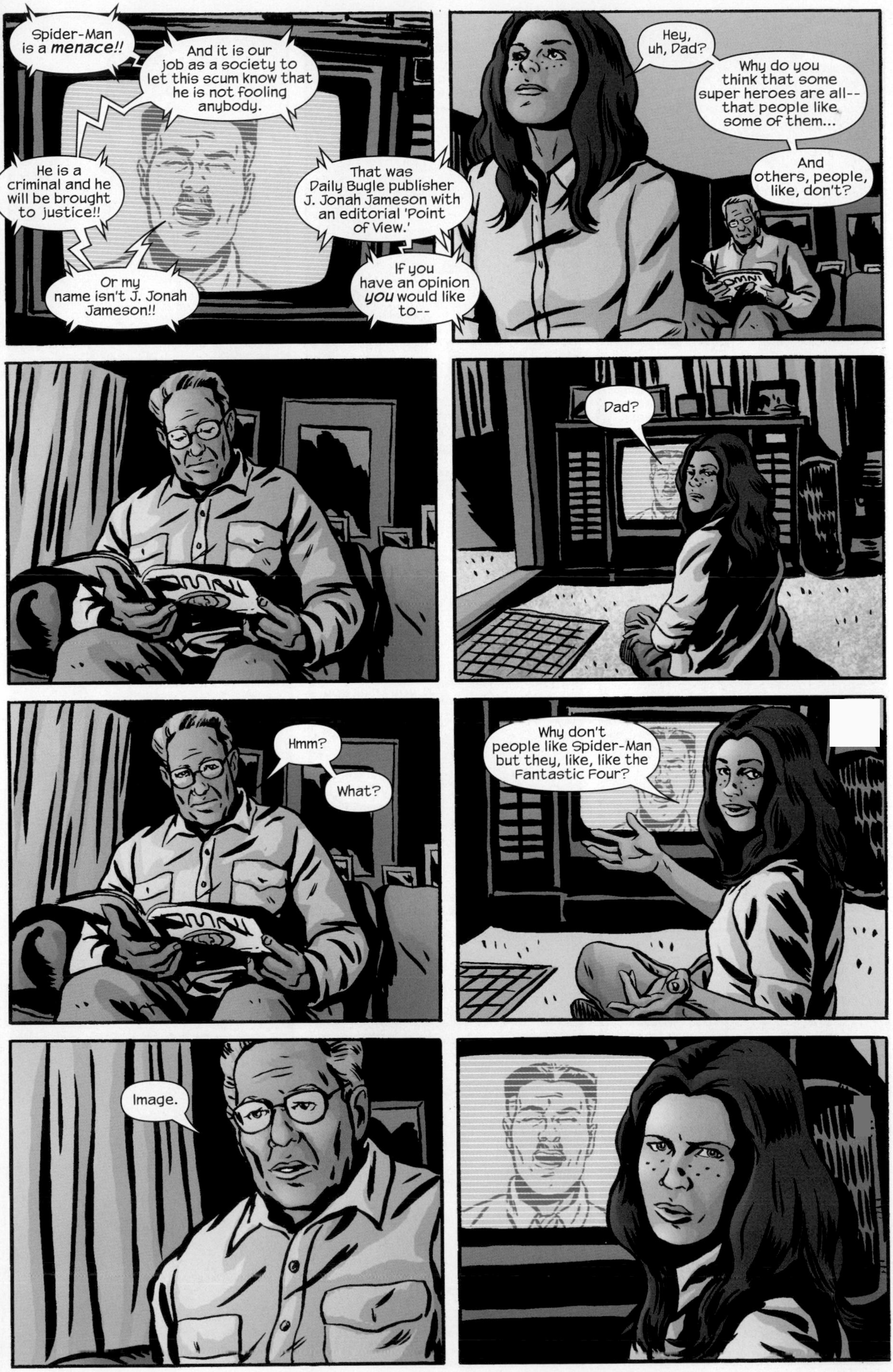
Spider-Man is a *menace!!*
And it is our job as a society to let this scum know that he is not fooling anybody.
He is a criminal and he will be brought to justice!!
Or my name isn't J. Jonah Jameson!!
That was Daily Bugle publisher J. Jonah Jameson with an editorial 'Point of View.'
If you have an opinion *you* would like to--
Hey, uh, Dad?
Why do you think that some super heroes are all-- that people like some of them...
And others, people, like, don't?
Dad?
Hmm?
What?
Why don't people like Spider-Man but they, like, like the Fantastic Four?
Image.

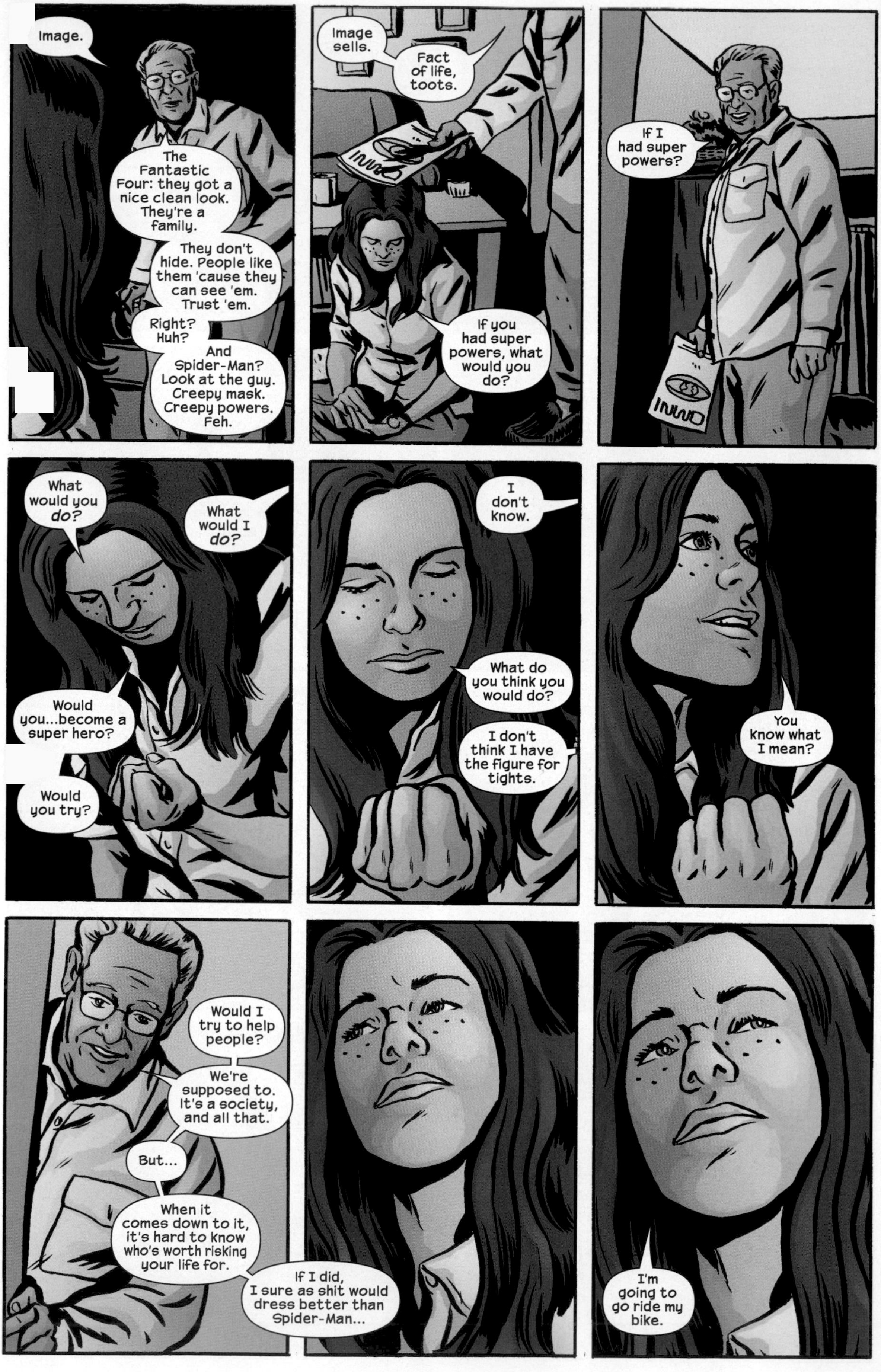
Image.
The Fantastic Four: they got a nice clean look. They're a family.
They don't hide. People like them 'cause they can see 'em. Trust 'em.
Right? Huh?
And Spider-Man? Look at the guy. Creepy mask. Creepy powers. Feh.
Image sells.
Fact of life, toots.
If you had super powers, what would you do?
If I had super powers?
What would you do?
What would I do?
Would you...become a super hero?
Would you try?
I don't know.
What do you think you would do?
I don't think I have the figure for tights.
You know what I mean?
Would I try to help people?
We're supposed to. It's a society, and all that.
But...
When it comes down to it, it's hard to know who's worth risking your life for.
If I did, I sure as shit would dress better than Spider-Man...
I'm going to go ride my bike.

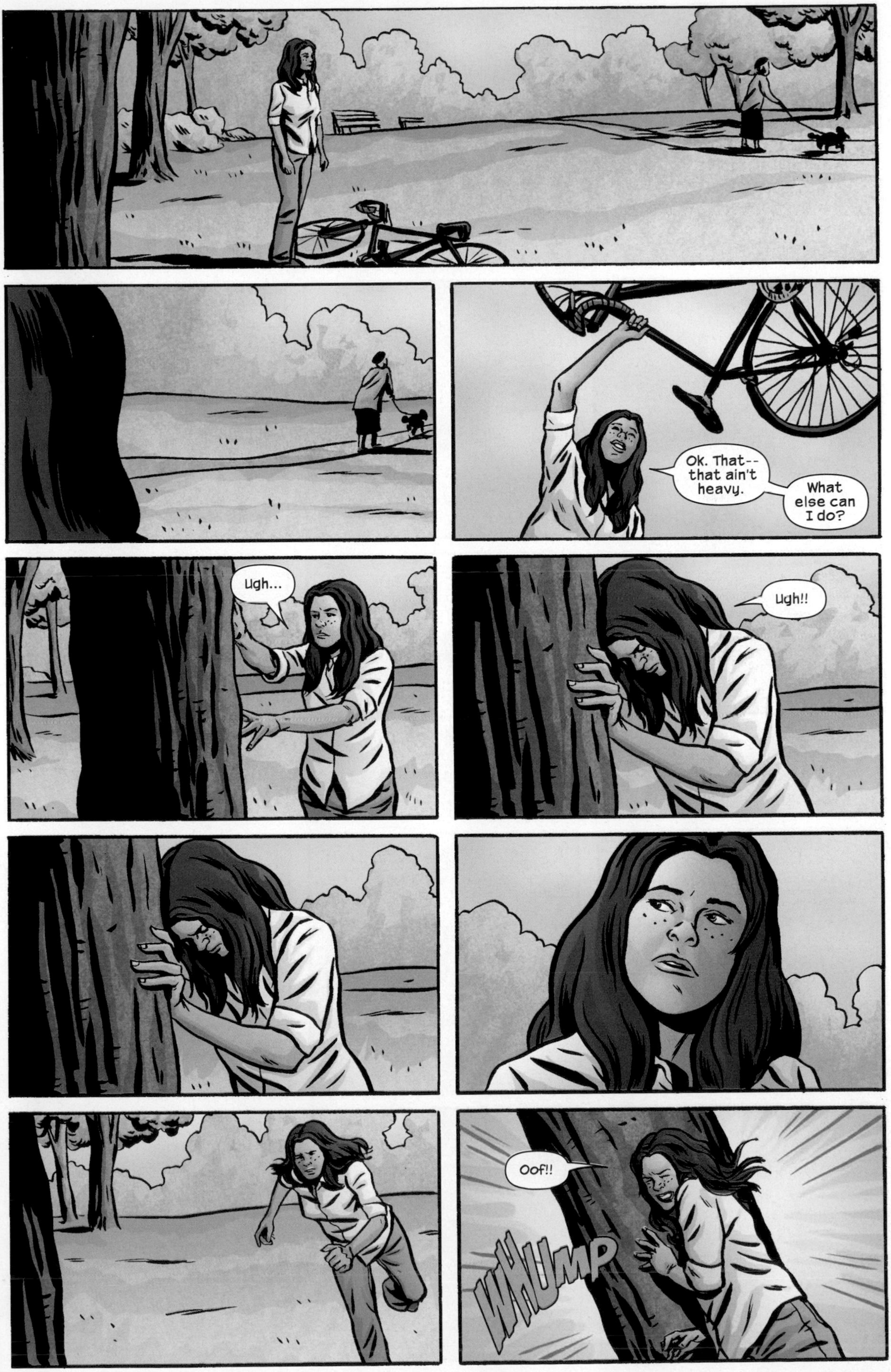
Ok. That--
that ain't
heavy.
What
else can
I do?
Ugh...
Ugh!!
Oof!!
WHUMP

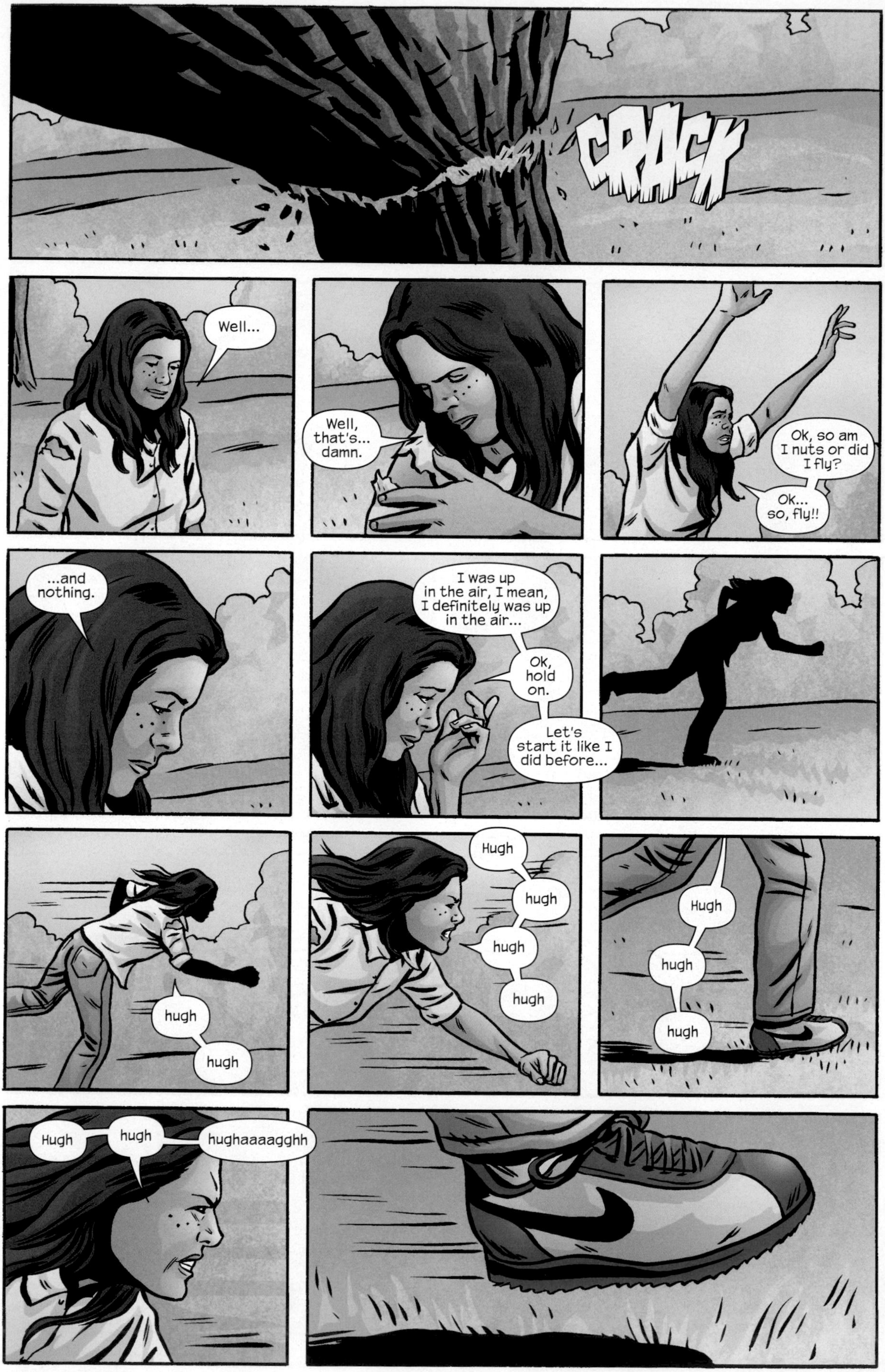
CRACK
Well...
Well, that's... damn.
Ok, so am I nuts or did I fly?
Ok... so, fly!!
...and nothing.
I was up in the air, I mean, I definitely was up in the air...
Ok, hold on.
Let's start it like I did before...
hugh
hugh
Hugh
hugh
hugh
hugh
Hugh
hugh
hugh
Hugh
hugh
hughaaaagghh

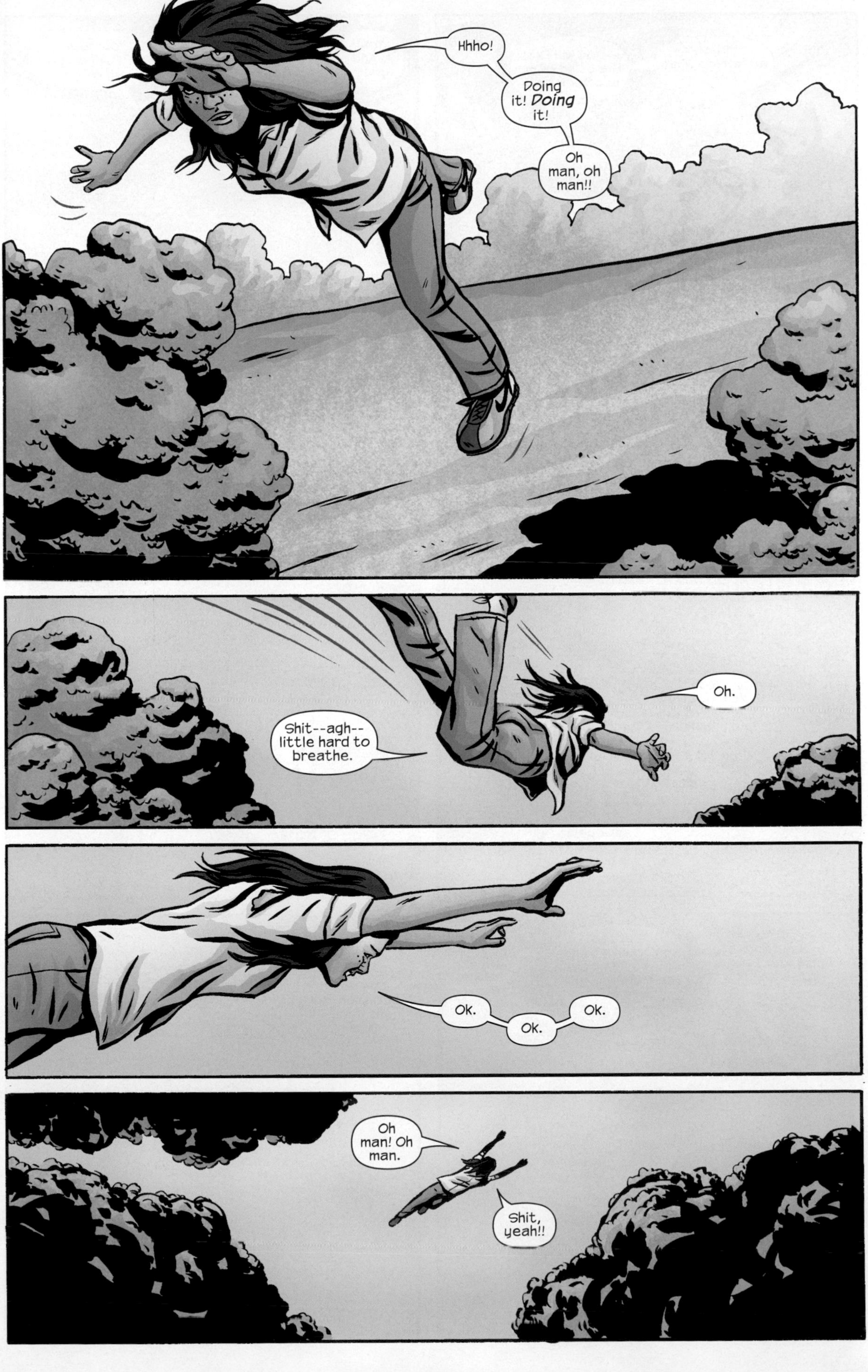
Hhho!
Doing it! *Doing* it!
Oh man, oh man!!
Oh.
Shit--agh--little hard to breathe.
Ok.
Ok.
Ok.
Oh man! Oh man.
Shit, yeah!!

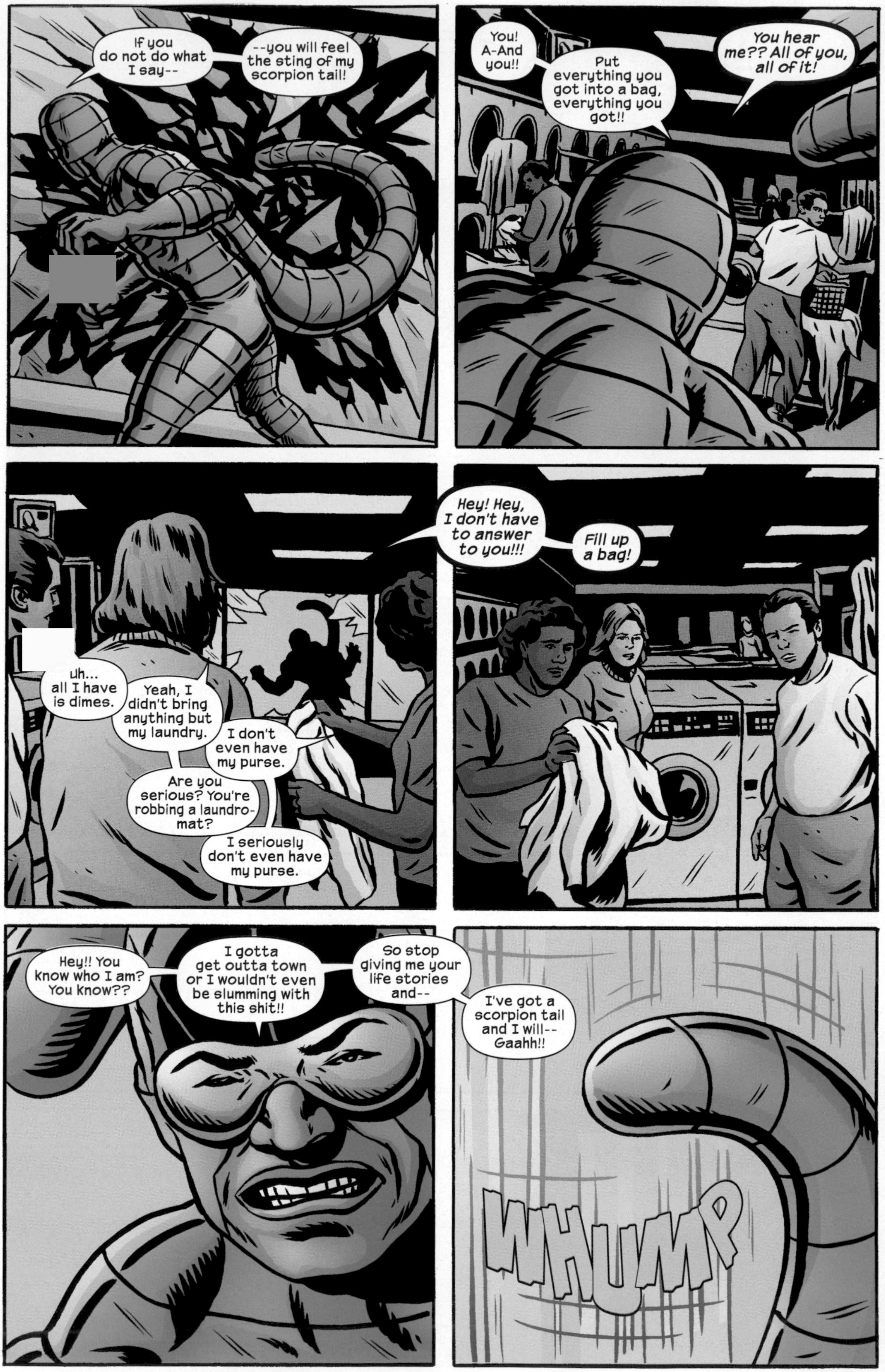

If you do not do what I say--
--you will feel the sting of my scorpion tail!
You! A-And you!!
Put everything you got into a bag, everything you got!!
You hear me?? All of you, all of it!
uh... all I have is dimes.
Yeah, I didn't bring anything but my laundry.
I don't even have my purse.
Are you serious? You're robbing a laundromat?
I seriously don't even have my purse.
Hey! Hey, I don't have to answer to you!!!
Fill up a bag!
Hey!! You know who I am? You know??
I gotta get outta town or I wouldn't even be slumming with this shit!!
So stop giving me your life stories and--
I've got a scorpion tail and I will-- Gaahh!!
WHUMP

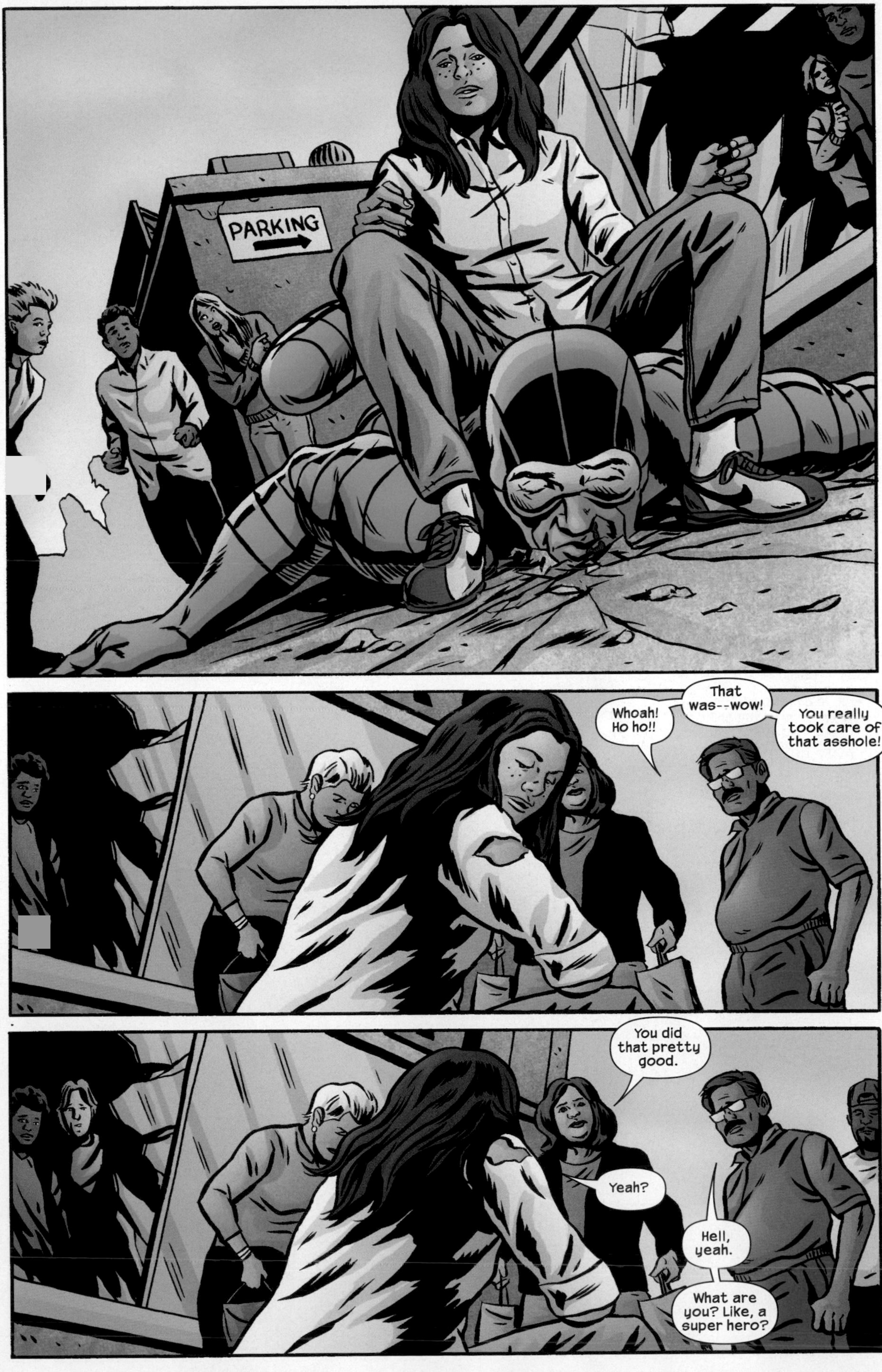
PARKING
Whoah! Ho ho!!
That was--wow!
You really took care of that asshole!
You did that pretty good.
Yeah?
Hell, yeah.
What are you? Like, a super hero?

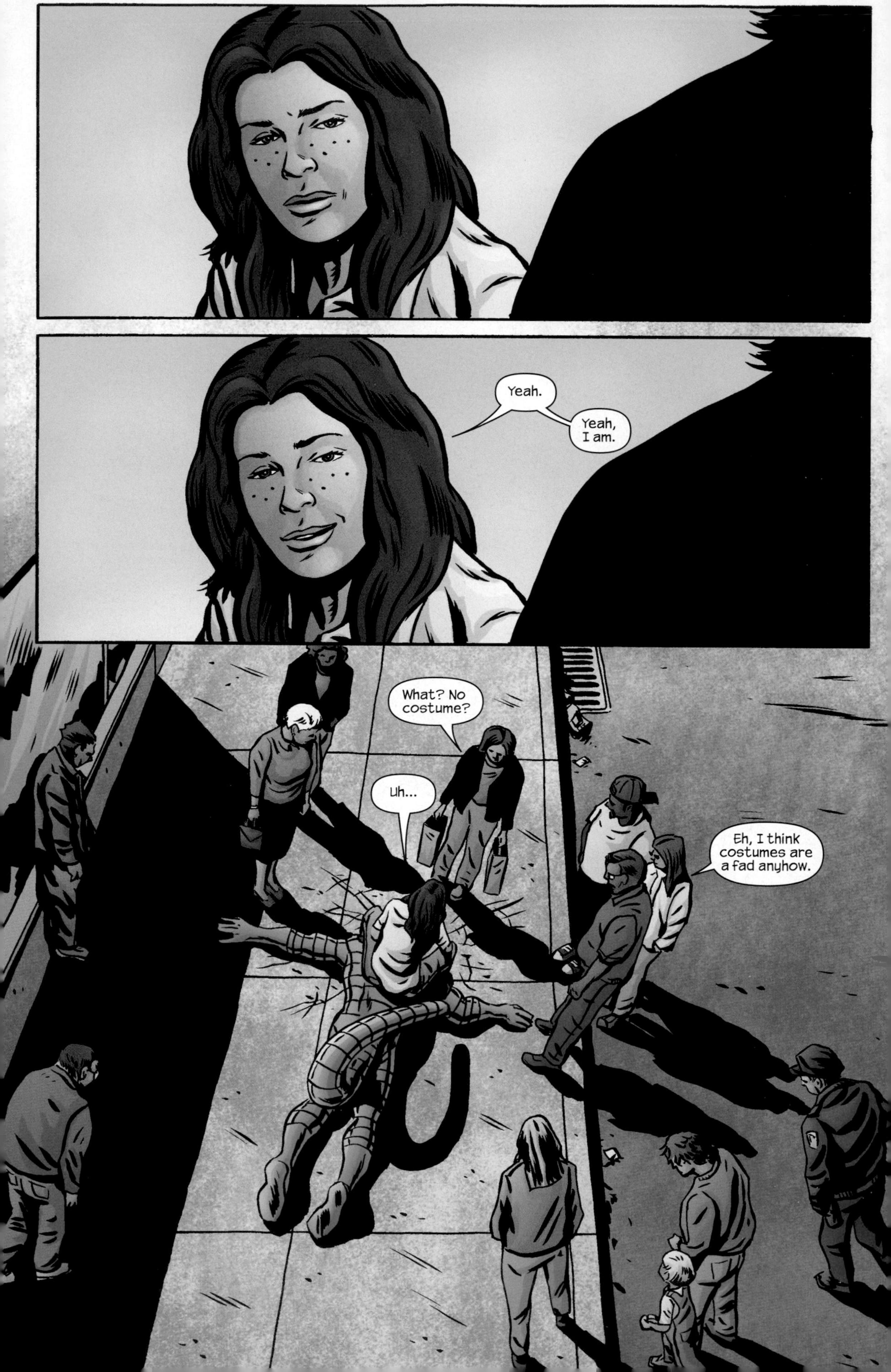
Yeah.
Yeah, I am.
What? No costume?
Uh...
Eh, I think costumes are a fad anyhow.

[redacted] R[redacted]E

ISSUE #24

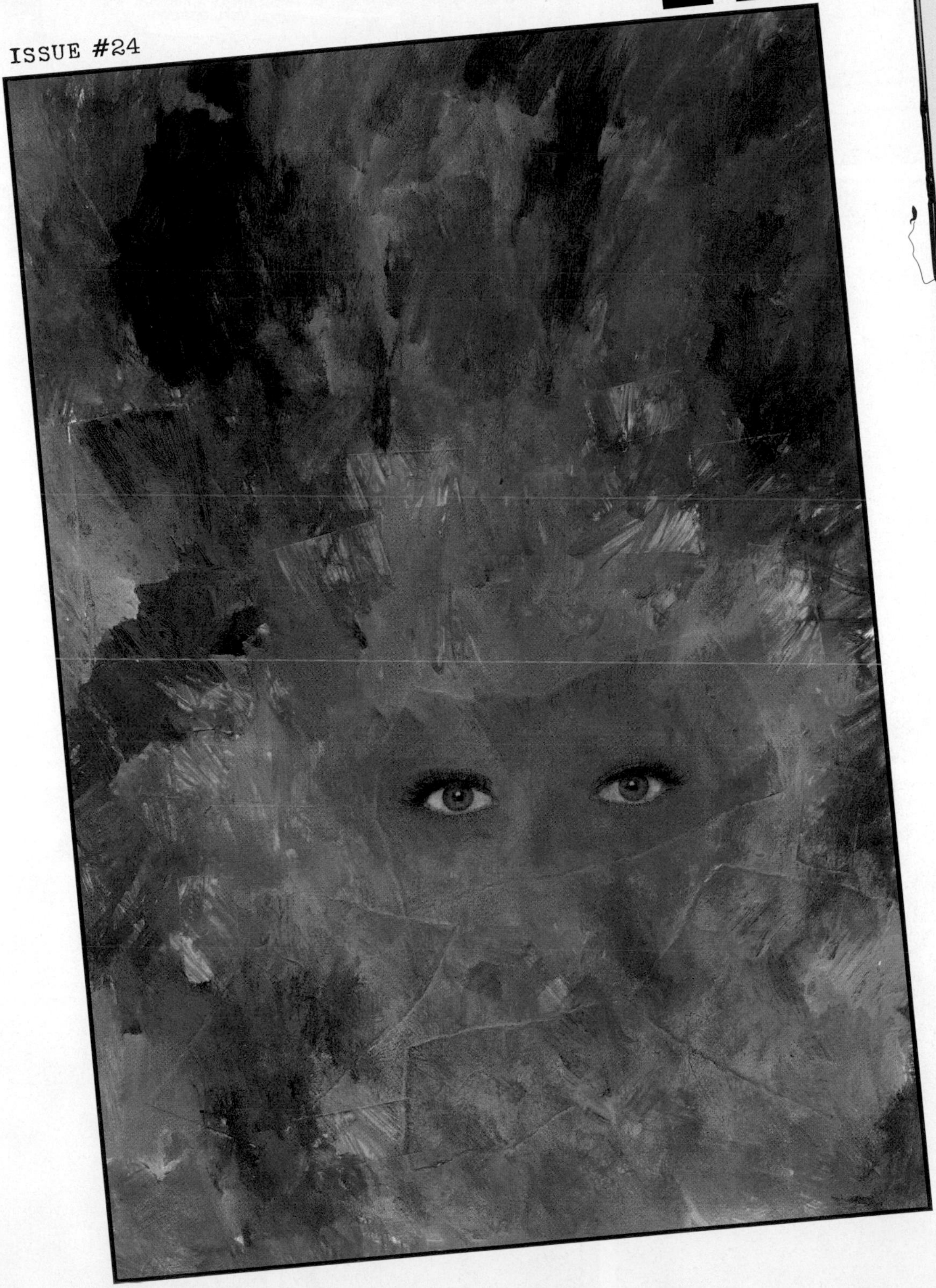

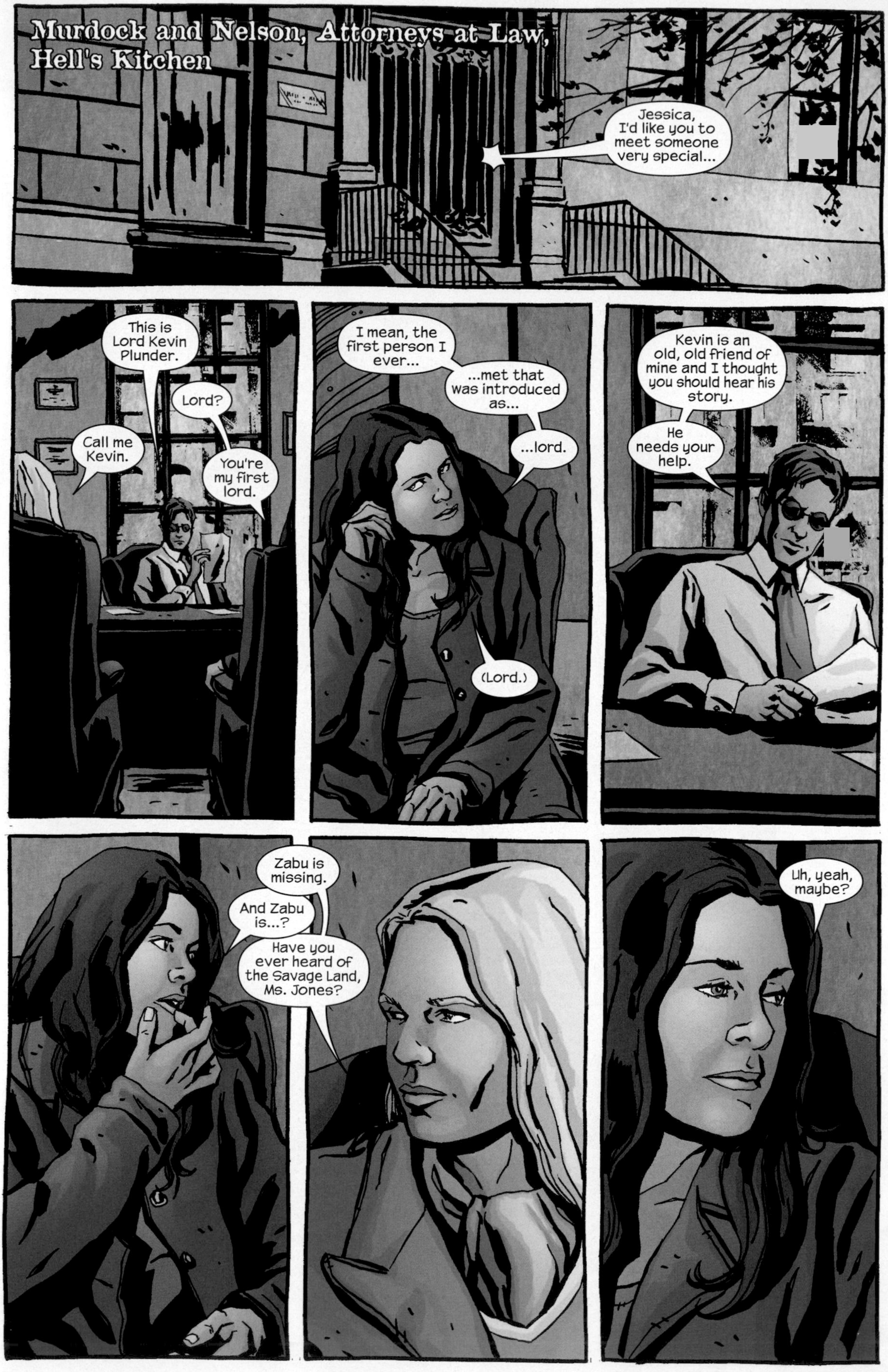
Murdock and Nelson, Attorneys at Law, Hell's Kitchen
Jessica, I'd like you to meet someone very special...
This is Lord Kevin Plunder.
Lord?
Call me Kevin.
You're my first lord.
I mean, the first person I ever...
...met that was introduced as...
...lord.
(Lord.)
Kevin is an old, old friend of mine and I thought you should hear his story.
He needs your help.
Zabu is missing.
And Zabu is...?
Have you ever heard of the Savage Land, Ms. Jones?
Uh, yeah, maybe?

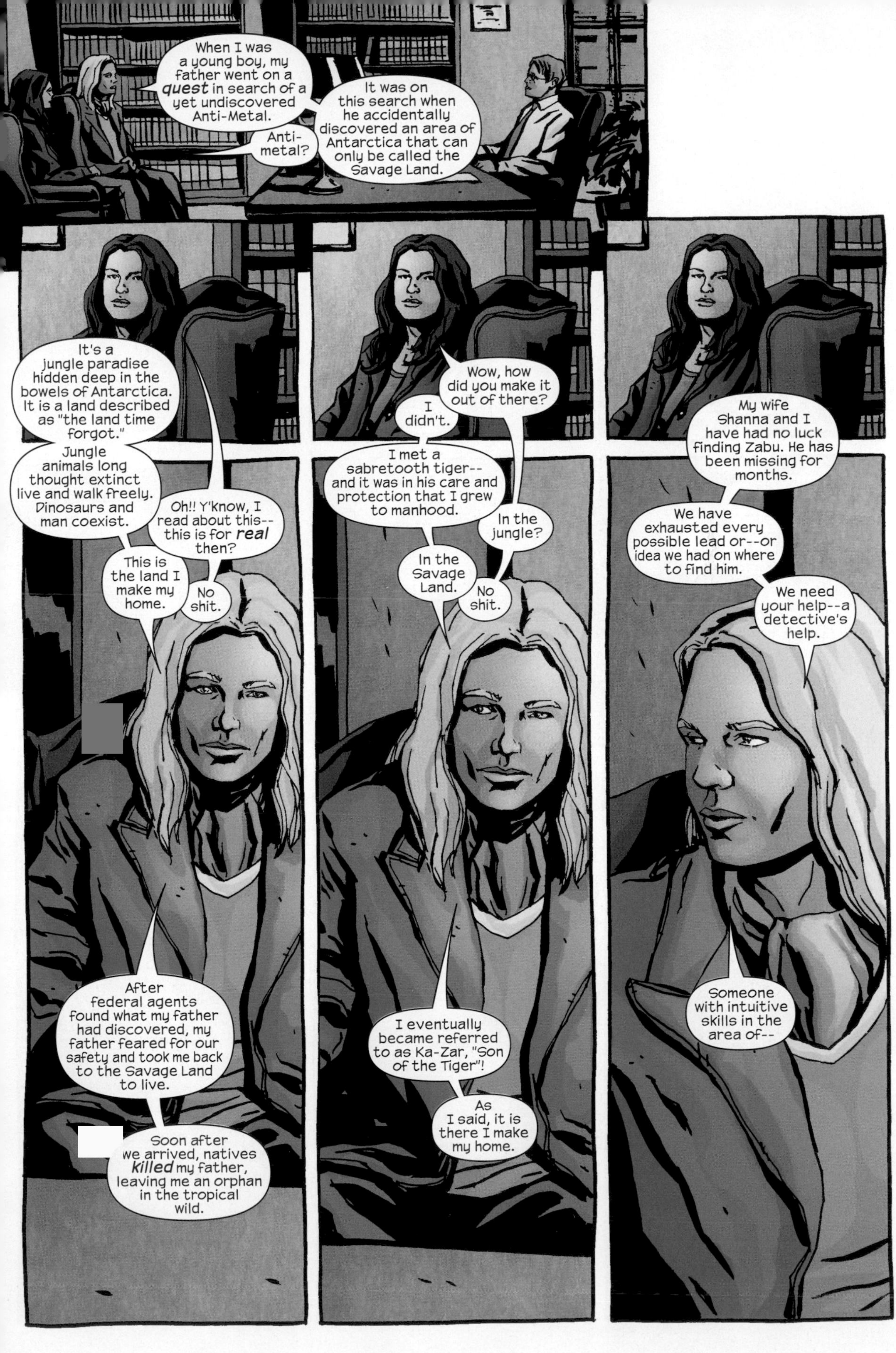
When I was a young boy, my father went on a quest in search of a yet undiscovered Anti-Metal.
Anti-metal?
It was on this search when he accidentally discovered an area of Antarctica that can only be called the Savage Land.
It's a jungle paradise hidden deep in the bowels of Antarctica. It is a land described as "the land time forgot."
Jungle animals long thought extinct live and walk freely. Dinosaurs and man coexist.
Oh!! Y'know, I read about this--this is for real then?
This is the land I make my home.
No shit.
After federal agents found what my father had discovered, my father feared for our safety and took me back to the Savage Land to live.
Soon after we arrived, natives killed my father, leaving me an orphan in the tropical wild.
Wow, how did you make it out of there?
I didn't.
I met a sabretooth tiger--and it was in his care and protection that I grew to manhood.
In the jungle?
In the Savage Land.
No shit.
I eventually became referred to as Ka-Zar, "Son of the Tiger"!
As I said, it is there I make my home.
My wife Shanna and I have had no luck finding Zabu. He has been missing for months.
We have exhausted every possible lead or--or idea we had on where to find him.
We need your help--a detective's help.
Someone with intuitive skills in the area of--

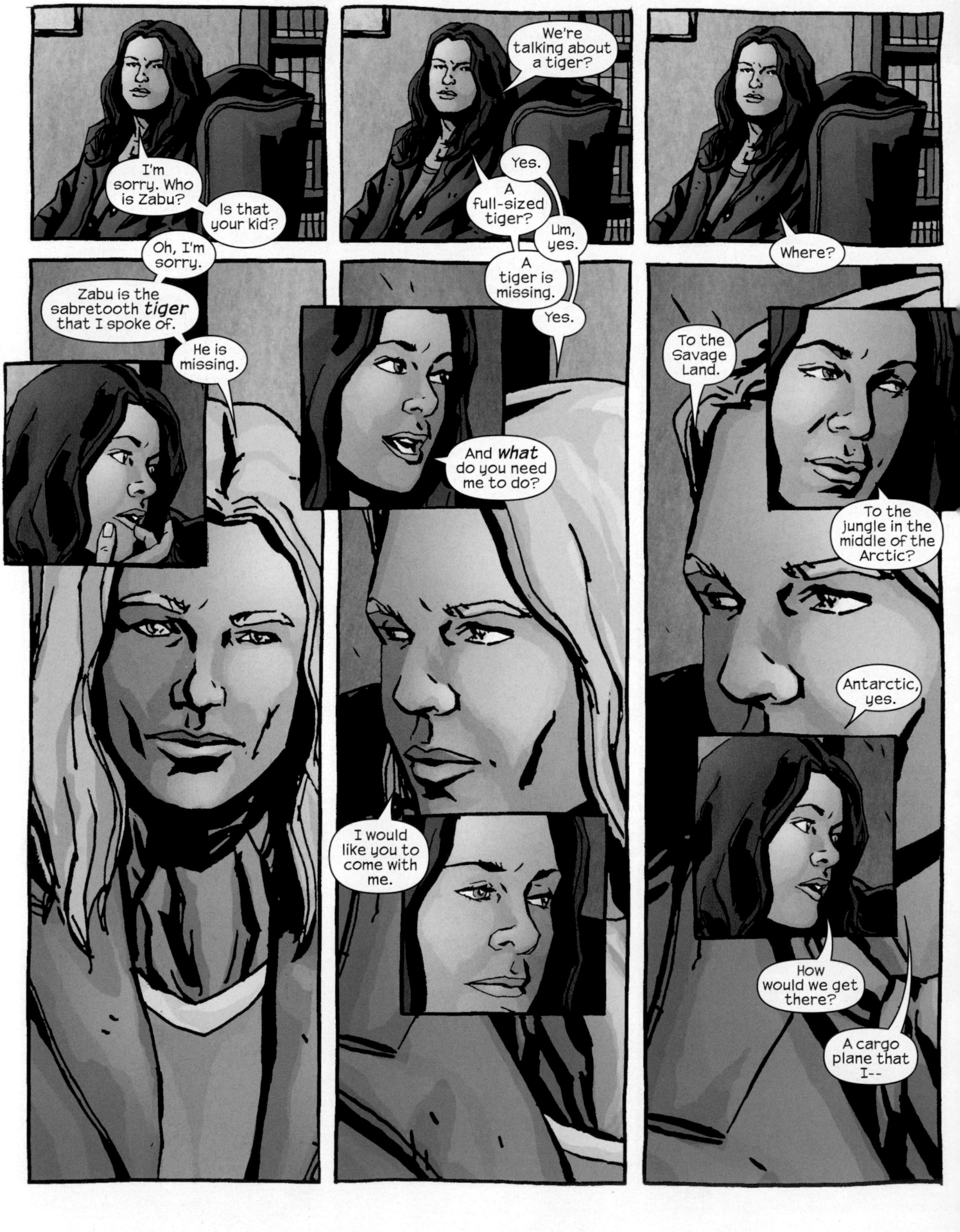
I'm sorry. Who is Zabu?
Is that your kid?
We're talking about a tiger?
Yes.
A full-sized tiger?
Um, yes.
A tiger is missing.
Yes.
Where?
Oh, I'm sorry.
Zabu is the sabretooth *tiger* that I spoke of.
He is missing.
And *what* do you need me to do?
I would like you to come with me.
To the Savage Land.
To the jungle in the middle of the Arctic?
Antarctic, yes.
How would we get there?
A cargo plane that I--

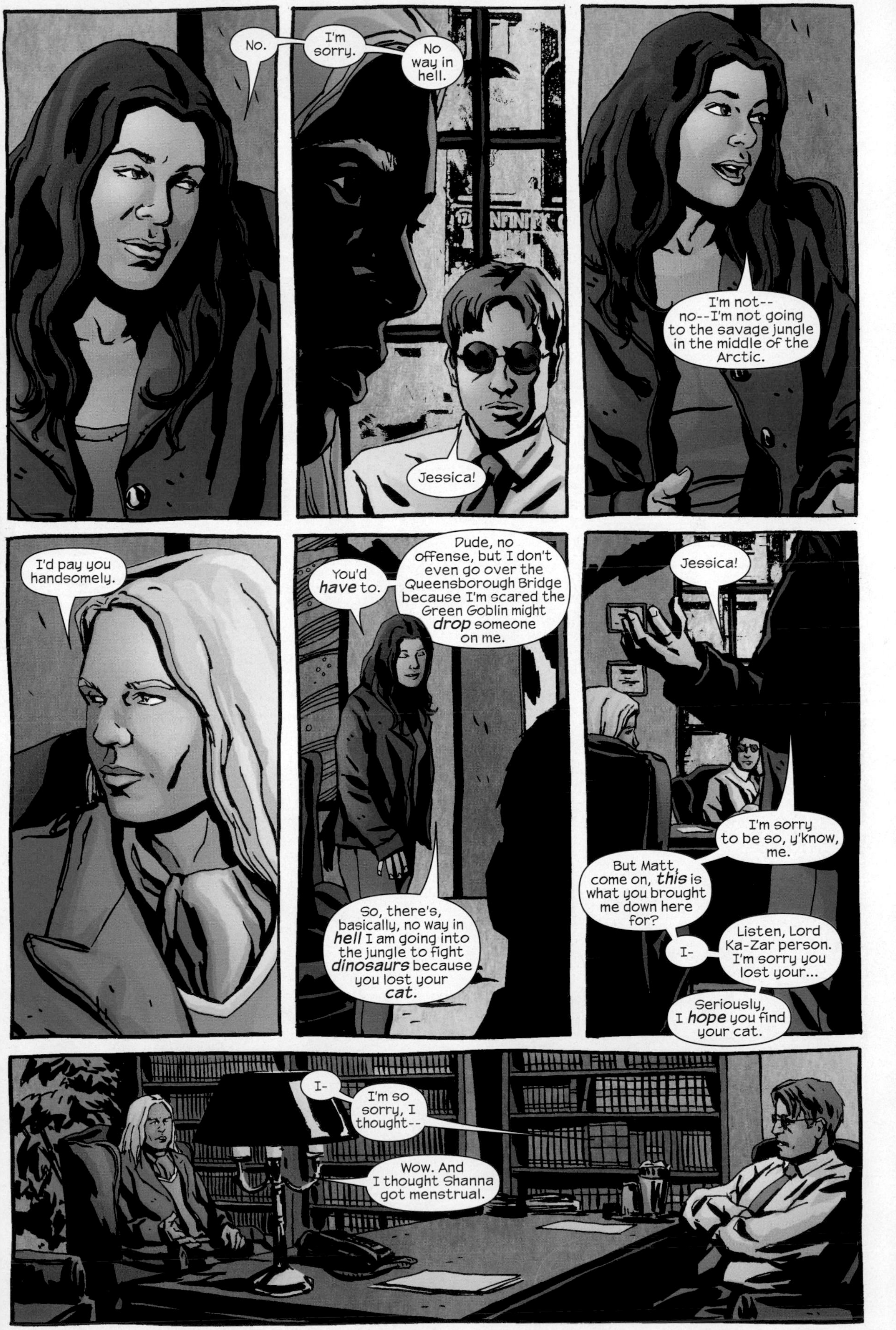
No.
I'm sorry.
No way in hell.
Jessica!
I'm not-- no--I'm not going to the savage jungle in the middle of the Arctic.
I'd pay you handsomely.
You'd have to.
Dude, no offense, but I don't even go over the Queensborough Bridge because I'm scared the Green Goblin might drop someone on me.
So, there's, basically, no way in hell I am going into the jungle to fight dinosaurs because you lost your cat.
Jessica!
I'm sorry to be so, y'know, me.
But Matt, come on, this is what you brought me down here for?
I-
Listen, Lord Ka-Zar person. I'm sorry you lost your...
Seriously, I hope you find your cat.
I-
I'm so sorry, I thought--
Wow. And I thought Shanna got menstrual.

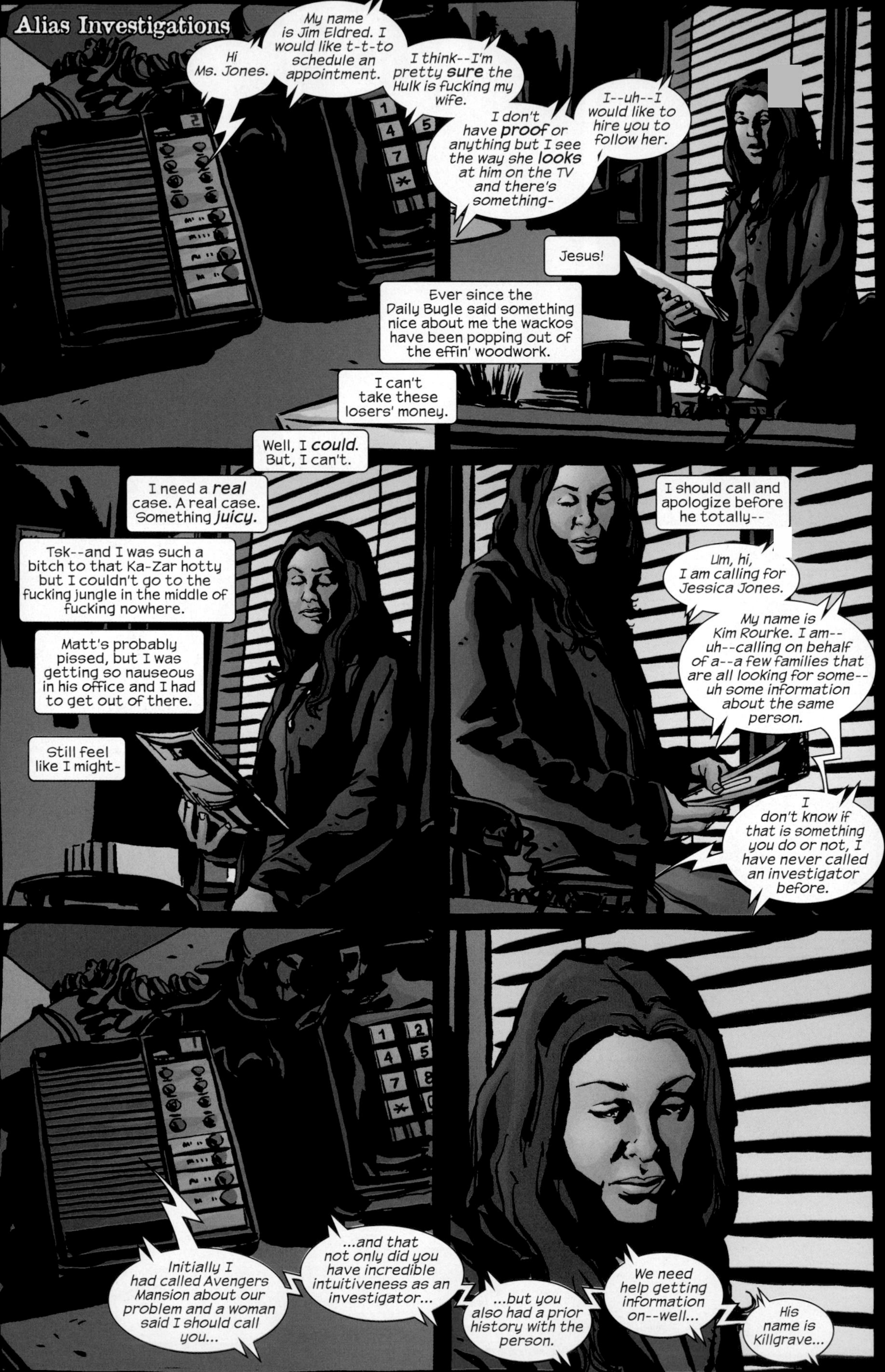
Alias Investigations
Hi Ms. Jones.
My name is Jim Eldred. I would like t-t-to schedule an appointment.
I think--I'm pretty sure the Hulk is fucking my wife.
I don't have proof or anything but I see the way she looks at him on the TV and there's something-
I--uh--I would like to hire you to follow her.
Jesus!
Ever since the Daily Bugle said something nice about me the wackos have been popping out of the effin' woodwork.
I can't take these losers' money.
Well, I could. But, I can't.
I need a real case. A real case. Something juicy.
Tsk--and I was such a bitch to that Ka-Zar hotty but I couldn't go to the fucking jungle in the middle of fucking nowhere.
Matt's probably pissed, but I was getting so nauseous in his office and I had to get out of there.
Still feel like I might-
I should call and apologize before he totally--
Um, hi, I am calling for Jessica Jones.
My name is Kim Rourke. I am--uh--calling on behalf of a--a few families that are all looking for some--uh some information about the same person.
I don't know if that is something you do or not, I have never called an investigator before.
Initially I had called Avengers Mansion about our problem and a woman said I should call you...
...and that not only did you have incredible intuitiveness as an investigator...
...but you also had a prior history with the person.
We need help getting information on--well...
His name is Killgrave...

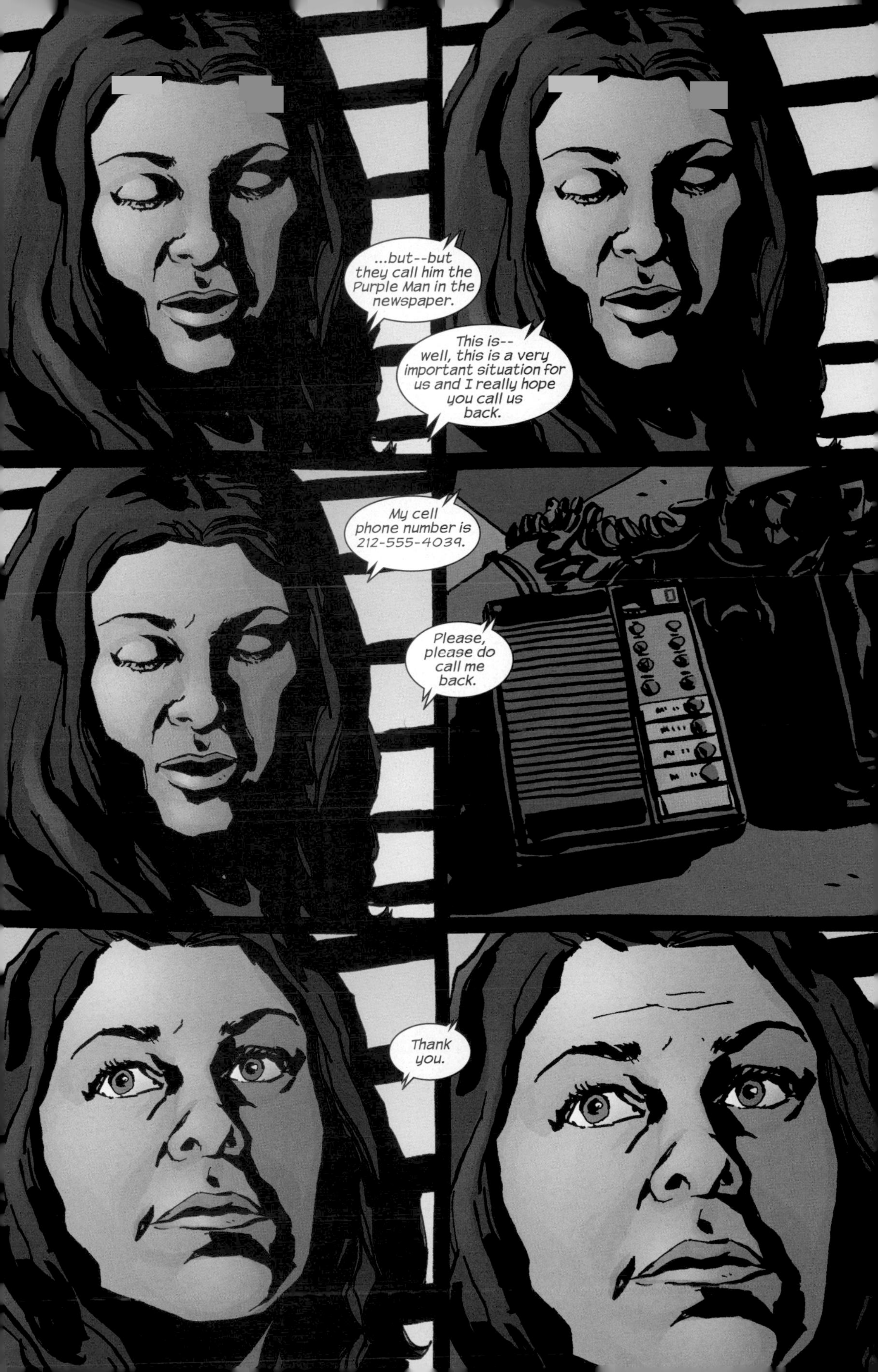

...but--but they call him the Purple Man in the newspaper.
This is-- well, this is a very important situation for us and I really hope you call us back.
My cell phone number is 212-555-4039.
Please, please do call me back.
Thank you.

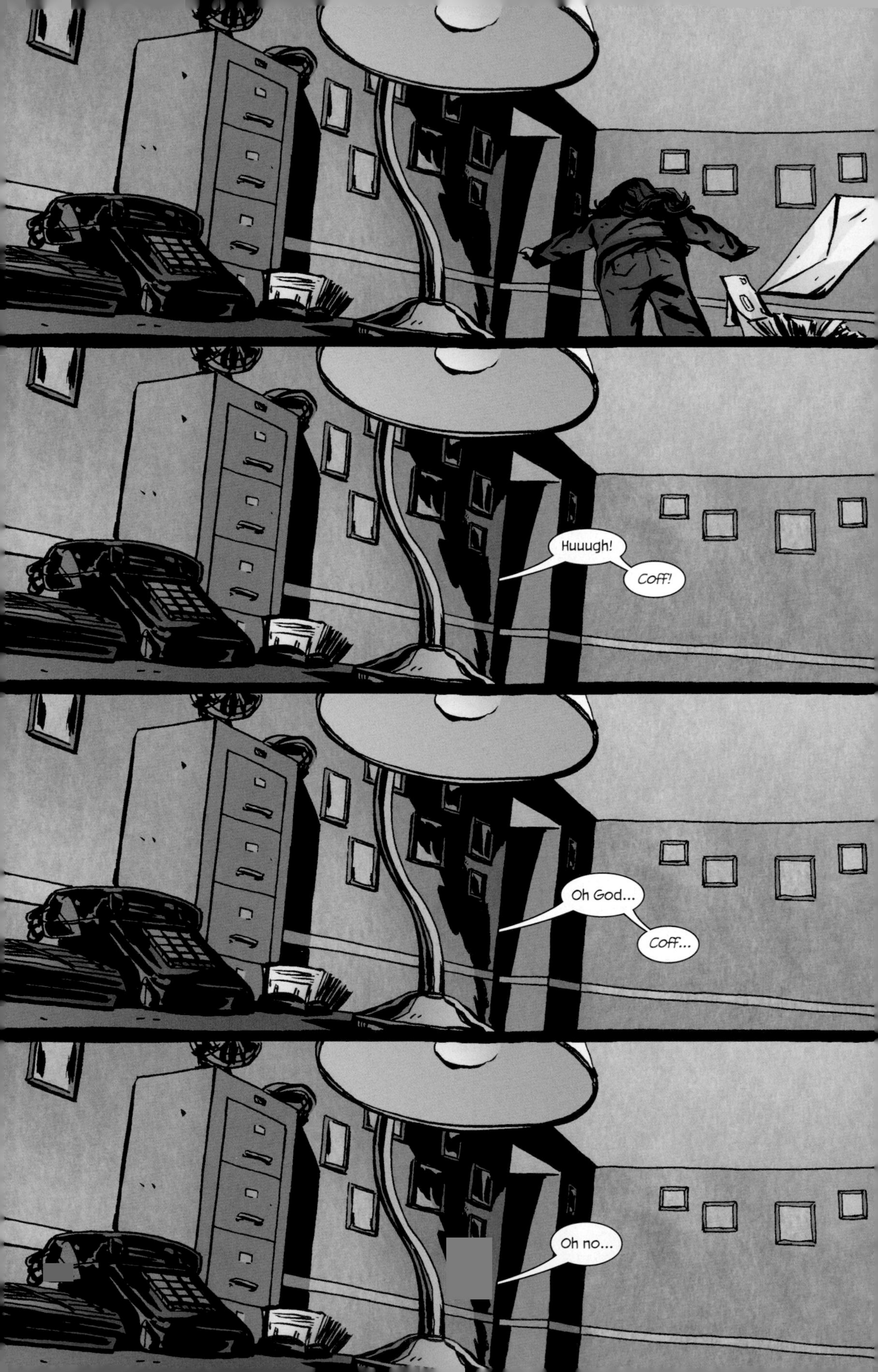
Huuugh!
Coff!
Oh God...
Coff...
Oh no...

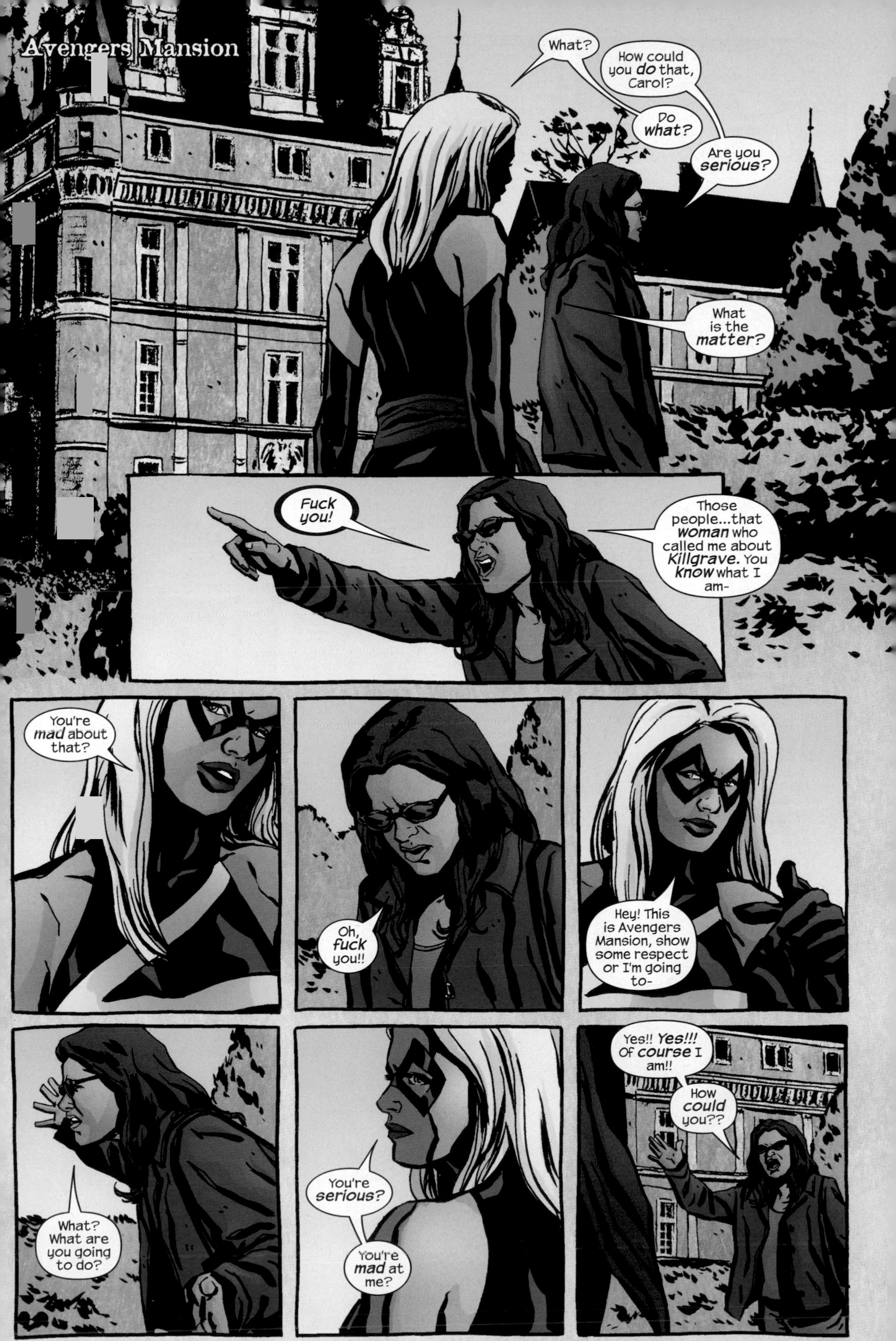
Avengers Mansion
What?
How could you do that, Carol?
Do what?
Are you serious?
What is the matter?
Fuck you!
Those people...that woman who called me about Killgrave. You know what I am-
You're mad about that?
Oh, fuck you!!
Hey! This is Avengers Mansion, show some respect or I'm going to-
What? What are you going to do?
You're serious?
You're mad at me?
Yes!! Yes!!! Of course I am!!
How could you??

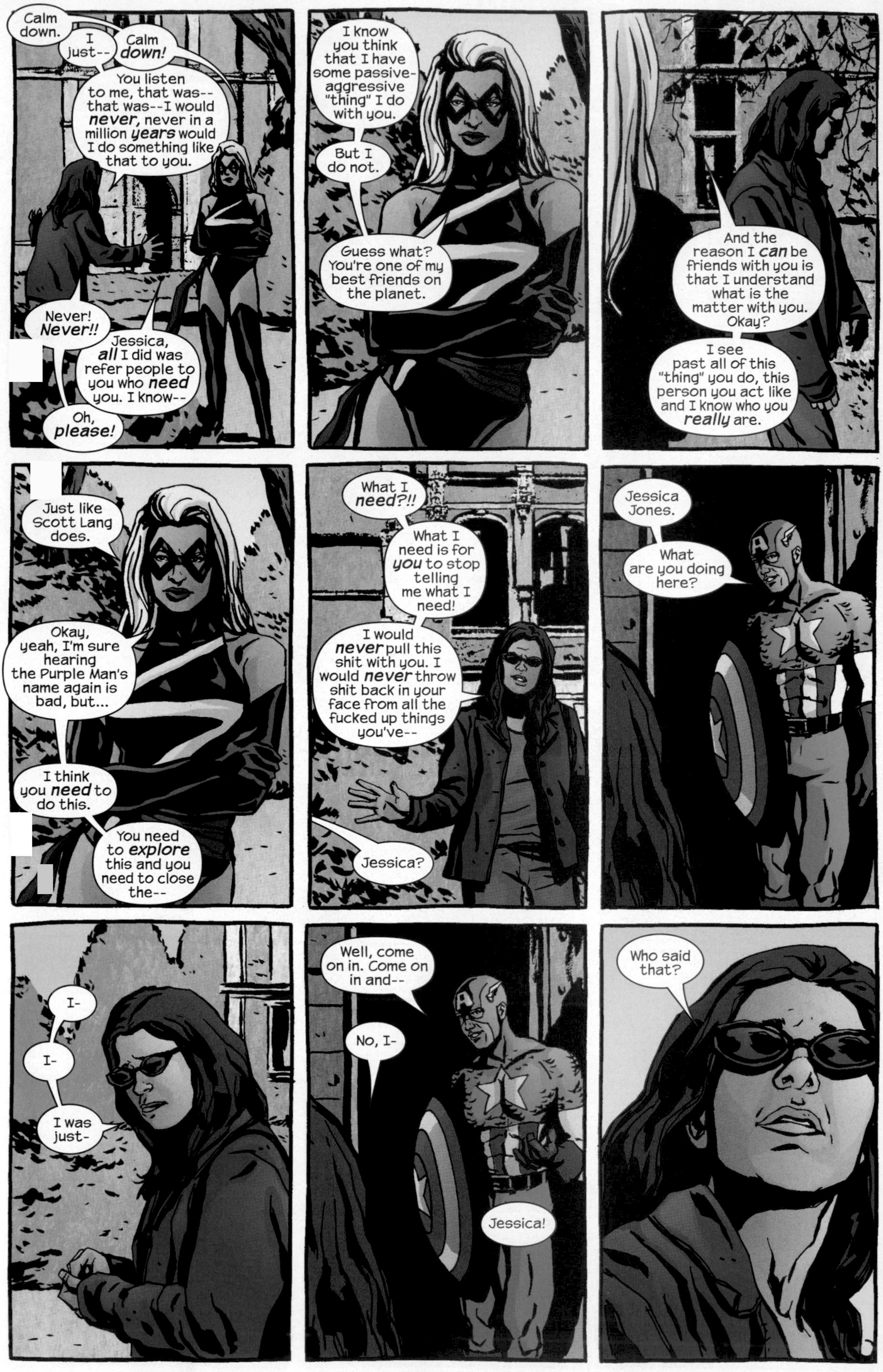
Calm down.
I just--
Calm down!
You listen to me, that was--that was--I would never, never in a million years would I do something like that to you.
Never! Never!!
Jessica, all I did was refer people to you who need you. I know--
Oh, please!
I know you think that I have some passive-aggressive "thing" I do with you.
But I do not.
Guess what? You're one of my best friends on the planet.
And the reason I can be friends with you is that I understand what is the matter with you. Okay?
I see past all of this "thing" you do, this person you act like and I know who you really are.
Just like Scott Lang does.
Okay, yeah, I'm sure hearing the Purple Man's name again is bad, but...
I think you need to do this.
You need to explore this and you need to close the--
What I need?!!
What I need is for you to stop telling me what I need!
I would never pull this shit with you. I would never throw shit back in your face from all the fucked up things you've--
Jessica?
Jessica Jones.
What are you doing here?
I-
I-
I was just-
Well, come on in. Come on in and--
No, I-
Jessica!
Who said that?

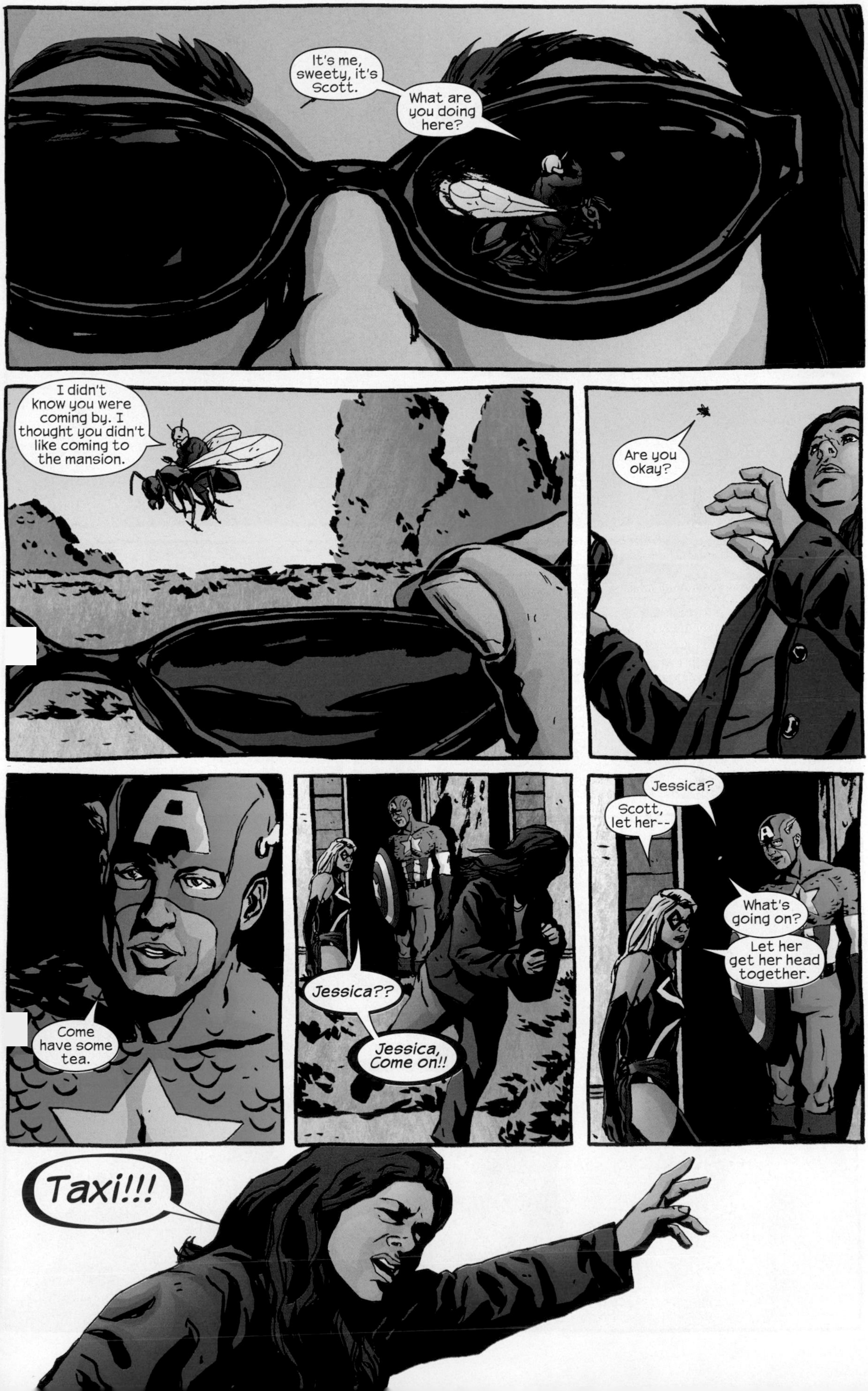
It's me, sweety, it's Scott.
What are you doing here?
I didn't know you were coming by. I thought you didn't like coming to the mansion.
Are you okay?
Come have some tea.
Jessica??
Jessica, Come on!!
Jessica?
Scott, let her--
What's going on?
Let her get her head together.
Taxi!!!

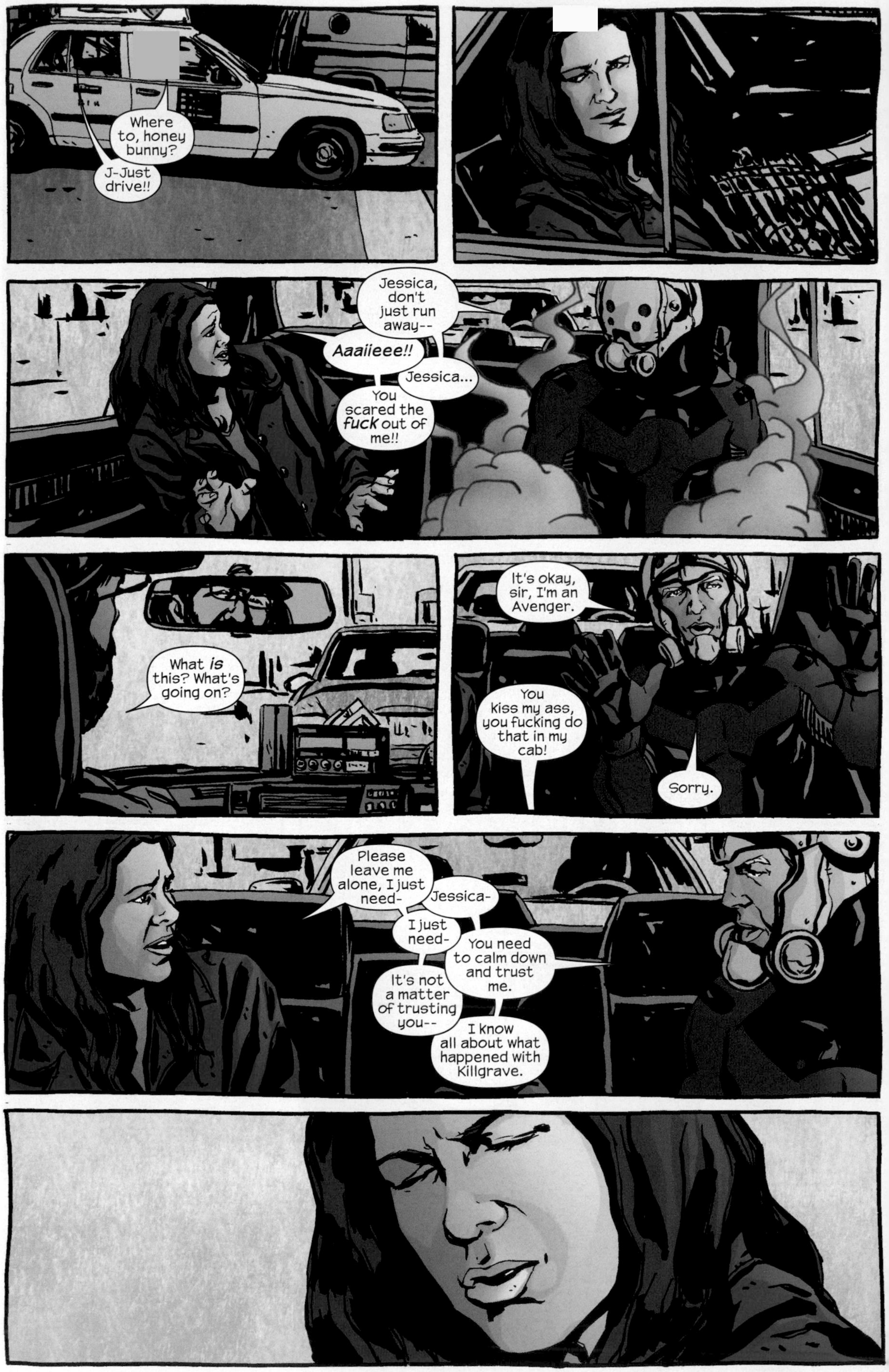
Where to, honey bunny?
J-Just drive!!
Jessica, don't just run away--
Aaaiieee!!
Jessica...
You scared the fuck out of me!!
What is this? What's going on?
It's okay, sir, I'm an Avenger.
You kiss my ass, you fucking do that in my cab!
Sorry.
Please leave me alone, I just need-
Jessica-
I just need-
You need to calm down and trust me.
It's not a matter of trusting you--
I know all about what happened with Killgrave.

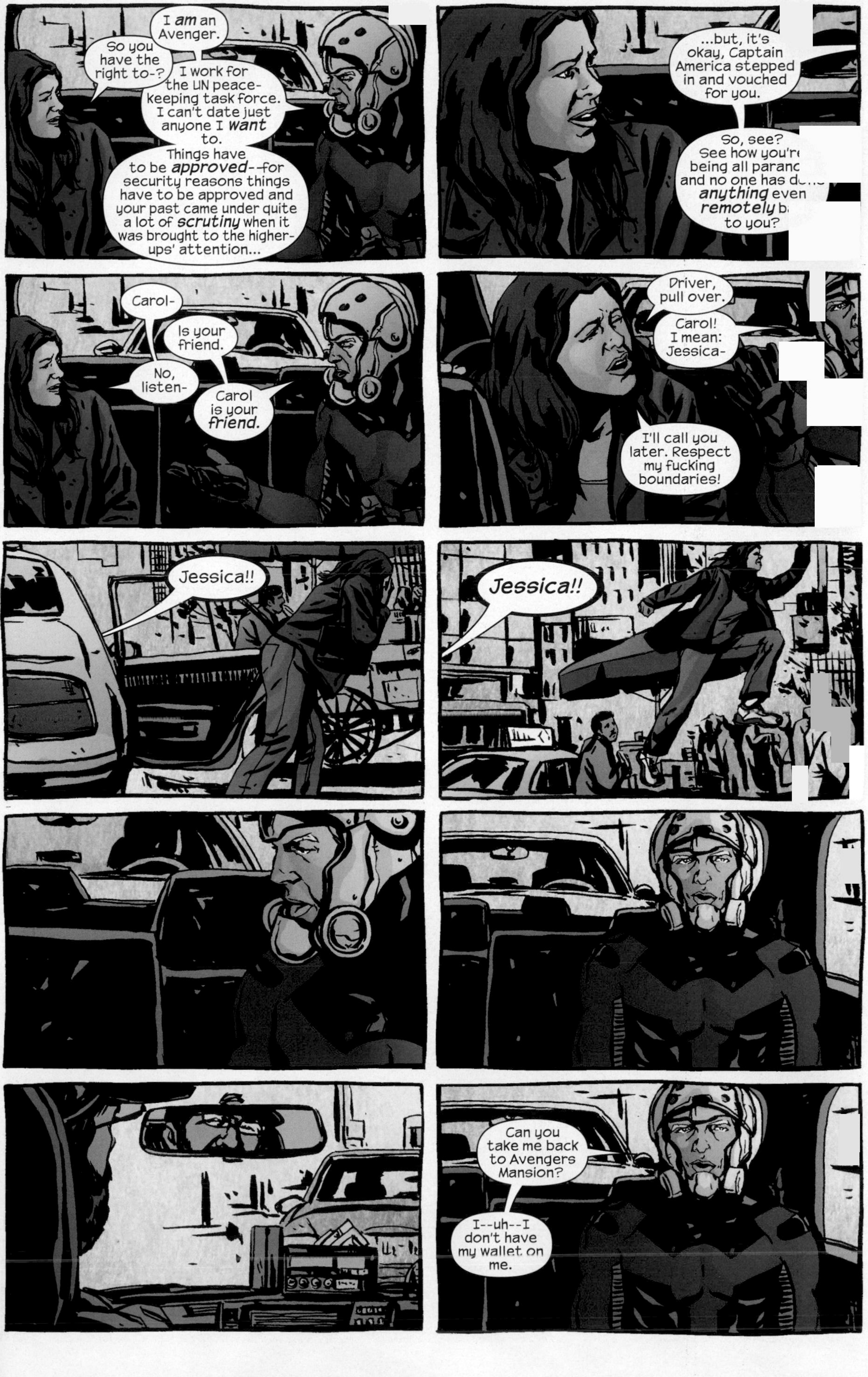
So you have the right to-?
I am an Avenger.
I work for the UN peace-keeping task force. I can't date just anyone I want to.
Things have to be approved--for security reasons things have to be approved and your past came under quite a lot of scrutiny when it was brought to the higher-ups' attention...
...but, it's okay, Captain America stepped in and vouched for you.
So, see? See how you'r being all paranc and no one has d anything even remotely b to you?
Carol-
Is your friend.
No, listen-
Carol is your friend.
Driver, pull over.
Carol! I mean: Jessica-
I'll call you later. Respect my fucking boundaries!
Jessica!!
Jessica!!
Can you take me back to Avengers Mansion?
I--uh--I don't have my wallet on me.

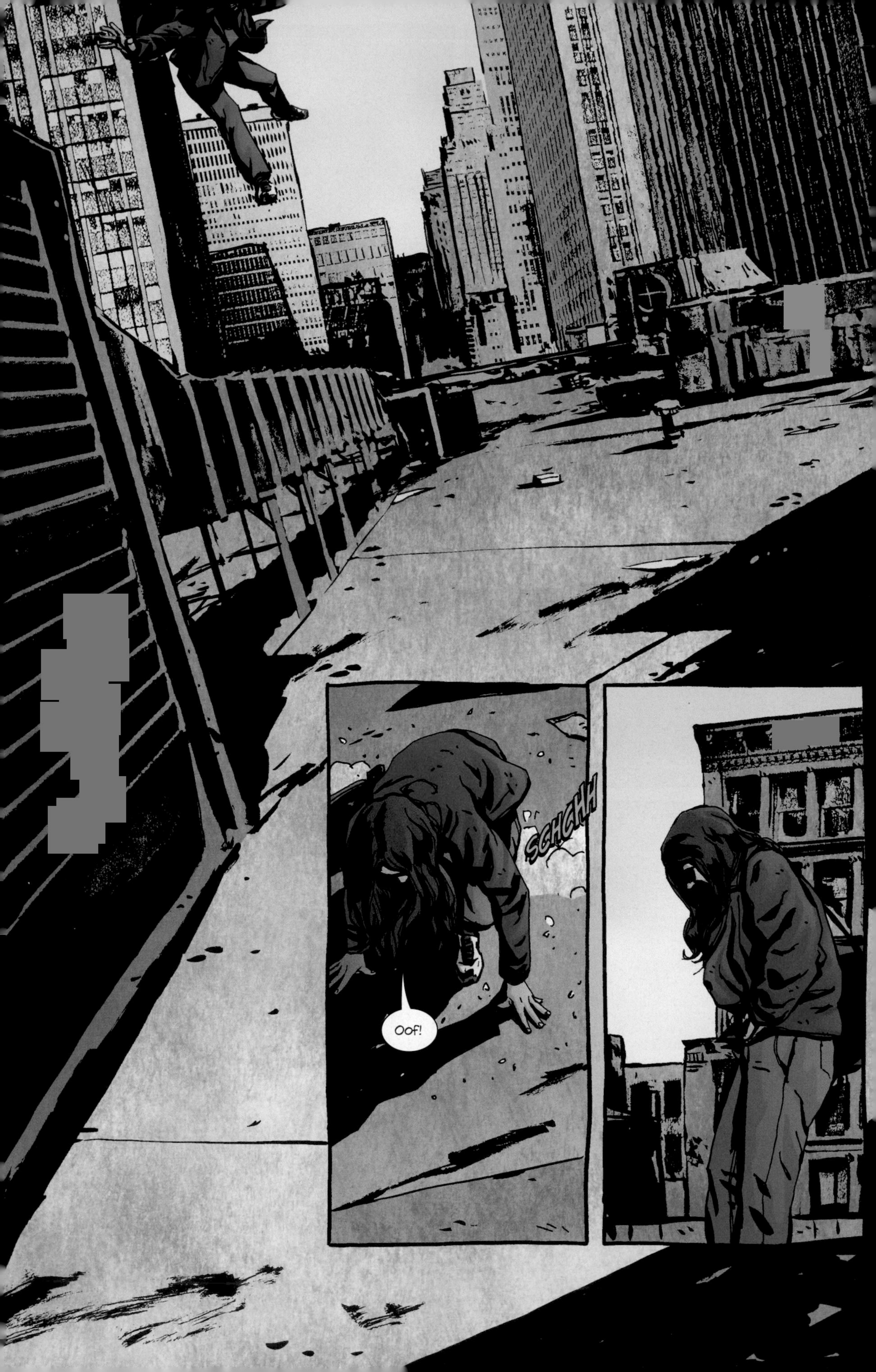
SCHCHH
Oof!

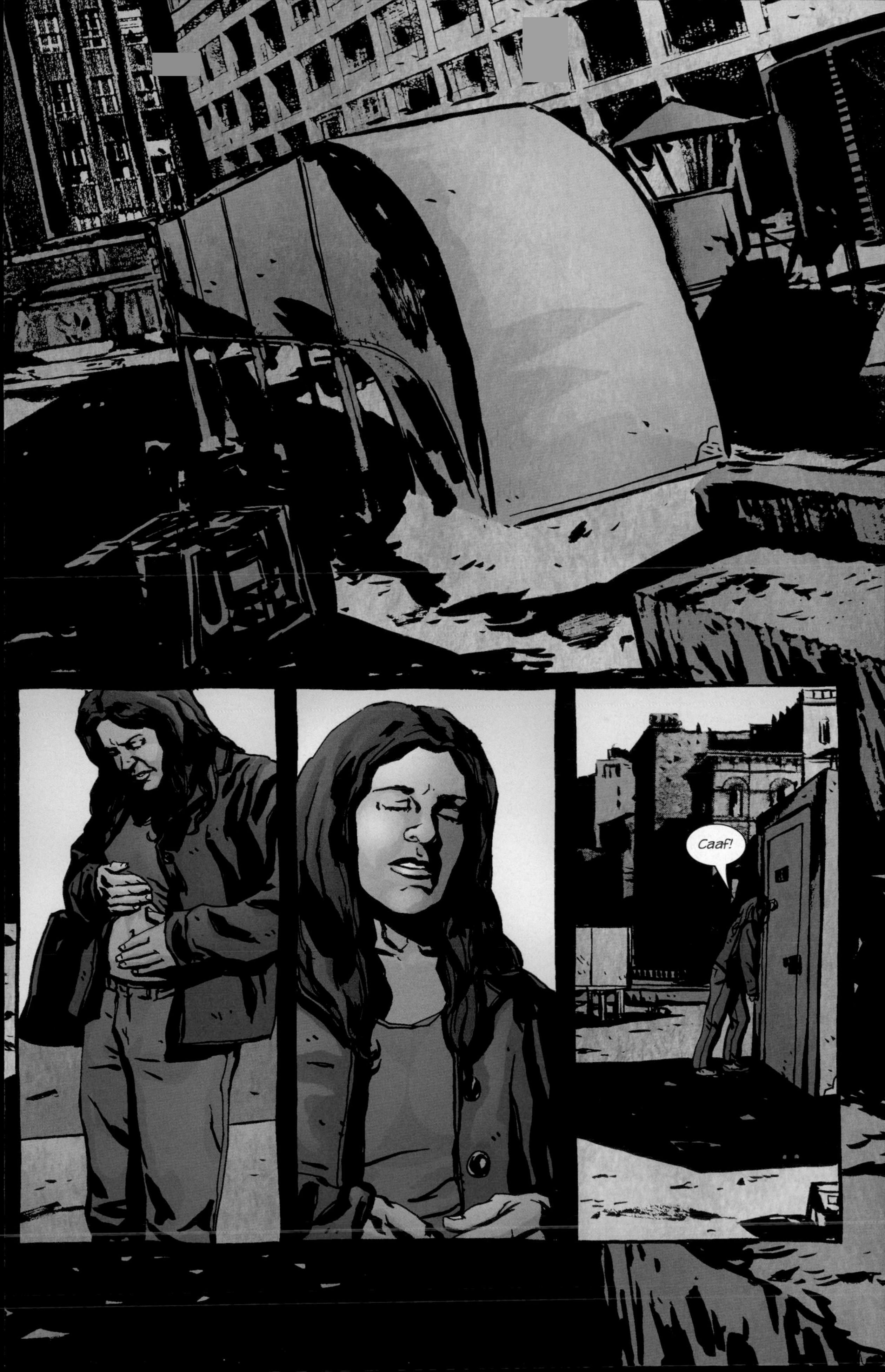
Caaf!

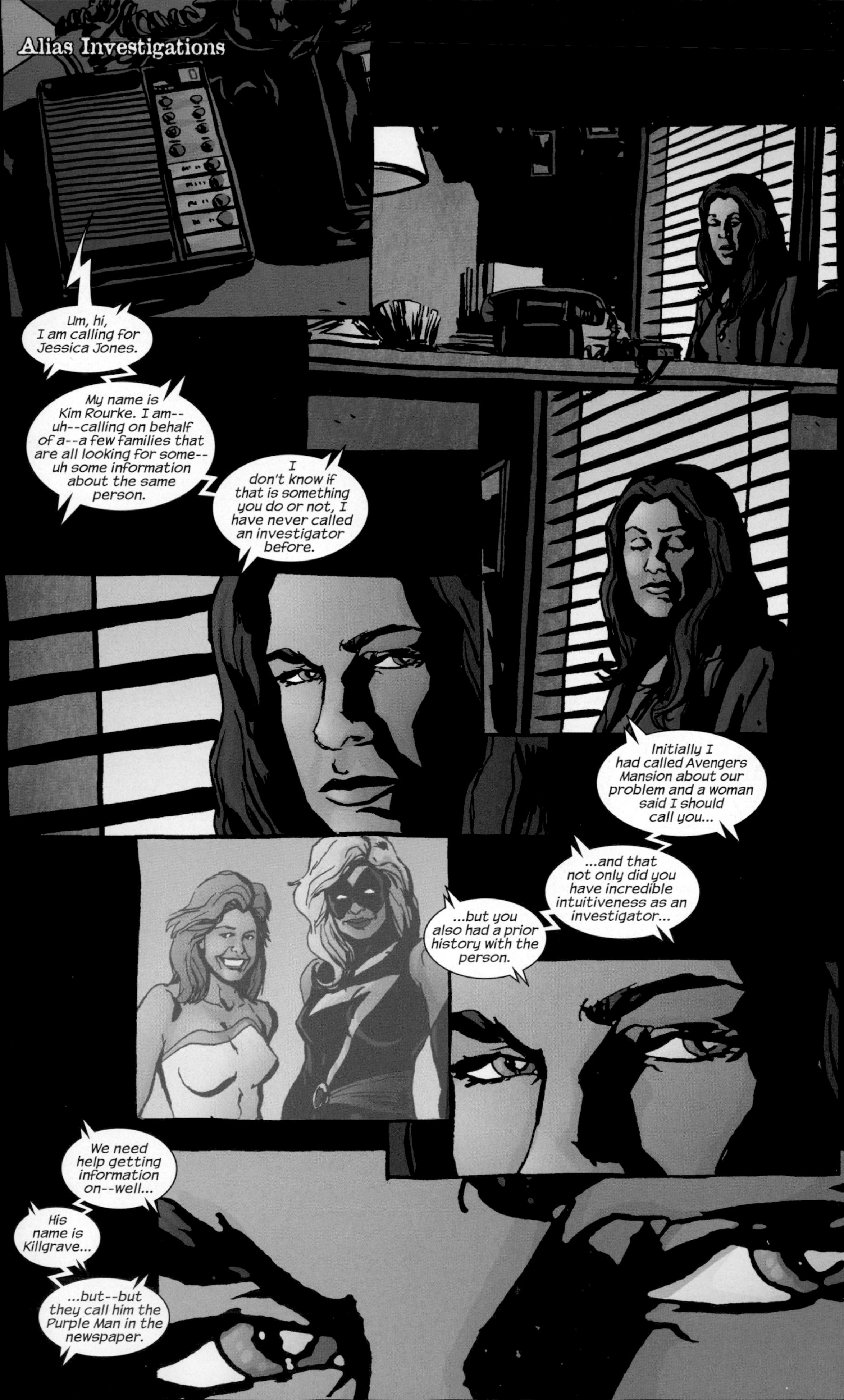

Alias Investigations
Um, hi, I am calling for Jessica Jones.
My name is Kim Rourke. I am--uh--calling on behalf of a--a few families that are all looking for some--uh some information about the same person.
I don't know if that is something you do or not, I have never called an investigator before.
Initially I had called Avengers Mansion about our problem and a woman said I should call you...
...and that not only did you have incredible intuitiveness as an investigator...
...but you also had a prior history with the person.
We need help getting information on--well...
His name is Killgrave...
...but--but they call him the Purple Man in the newspaper.

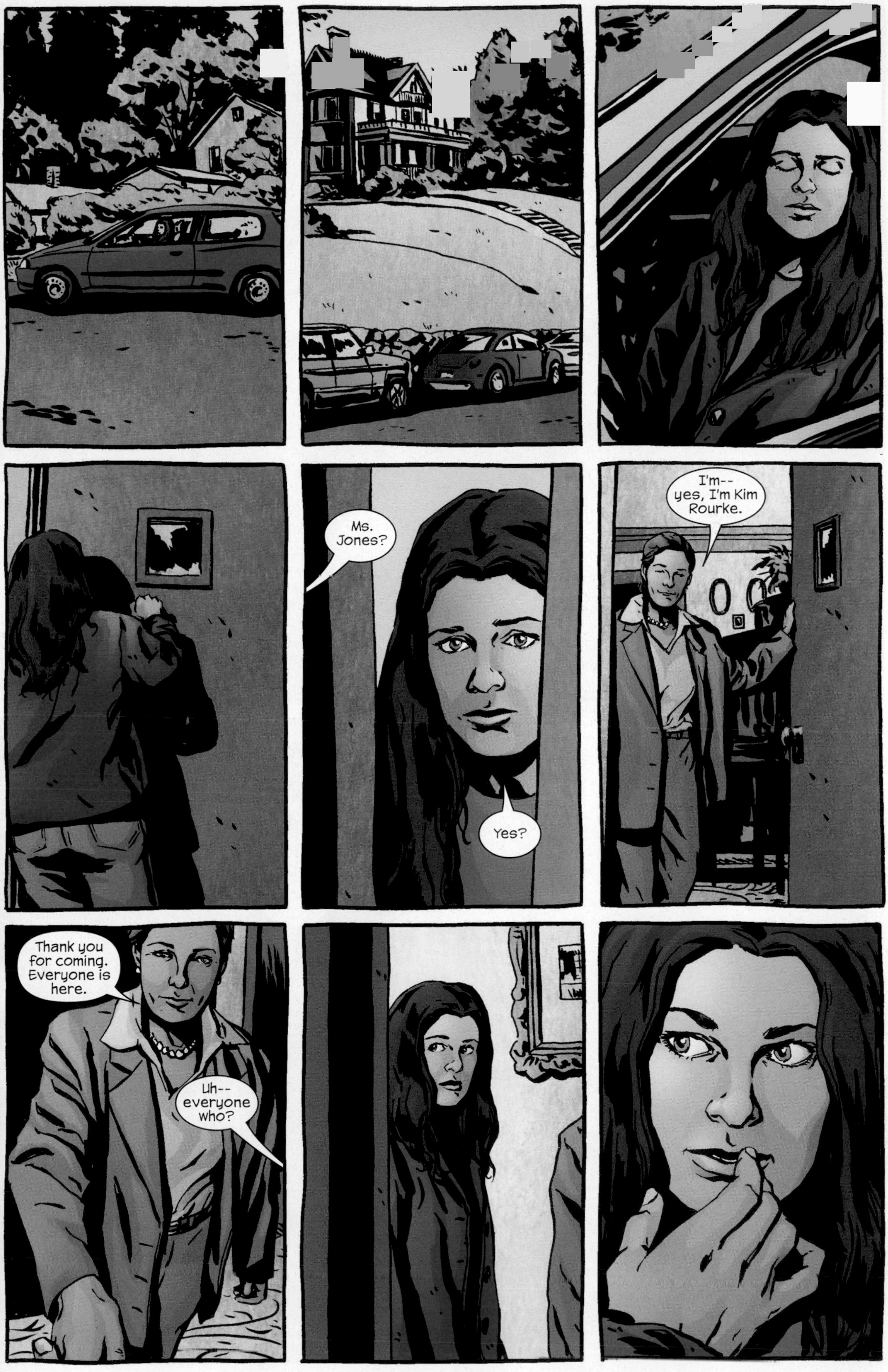
Ms. Jones?
Yes?
I'm-- yes, I'm Kim Rourke.
Thank you for coming. Everyone is here.
Uh-- everyone who?

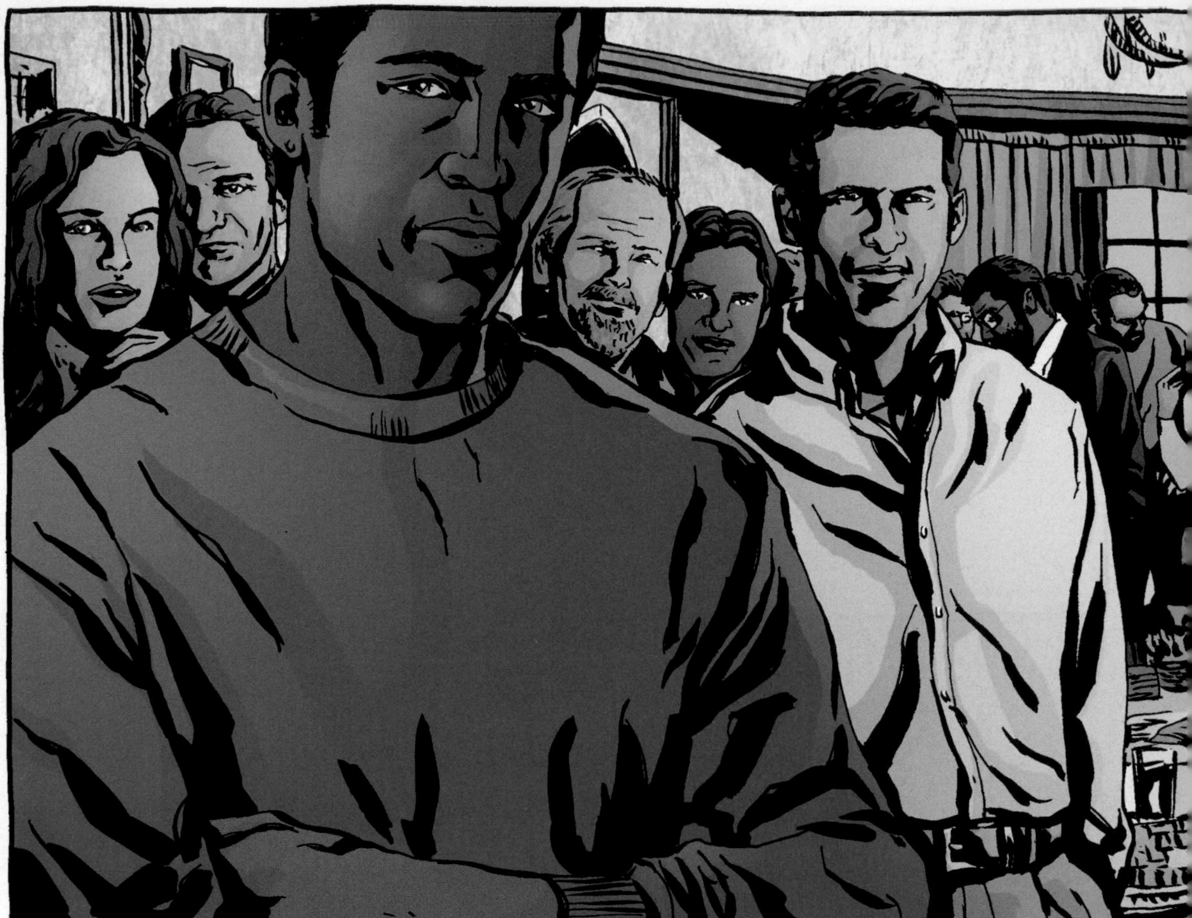

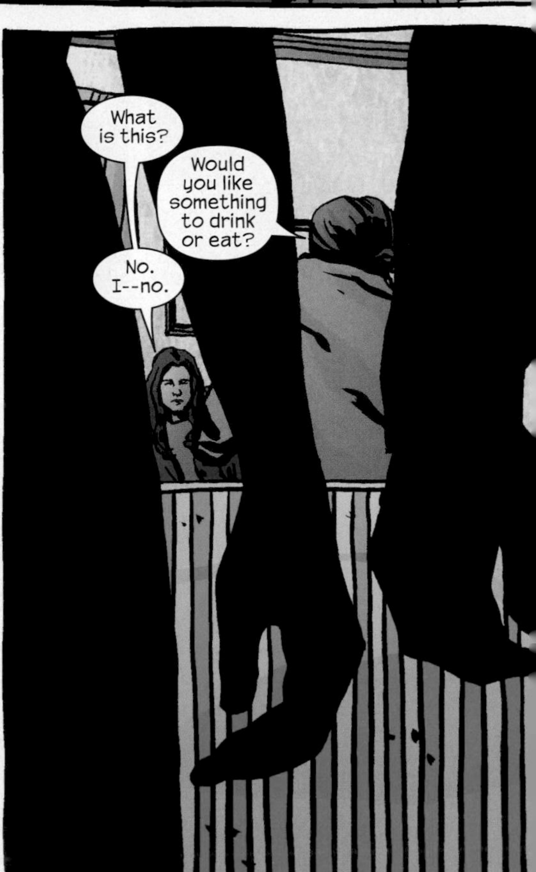
What is this?
Would you like something to drink or eat?
No. I--no.

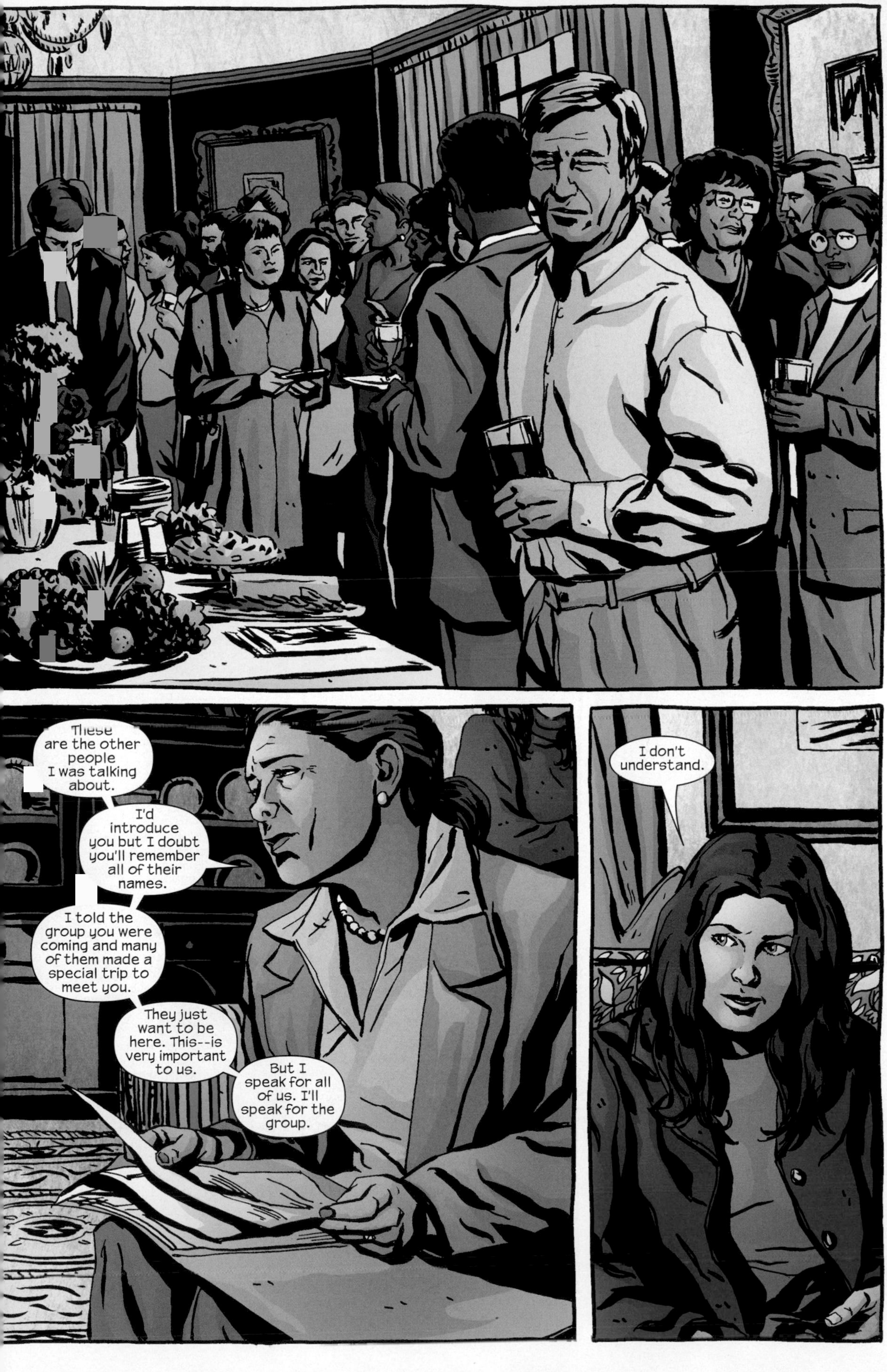
These are the other people I was talking about.
I'd introduce you but I doubt you'll remember all of their names.
I told the group you were coming and many of them made a special trip to meet you.
They just want to be here. This--is very important to us.
But I speak for all of us. I'll speak for the group.
I don't understand.

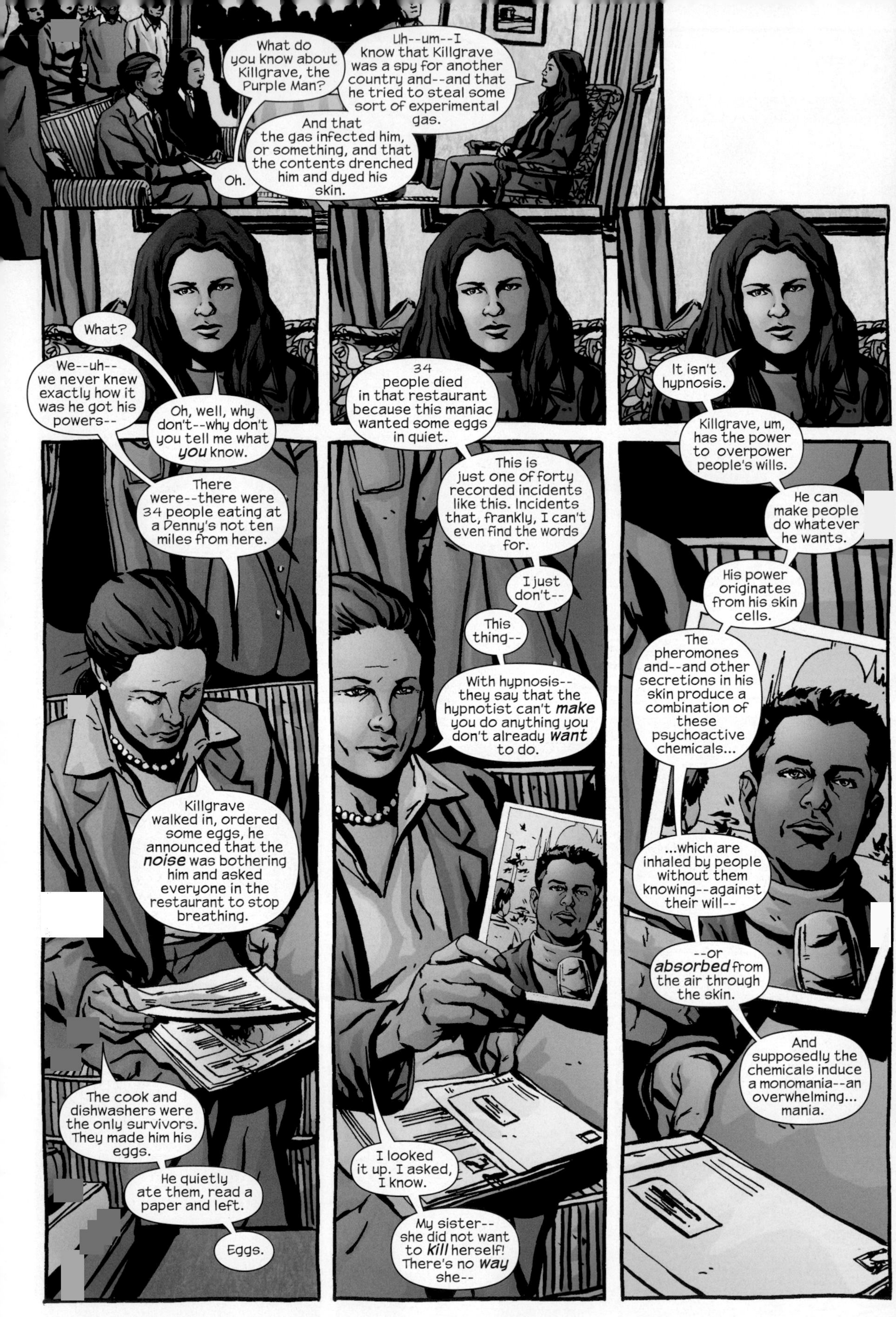

What do you know about Killgrave, the Purple Man?
Uh--um--I know that Killgrave was a spy for another country and--and that he tried to steal some sort of experimental gas.
And that the gas infected him, or something, and that the contents drenched him and dyed his skin.
Oh.
What?
We--uh--we never knew exactly how it was he got his powers--
Oh, well, why don't--why don't you tell me what *you* know.
There were--there were 34 people eating at a Denny's not ten miles from here.
Killgrave walked in, ordered some eggs, he announced that the *noise* was bothering him and asked everyone in the restaurant to stop breathing.
The cook and dishwashers were the only survivors. They made him his eggs.
He quietly ate them, read a paper and left.
Eggs.
34 people died in that restaurant because this maniac wanted some eggs in quiet.
This is just one of forty recorded incidents like this. Incidents that, frankly, I can't even find the words for.
I just don't--
This thing--
With hypnosis--they say that the hypnotist can't *make* you do anything you don't already *want* to do.
I looked it up. I asked, I know.
My sister--she did not want to *kill* herself! There's no *way* she--
It isn't hypnosis.
Killgrave, um, has the power to overpower people's wills.
He can make people do whatever he wants.
His power originates from his skin cells.
The pheromones and--and other secretions in his skin produce a combination of these psychoactive chemicals...
...which are inhaled by people without them knowing--against their will--
--or *absorbed* from the air through the skin.
And supposedly the chemicals induce a monomania--an overwhelming... mania.

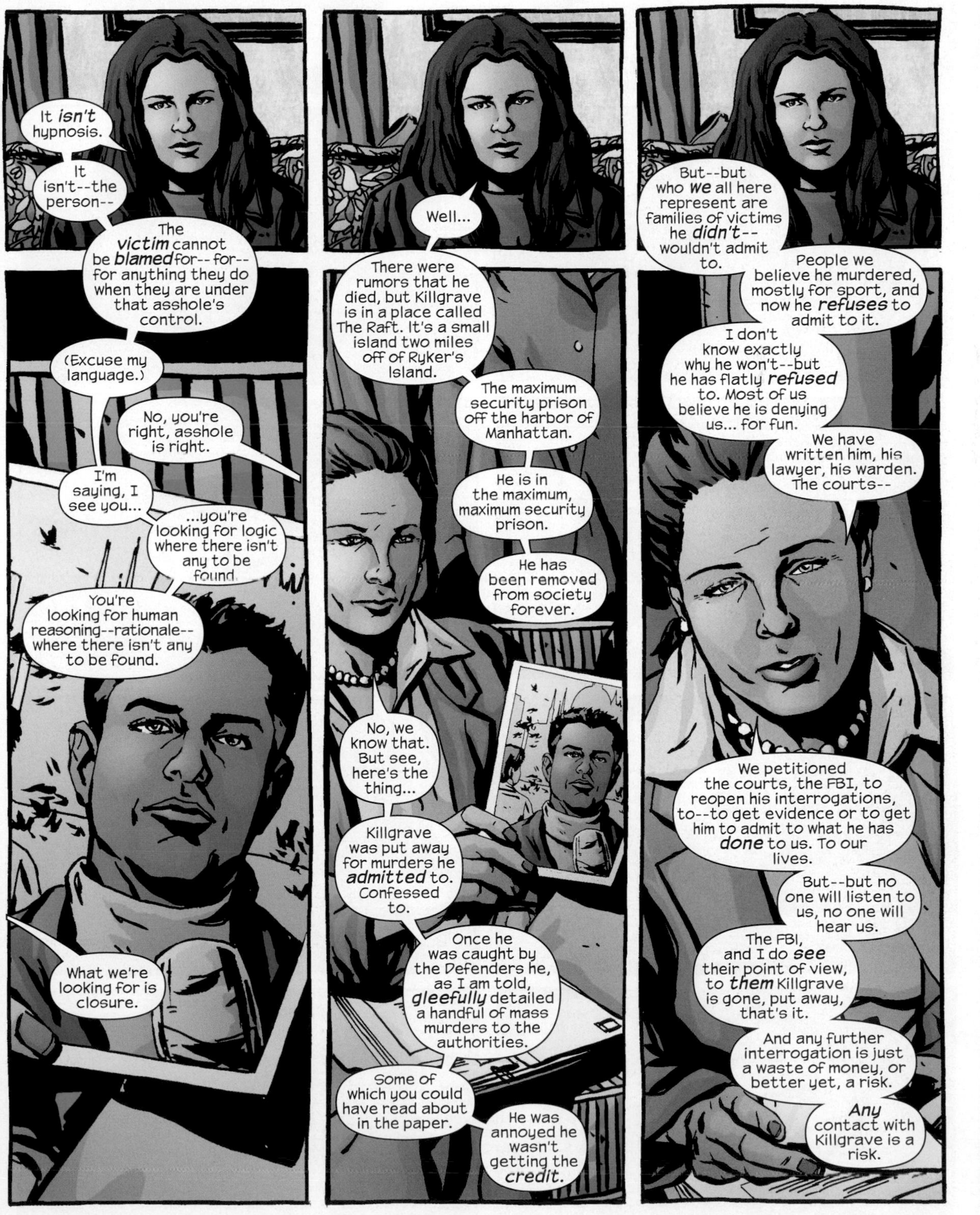

It isn't hypnosis.
It isn't--the person--
The victim cannot be blamed for-- for-- for anything they do when they are under that asshole's control.
(Excuse my language.)
No, you're right, asshole is right.
I'm saying, I see you...
...you're looking for logic where there isn't any to be found.
You're looking for human reasoning--rationale-- where there isn't any to be found.
What we're looking for is closure.
Well...
There were rumors that he died, but Killgrave is in a place called The Raft. It's a small island two miles off of Ryker's Island.
The maximum security prison off the harbor of Manhattan.
He is in the maximum, maximum security prison.
He has been removed from society forever.
No, we know that. But see, here's the thing...
Killgrave was put away for murders he admitted to. Confessed to.
Once he was caught by the Defenders he, as I am told, gleefully detailed a handful of mass murders to the authorities.
Some of which you could have read about in the paper.
He was annoyed he wasn't getting the credit.
But--but who we all here represent are families of victims he didn't-- wouldn't admit to.
People we believe he murdered, mostly for sport, and now he refuses to admit to it.
I don't know exactly why he won't--but he has flatly refused to. Most of us believe he is denying us... for fun.
We have written him, his lawyer, his warden. The courts--
We petitioned the courts, the FBI, to reopen his interrogations, to--to get evidence or to get him to admit to what he has done to us. To our lives.
But--but no one will listen to us, no one will hear us.
The FBI, and I do see their point of view, to them Killgrave is gone, put away, that's it.
And any further interrogation is just a waste of money, or better yet, a risk.
Any contact with Killgrave is a risk.

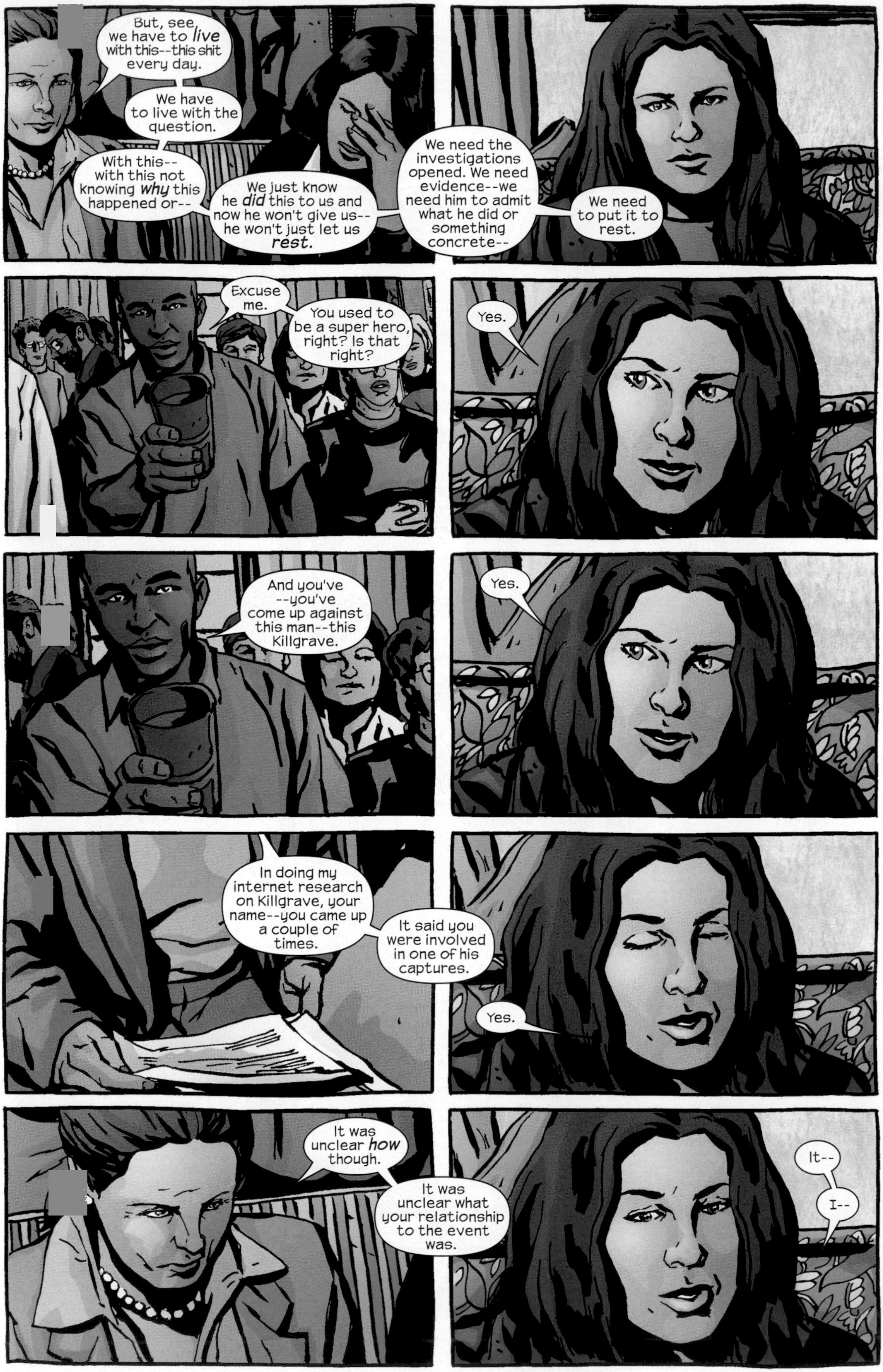

But, see, we have to *live* with this--this shit every day.
We have to live with the question.
With this--with this not knowing *why* this happened or--
We just know he *did* this to us and now he won't give us--he won't just let us *rest.*
We need the investigations opened. We need evidence--we need him to admit what he did or something concrete--
We need to put it to rest.
Excuse me.
You used to be a super hero, right? Is that right?
Yes.
And you've--you've come up against this man--this Killgrave.
Yes.
In doing my internet research on Killgrave, your name--you came up a couple of times.
It said you were involved in one of his captures.
Yes.
It was unclear *how* though.
It was unclear what your relationship to the event was.
It--
I--

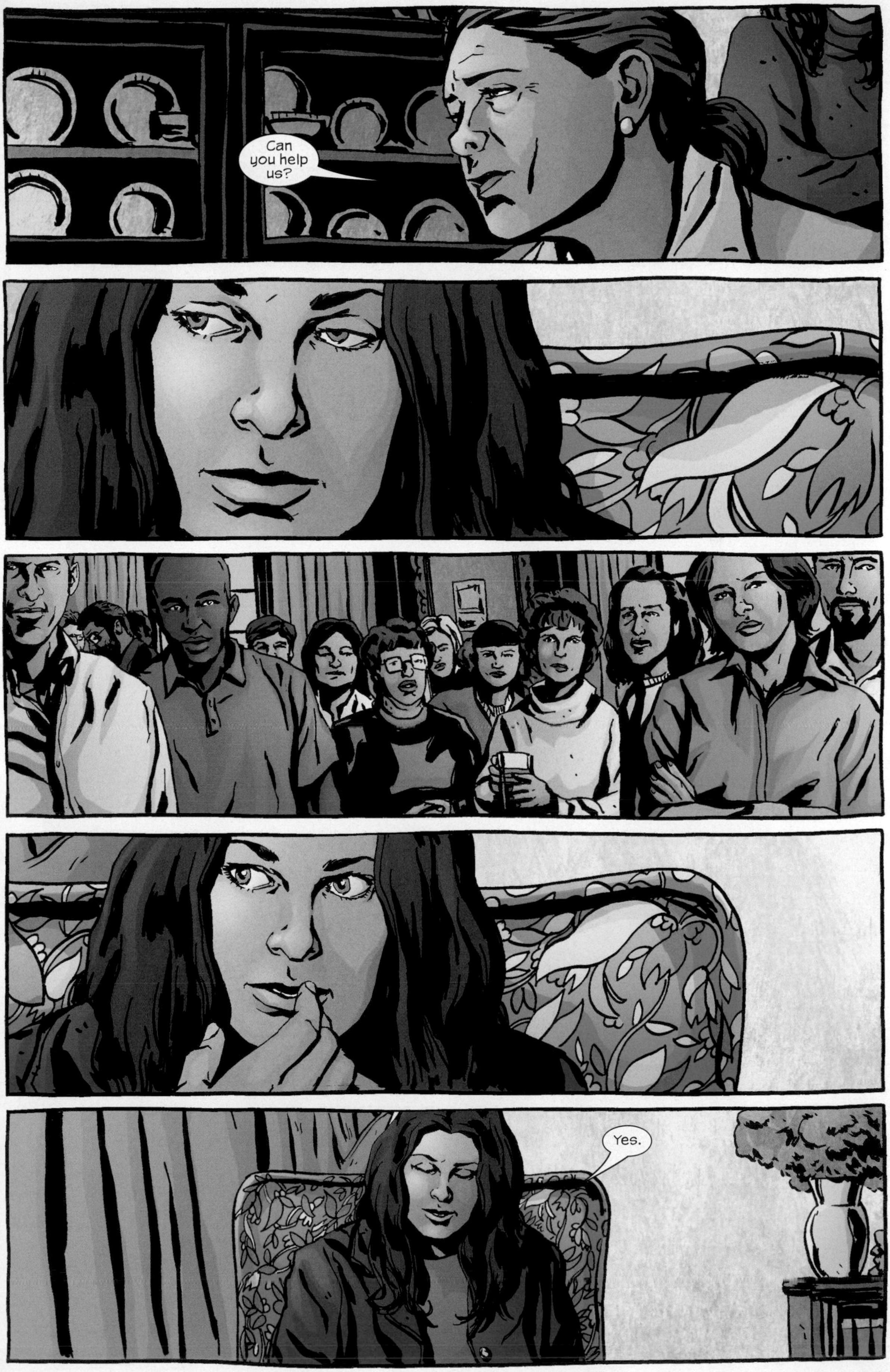
Can you help us?
Yes.

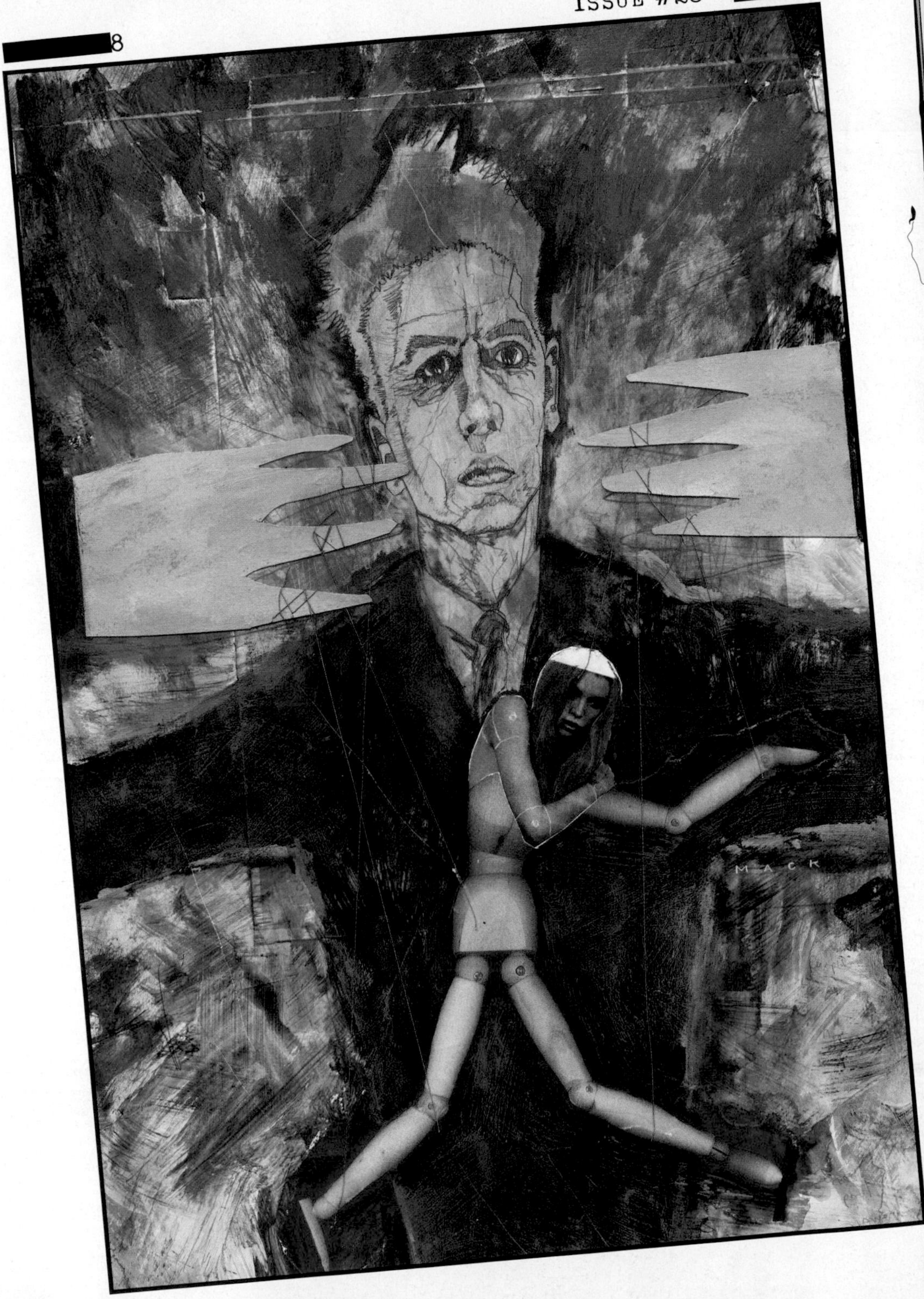

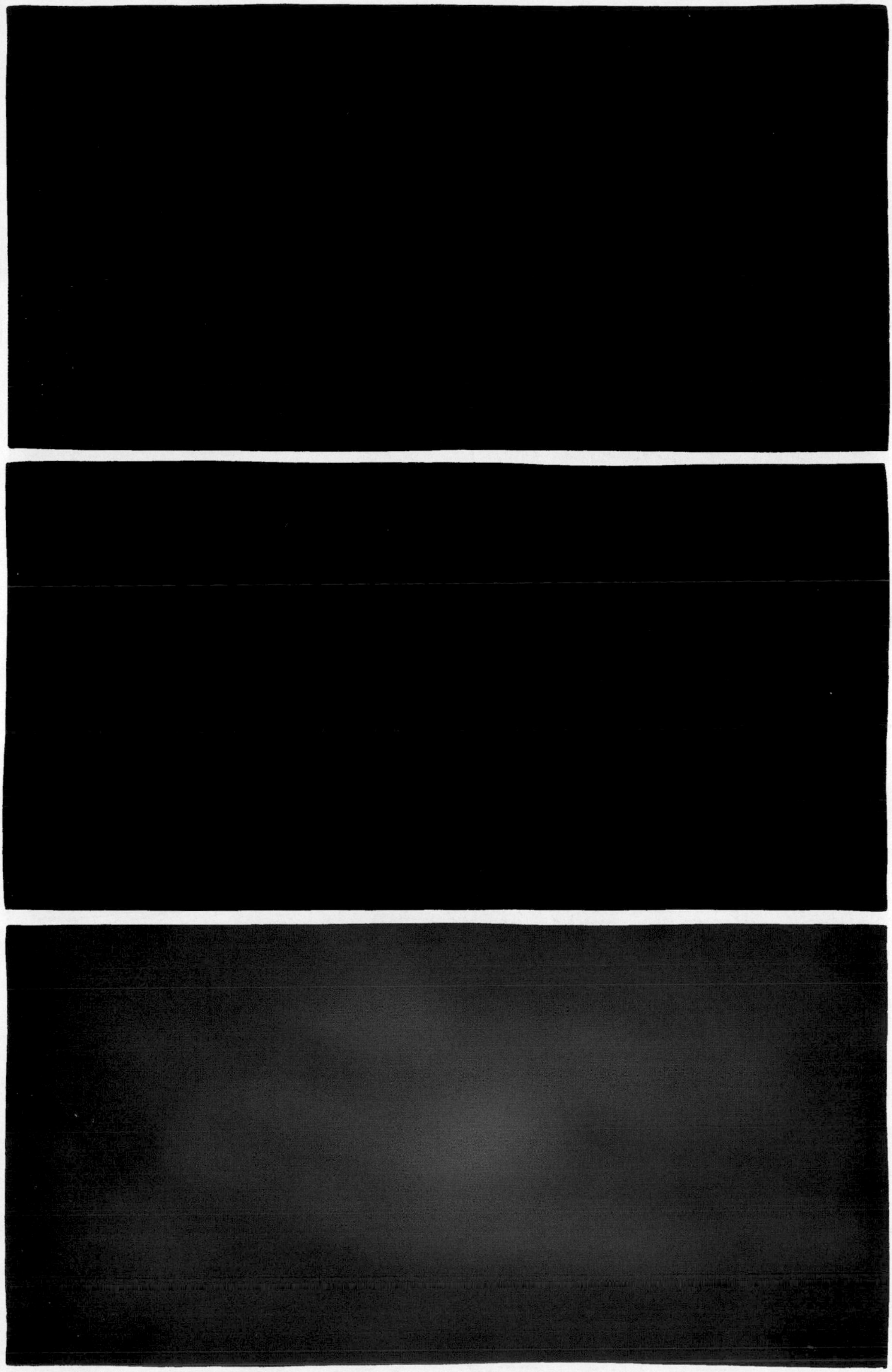

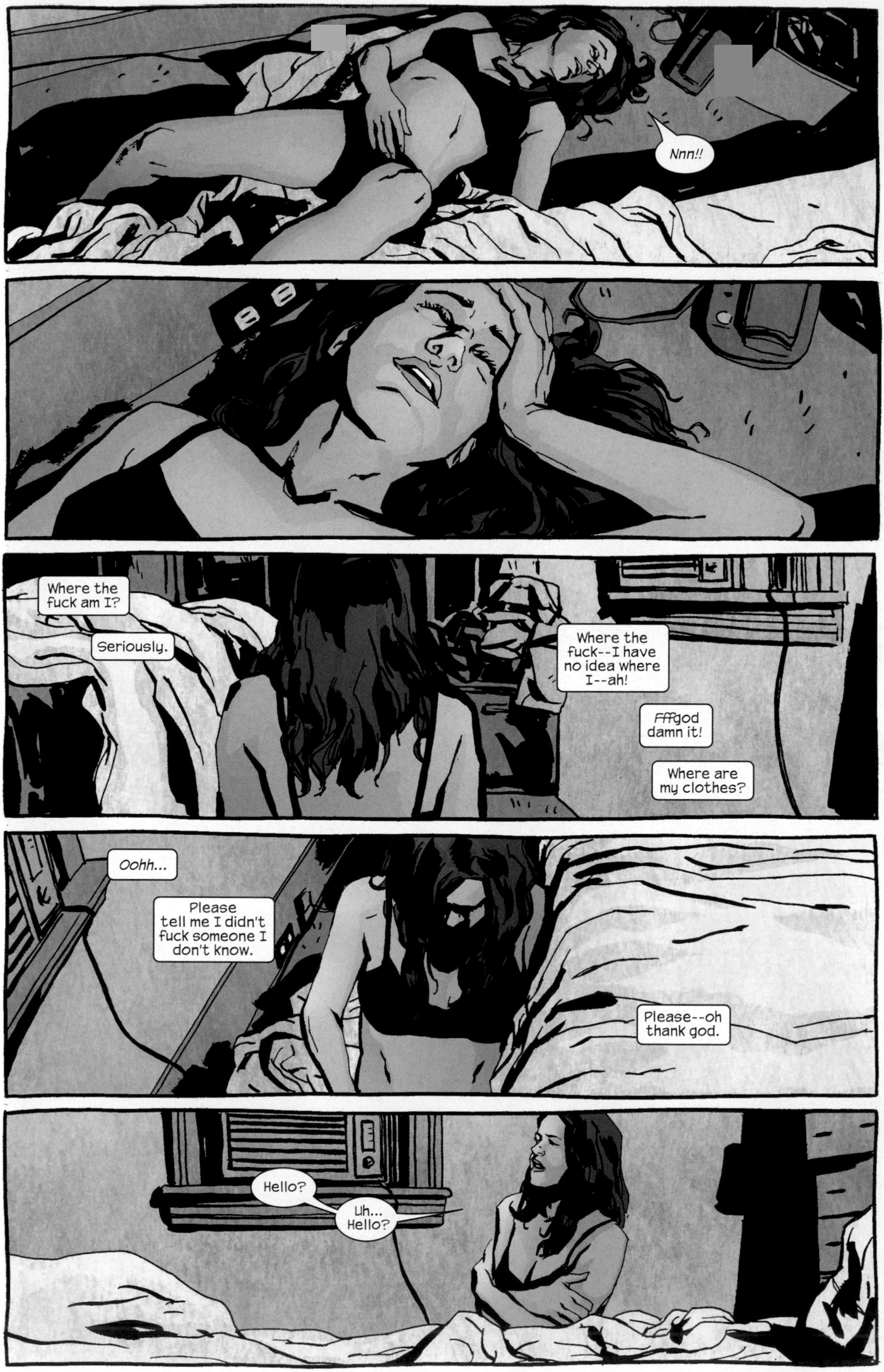
Nnn!!
Where the fuck am I?
Seriously.
Where the fuck--I have no idea where I--ah!
Fffgod damn it!
Where are my clothes?
Oohh...
Please tell me I didn't fuck someone I don't know.
Please--oh thank god.
Hello?
Uh... Hello?

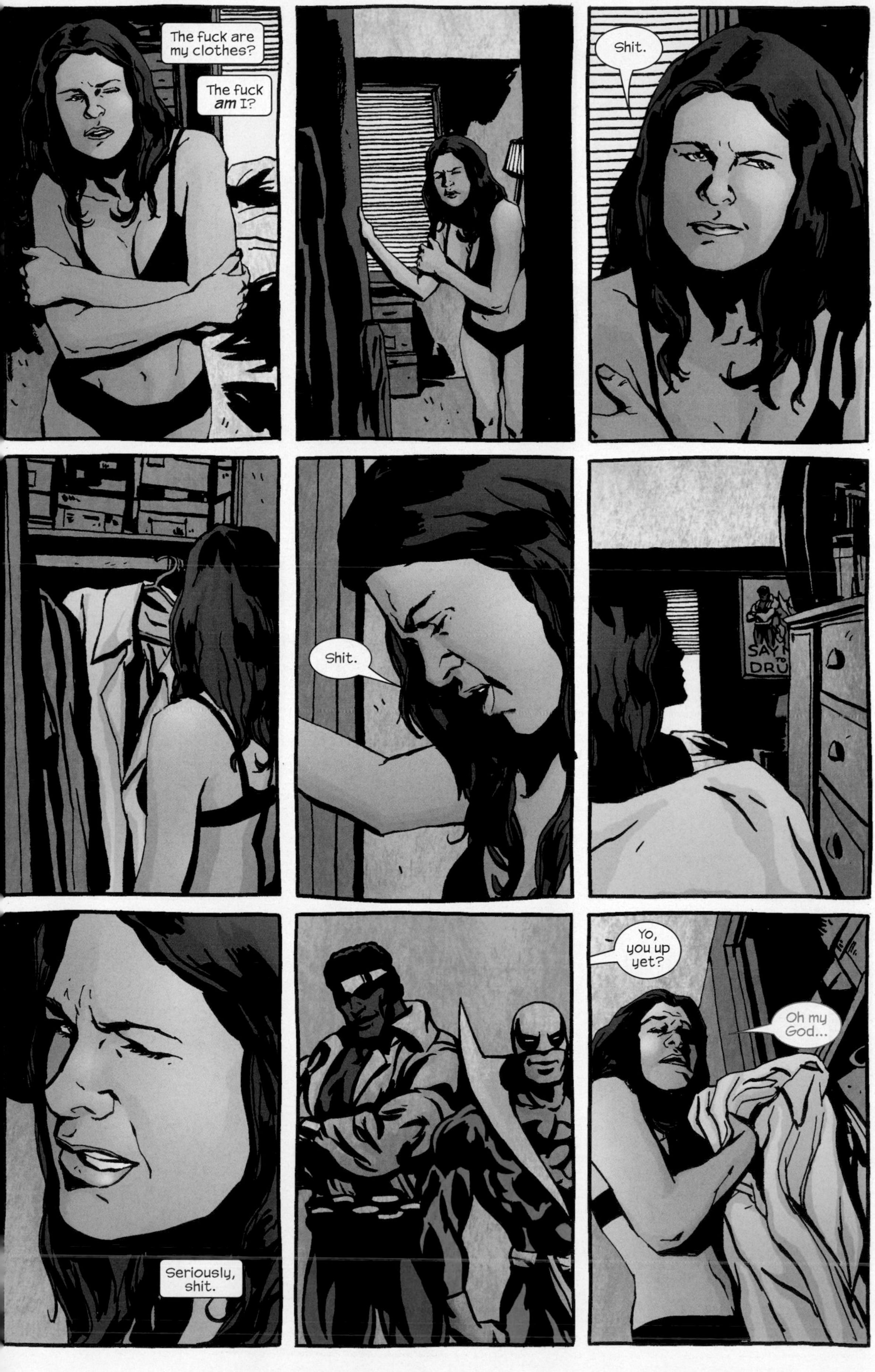
The fuck are my clothes?
The fuck *am* I?
Shit.
Shit.
Seriously, shit.
Yo, you up yet?
Oh my God...

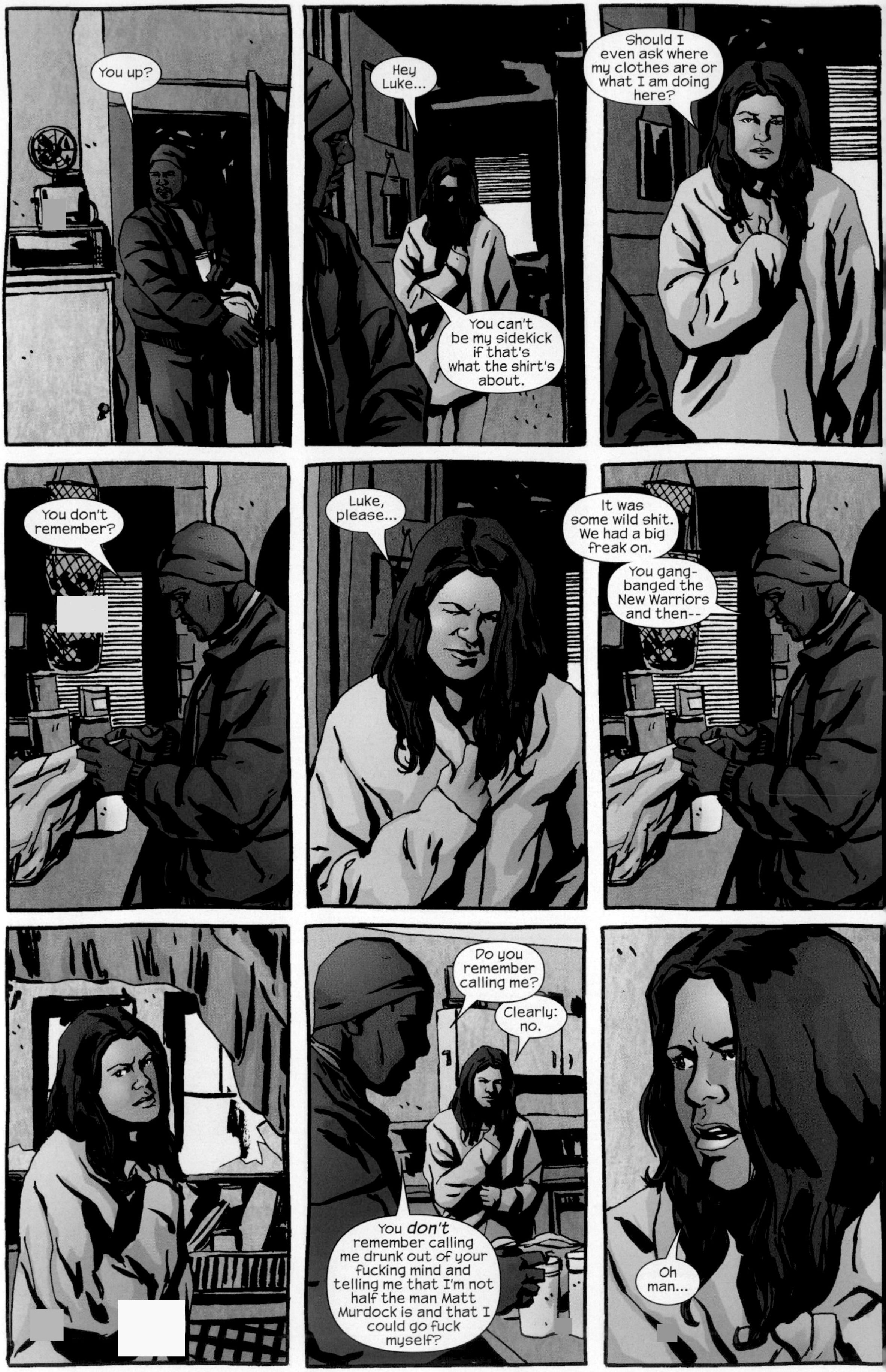
You up?
Hey Luke...
You can't be my sidekick if that's what the shirt's about.
Should I even ask where my clothes are or what I am doing here?
You don't remember?
Luke, please...
It was some wild shit. We had a big freak on.
You gang-banged the New Warriors and then--
Do you remember calling me?
Clearly: no.
You don't remember calling me drunk out of your fucking mind and telling me that I'm not half the man Matt Murdock is and that I could go fuck myself?
Oh man...

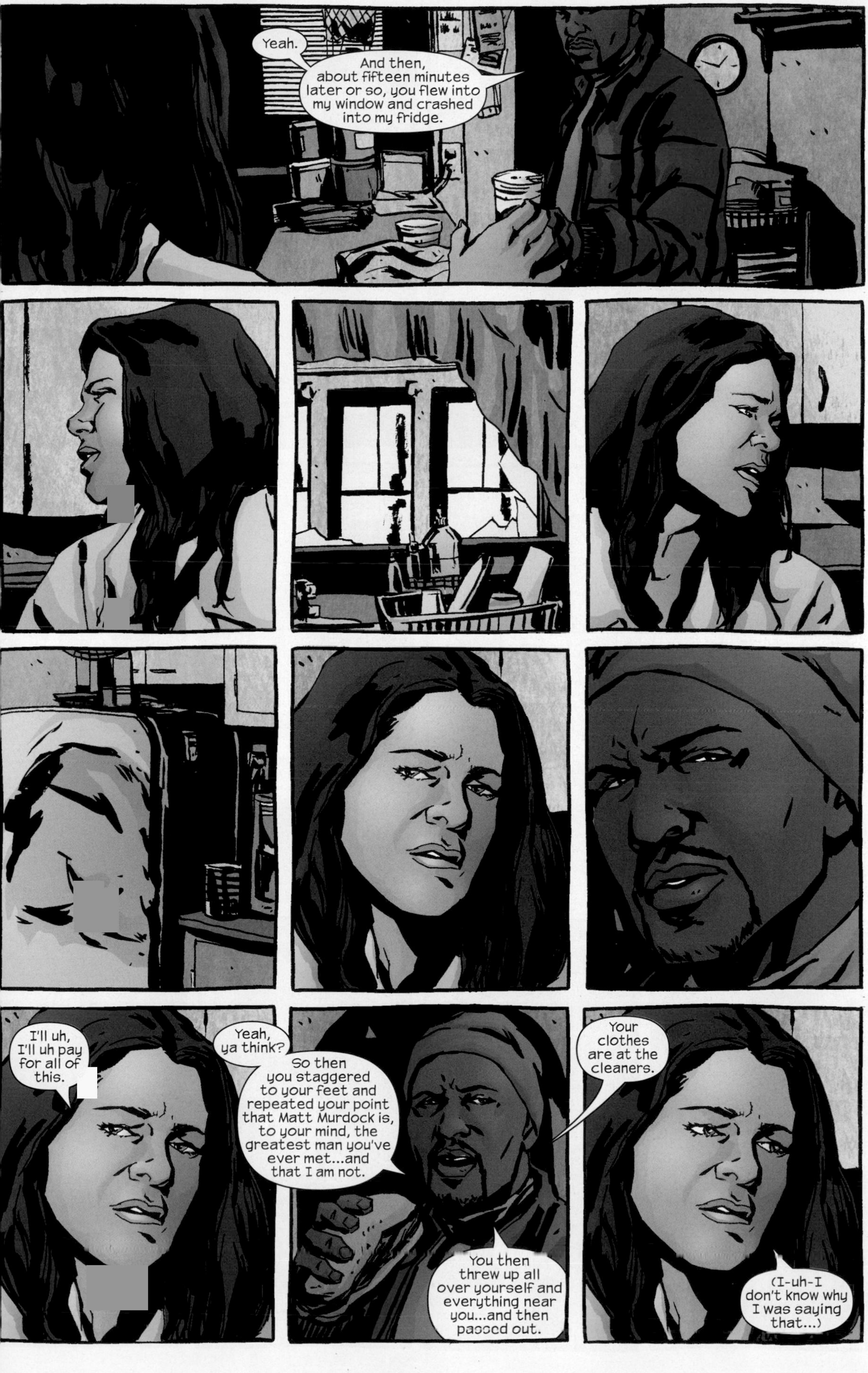
Yeah.
And then, about fifteen minutes later or so, you flew into my window and crashed into my fridge.
I'll uh, I'll uh pay for all of this.
Yeah, ya think?
So then you staggered to your feet and repeated your point that Matt Murdock is, to your mind, the greatest man you've ever met...and that I am not.
You then threw up all over yourself and everything near you...and then passed out.
Your clothes are at the cleaners.
(I-uh-I don't know why I was saying that...)

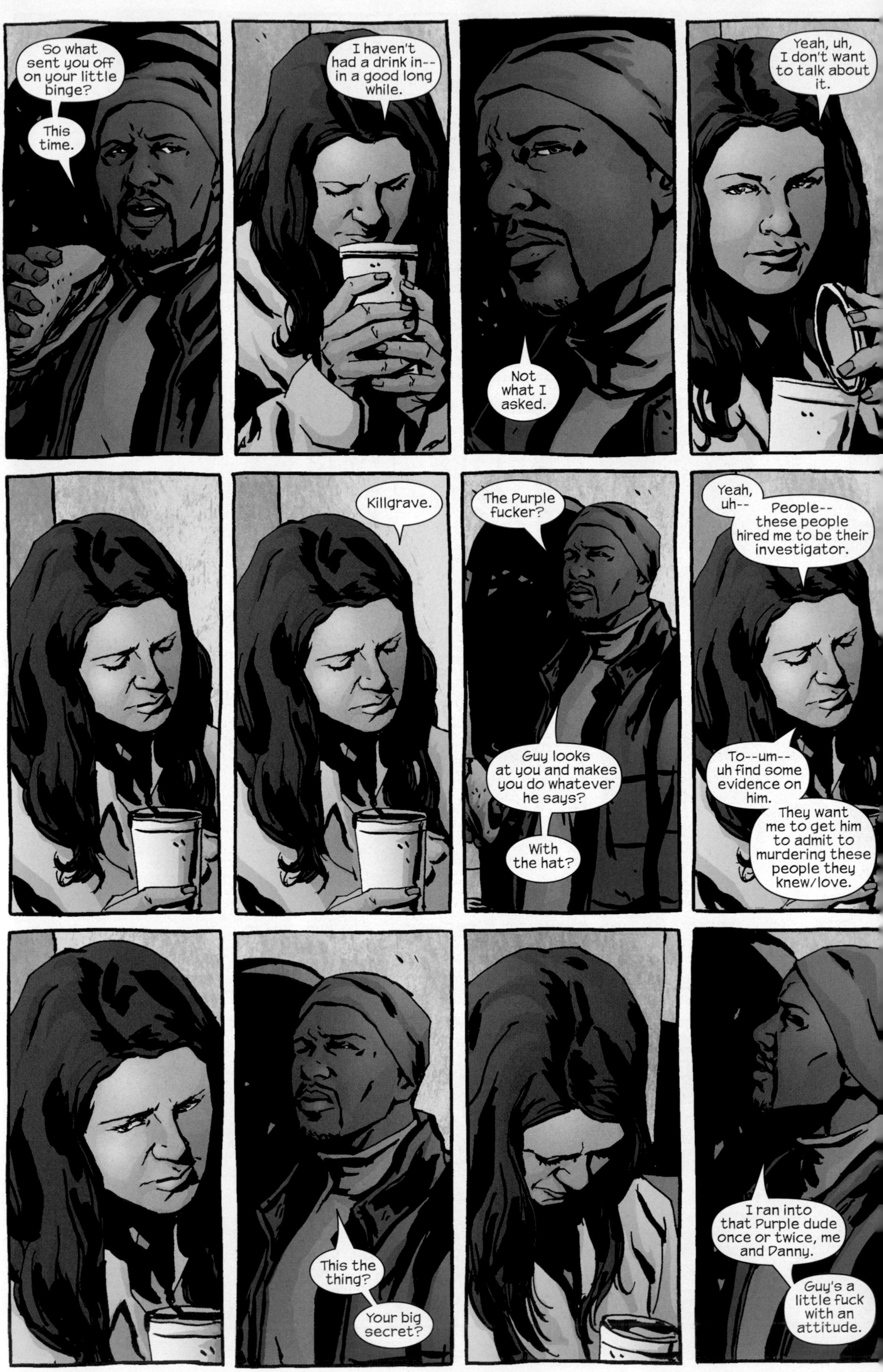
So what sent you off on your little binge?
This time.
I haven't had a drink in-- in a good long while.
Not what I asked.
Yeah, uh, I don't want to talk about it.
Killgrave.
The Purple fucker?
Guy looks at you and makes you do whatever he says?
With the hat?
Yeah, uh--
People-- these people hired me to be their investigator.
To--um-- uh find some evidence on him.
They want me to get him to admit to murdering these people they knew/love.
This the thing?
Your big secret?
I ran into that Purple dude once or twice, me and Danny.
Guy's a little fuck with an attitude.

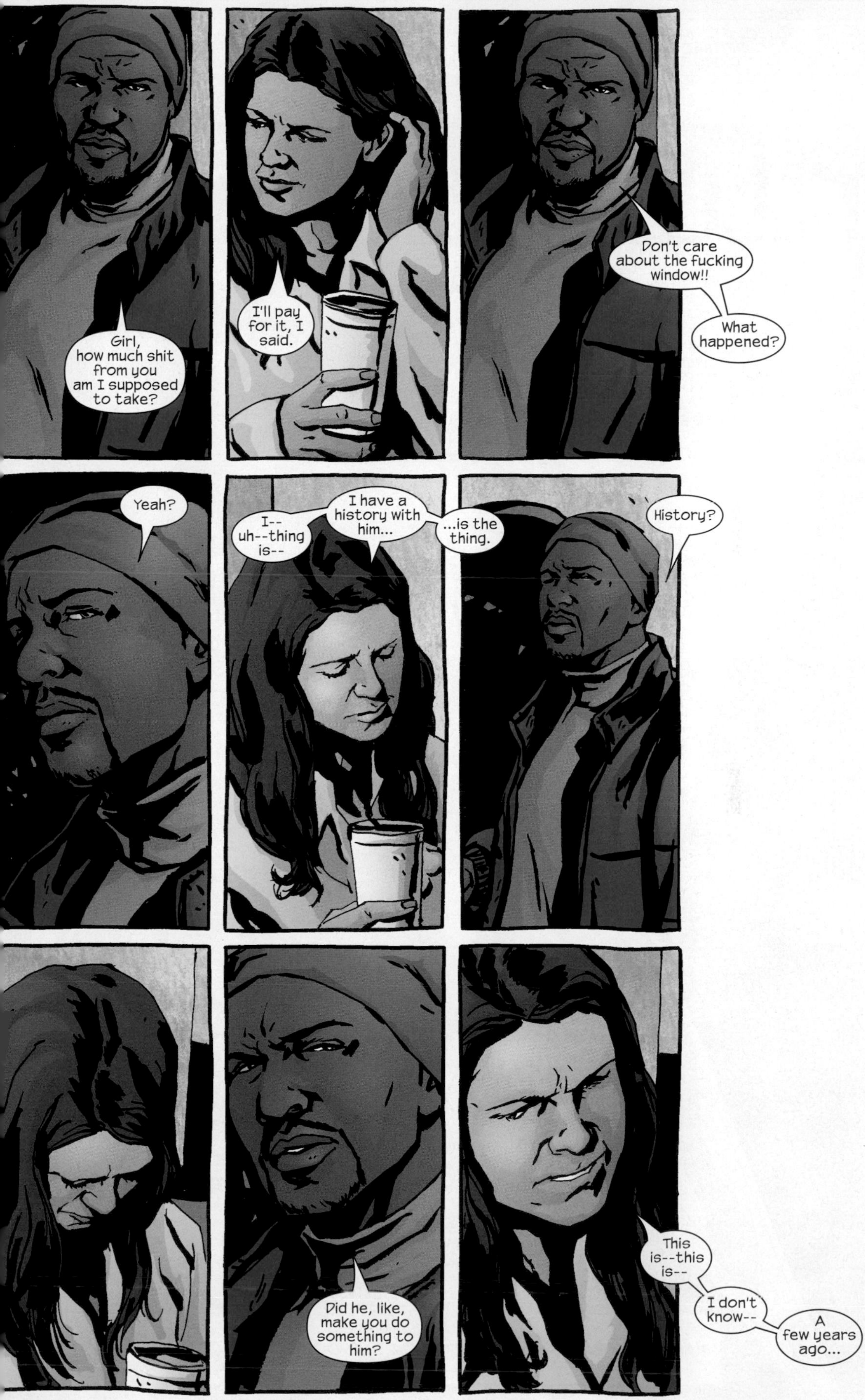
Girl, how much shit from you am I supposed to take?
I'll pay for it, I said.
Don't care about the fucking window!!
What happened?
Yeah?
I-- uh--thing is--
I have a history with him...
...is the thing.
History?
Did he, like, make you do something to him?
This is--this is--
I don't know--
A few years ago...

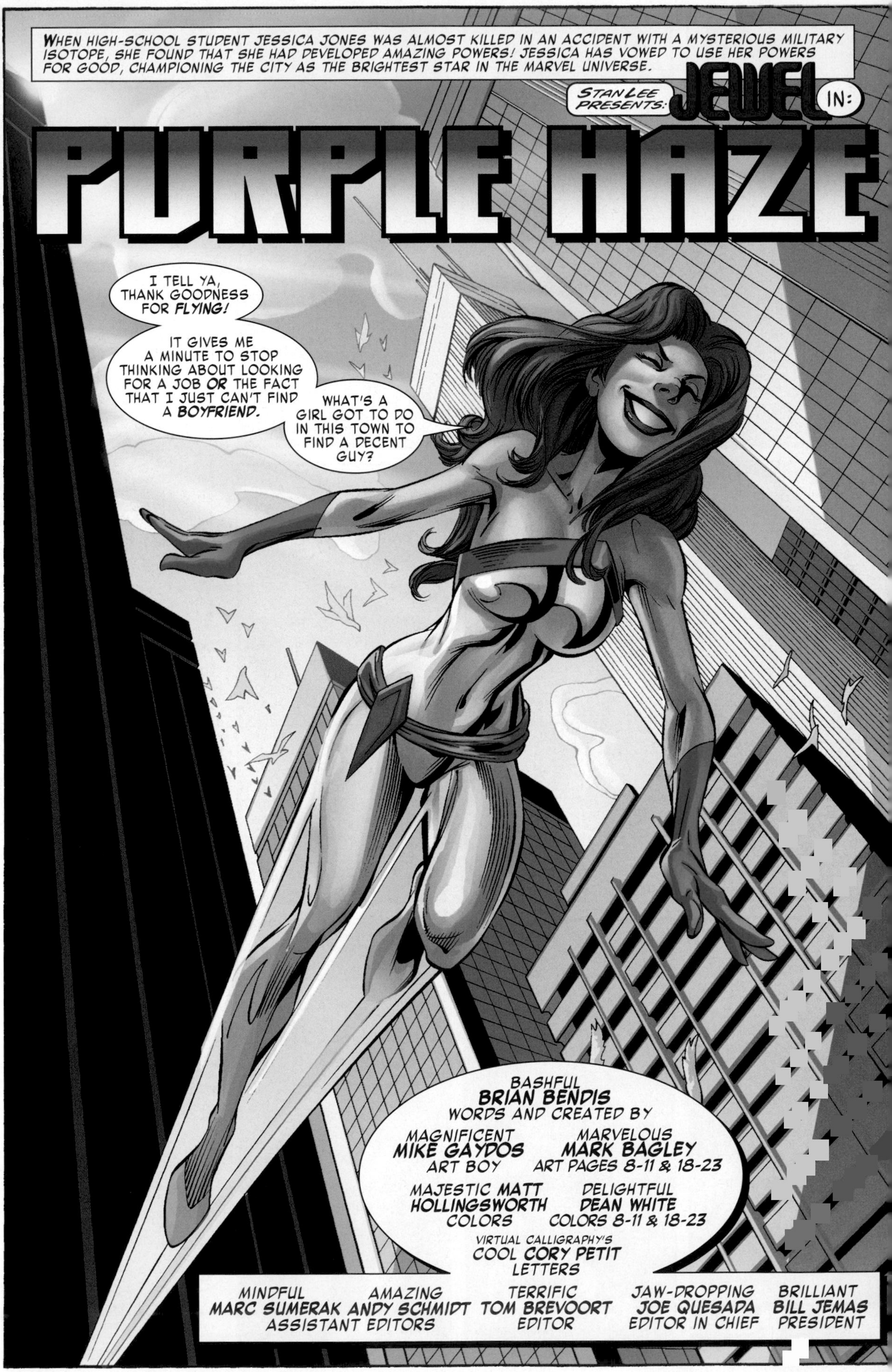
WHEN HIGH-SCHOOL STUDENT JESSICA JONES WAS ALMOST KILLED IN AN ACCIDENT WITH A MYSTERIOUS MILITARY ISOTOPE, SHE FOUND THAT SHE HAD DEVELOPED AMAZING POWERS! JESSICA HAS VOWED TO USE HER POWERS FOR GOOD, CHAMPIONING THE CITY AS THE BRIGHTEST STAR IN THE MARVEL UNIVERSE.
STAN LEE PRESENTS: JEWEL IN:
PURPLE HAZE
I TELL YA, THANK GOODNESS FOR FLYING!
IT GIVES ME A MINUTE TO STOP THINKING ABOUT LOOKING FOR A JOB OR THE FACT THAT I JUST CAN'T FIND A BOYFRIEND.
WHAT'S A GIRL GOT TO DO IN THIS TOWN TO FIND A DECENT GUY?
BASHFUL BRIAN BENDIS WORDS AND CREATED BY
MAGNIFICENT MIKE GAYDOS ART BOY
MARVELOUS MARK BAGLEY ART PAGES 8-11 & 18-23
MAJESTIC MATT HOLLINGSWORTH COLORS
DELIGHTFUL DEAN WHITE COLORS 8-11 & 18-23
VIRTUAL CALLIGRAPHY'S COOL CORY PETIT LETTERS
MINDFUL MARC SUMERAK AMAZING ANDY SCHMIDT ASSISTANT EDITORS
TERRIFIC TOM BREVOORT EDITOR
JAW-DROPPING JOE QUESADA EDITOR IN CHIEF
BRILLIANT BILL JEMAS PRESIDENT

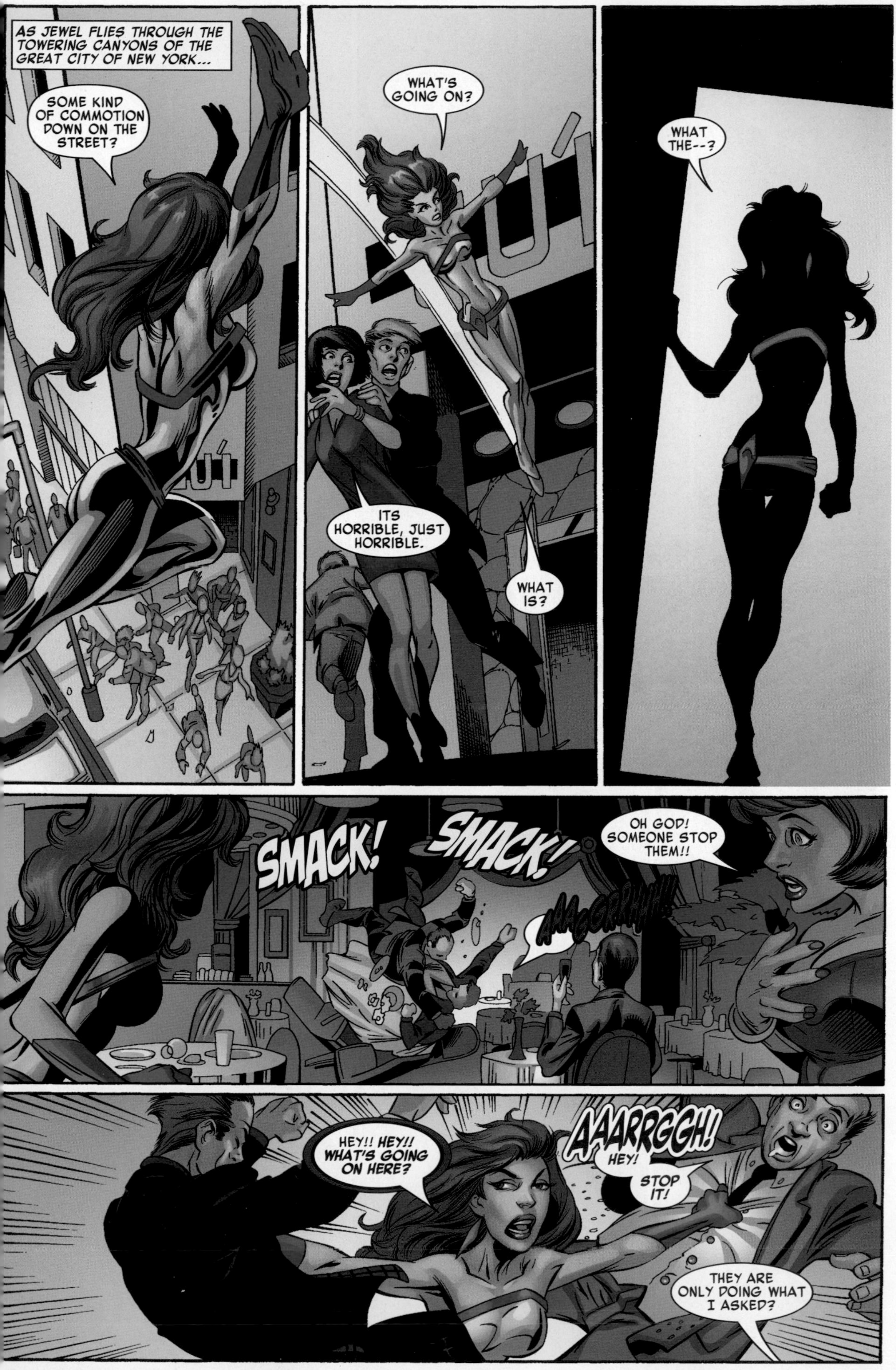
AS JEWEL FLIES THROUGH THE TOWERING CANYONS OF THE GREAT CITY OF NEW YORK...
SOME KIND OF COMMOTION DOWN ON THE STREET?
WHAT'S GOING ON?
ITS HORRIBLE, JUST HORRIBLE.
WHAT IS?
WHAT THE--?
SMACK!
SMACK!
OH GOD! SOMEONE STOP THEM!!
HEY!! HEY!! WHAT'S GOING ON HERE?
AAARRGGH!
HEY! STOP IT!
THEY ARE ONLY DOING WHAT I ASKED?

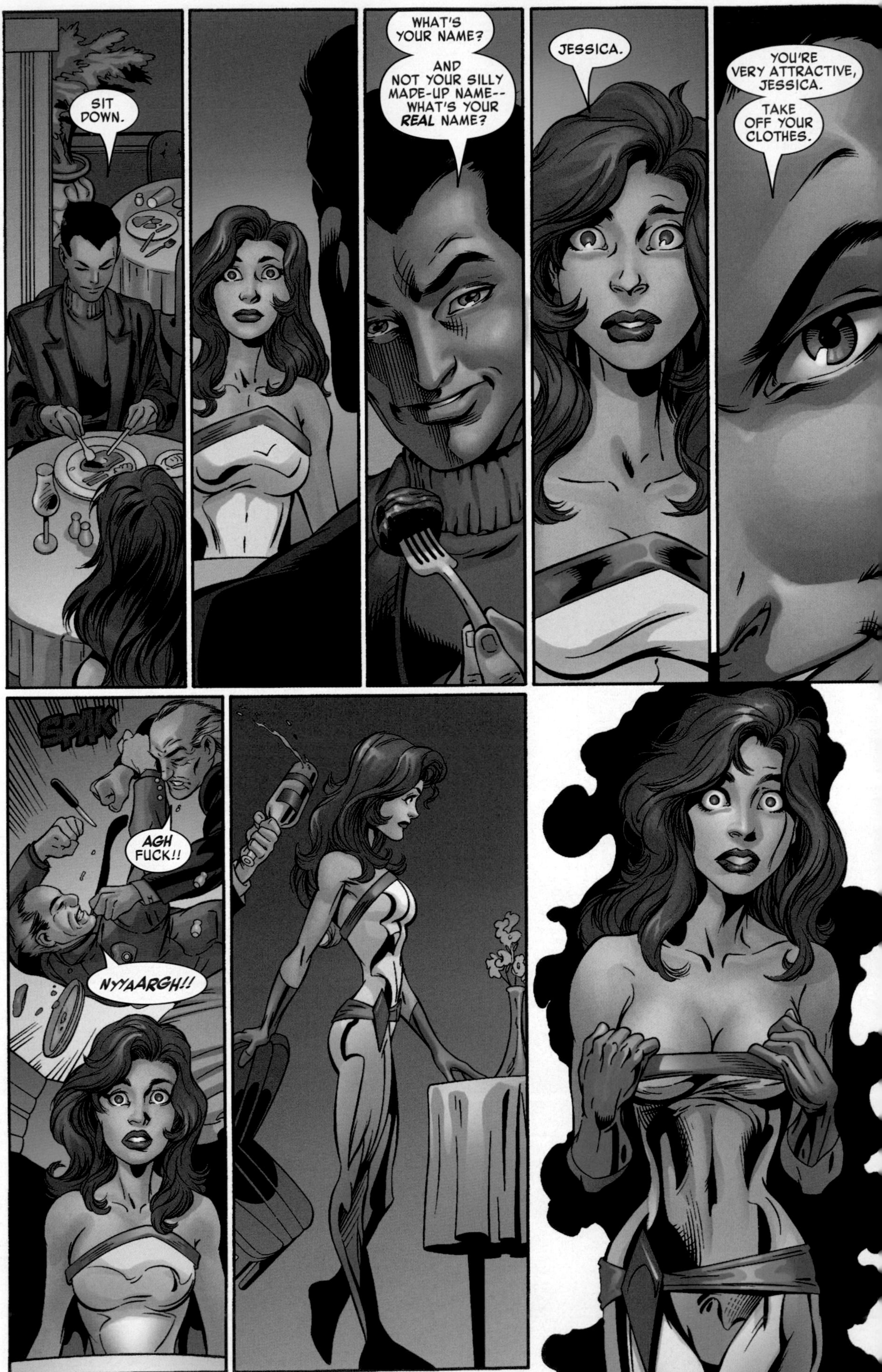
SIT DOWN.
WHAT'S YOUR NAME?
AND NOT YOUR SILLY MADE-UP NAME-- WHAT'S YOUR *REAL* NAME?
JESSICA.
YOU'RE VERY ATTRACTIVE, JESSICA.
TAKE OFF YOUR CLOTHES.
SPAK
AGH FUCK!!
NYYAARGH!!

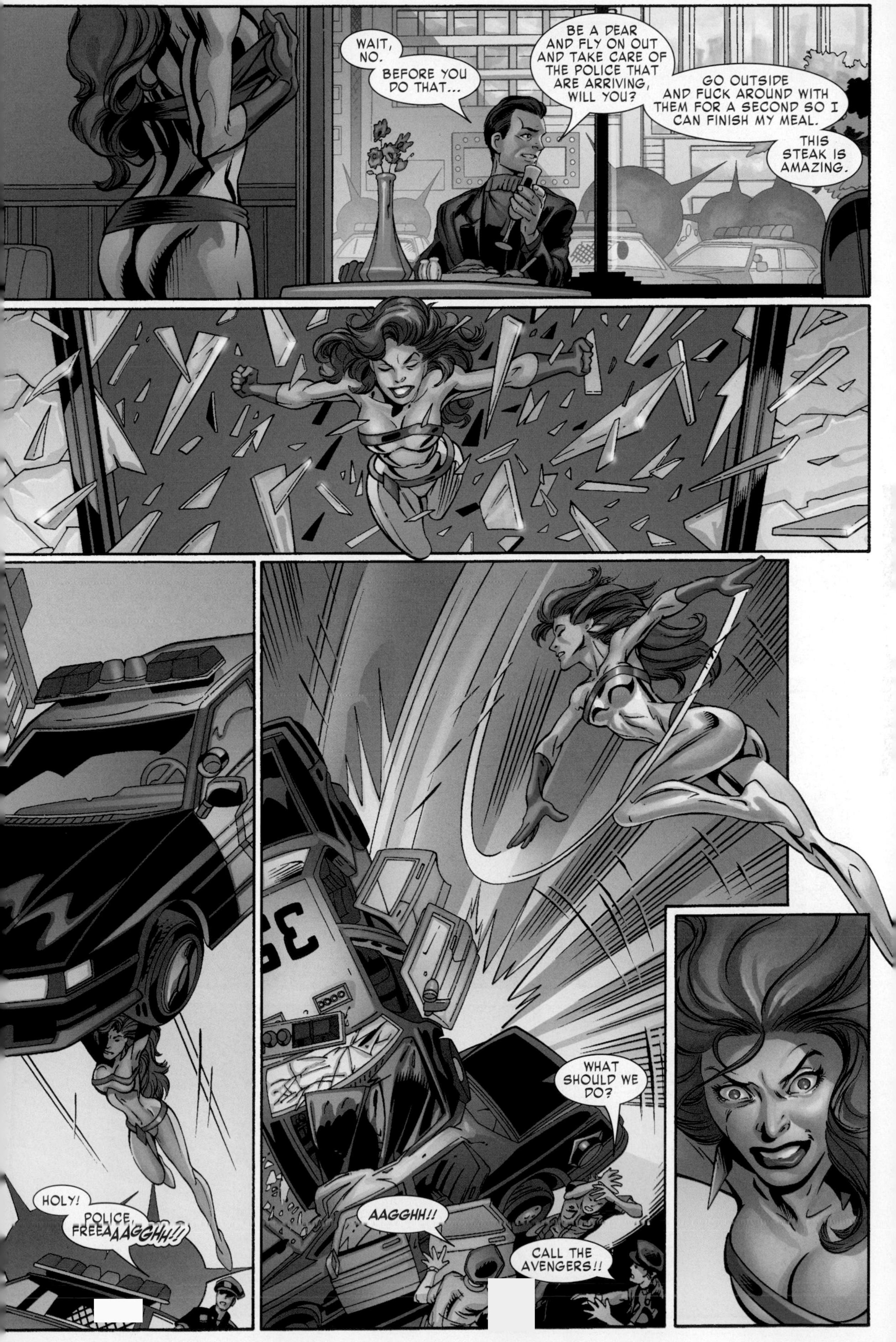
WAIT, NO.
BEFORE YOU DO THAT...
BE A DEAR AND FLY ON OUT AND TAKE CARE OF THE POLICE THAT ARE ARRIVING, WILL YOU?
GO OUTSIDE AND FUCK AROUND WITH THEM FOR A SECOND SO I CAN FINISH MY MEAL.
THIS STEAK IS AMAZING.
HOLY!
POLICE, FREEAAAGGHH!!
AAGGHH!!
WHAT SHOULD WE DO?
CALL THE AVENGERS!!

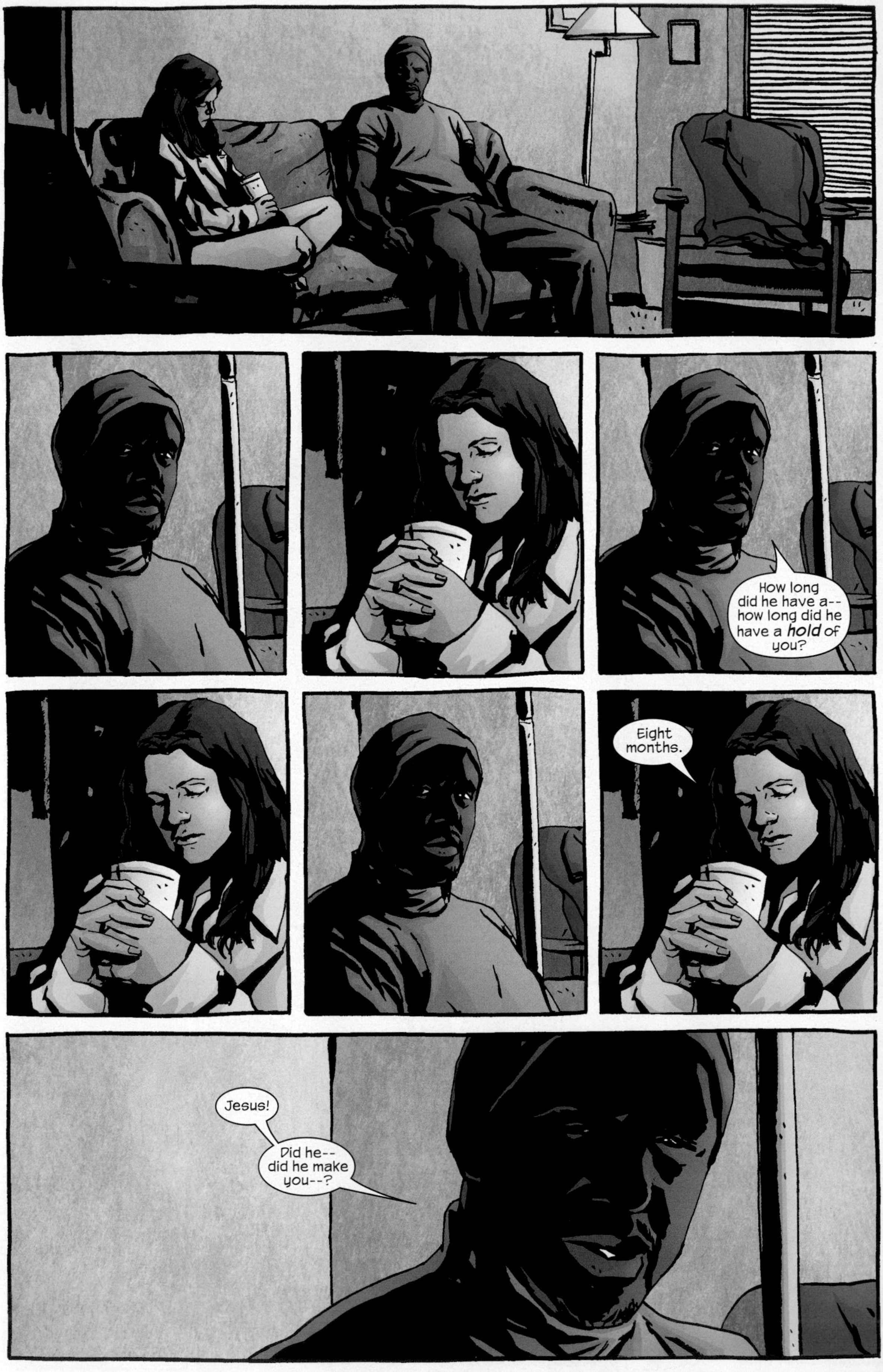
How long did he have a-- how long did he have a *hold* of you?
Eight months.
Jesus!
Did he-- did he make you--?

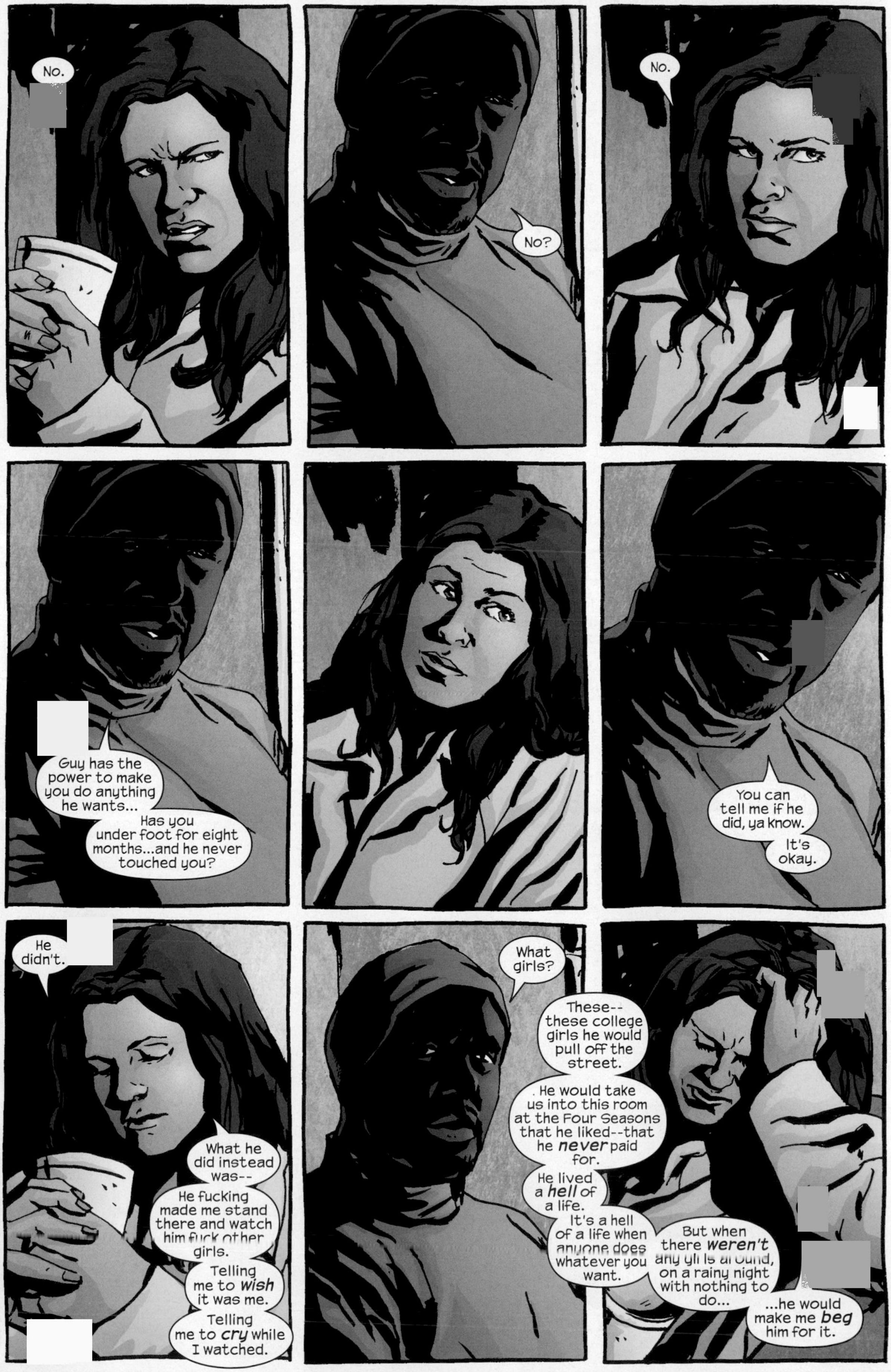
No.
No?
No.
Guy has the power to make you do anything he wants...
Has you under foot for eight months...and he never touched you?
You can tell me if he did, ya know.
It's okay.
He didn't.
What he did instead was--
He fucking made me stand there and watch him fuck other girls.
Telling me to *wish* it was me.
Telling me to *cry* while I watched.
What girls?
These-- these college girls he would pull off the street.
He would take us into this room at the Four Seasons that he liked--that he *never* paid for.
He lived a *hell* of a life.
It's a hell of a life when anyone does whatever you want.
But when there *weren't* any girls around, on a rainy night with nothing to do...
...he would make me *beg* him for it.

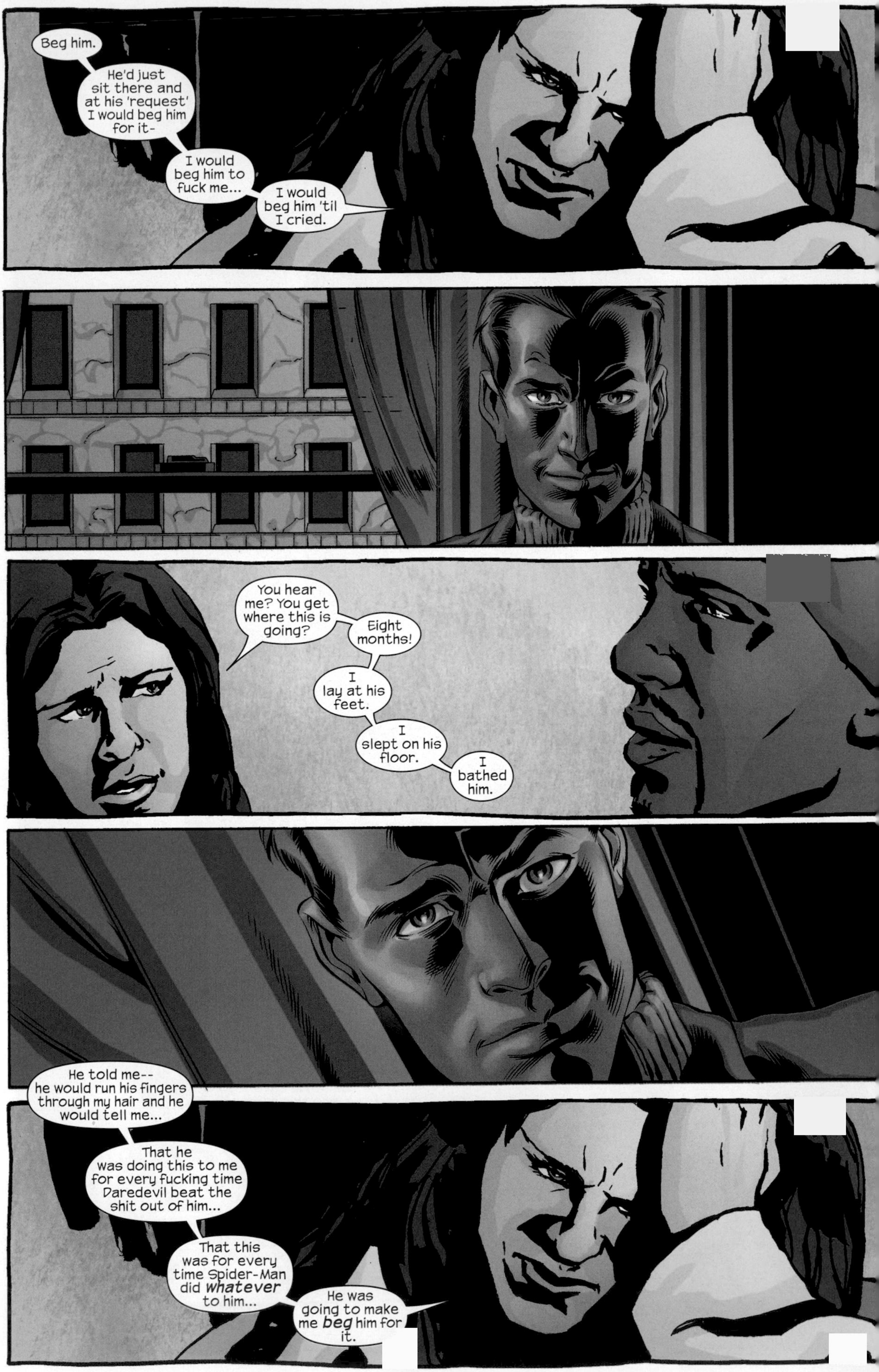
Beg him.
He'd just sit there and at his 'request' I would beg him for it-
I would beg him to fuck me...
I would beg him 'til I cried.
You hear me? You get where this is going?
Eight months!
I lay at his feet.
I slept on his floor.
I bathed him.
He told me-- he would run his fingers through my hair and he would tell me...
That he was doing this to me for every fucking time Daredevil beat the shit out of him...
That this was for every time Spider-Man did *whatever* to him...
He was going to make me **beg** him for it.

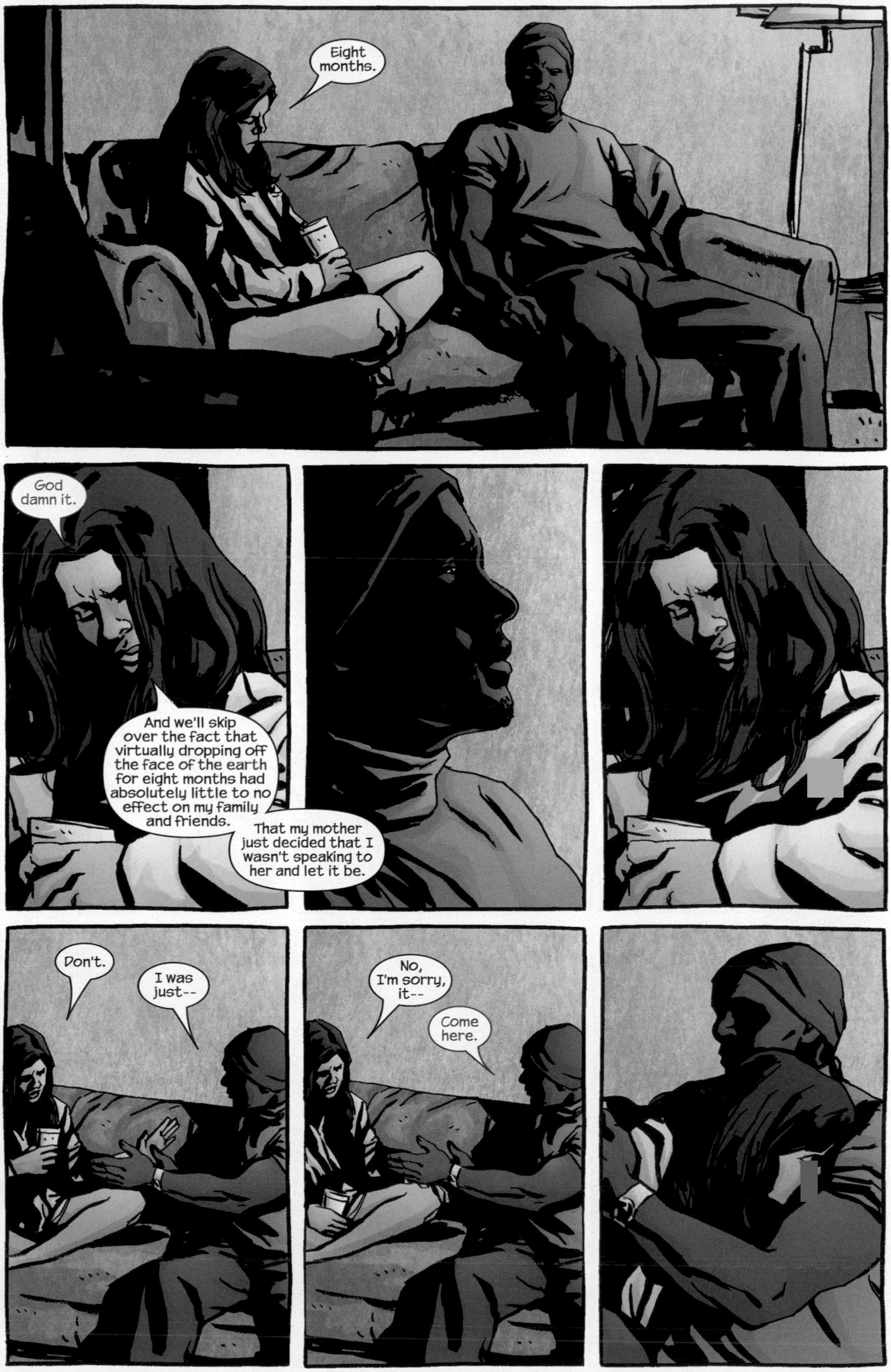
Eight months.
God damn it.
And we'll skip over the fact that virtually dropping off the face of the earth for eight months had absolutely little to no effect on my family and friends.
That my mother just decided that I wasn't speaking to her and let it be.
Don't.
I was just--
No, I'm sorry, it--
Come here.

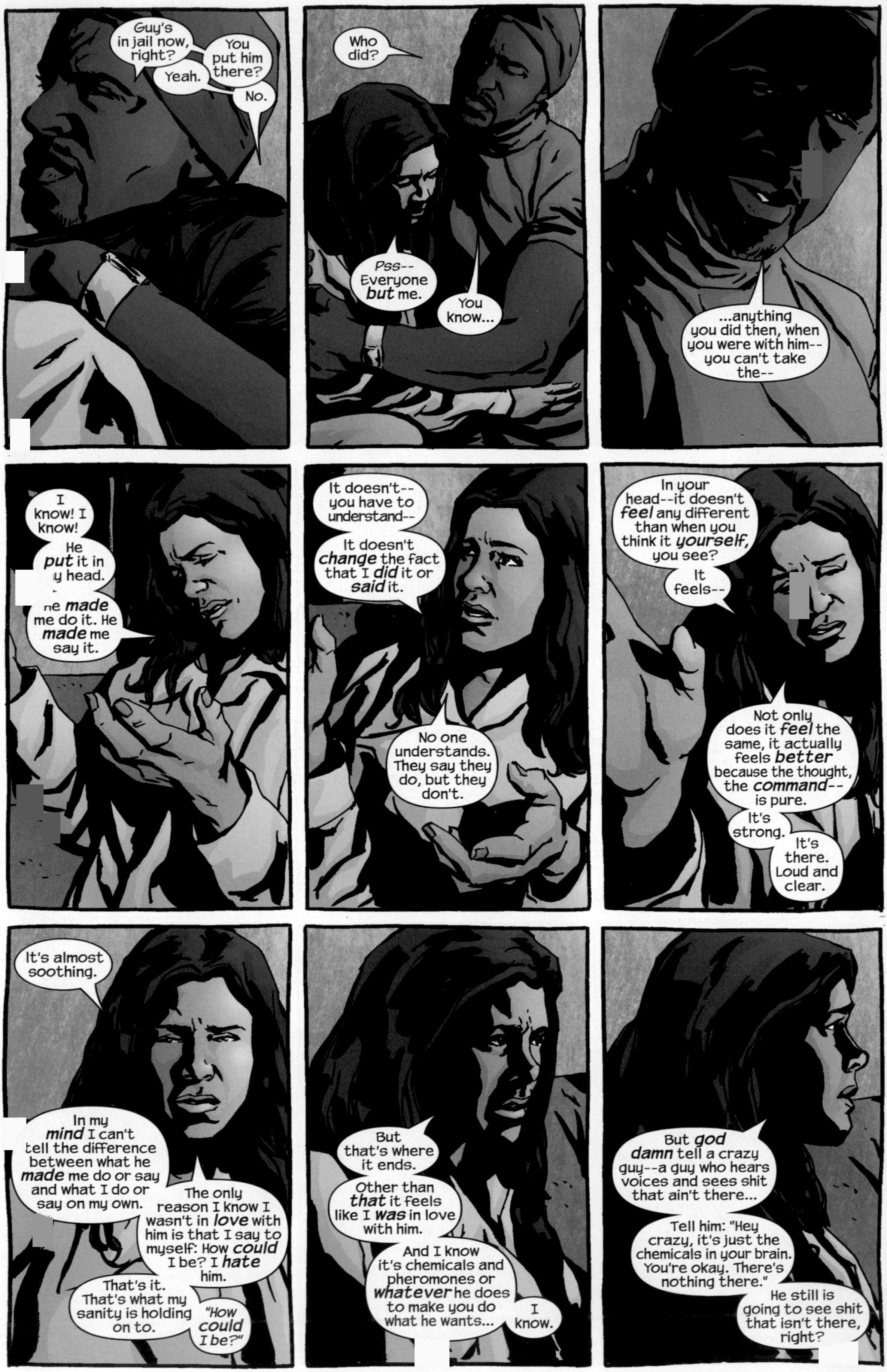
Guy's in jail now, right?
You put him there?
Yeah.
No.
Who did?
Pss-- Everyone but me.
You know...
...anything you did then, when you were with him-- you can't take the--
I know! I know!
He put it in y head.
e made me do it. He made me say it.
It doesn't-- you have to understand--
It doesn't change the fact that I did it or said it.
No one understands. They say they do, but they don't.
In your head--it doesn't feel any different than when you think it yourself, you see?
It feels--
Not only does it feel the same, it actually feels better because the thought, the command-- is pure.
It's strong.
It's there. Loud and clear.
It's almost soothing.
In my mind I can't tell the difference between what he made me do or say and what I do or say on my own.
The only reason I know I wasn't in love with him is that I say to myself: How could I be? I hate him.
That's it. That's what my sanity is holding on to.
"How could I be?"
But that's where it ends.
Other than that it feels like I was in love with him.
And I know it's chemicals and pheromones or whatever he does to make you do what he wants...
I know.
But god damn tell a crazy guy--a guy who hears voices and sees shit that ain't there...
Tell him: "Hey crazy, it's just the chemicals in your brain. You're okay. There's nothing there."
He still is going to see shit that isn't there, right?

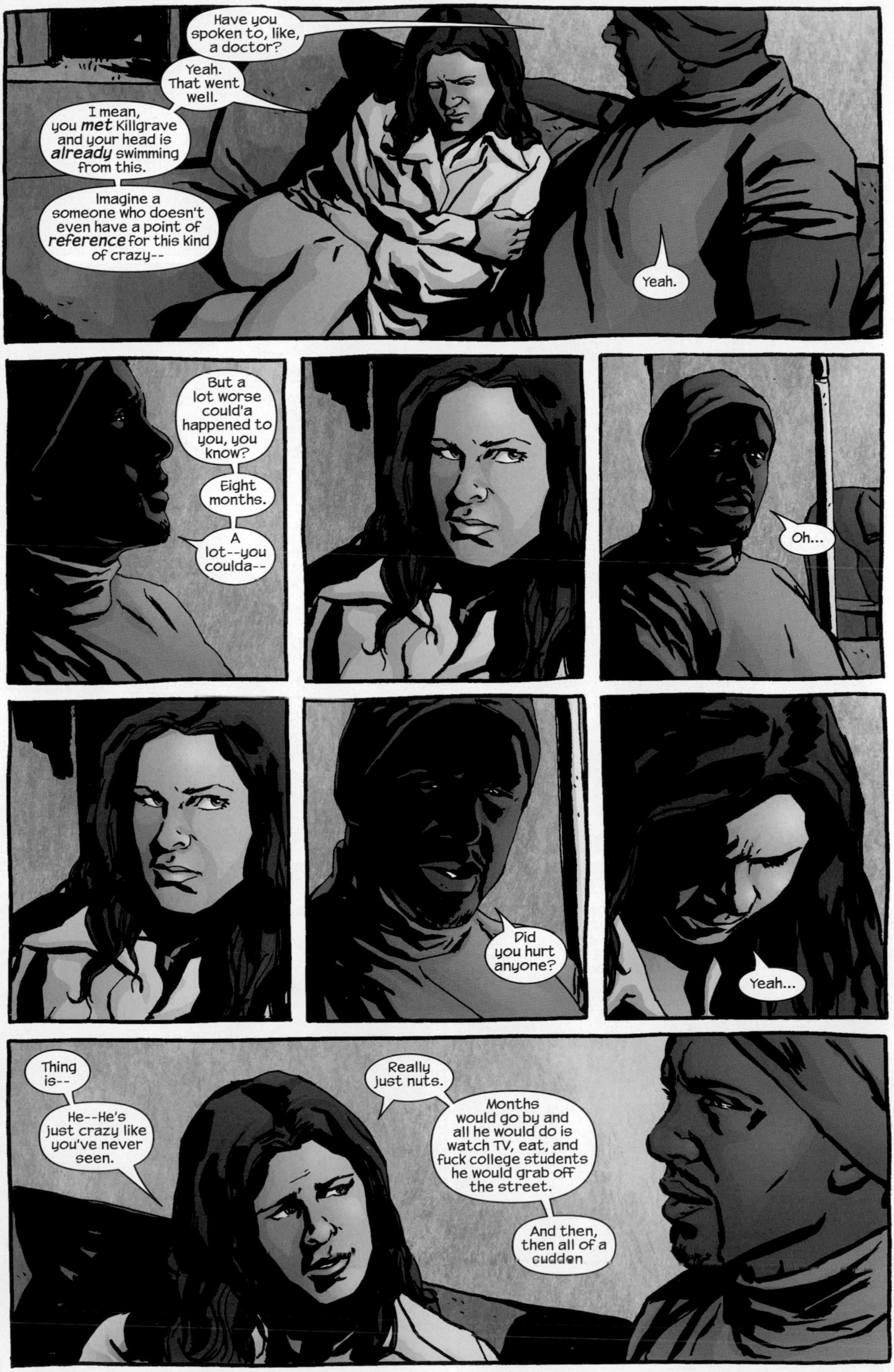
Have you spoken to, like, a doctor?
Yeah. That went well.
I mean, you met Killgrave and your head is already swimming from this.
Imagine a someone who doesn't even have a point of reference for this kind of crazy--
Yeah.
But a lot worse could'a happened to you, you know?
Eight months.
A lot--you coulda--
Oh...
Did you hurt anyone?
Yeah...
Thing is--
He--He's just crazy like you've never seen.
Really just nuts.
Months would go by and all he would do is watch TV, eat, and fuck college students he would grab off the street.
And then, then all of a cudden

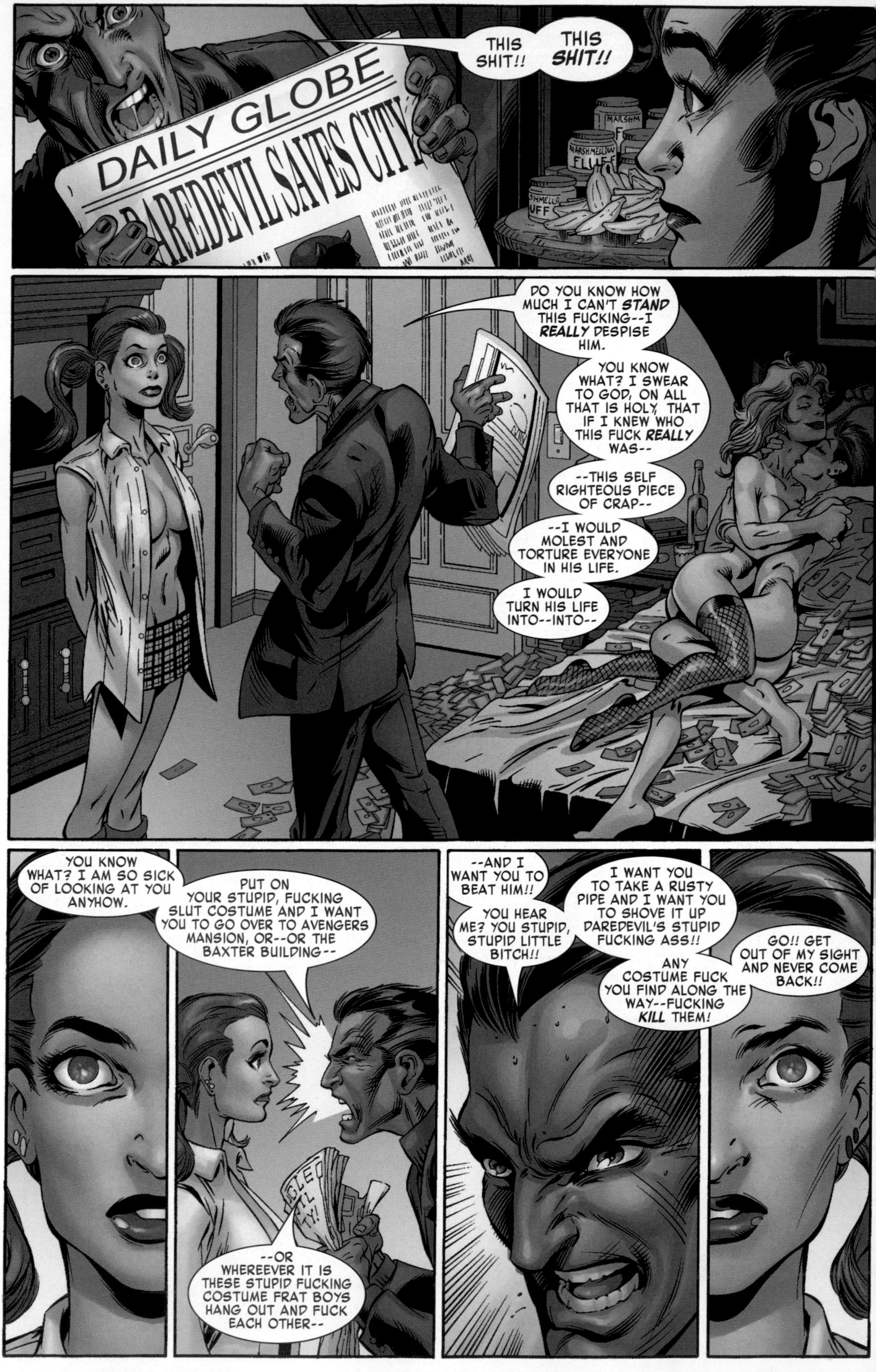
THIS SHIT!!
THIS SHIT!!
DAILY GLOBE
DAREDEVIL SAVES CITY
MARSHMELLOW FLUFF
DO YOU KNOW HOW MUCH I CAN'T STAND THIS FUCKING--I REALLY DESPISE HIM.
YOU KNOW WHAT? I SWEAR TO GOD, ON ALL THAT IS HOLY, THAT IF I KNEW WHO THIS FUCK REALLY WAS--
--THIS SELF RIGHTEOUS PIECE OF CRAP--
--I WOULD MOLEST AND TORTURE EVERYONE IN HIS LIFE.
I WOULD TURN HIS LIFE INTO--INTO--
YOU KNOW WHAT? I AM SO SICK OF LOOKING AT YOU ANYHOW.
PUT ON YOUR STUPID, FUCKING SLUT COSTUME AND I WANT YOU TO GO OVER TO AVENGERS MANSION, OR--OR THE BAXTER BUILDING--
--OR WHEREEVER IT IS THESE STUPID FUCKING COSTUME FRAT BOYS HANG OUT AND FUCK EACH OTHER--
--AND I WANT YOU TO BEAT HIM!!
YOU HEAR ME? YOU STUPID, STUPID LITTLE BITCH!!
I WANT YOU TO TAKE A RUSTY PIPE AND I WANT YOU TO SHOVE IT UP DAREDEVIL'S STUPID FUCKING ASS!!
ANY COSTUME FUCK YOU FIND ALONG THE WAY--FUCKING KILL THEM!
GO!! GET OUT OF MY SIGHT AND NEVER COME BACK!!

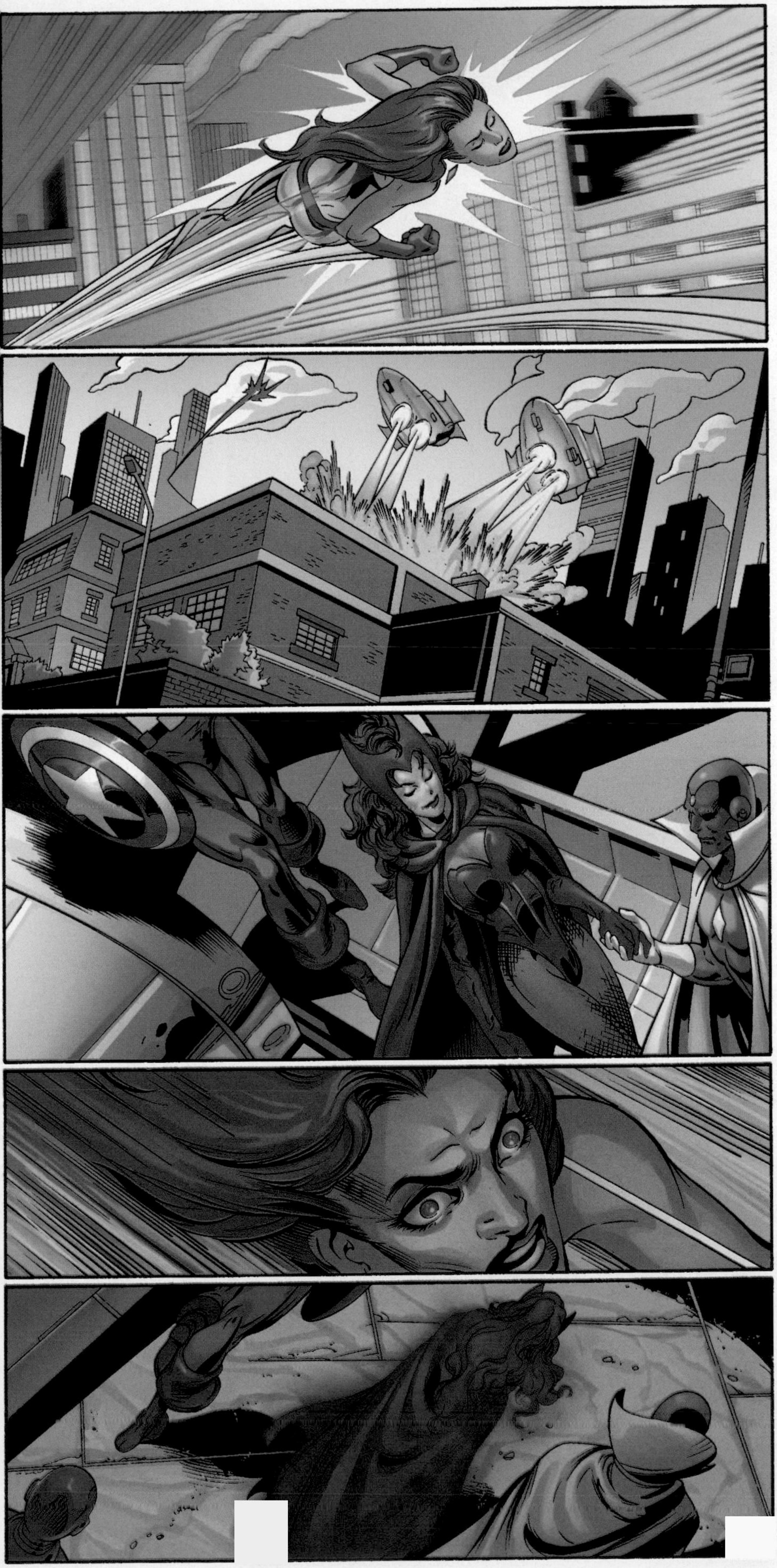

Now, the second I'm out of range of Killgrave's chemical bombardment of my brain...

The ***second*** I get the hell away from him, I start coming out of it.

Finally.

The ***brainwashing***, or whatever the fuck it is, starts wearing off.

And it wasn't a pleasant experience.

I mean, this mind control shit he's been pumping into me has ***been*** there for eight months.

Every day, every night: eight months.

And so as soon as Killgrave ***wasn't*** there, my body, my brain--it had no fucking idea what to do!!

I was having some kind of a nervous breakdown.

I found myself ***still*** determined to do what he told me to do, but now I could feel my body trying to stop.

But I'm still going ahead with my mission.

I knew what I was doing was fucked up, but I couldn't--stop--***doing***--it.

I bolt right towards Avengers Mansion looking for Daredevil, just like he told me to...

(Even though I know as well as anyone on the planet that Daredevil isn't there, shouldn't be there, and I don't think has ***ever*** been there).

But I can't ***stop*** doing what Killgrave told me to do.

I ***can't*** stop.

I can't ***stop.***

Also now, I can't ***see*** straight. My head is ***throbbing.*** I--I can hear my heart looking for a way right the fuck out of my chest!

And I ***still*** don't ***stop*** what I'm doing.

So just--just as I am getting there, a couple of those Avengers jet things are coming in for a landing.

The Avengers are just coming home from some big mission.

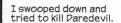

And here I am, all whacked out.

And I know I sound like a retard, but from my fucked up point of view I was doing what Killgrave asked.

I swooped down and tried to kill Daredevil.

Except it wasn't Daredevil, not even close. It was the Scarlet Witch...

(Who I happen to be a *huge* fan of)

And she was totally caught off guard and I'm god damn lucky I didn't take her head off.

And, I don't know if it was just the act. The hitting.

But the second I *hit* her--I was *finally* awake!

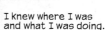

I knew where I was and what I was doing.

More importantly-- I knew what I just did and what it *looked* like.

It all happened in a *second*!!

I mean, a *second*.

There I am surrounded by not only the Avengers, who are just shocked to shit to find themselves coming home from some huge cosmic whatever...

(where they probably saved the whole fucking universe...)

...and there they are looking at some costumed bimbo who just swooped down and *hit* one of them!!

Who, now, was just standing there with a stupid look on her face.

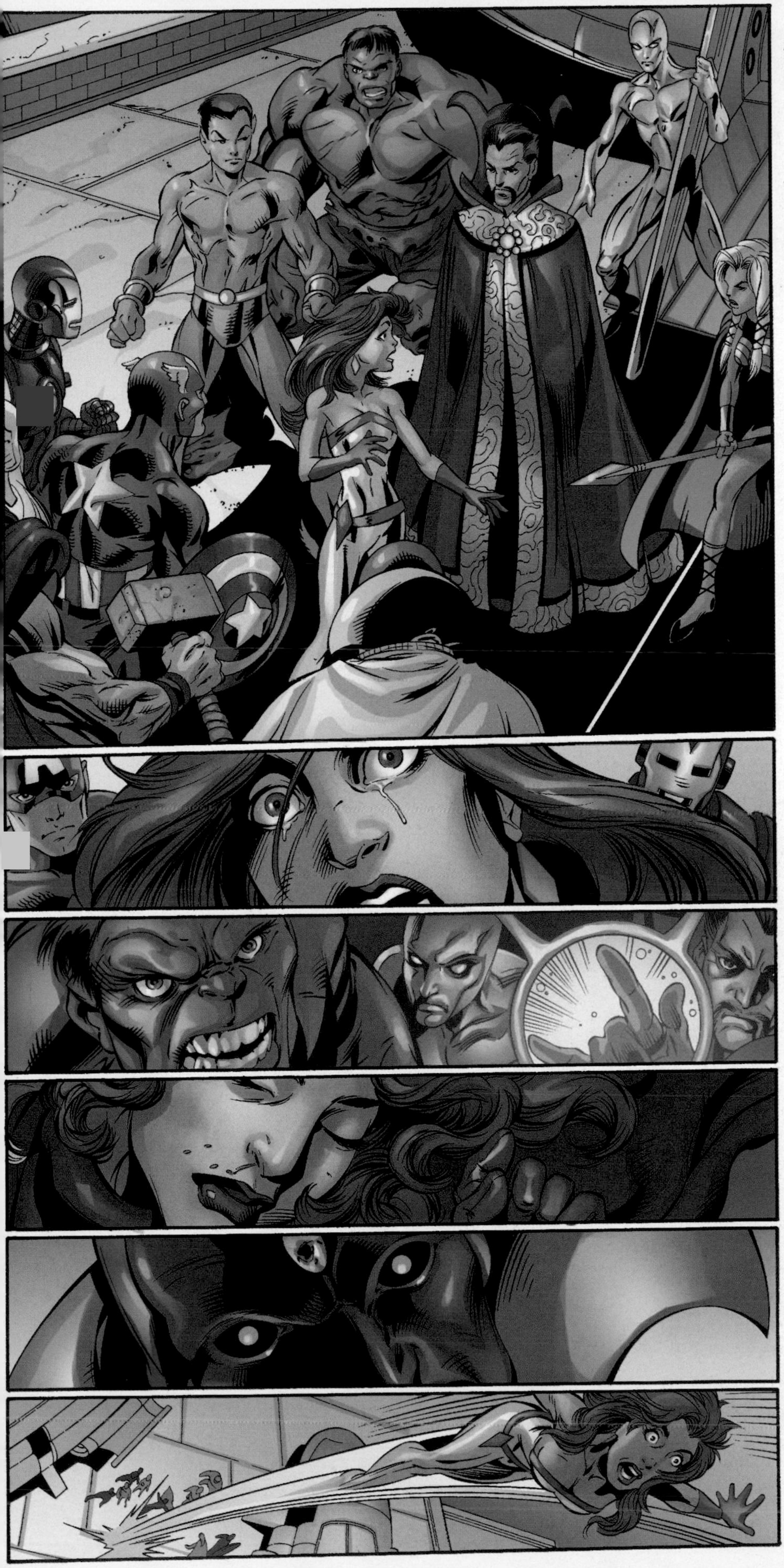

And, oh yeah, not only was it the Avengers that I happen to side swipe...

But I pick a day where the Avengers ***and*** the Defenders, the old school classic Defenders, are doing some big ***team-up.***

So not only do I got Captain America, Thor, Iron Man, and the Scarlet Witch's husband ready to just beat my ass...

...but now I got the fucking Incredible Hulk, that Dr. Strange dude, the Namor guy...

All of 'em.

I mean, I was--I was so ***fucked*** it wasn't even funny.

And I could--I could imagine in my mind's eye the scene where I try to say: 'I'm sorry everyone, I thought she was Daredevil and I think I was under someone else's mind control, but now I'm not. I'm okay now.'

I could hear my brain trying to form the explanation and I heard how fucked it sounded, so I just...

I mean, what the hell could I do?

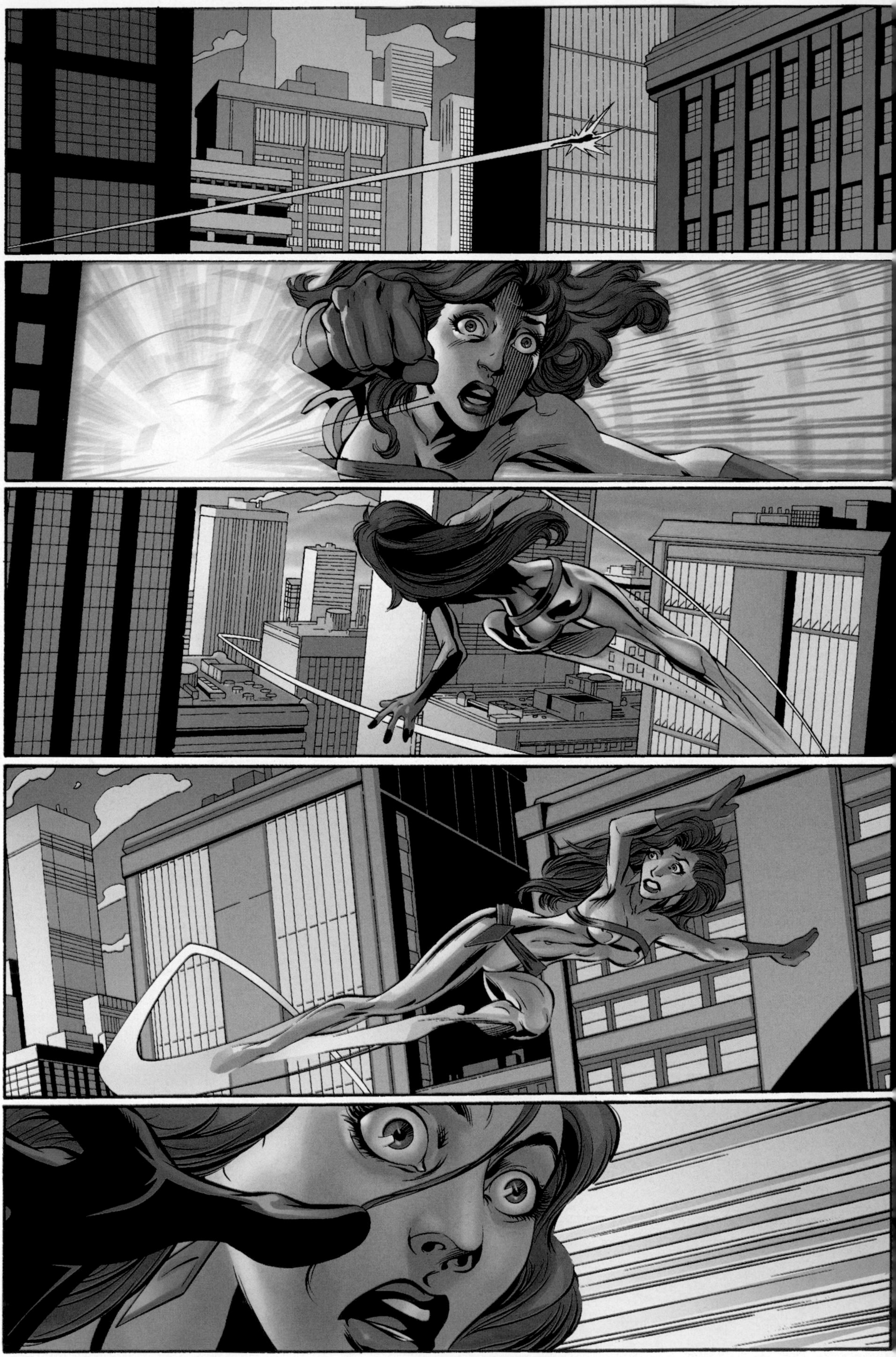

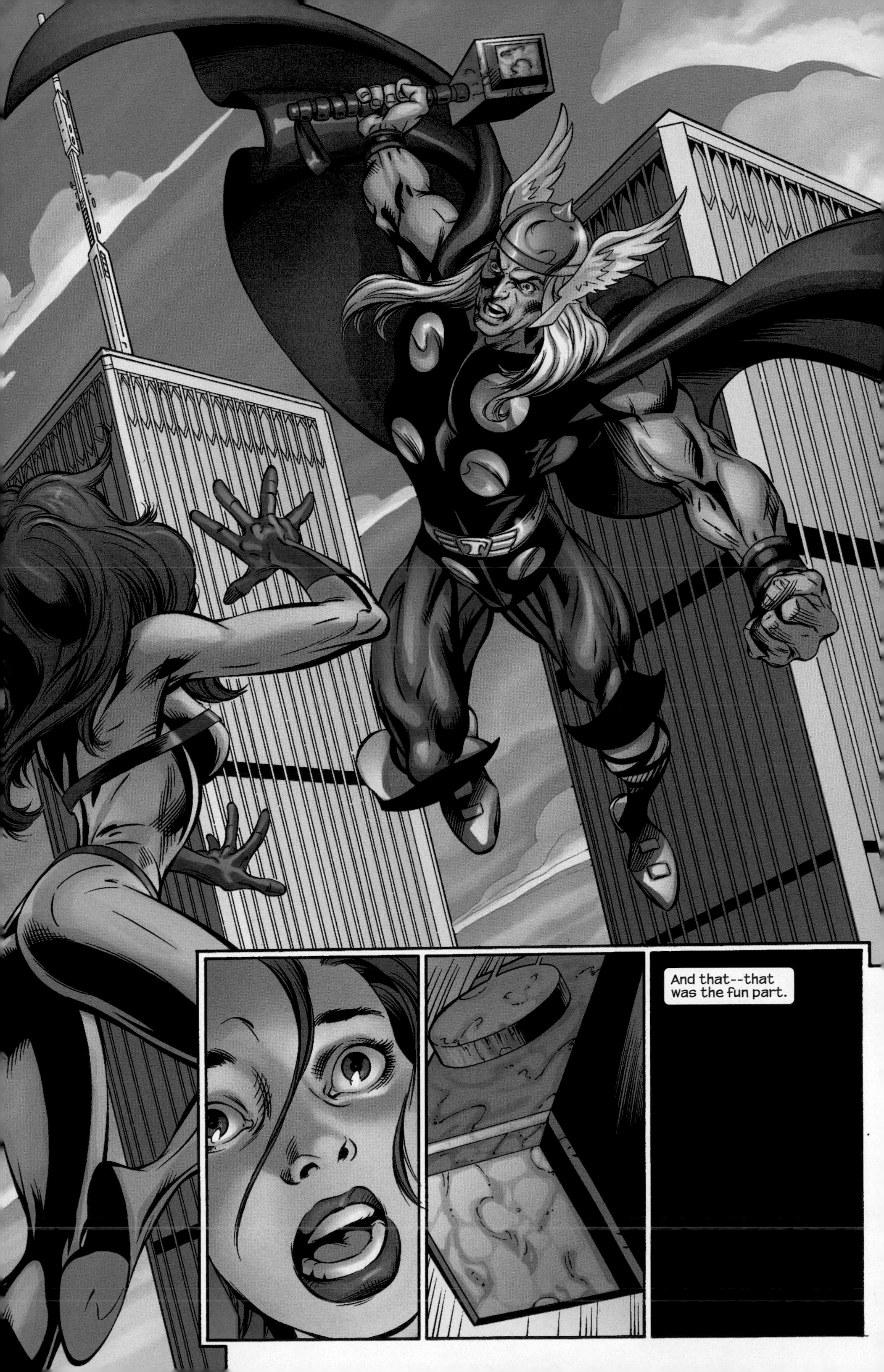
And that--that
was the fun part.

CONFIDENTIAL

ISSUE #26

AV[redacted]S

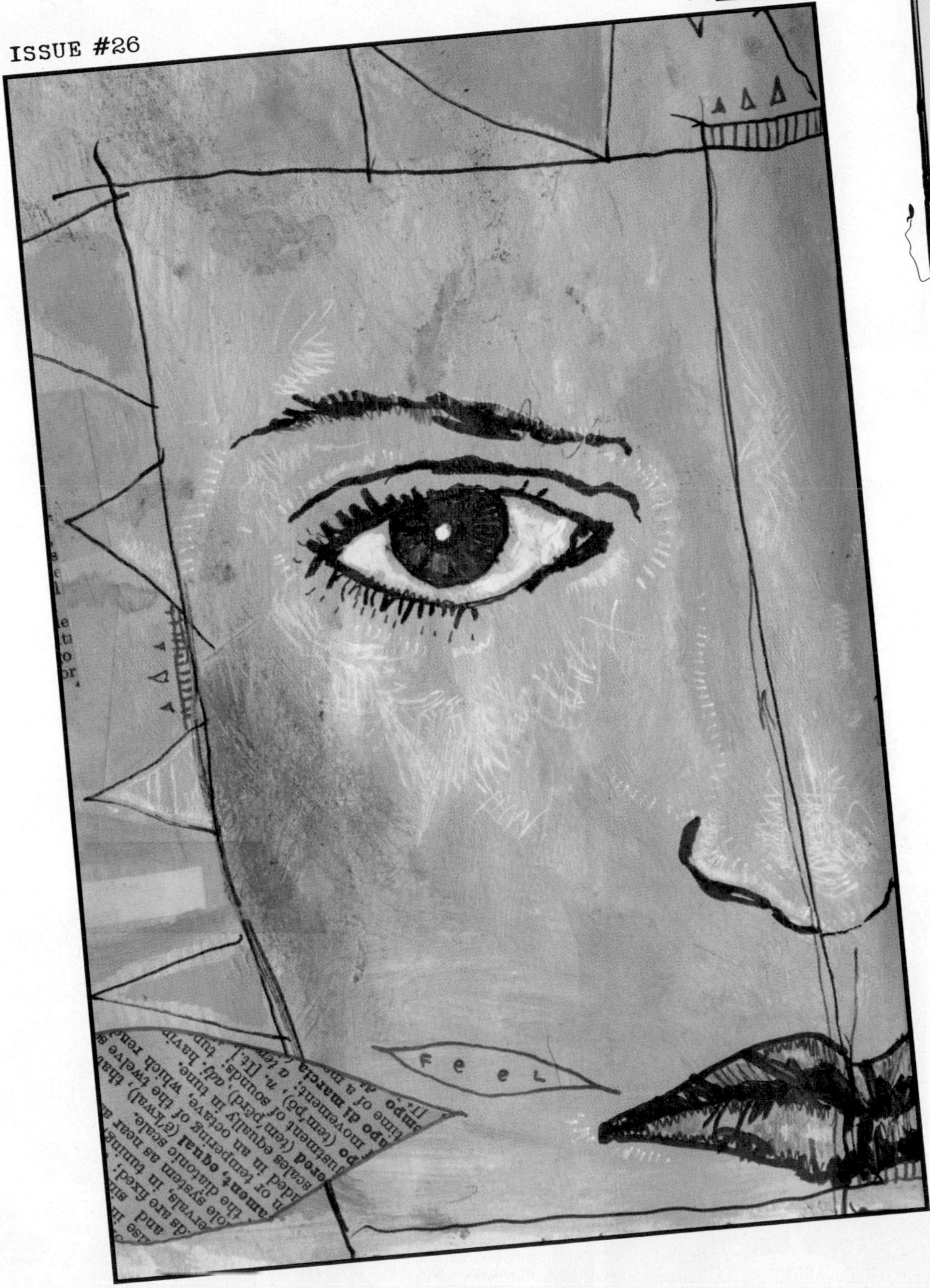

feel

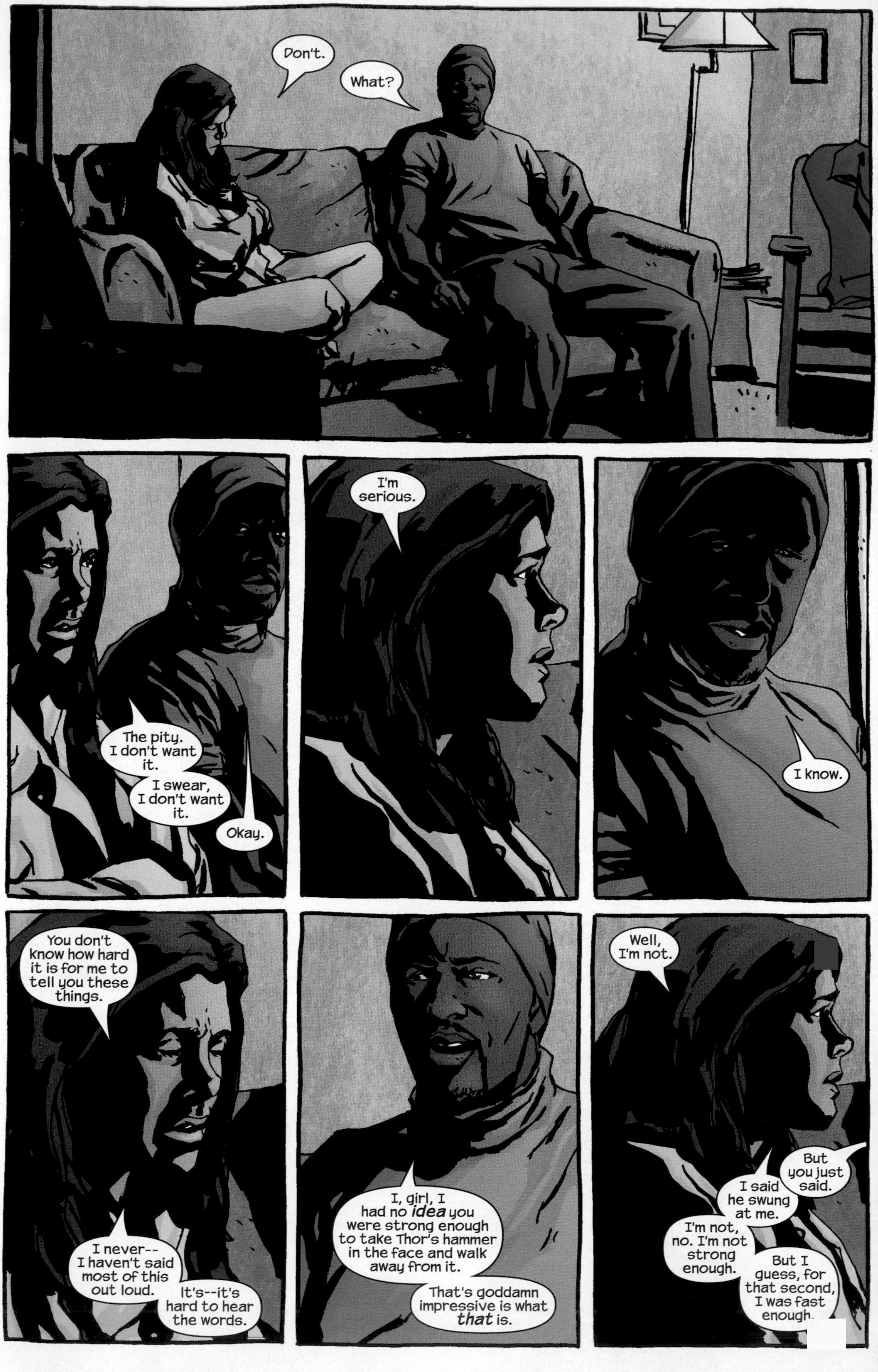
Don't.
What?
The pity. I don't want it.
I swear, I don't want it.
Okay.
I'm serious.
I know.
You don't know how hard it is for me to tell you these things.
I never-- I haven't said most of this out loud.
It's--it's hard to hear the words.
I, girl, I had no idea you were strong enough to take Thor's hammer in the face and walk away from it.
That's goddamn impressive is what that is.
Well, I'm not.
But you just said.
I said he swung at me.
I'm not, no. I'm not strong enough.
But I guess, for that second, I was fast enough.

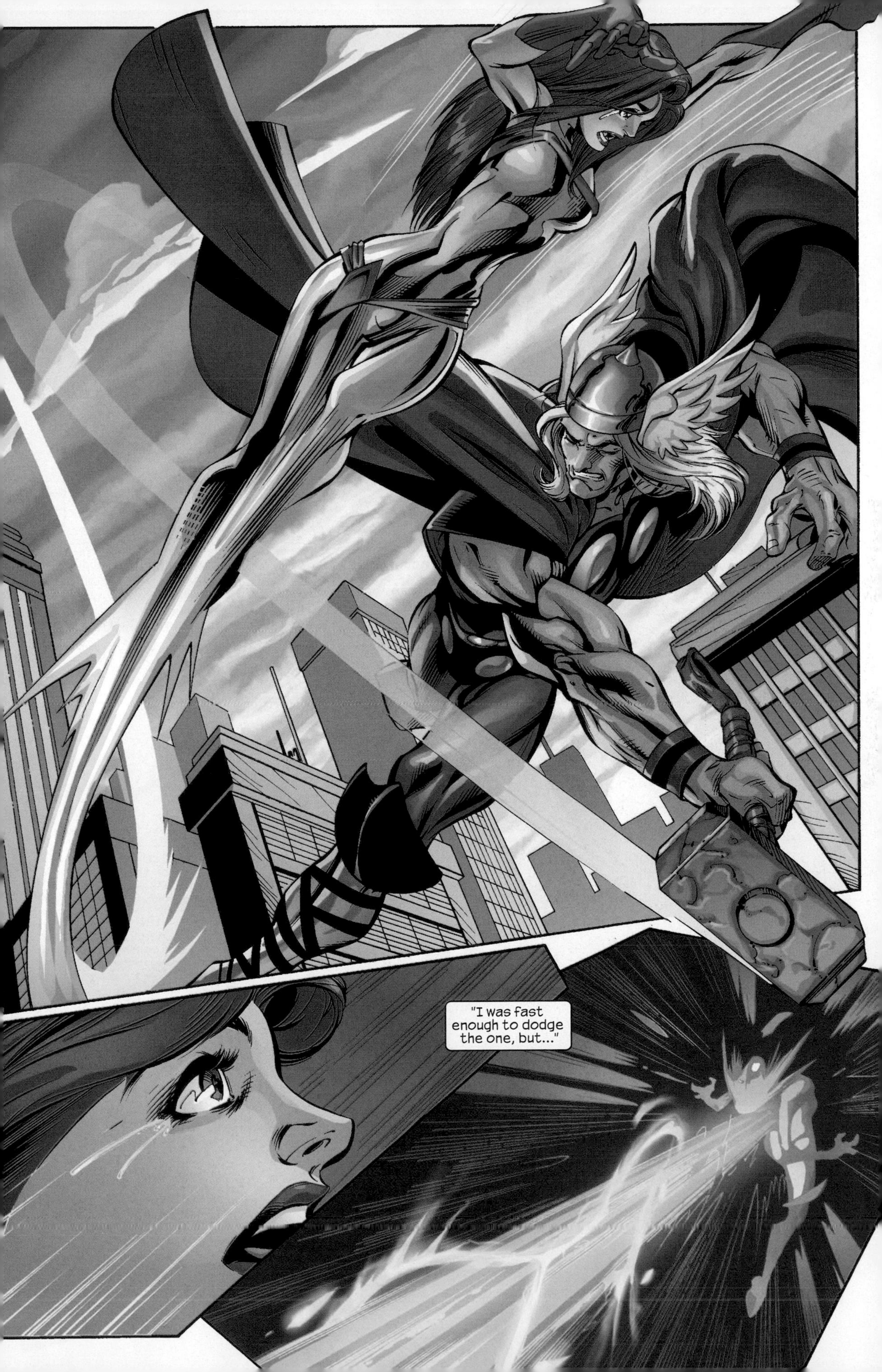
"I was fast enough to dodge the one, but..."

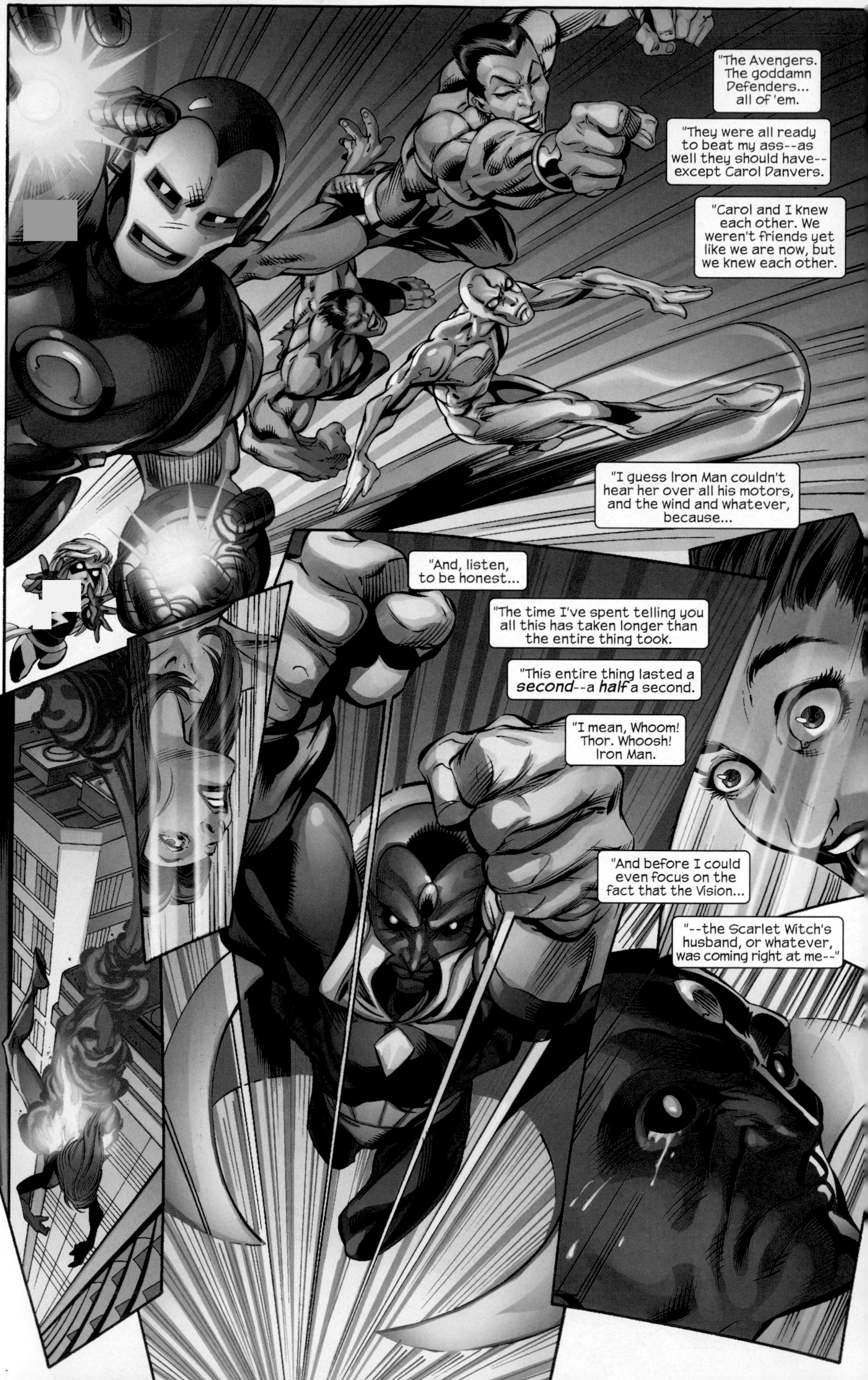
"The Avengers. The goddamn Defenders... all of 'em.
"They were all ready to beat my ass--as well they should have--except Carol Danvers.
"Carol and I knew each other. We weren't friends yet like we are now, but we knew each other.
"I guess Iron Man couldn't hear her over all his motors, and the wind and whatever, because...
"And, listen, to be honest...
"The time I've spent telling you all this has taken longer than the entire thing took.
"This entire thing lasted a *second*--a *half* a second.
"I mean, Whoom! Thor. Whoosh! Iron Man.
"And before I could even focus on the fact that the Vision...
"--the Scarlet Witch's husband, or whatever, was coming right at me--"

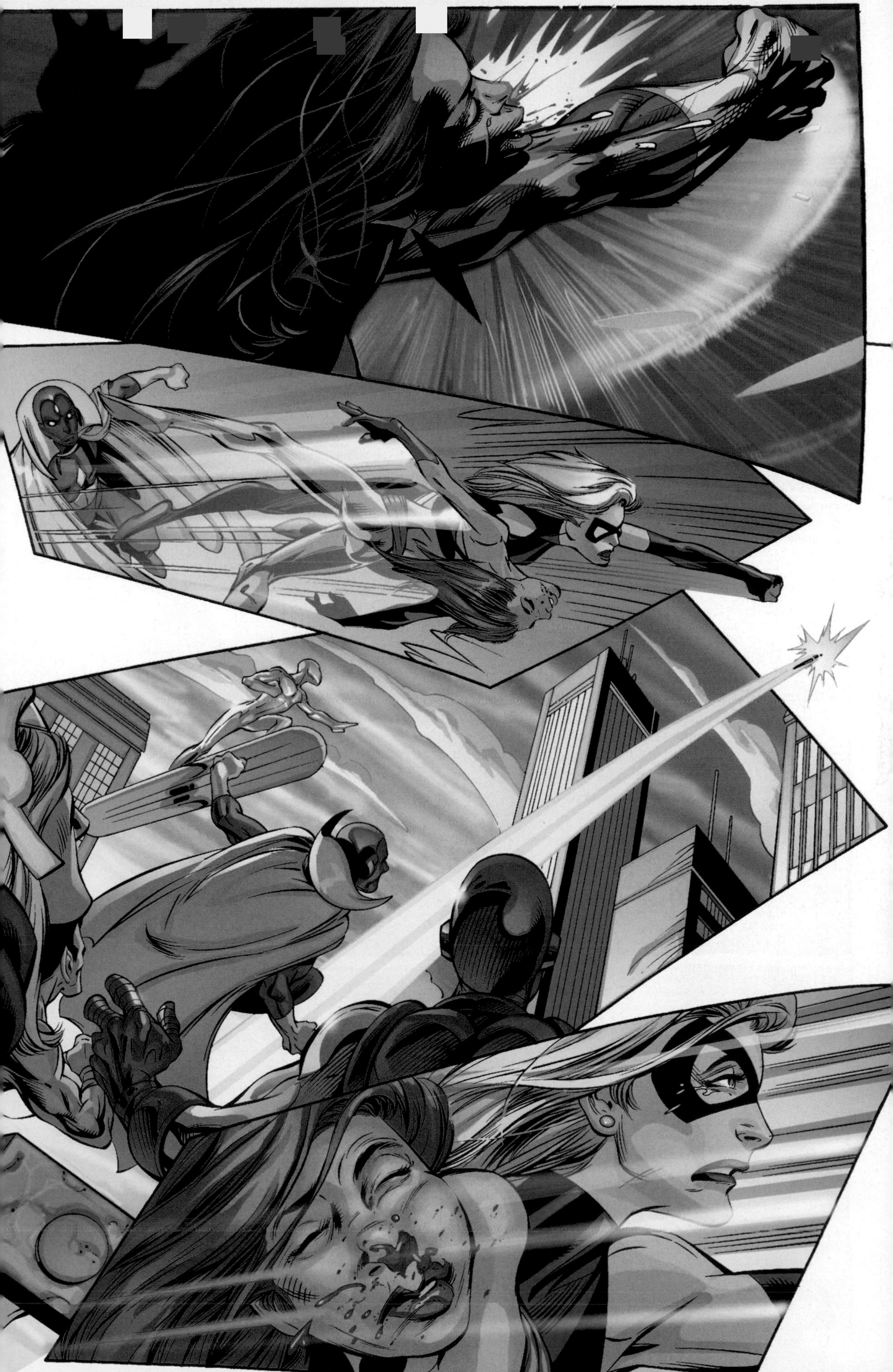

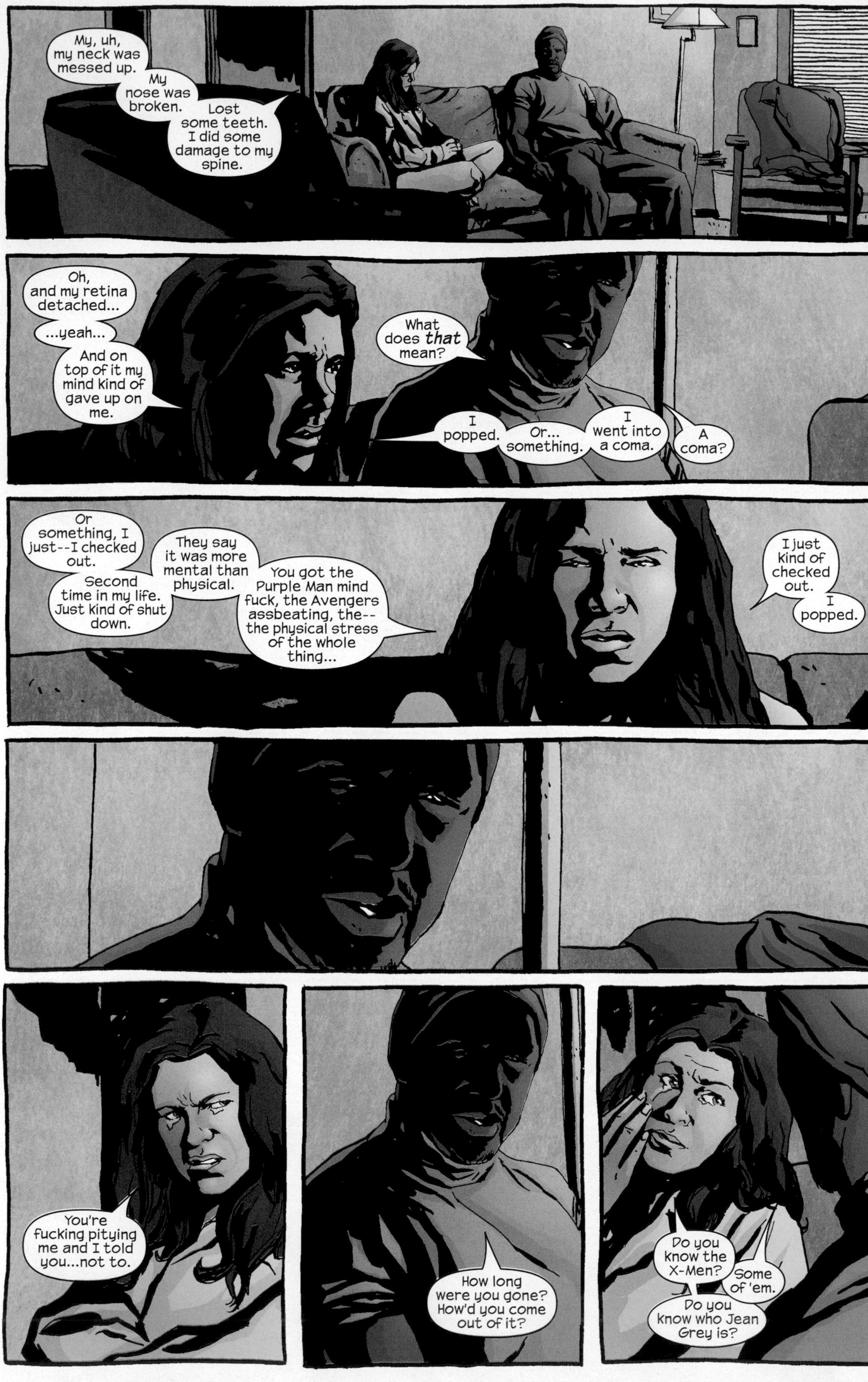

My, uh, my neck was messed up.
My nose was broken.
Lost some teeth. I did some damage to my spine.
Oh, and my retina detached...
...yeah...
And on top of it my mind kind of gave up on me.
What does *that* mean?
I popped.
Or... something.
I went into a coma.
A coma?
Or something, I just--I checked out.
Second time in my life. Just kind of shut down.
They say it was more mental than physical.
You got the Purple Man mind fuck, the Avengers assbeating, the--the physical stress of the whole thing...
I just kind of checked out.
I popped.
You're fucking pitying me and I told you...not to.
How long were you gone? How'd you come out of it?
Do you know the X-Men?
Some of 'em.
Do you know who Jean Grey is?

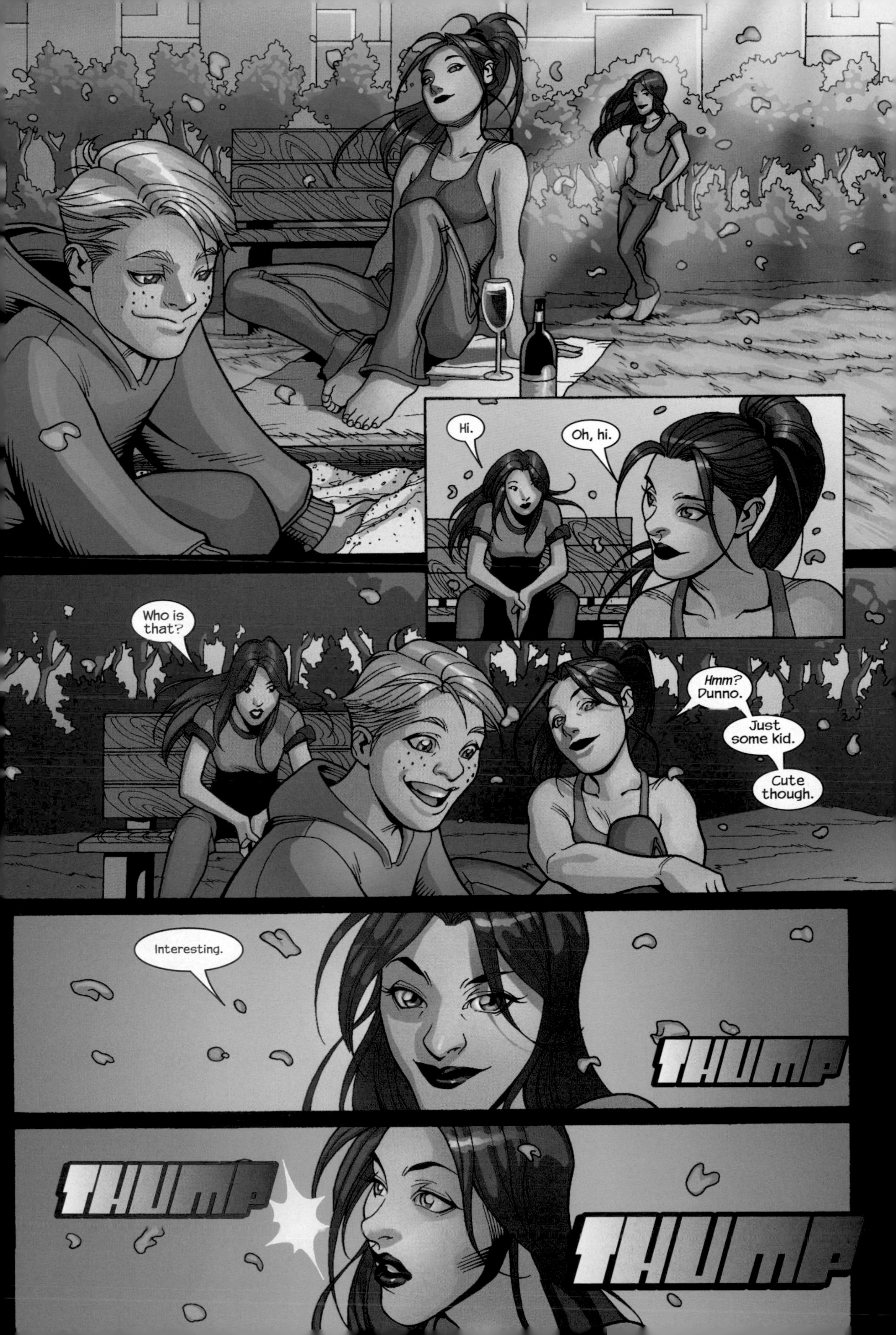
Hi.
Oh, hi.
Who is that?
Hmm? Dunno.
Just some kid.
Cute though.
Interesting.
THUMP
THUMP
THUMP

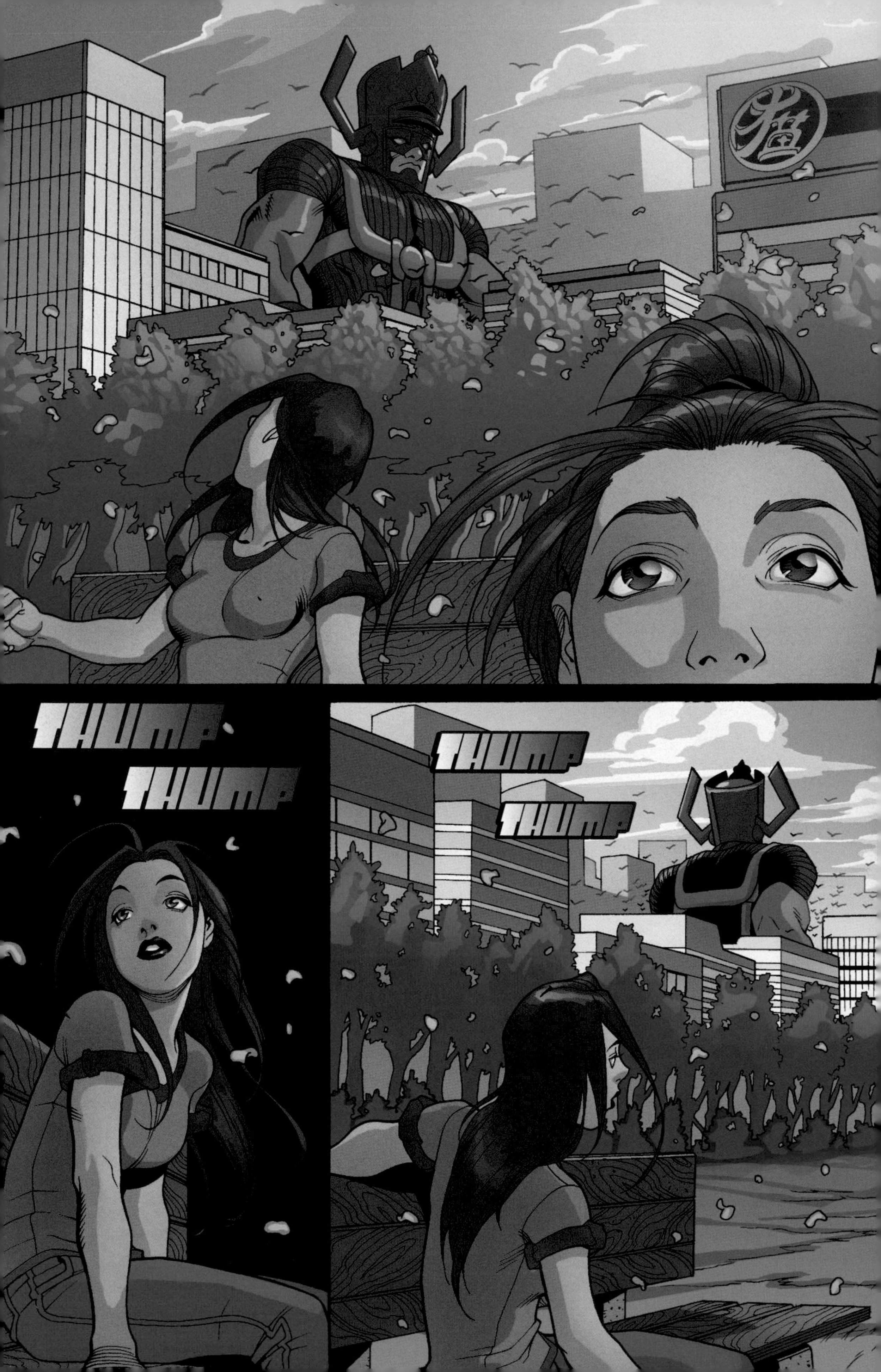
THUMP
THUMP
THUMP
THUMP

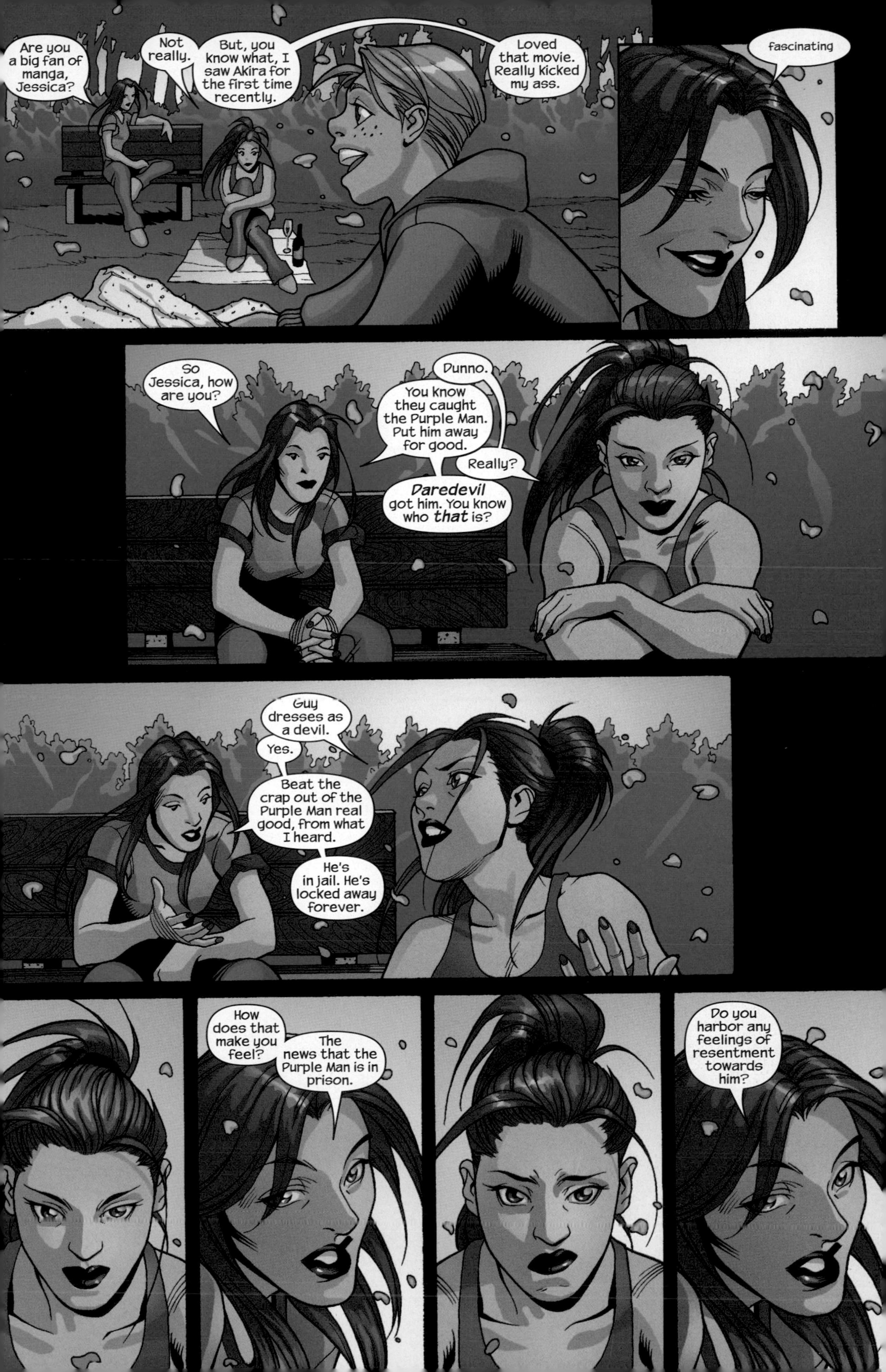
Are you a big fan of manga, Jessica?
Not really.
But, you know what, I saw Akira for the first time recently.
Loved that movie. Really kicked my ass.
fascinating
So Jessica, how are you?
Dunno.
You know they caught the Purple Man. Put him away for good.
Really?
Daredevil got him. You know who *that* is?
Guy dresses as a devil.
Yes.
Beat the crap out of the Purple Man real good, from what I heard.
He's in jail. He's locked away forever.
How does that make you feel?
The news that the Purple Man is in prison.
Do you harbor any feelings of resentment towards him?

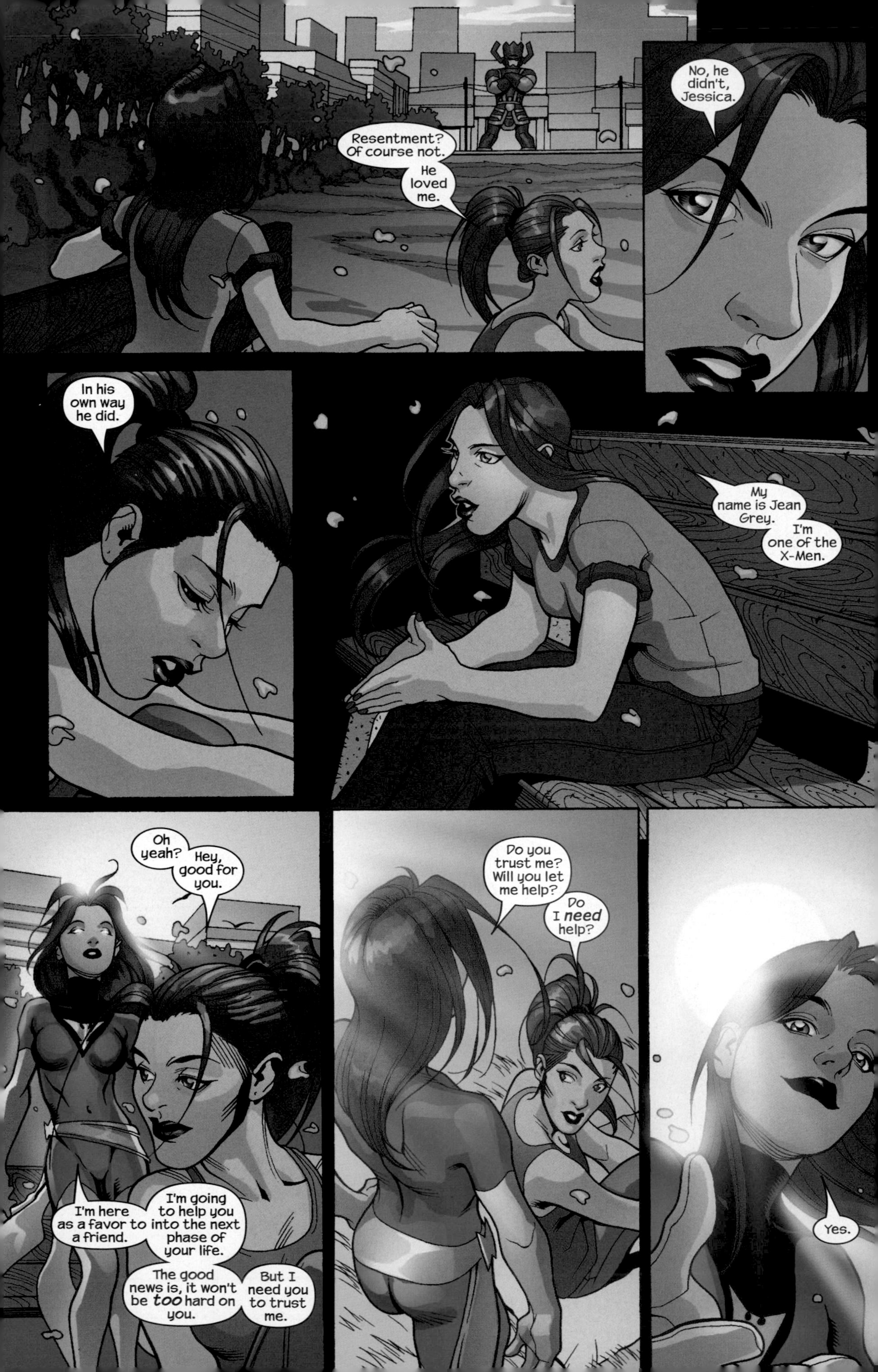
Resentment? Of course not.
He loved me.
No, he didn't, Jessica.
In his own way he did.
My name is Jean Grey.
I'm one of the X-Men.
Oh yeah?
Hey, good for you.
I'm here as a favor to a friend.
I'm going to help you into the next phase of your life.
The good news is, it won't be *too* hard on you.
But I need you to trust me.
Do you trust me? Will you let me help?
Do I *need* help?
Yes.

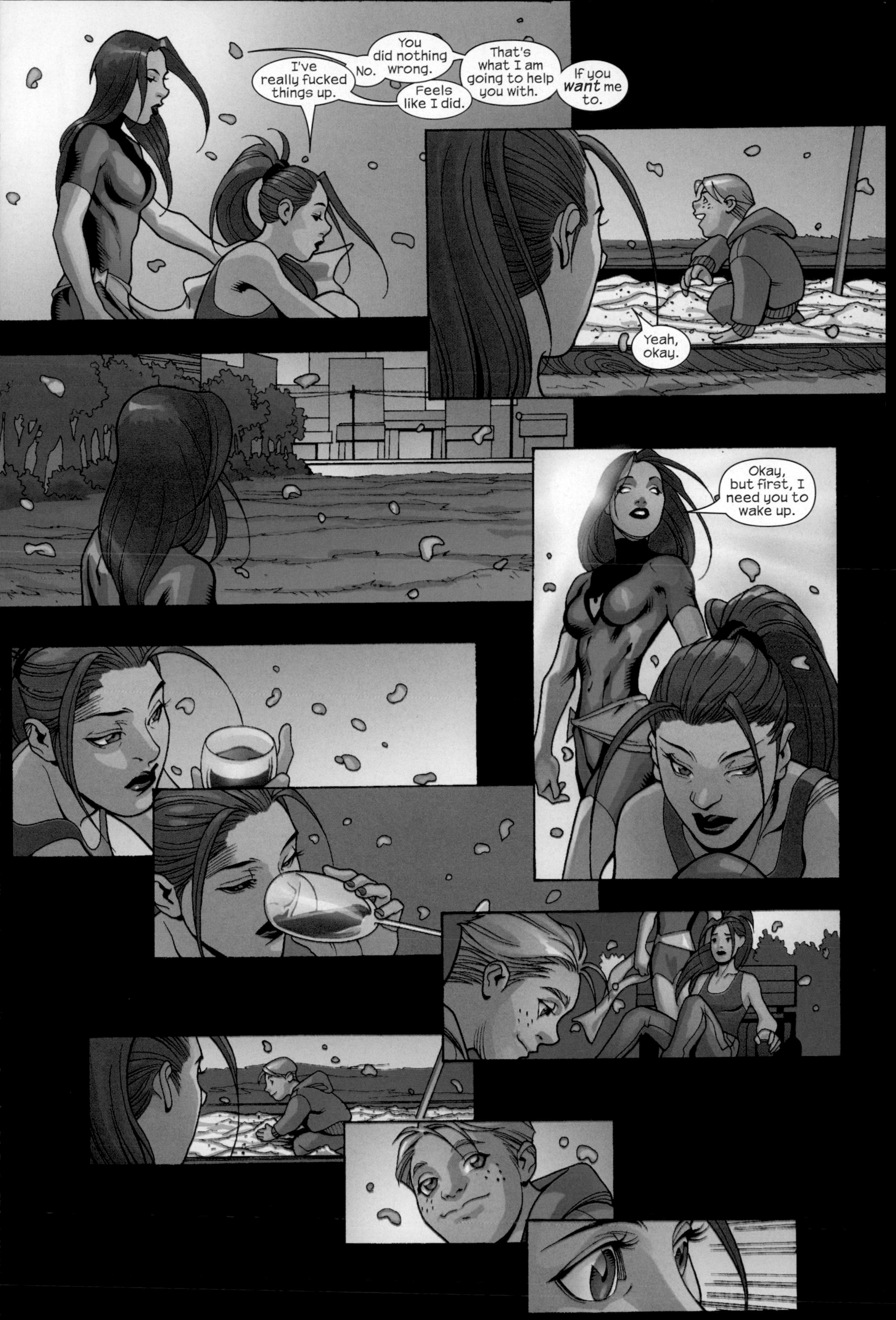

I've really fucked things up.
No.
You did nothing wrong.
Feels like I did.
That's what I am going to help you with.
If you *want* me to.
Yeah, okay.
Okay, but first, I need you to wake up.

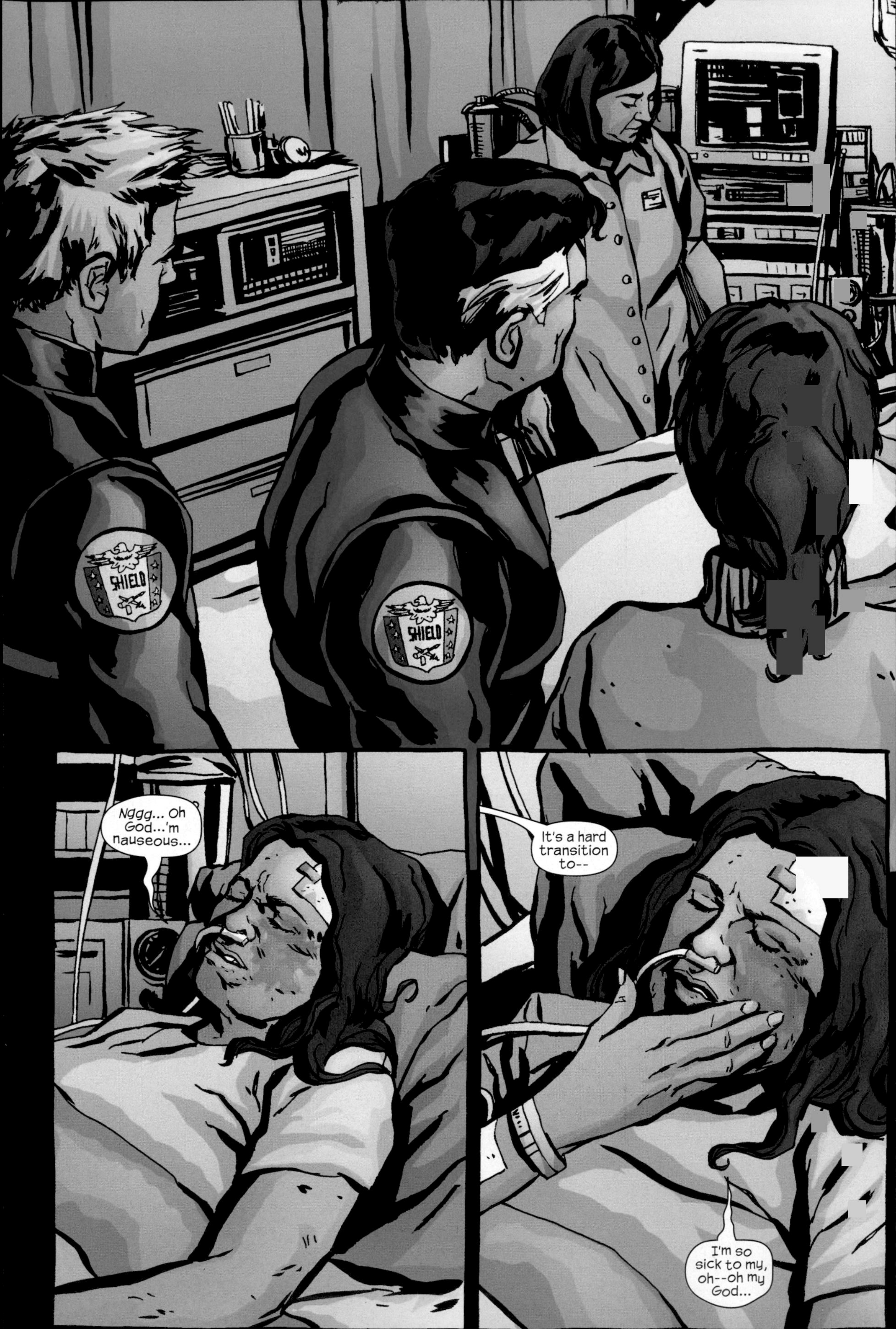
SHIELD
SHIELD
Nggg... Oh God...'m nauseous...
It's a hard transition to--
I'm so sick to my, oh--oh my God...

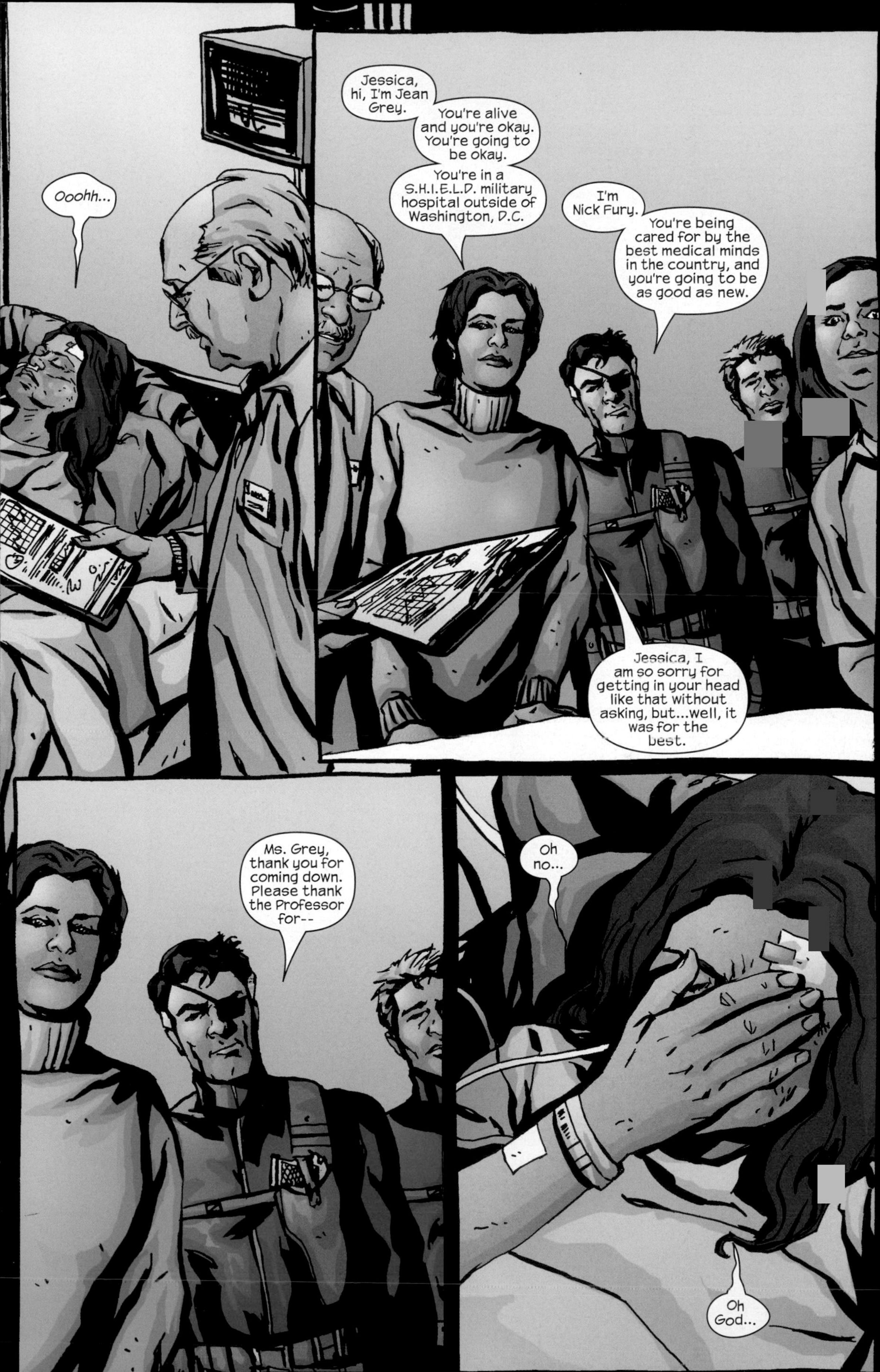
Ooohh...
Jessica, hi, I'm Jean Grey.
You're alive and you're okay. You're going to be okay.
You're in a S.H.I.E.L.D. military hospital outside of Washington, D.C.
I'm Nick Fury.
You're being cared for by the best medical minds in the country, and you're going to be as good as new.
Jessica, I am so sorry for getting in your head like that without asking, but...well, it was for the best.
Ms. Grey, thank you for coming down. Please thank the Professor for--
Oh no...
Oh God...

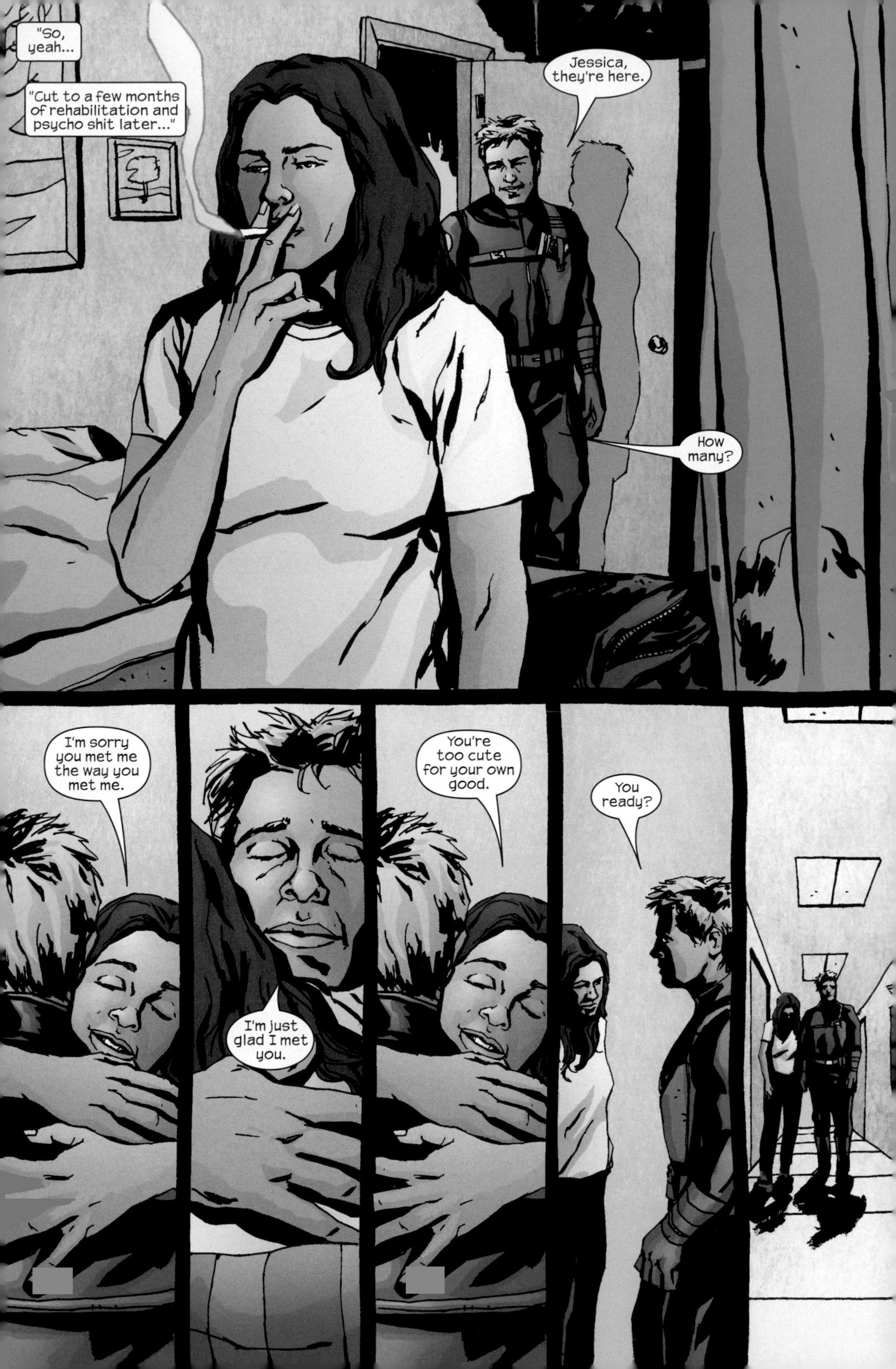
"So, yeah...
"Cut to a few months of rehabilitation and psycho shit later..."
Jessica, they're here.
How many?
I'm sorry you met me the way you met me.
I'm just glad I met you.
You're too cute for your own good.
You ready?

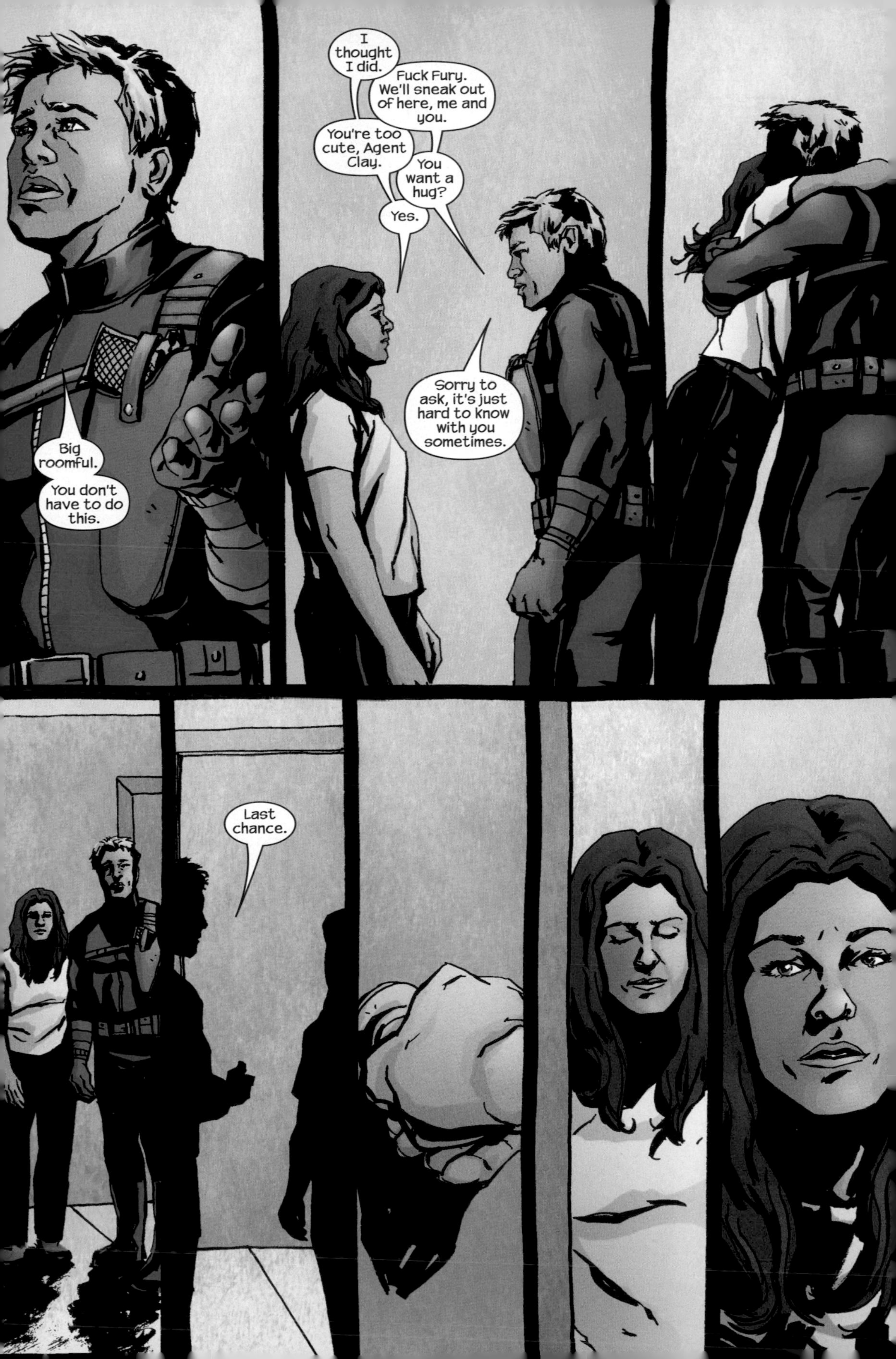
Big roomful.
You don't have to do this.
I thought I did.
Fuck Fury. We'll sneak out of here, me and you.
You're too cute, Agent Clay.
You want a hug?
Yes.
Sorry to ask, it's just hard to know with you sometimes.
Last chance.

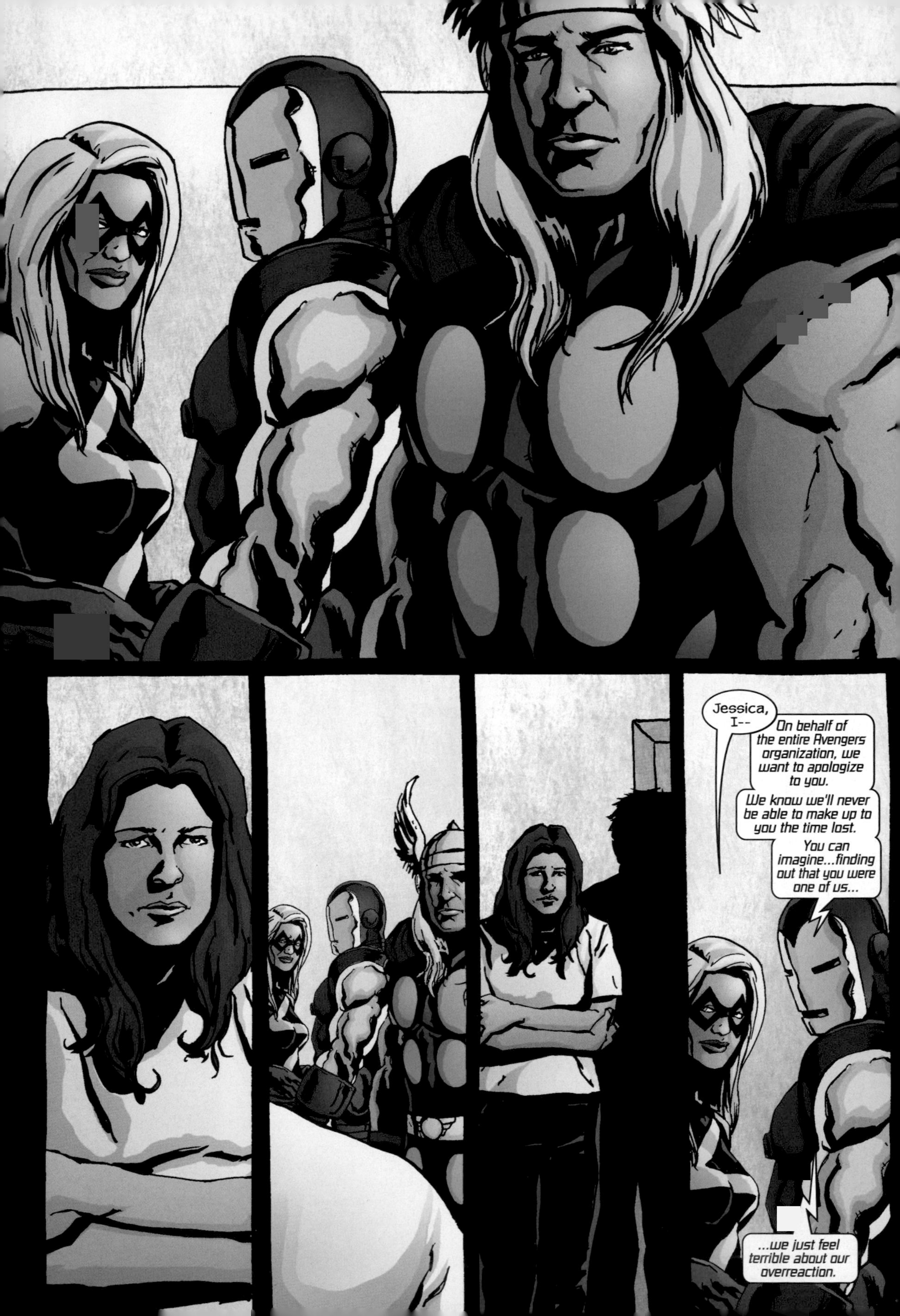
Jessica, I--
On behalf of the entire Avengers organization, we want to apologize to you.
We know we'll never be able to make up to you the time lost.
You can imagine...finding out that you were one of us...
...we just feel terrible about our overreaction.

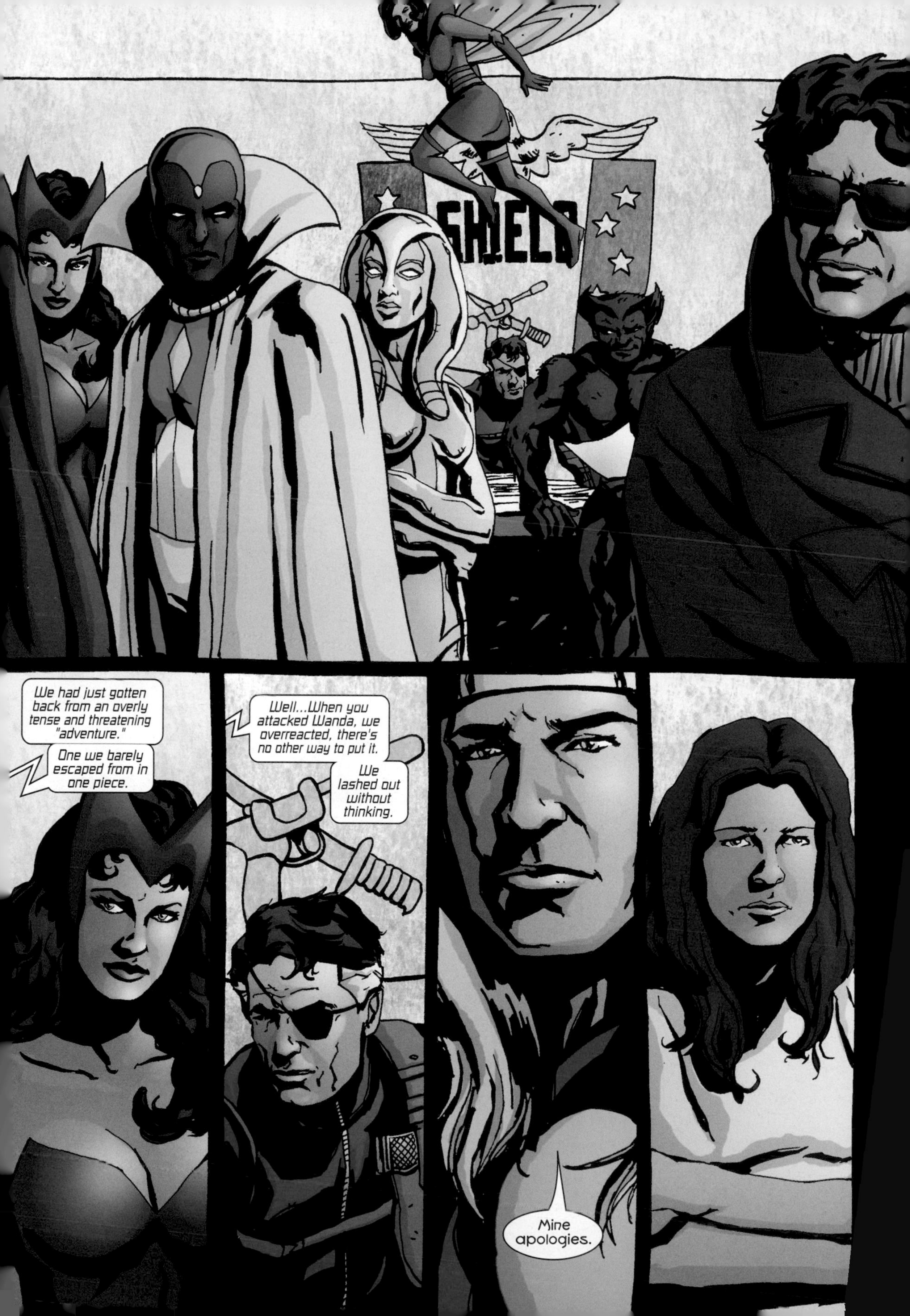

We had just gotten back from an overly tense and threatening "adventure."
One we barely escaped from in one piece.
Well...When you attacked Wanda, we overreacted, there's no other way to put it.
We lashed out without thinking.
Mine apologies.

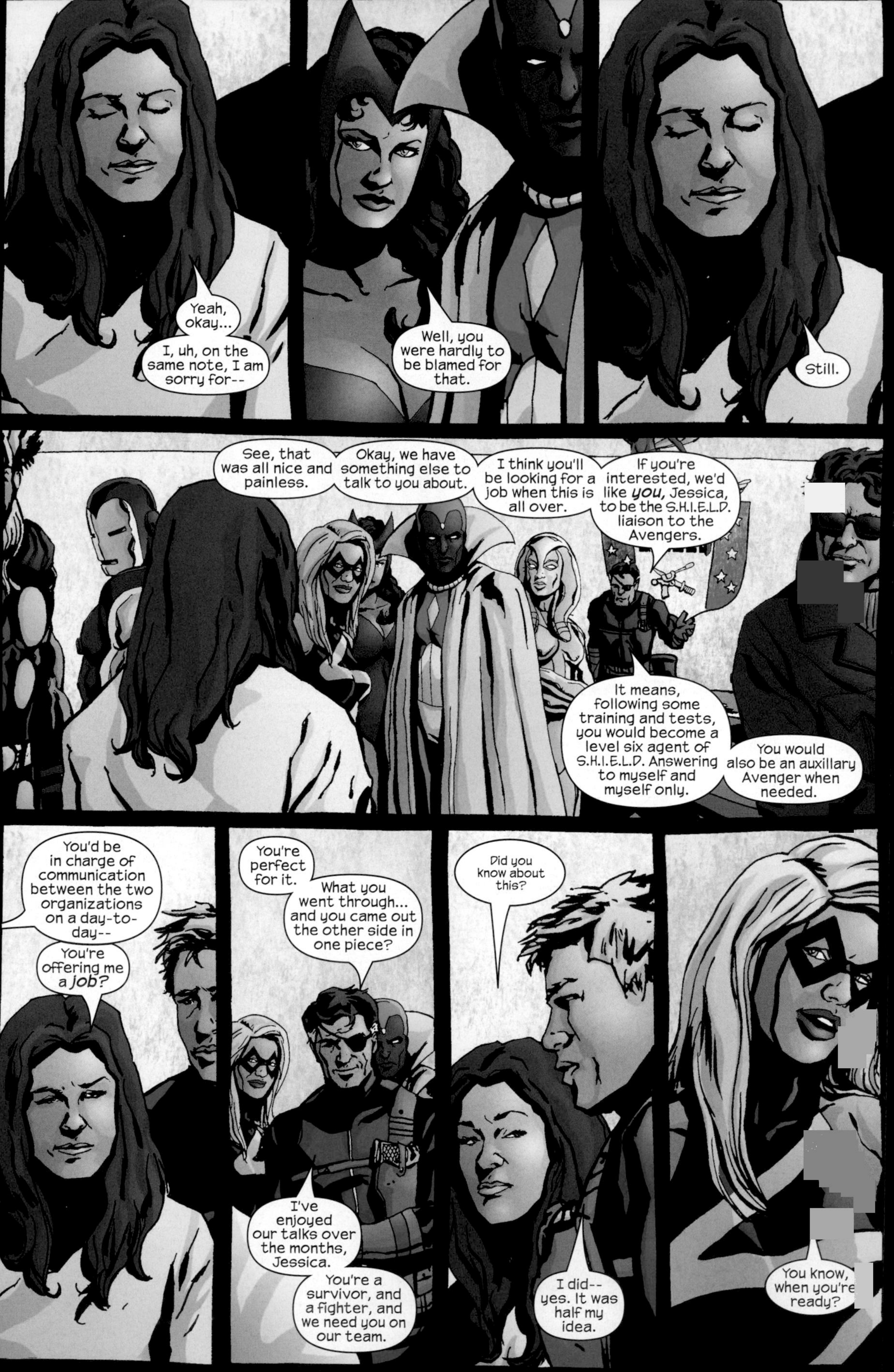
Yeah, okay...
I, uh, on the same note, I am sorry for--
Well, you were hardly to be blamed for that.
Still.
See, that was all nice and painless.
Okay, we have something else to talk to you about.
I think you'll be looking for a job when this is all over.
If you're interested, we'd like *you,* Jessica, to be the S.H.I.E.L.D. liaison to the Avengers.
It means, following some training and tests, you would become a level six agent of S.H.I.E.L.D. Answering to myself and myself only.
You would also be an auxillary Avenger when needed.
You'd be in charge of communication between the two organizations on a day-to-day--
You're offering me a *job?*
You're perfect for it.
What you went through... and you came out the other side in one piece?
I've enjoyed our talks over the months, Jessica.
You're a survivor, and a fighter, and we need you on our team.
Did you know about this?
I did-- yes. It was half my idea.
You know, when you're ready?

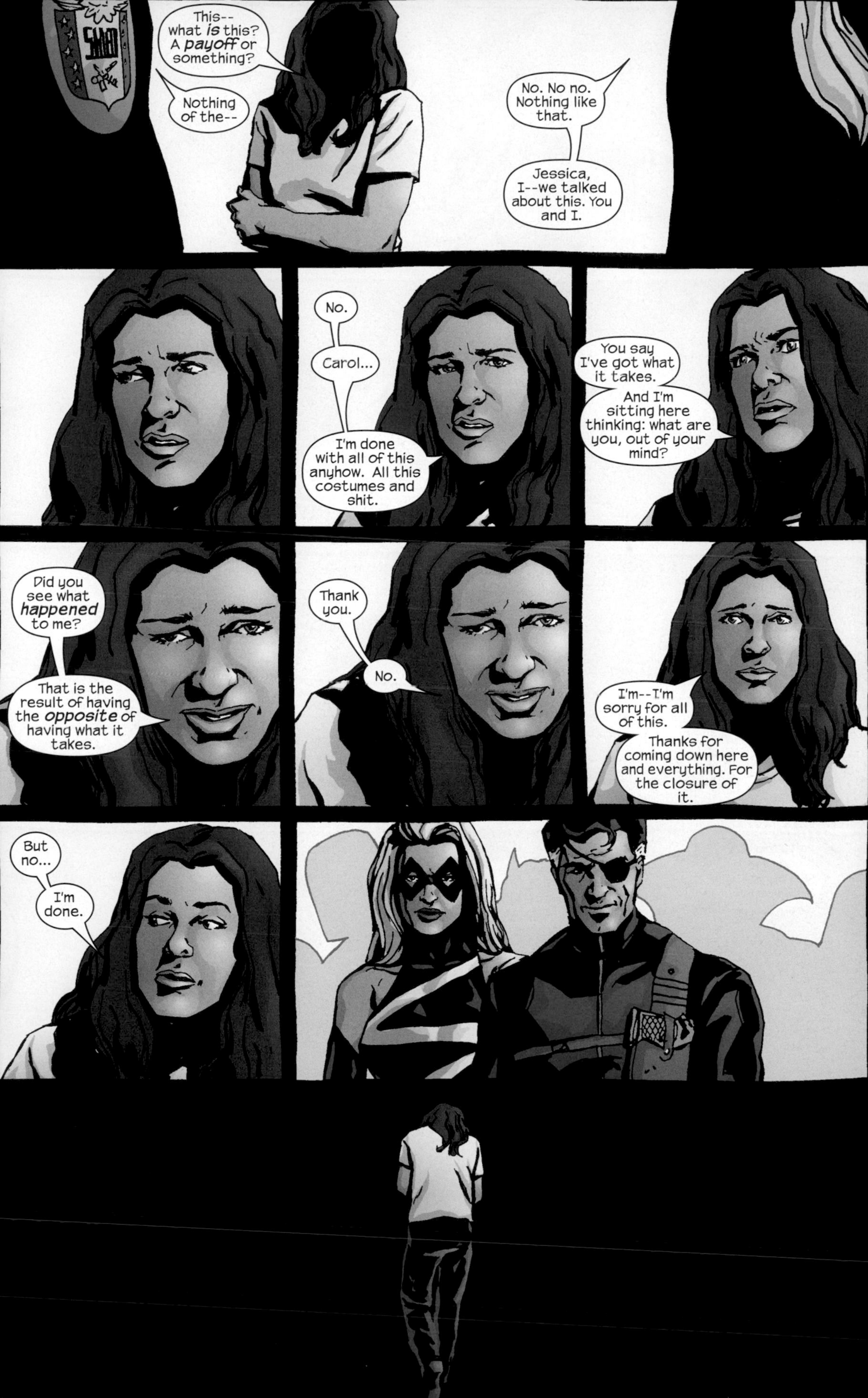

This-- what *is* this? A *payoff* or something?
Nothing of the--
No. No no. Nothing like that.
Jessica, I--we talked about this. You and I.
No.
Carol...
I'm done with all of this anyhow. All this costumes and shit.
You say I've got what it takes.
And I'm sitting here thinking: what are you, out of your mind?
Did you see what *happened* to me?
That is the result of having the *opposite* of having what it takes.
Thank you.
No.
I'm--I'm sorry for all of this.
Thanks for coming down here and everything. For the closure of it.
But no...
I'm done.

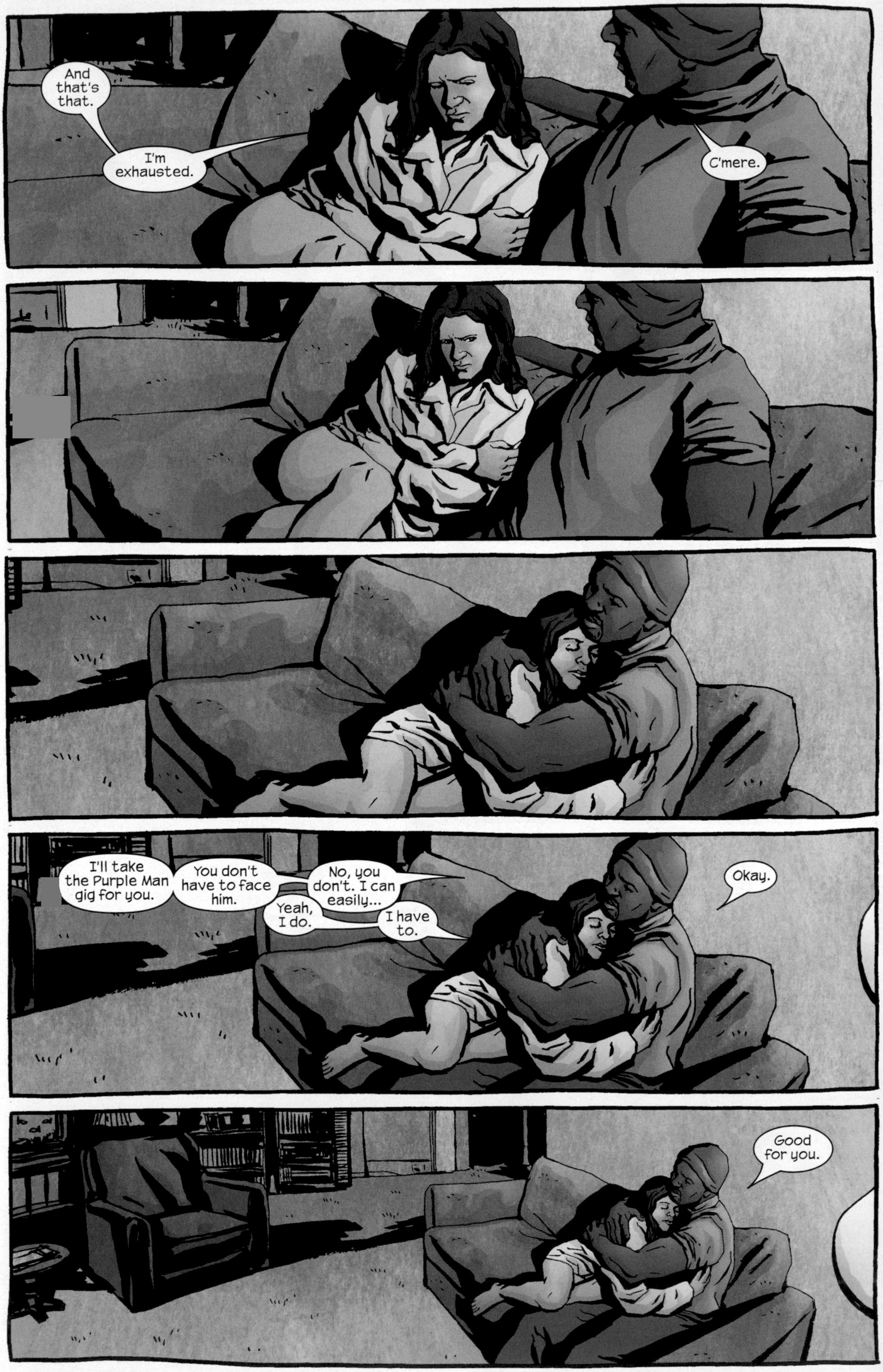

And that's that.
I'm exhausted.
C'mere.
I'll take the Purple Man gig for you.
You don't have to face him.
No, you don't. I can easily...
Yeah, I do.
I have to.
Okay.
Good for you.

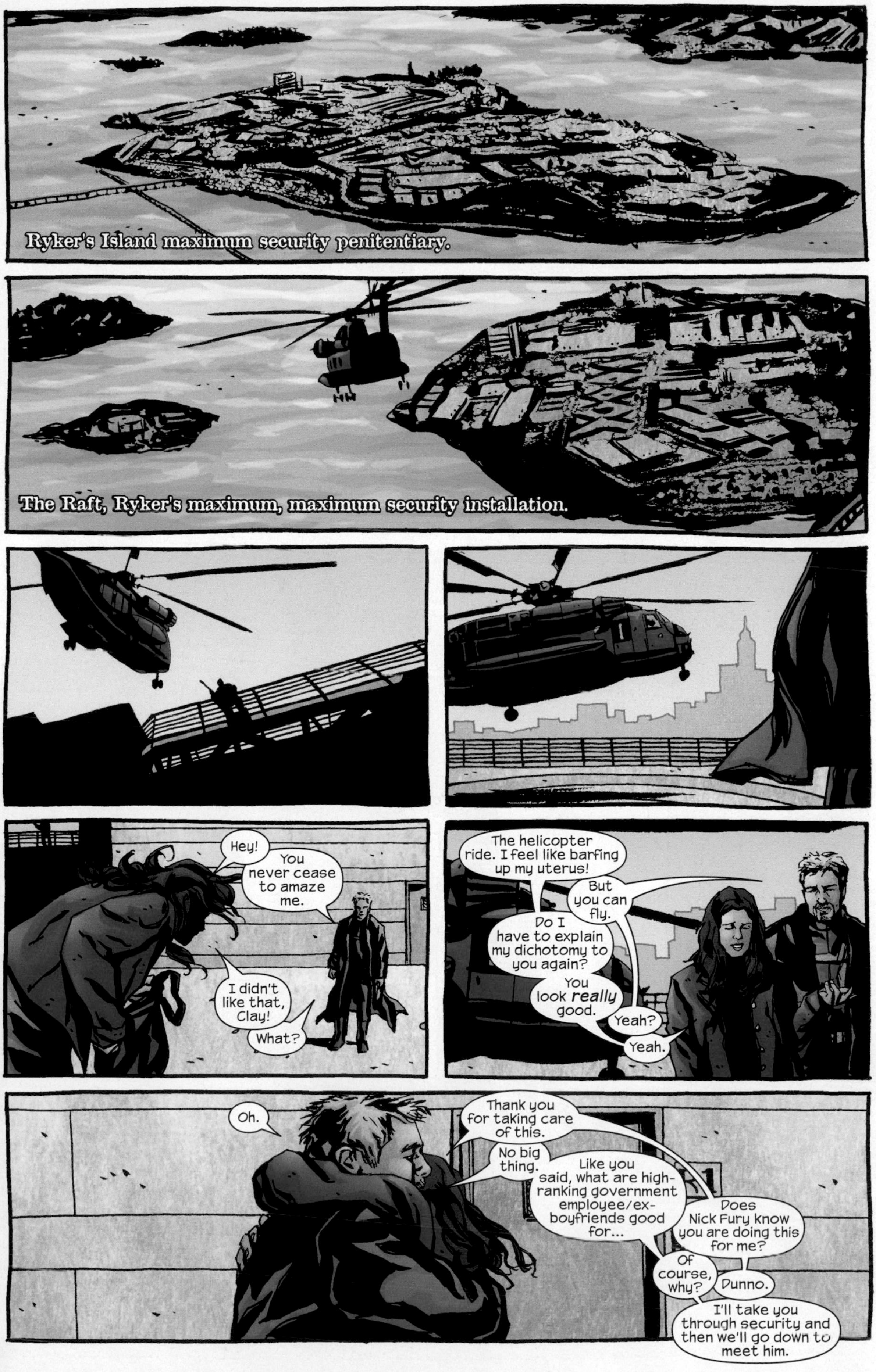
Ryker's Island maximum security penitentiary.
The Raft, Ryker's maximum, maximum security installation.
Hey!
You never cease to amaze me.
I didn't like that, Clay!
What?
The helicopter ride. I feel like barfing up my uterus!
But you can fly.
Do I have to explain my dichotomy to you again?
You look *really* good.
Yeah?
Yeah.
Oh.
Thank you for taking care of this.
No big thing.
Like you said, what are high-ranking government employee/ex-boyfriends good for...
Does Nick Fury know you are doing this for me?
Of course, why?
Dunno.
I'll take you through security and then we'll go down to meet him.

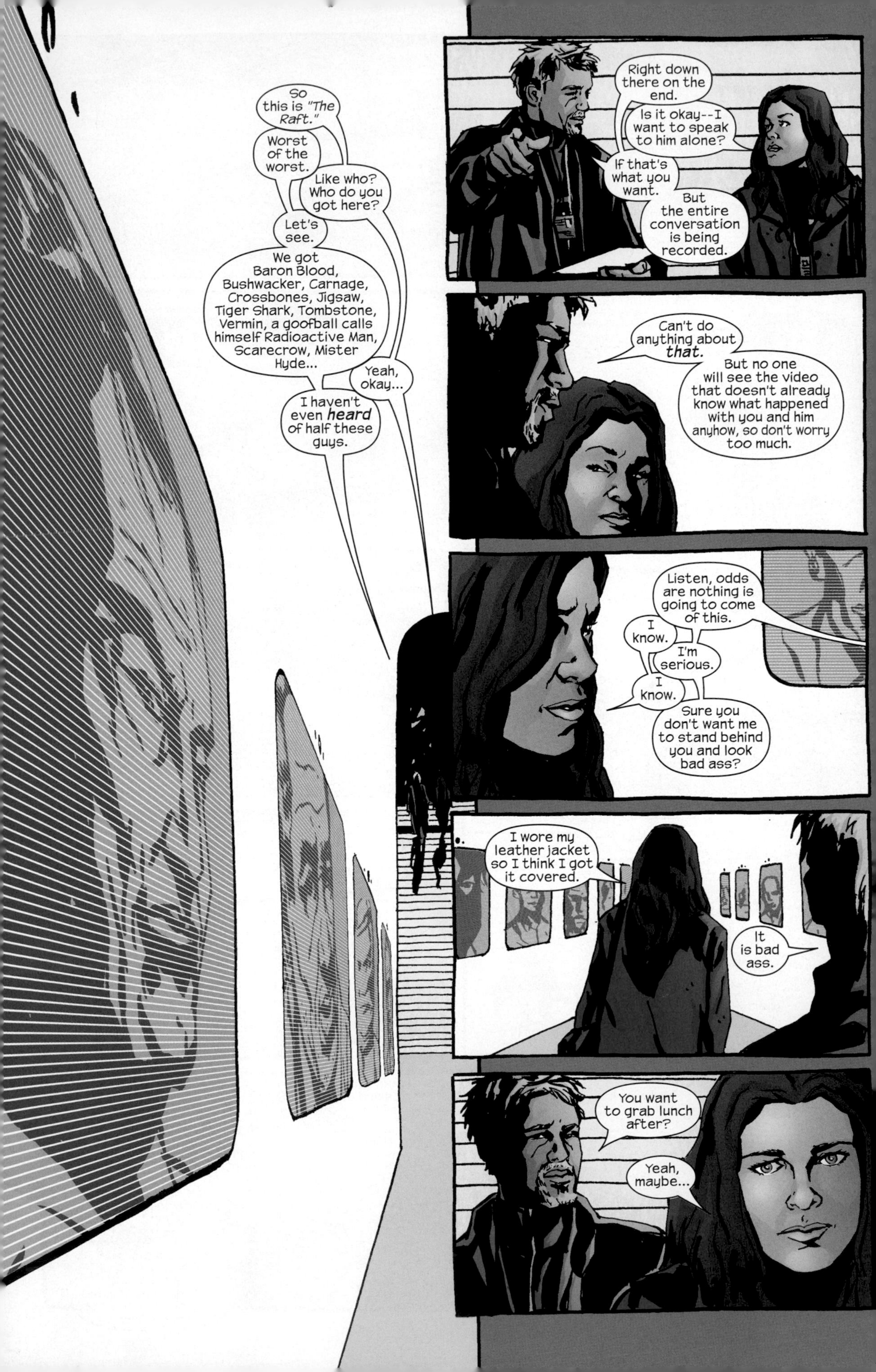
So this is "The Raft."
Worst of the worst.
Like who? Who do you got here?
Let's see.
We got Baron Blood, Bushwacker, Carnage, Crossbones, Jigsaw, Tiger Shark, Tombstone, Vermin, a goofball calls himself Radioactive Man, Scarecrow, Mister Hyde...
Yeah, okay...
I haven't even heard of half these guys.
Right down there on the end.
Is it okay--I want to speak to him alone?
If that's what you want.
But the entire conversation is being recorded.
Can't do anything about that.
But no one will see the video that doesn't already know what happened with you and him anyhow, so don't worry too much.
Listen, odds are nothing is going to come of this.
I know.
I'm serious.
I know.
Sure you don't want me to stand behind you and look bad ass?
I wore my leather jacket so I think I got it covered.
It is bad ass.
You want to grab lunch after?
Yeah, maybe...

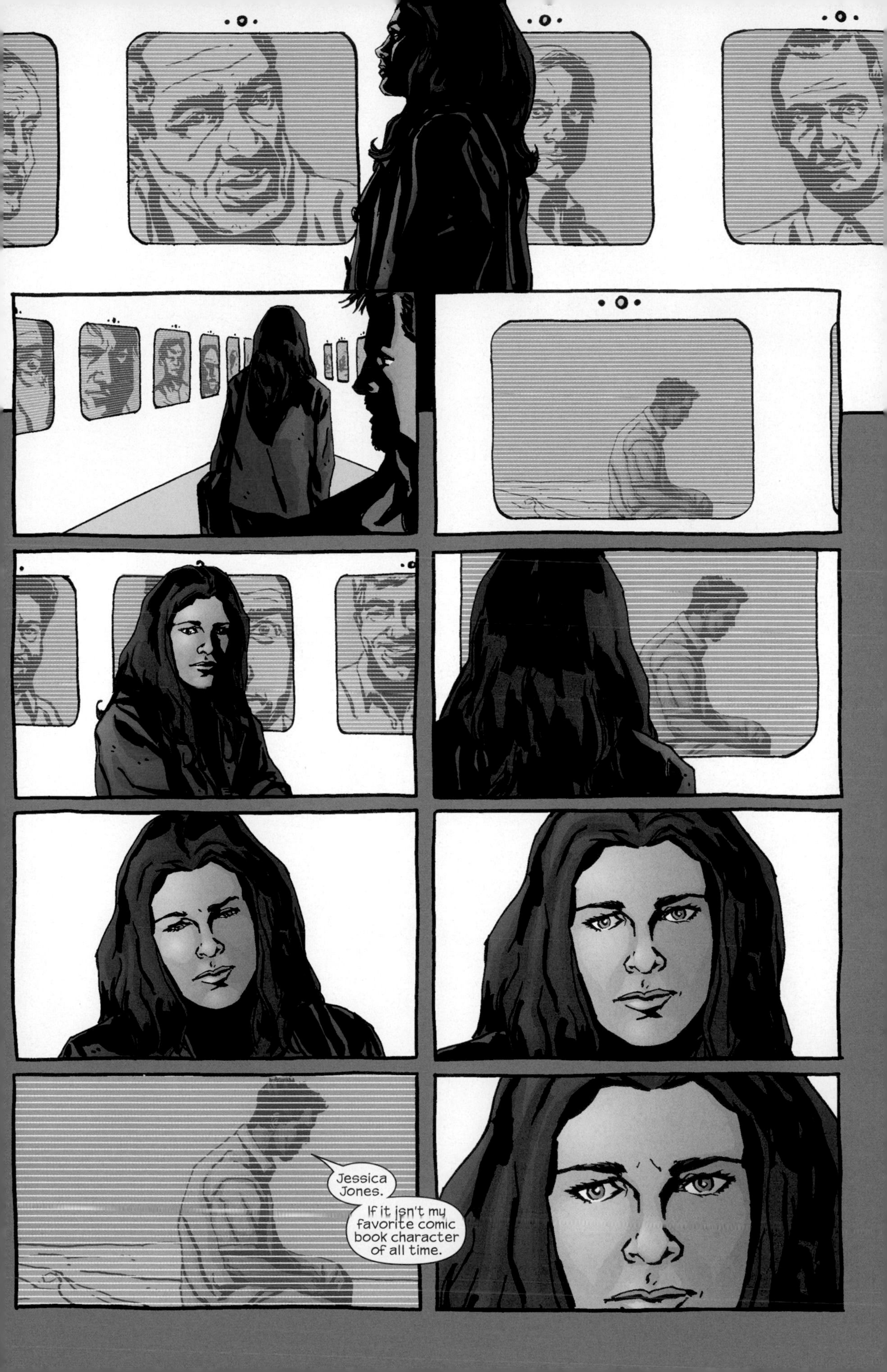
Jessica Jones.
If it isn't my favorite comic book character of all time.

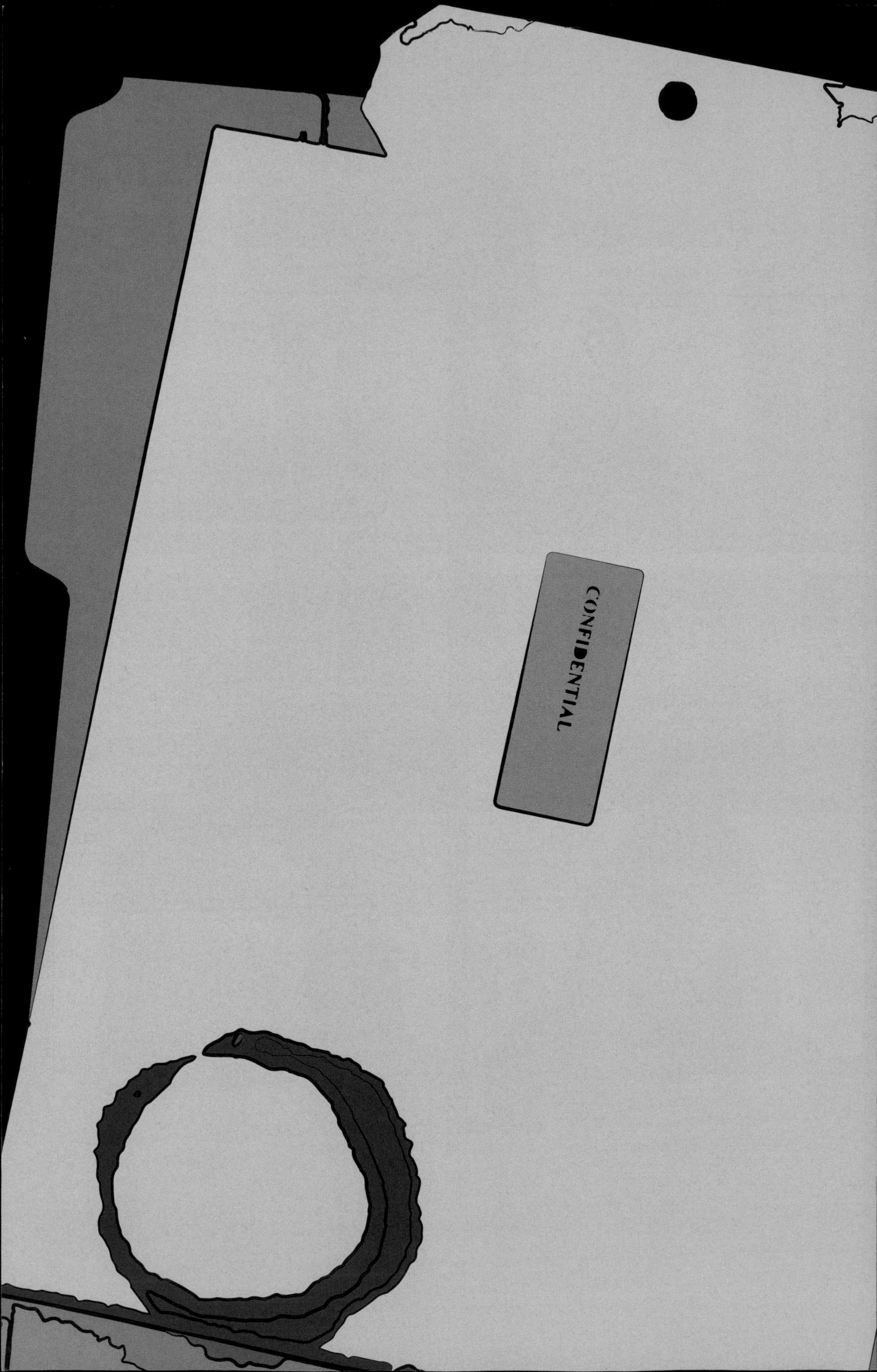
CONFIDENTIAL

THE RA[redacted]ER'S [redacted]

ISSUE #27

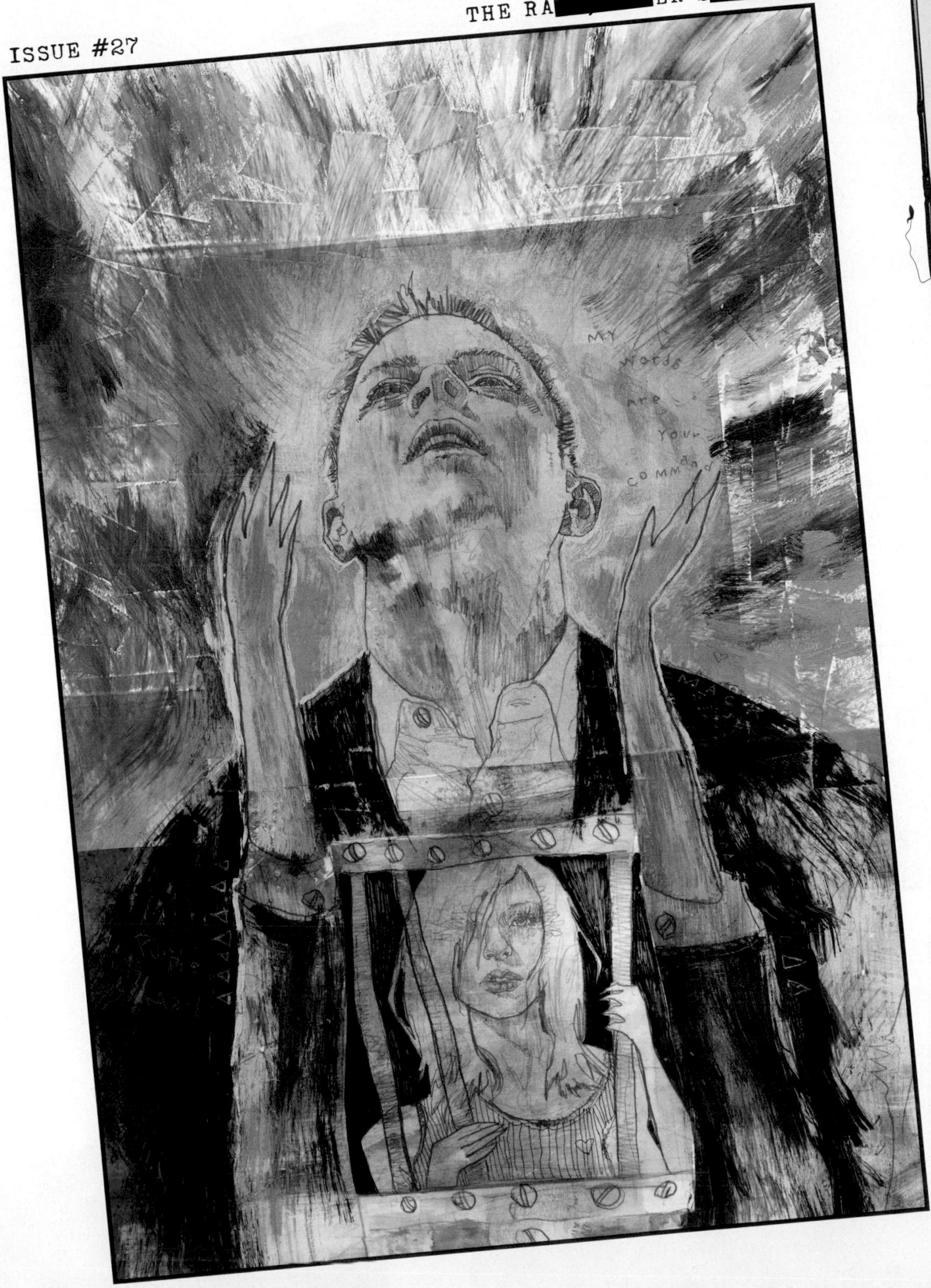
MY words are your command

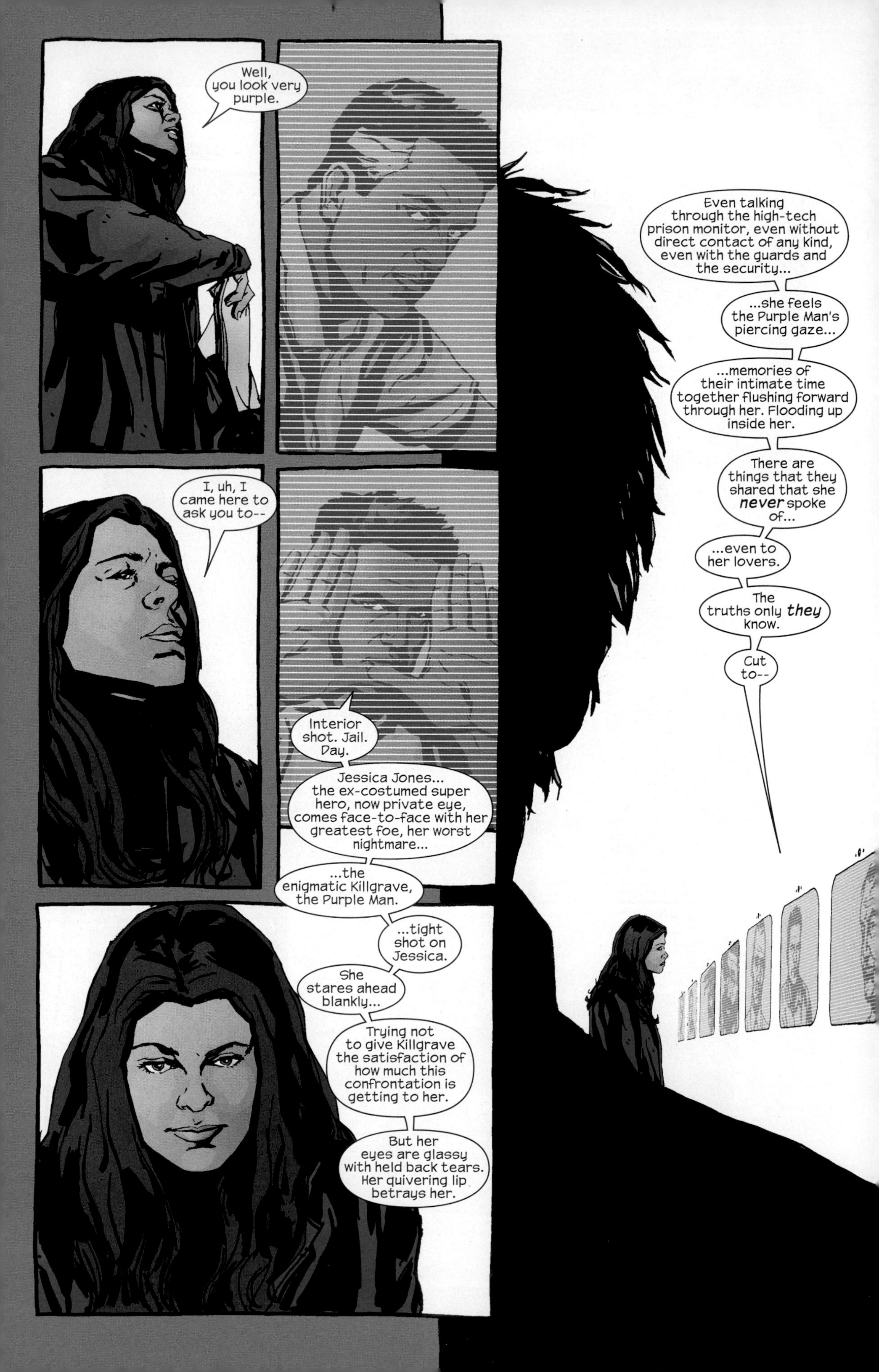
Well, you look very purple.
I, uh, I came here to ask you to--
Interior shot. Jail. Day.
Jessica Jones... the ex-costumed super hero, now private eye, comes face-to-face with her greatest foe, her worst nightmare...
...the enigmatic Killgrave, the Purple Man.
...tight shot on Jessica.
She stares ahead blankly...
Trying not to give Killgrave the satisfaction of how much this confrontation is getting to her.
But her eyes are glassy with held back tears. Her quivering lip betrays her.
Even talking through the high-tech prison monitor, even without direct contact of any kind, even with the guards and the security...
...she feels the Purple Man's piercing gaze...
...memories of their intimate time together flushing forward through her. Flooding up inside her.
There are things that they shared that she never spoke of...
...even to her lovers.
The truths only they know.
Cut to--

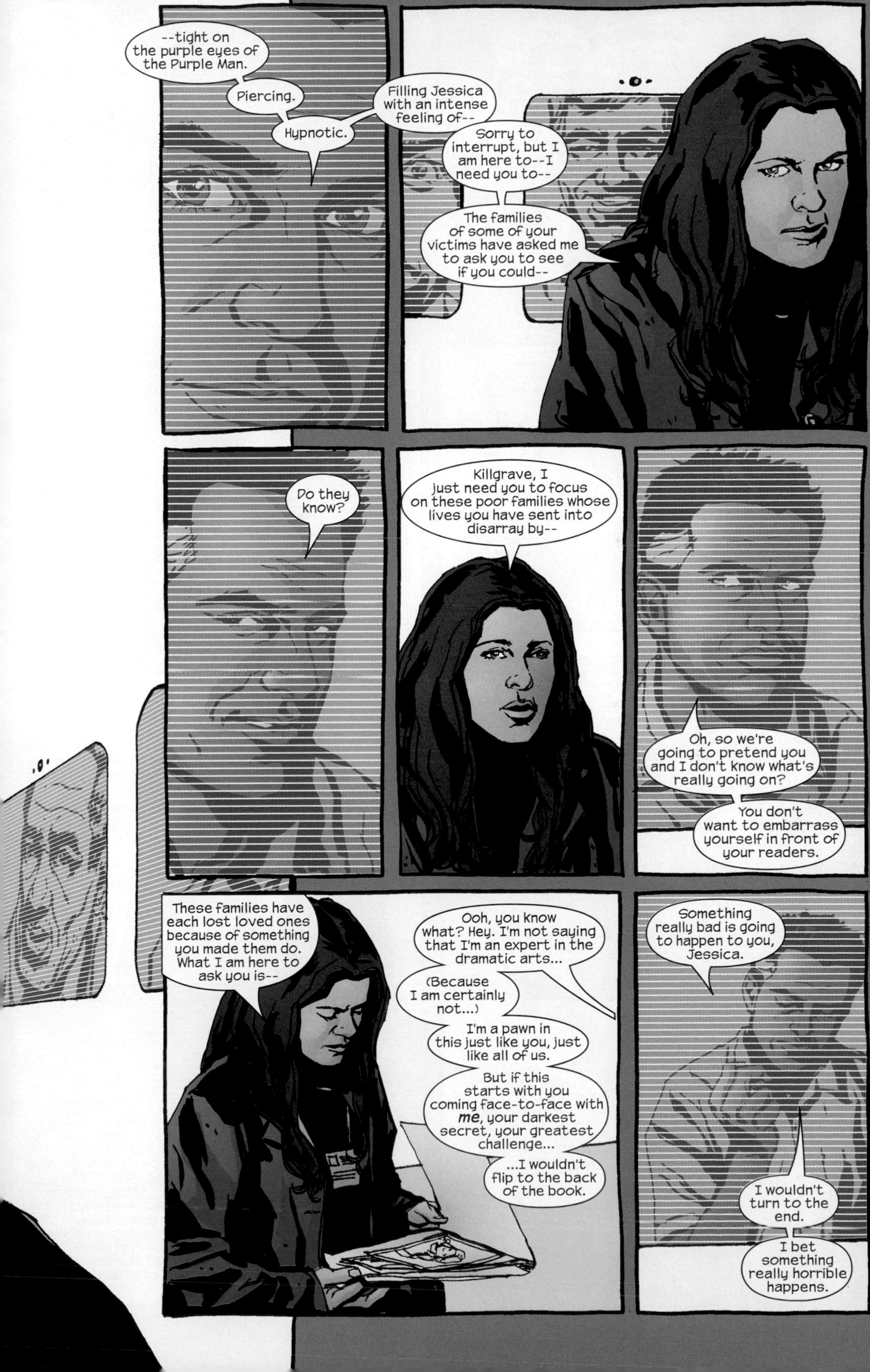
--tight on the purple eyes of the Purple Man.
Piercing.
Hypnotic.
Filling Jessica with an intense feeling of--
Sorry to interrupt, but I am here to--I need you to--
The families of some of your victims have asked me to ask you to see if you could--
Do they know?
Killgrave, I just need you to focus on these poor families whose lives you have sent into disarray by--
Oh, so we're going to pretend you and I don't know what's really going on?
You don't want to embarrass yourself in front of your readers.
These families have each lost loved ones because of something you made them do. What I am here to ask you is--
Ooh, you know what? Hey. I'm not saying that I'm an expert in the dramatic arts...
(Because I am certainly not...)
I'm a pawn in this just like you, just like all of us.
But if this starts with you coming face-to-face with *me*, your darkest secret, your greatest challenge...
...I wouldn't flip to the back of the book.
Something really bad is going to happen to you, Jessica.
I wouldn't turn to the end.
I bet something really horrible happens.

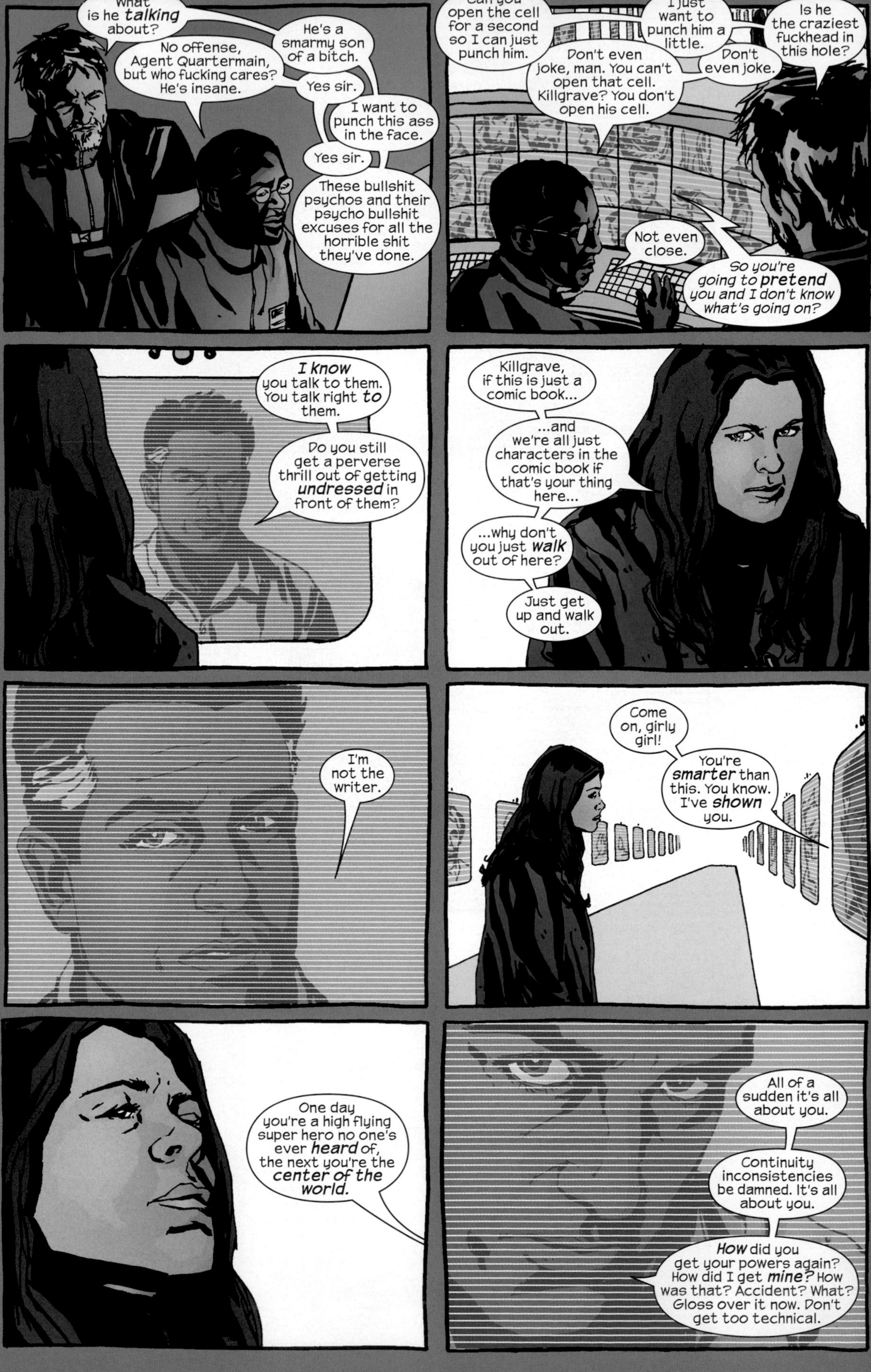
What is he talking about?
No offense, Agent Quartermain, but who fucking cares? He's insane.
He's a smarmy son of a bitch.
Yes sir.
I want to punch this ass in the face.
Yes sir.
These bullshit psychos and their psycho bullshit excuses for all the horrible shit they've done.
Can you open the cell for a second so I can just punch him.
I just want to punch him a little.
Don't even joke, man. You can't open that cell. Killgrave? You don't open his cell.
Don't even joke.
Is he the craziest fuckhead in this hole?
Not even close.
So you're going to pretend you and I don't know what's going on?
I know you talk to them. You talk right to them.
Do you still get a perverse thrill out of getting undressed in front of them?
Killgrave, if this is just a comic book...
...and we're all just characters in the comic book if that's your thing here...
...why don't you just walk out of here?
Just get up and walk out.
I'm not the writer.
Come on, girly girl!
You're smarter than this. You know. I've shown you.
One day you're a high flying super hero no one's ever heard of, the next you're the center of the world.
All of a sudden it's all about you.
Continuity inconsistencies be damned. It's all about you.
How did you get your powers again? How did I get mine? How was that? Accident? What? Gloss over it now. Don't get too technical.

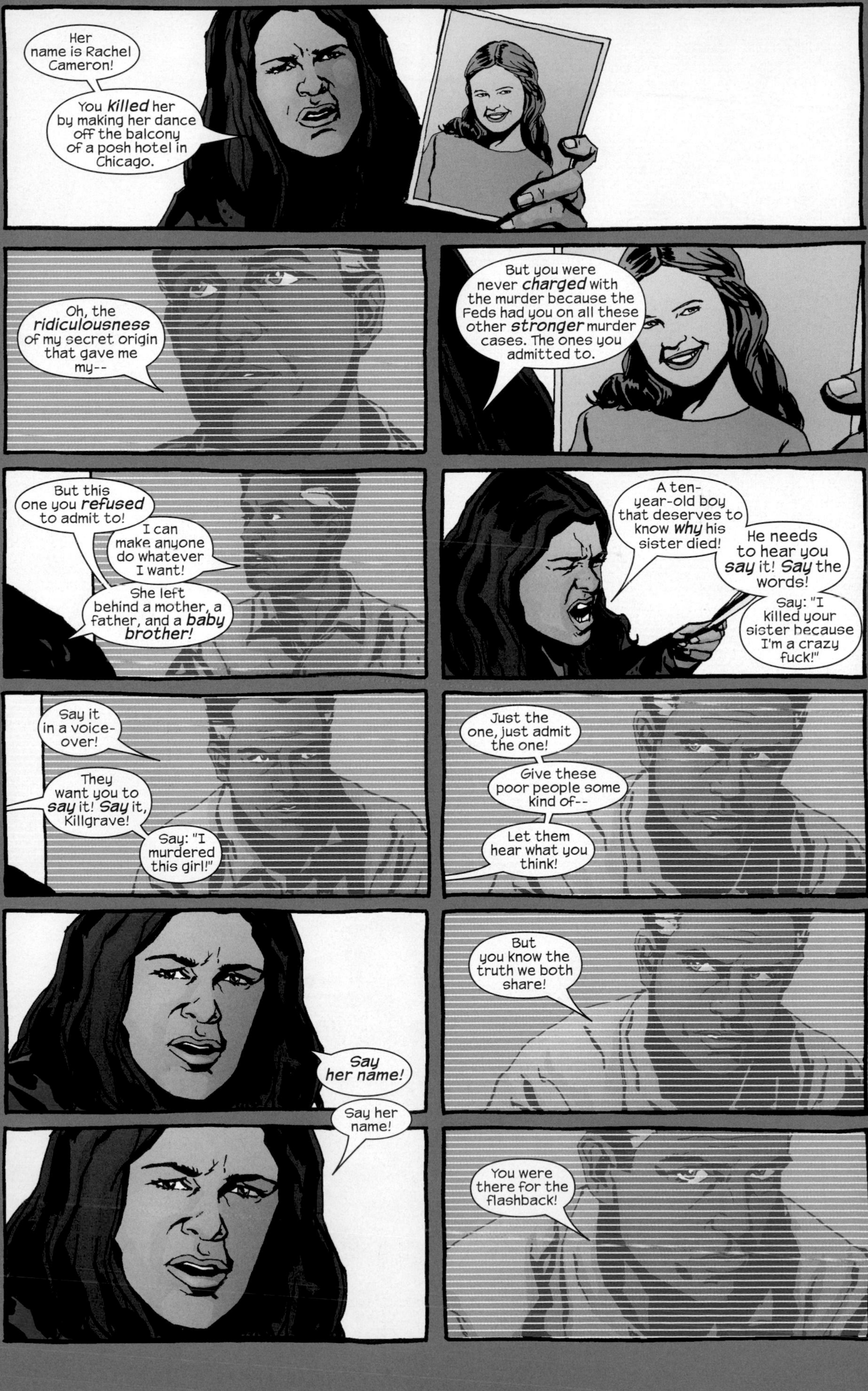

Her name is Rachel Cameron!
You *killed* her by making her dance off the balcony of a posh hotel in Chicago.
Oh, the *ridiculousness* of my secret origin that gave me my--
But you were never *charged* with the murder because the Feds had you on all these other *stronger* murder cases. The ones you admitted to.
But this one you *refused* to admit to!
I can make anyone do whatever I want!
She left behind a mother, a father, and a *baby brother!*
A ten-year-old boy that deserves to know *why* his sister died!
He needs to hear you *say* it! *Say* the words!
Say: "I killed your sister because I'm a crazy fuck!"
Say it in a voice-over!
They want you to *say* it! *Say* it, Killgrave!
Say: "I murdered this girl!"
Just the one, just admit the one!
Give these poor people some kind of--
Let them hear what you think!
Say her name!
But you know the truth we both share!
Say her name!
You were there for the flashback!

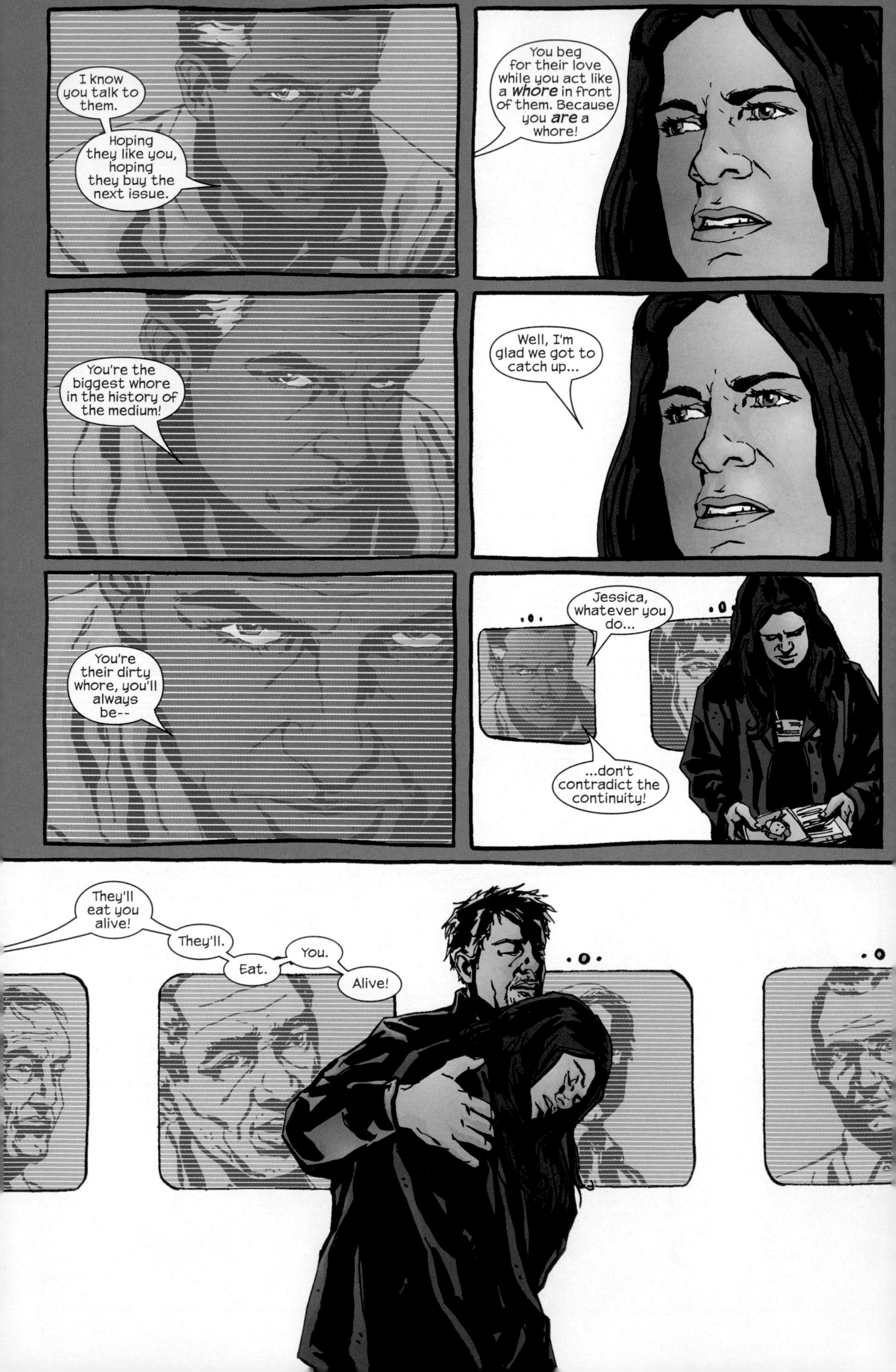
I know you talk to them.
Hoping they like you, hoping they buy the next issue.
You beg for their love while you act like a ***whore*** in front of them. Because you ***are*** a whore!
You're the biggest whore in the history of the medium!
Well, I'm glad we got to catch up...
You're their dirty whore, you'll always be--
Jessica, whatever you do...
...don't contradict the continuity!
They'll eat you alive!
They'll.
Eat.
You.
Alive!

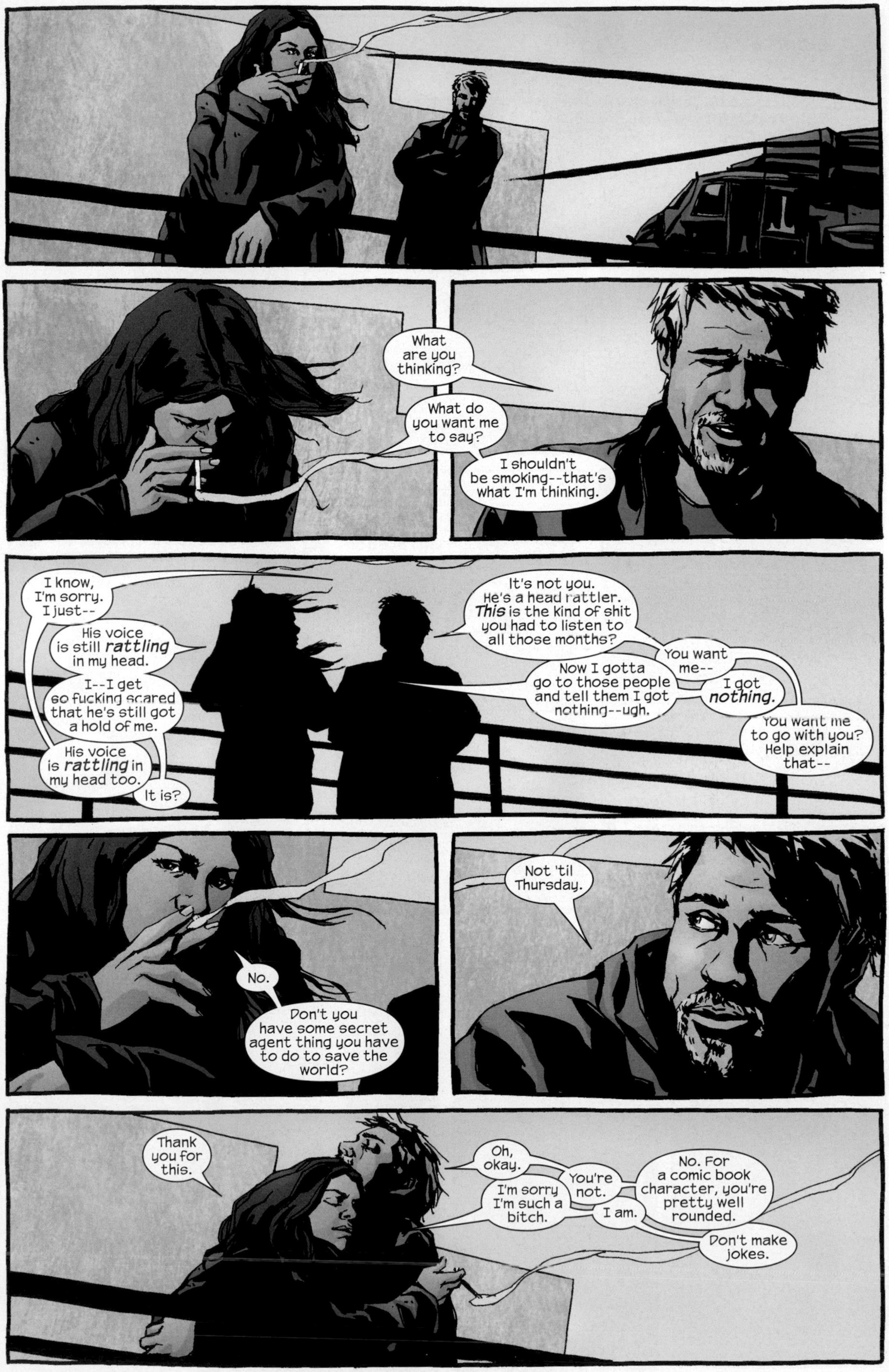
What are you thinking?
What do you want me to say?
I shouldn't be smoking--that's what I'm thinking.
I know, I'm sorry. I just--
His voice is still *rattling* in my head.
I--I get so fucking scared that he's still got a hold of me.
His voice is *rattling* in my head too.
It is?
It's not you. He's a head rattler. *This* is the kind of shit you had to listen to all those months?
Now I gotta go to those people and tell them I got nothing--ugh.
You want me--
I got *nothing.*
You want me to go with you? Help explain that--
Not 'til Thursday.
No.
Don't you have some secret agent thing you have to do to save the world?
Thank you for this.
Oh, okay.
I'm sorry I'm such a bitch.
You're not.
I am.
No. For a comic book character, you're pretty well rounded.
Don't make jokes.

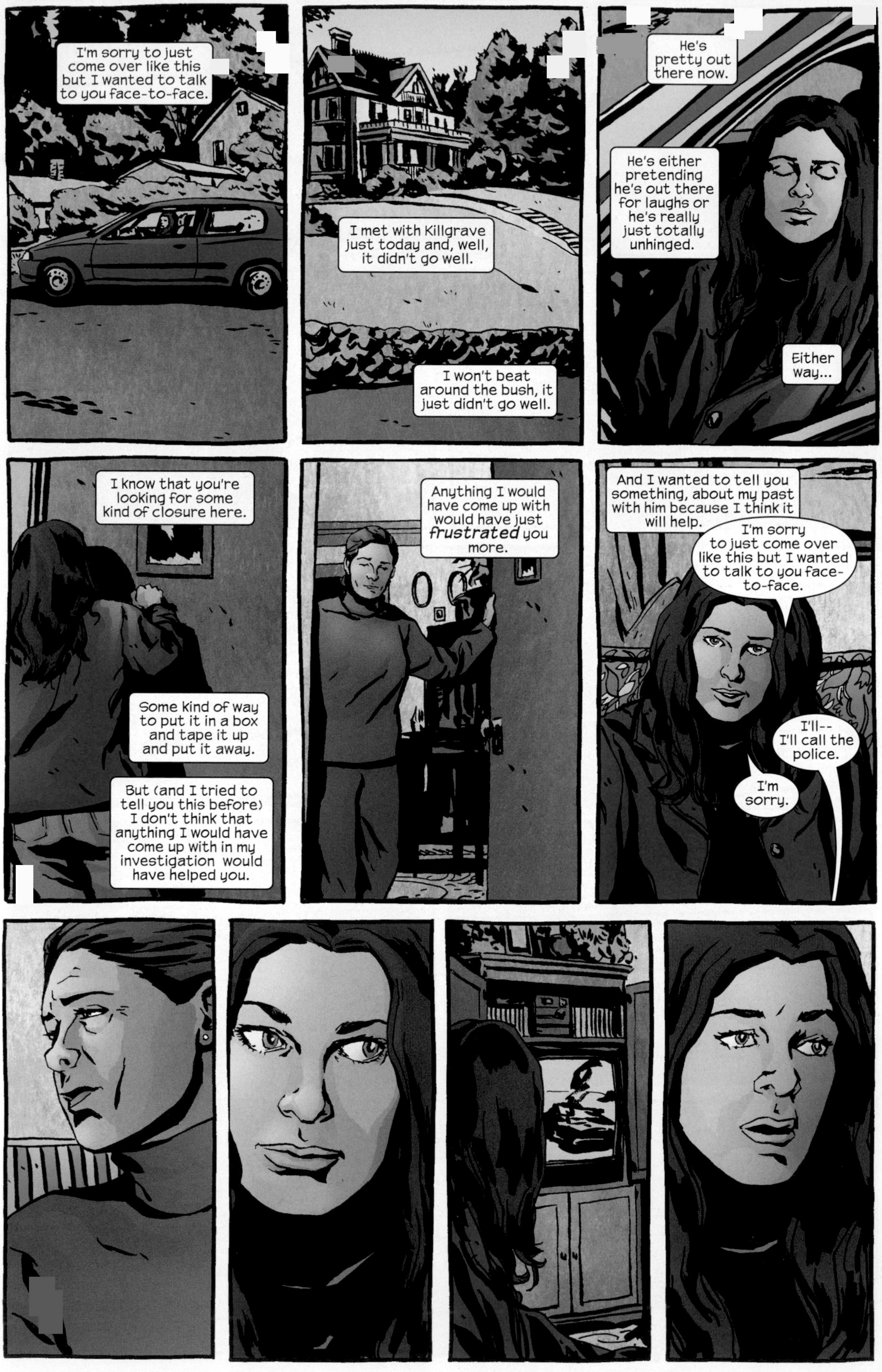

I'm sorry to just come over like this but I wanted to talk to you face-to-face.
I met with Killgrave just today and, well, it didn't go well.
I won't beat around the bush, it just didn't go well.
He's pretty out there now.
He's either pretending he's out there for laughs or he's really just totally unhinged.
Either way...
I know that you're looking for some kind of closure here.
Some kind of way to put it in a box and tape it up and put it away.
But (and I tried to tell you this before) I don't think that anything I would have come up with in my investigation would have helped you.
Anything I would have come up with would have just *frustrated* you more.
And I wanted to tell you something, about my past with him because I think it will help.
I'm sorry to just come over like this but I wanted to talk to you face-to-face.
I'll-- I'll call the police.
I'm sorry.

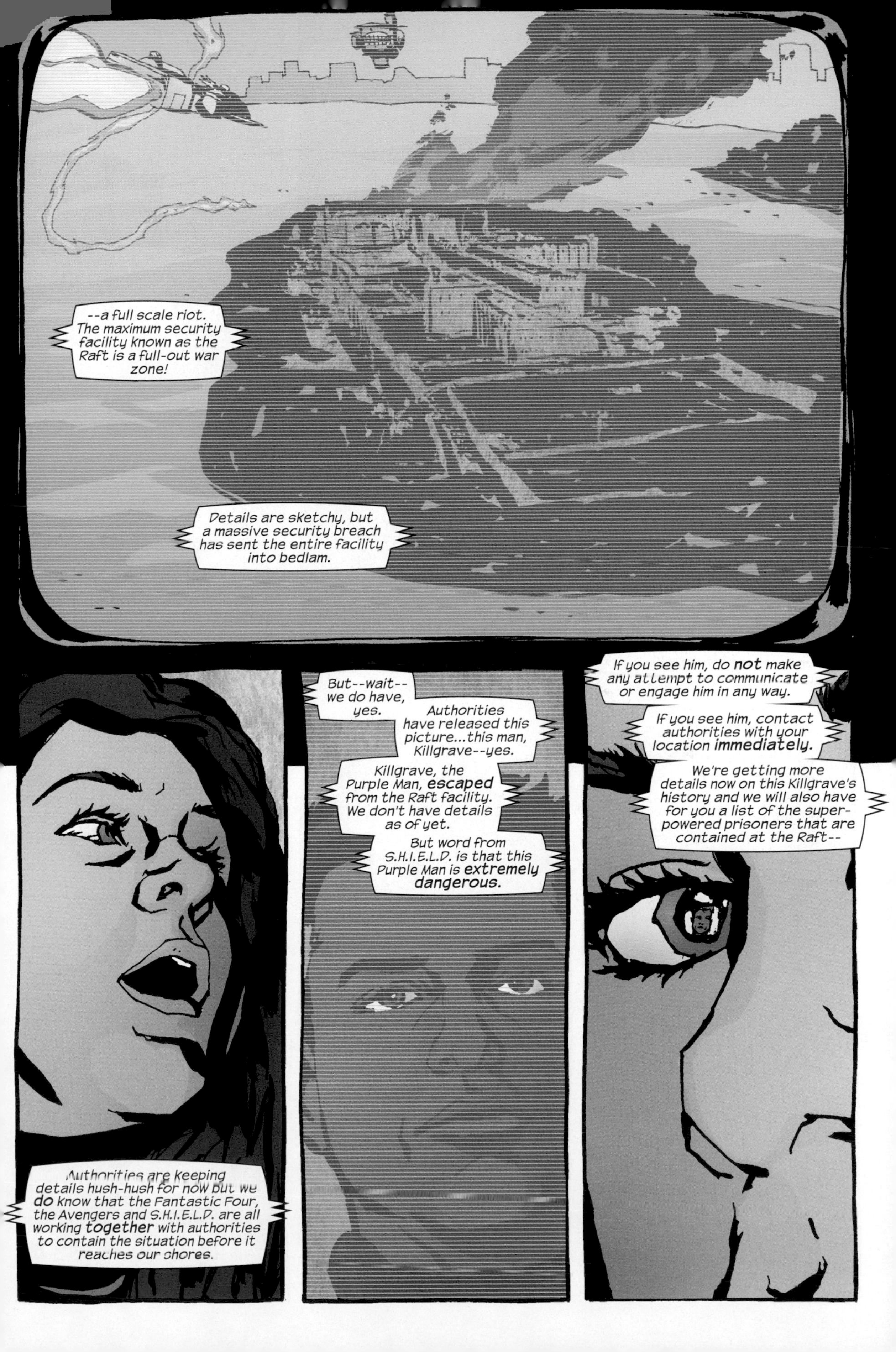
--a full scale riot. The maximum security facility known as the Raft is a full-out war zone!
Details are sketchy, but a massive security breach has sent the entire facility into bedlam.
Authorities are keeping details hush-hush for now but we do know that the Fantastic Four, the Avengers and S.H.I.E.L.D. are all working together with authorities to contain the situation before it reaches our shores.
But--wait-- we do have, yes.
Authorities have released this picture...this man, Killgrave--yes.
Killgrave, the Purple Man, escaped from the Raft facility. We don't have details as of yet.
But word from S.H.I.E.L.D. is that this Purple Man is extremely dangerous.
If you see him, do not make any attempt to communicate or engage him in any way.
If you see him, contact authorities with your location immediately.
We're getting more details now on this Killgrave's history and we will also have for you a list of the super-powered prisoners that are contained at the Raft--

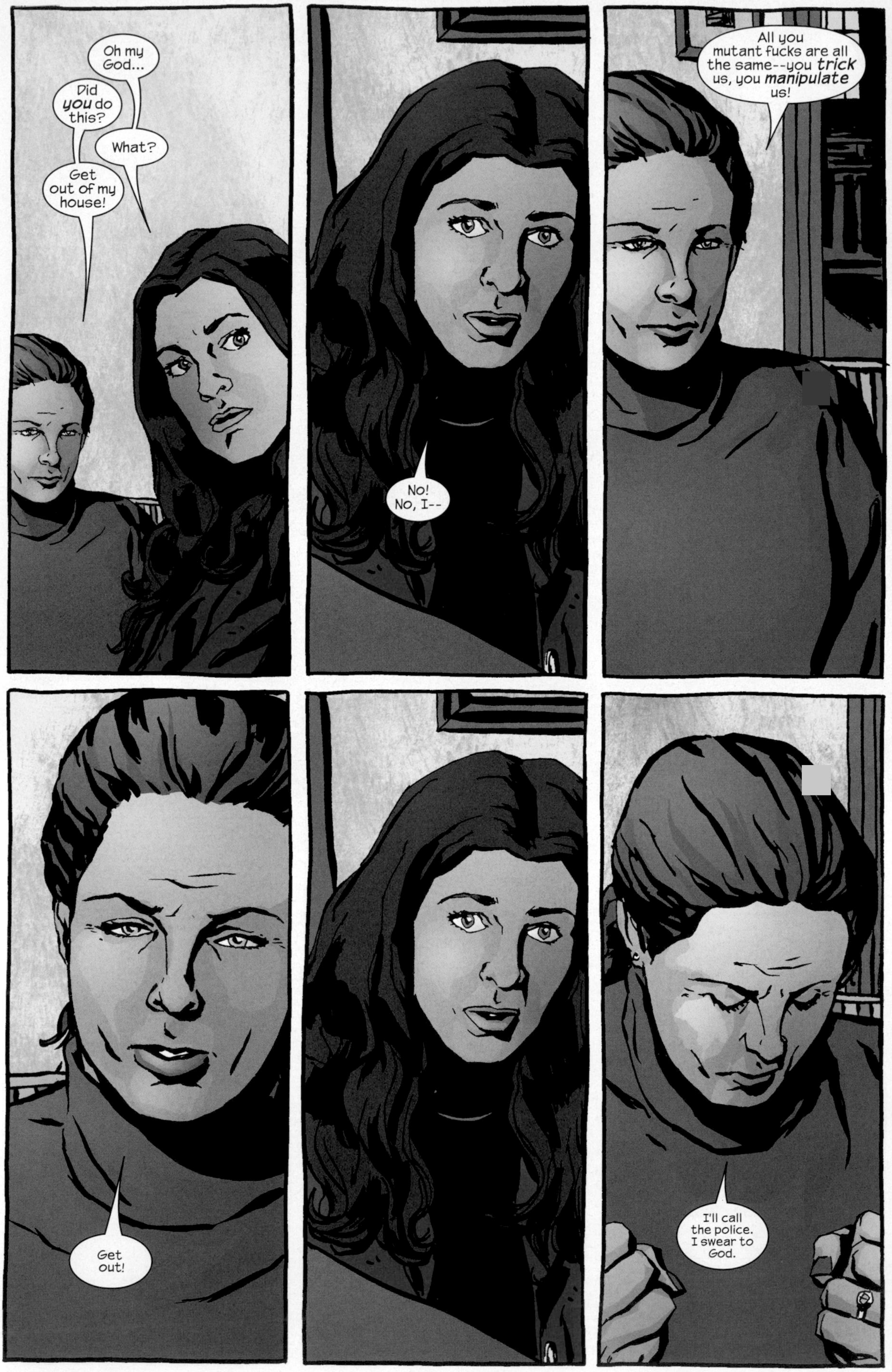
Oh my God...
Did you do this?
What?
Get out of my house!
No! No, I--
All you mutant fucks are all the same--you trick us, you manipulate us!
Get out!
I'll call the police. I swear to God.

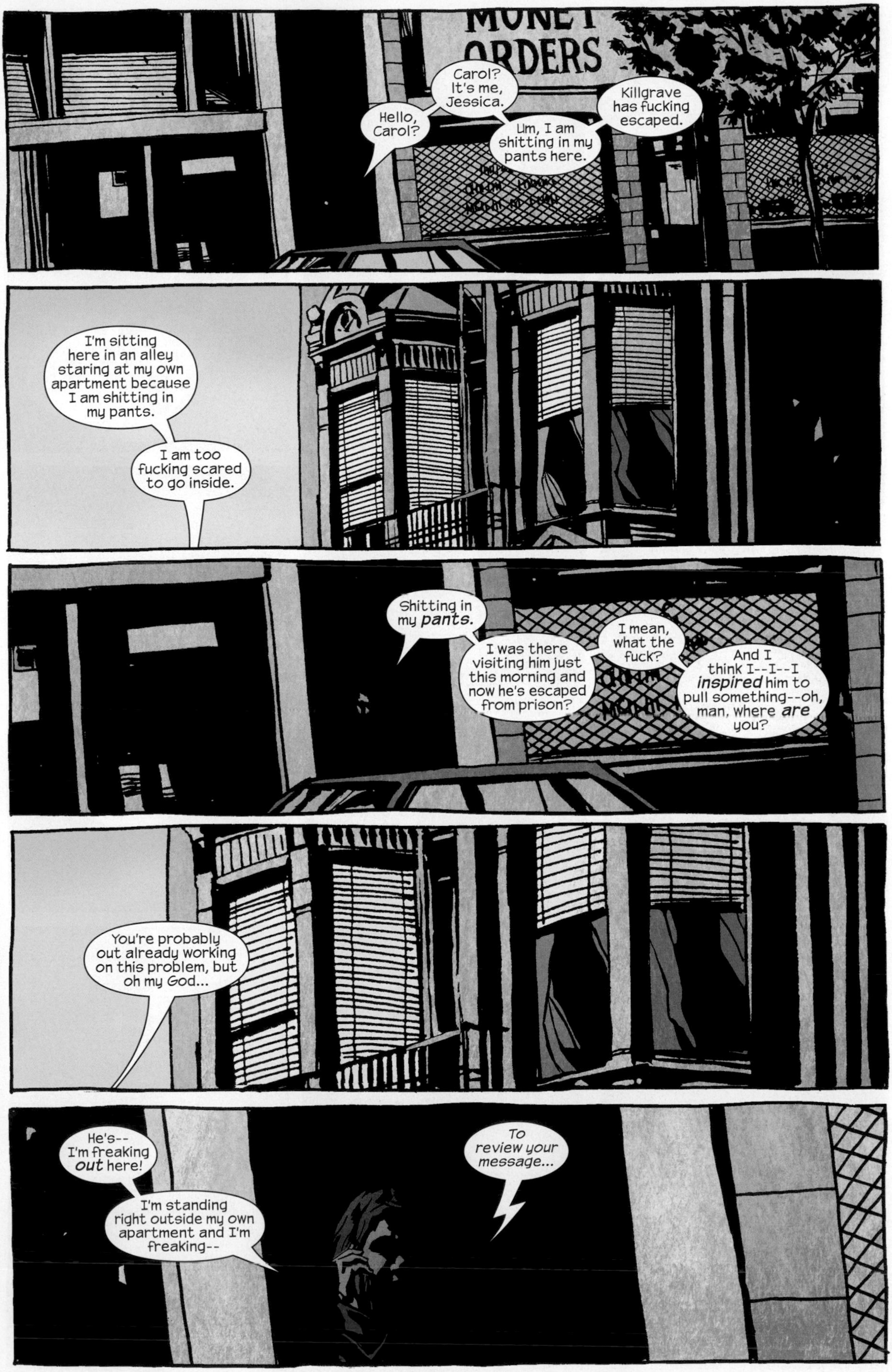
MONEY ORDERS
Hello, Carol?
Carol? It's me, Jessica.
Um, I am shitting in my pants here.
Killgrave has fucking escaped.
I'm sitting here in an alley staring at my own apartment because I am shitting in my pants.
I am too fucking scared to go inside.
Shitting in my *pants.*
I was there visiting him just this morning and now he's escaped from prison?
I mean, what the fuck?
And I think I--I--I *inspired* him to pull something--oh, man, where *are* you?
You're probably out already working on this problem, but oh my God...
He's-- I'm freaking *out* here!
I'm standing right outside my own apartment and I'm freaking--
To review your message...

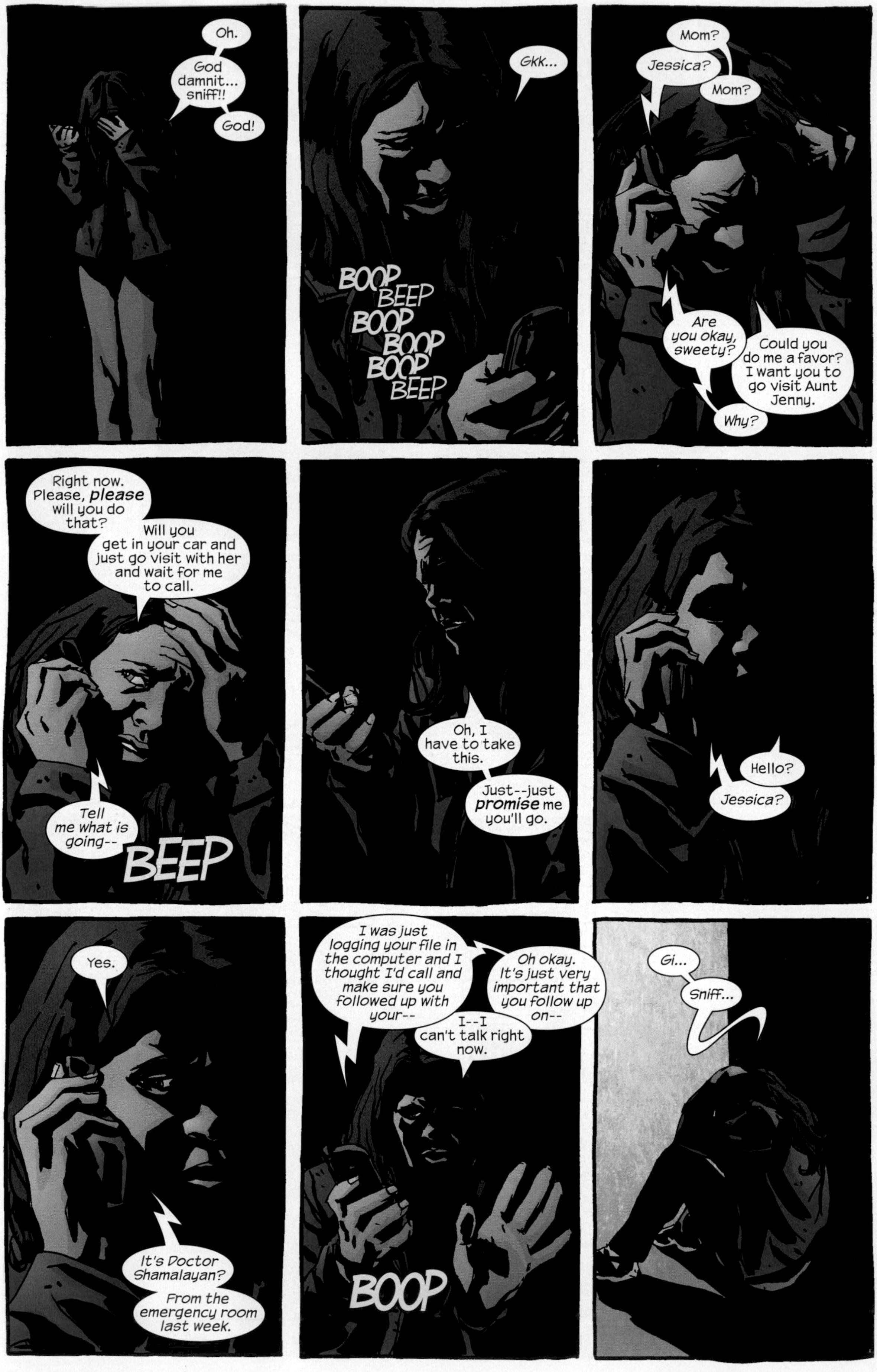
Oh.
God damnit... sniff!!
God!
Gkk...
BOOP BEEP BOOP BOOP BOOP BEEP
Mom?
Jessica?
Mom?
Are you okay, sweety?
Could you do me a favor? I want you to go visit Aunt Jenny.
Why?
Right now. Please, *please* will you do that?
Will you get in your car and just go visit with her and wait for me to call.
Tell me what is going--
BEEP
Oh, I have to take this.
Just--just *promise* me you'll go.
Hello?
Jessica?
Yes.
It's Doctor Shamalayan?
From the emergency room last week.
I was just logging your file in the computer and I thought I'd call and make sure you followed up with your--
Oh okay. It's just very important that you follow up on--
I--I can't talk right now.
BOOP
Gi...
Sniff...

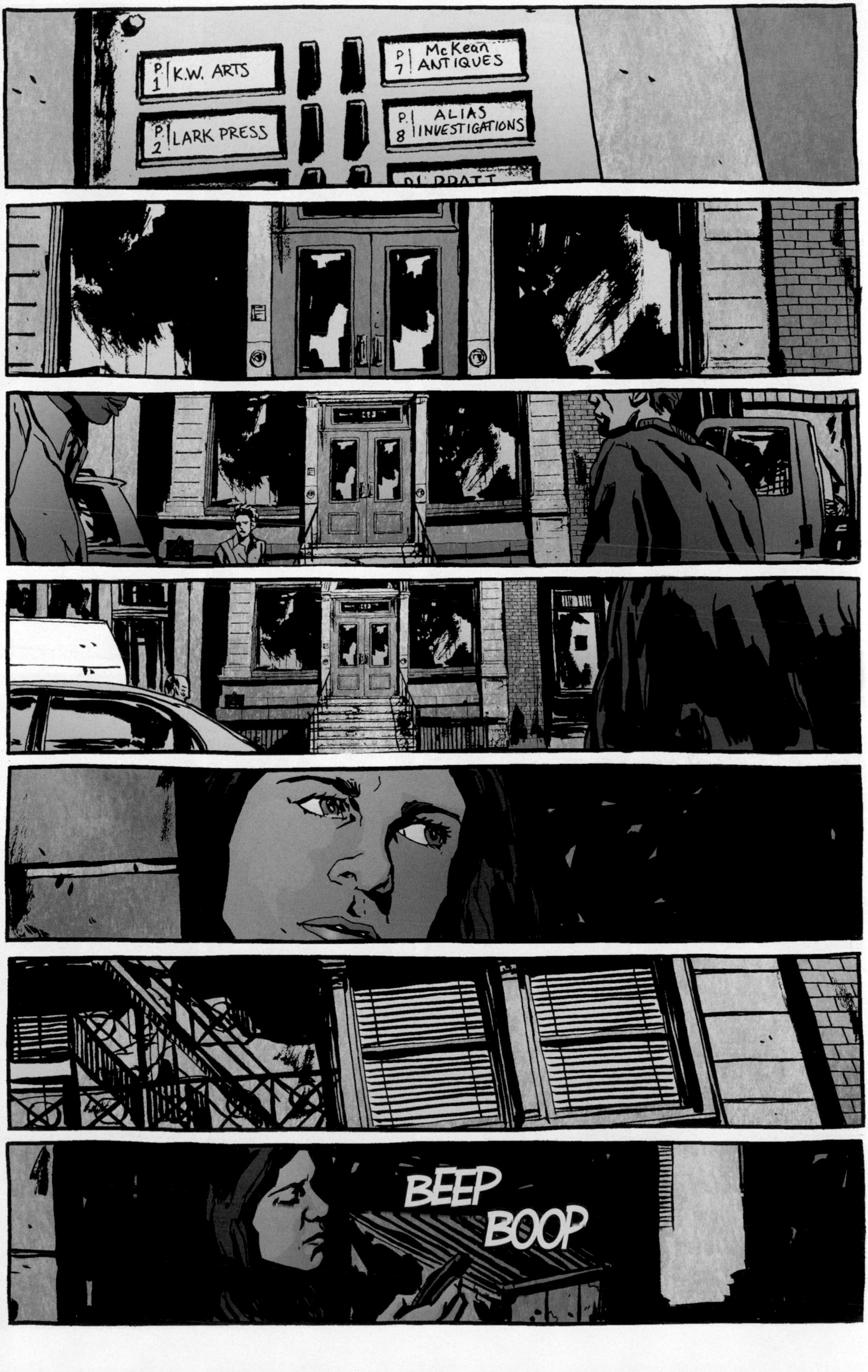

P. 1 K.W. ARTS
P. 7 McKean ANTIQUES
P. 2 LARK PRESS
P. 8 ALIAS INVESTIGATIONS
BEEP
BOOP

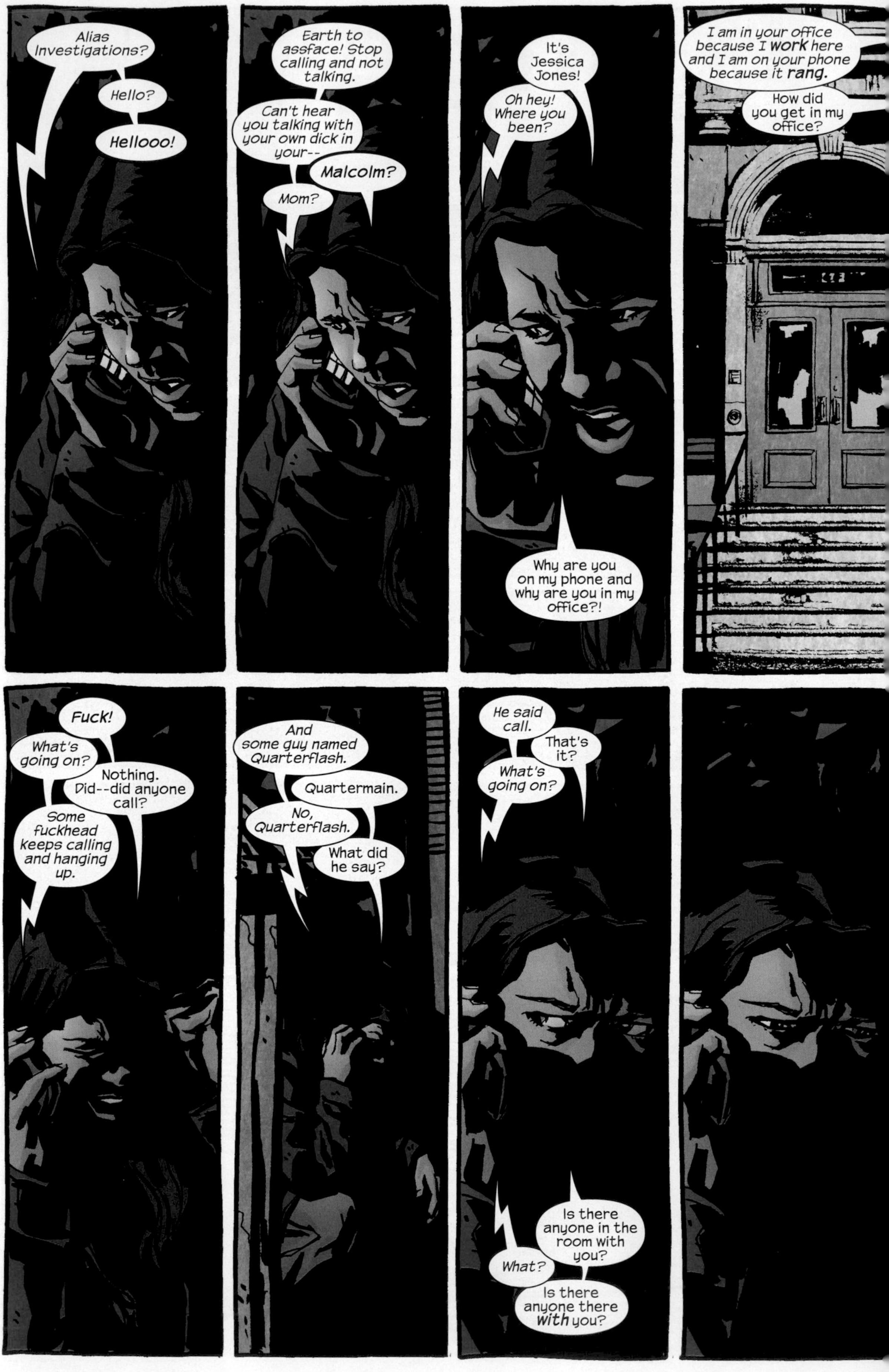
Alias Investigations?
Hello?
Hellooo!
Earth to assface! Stop calling and not talking.
Can't hear you talking with your own dick in your--
Malcolm?
Mom?
It's Jessica Jones!
Oh hey! Where you been?
Why are you on my phone and why are you in my office?!
I am in your office because I work here and I am on your phone because it rang.
How did you get in my office?
Fuck!
What's going on?
Nothing. Did--did anyone call?
Some fuckhead keeps calling and hanging up.
And some guy named Quarterflash.
Quartermain.
No, Quarterflash.
What did he say?
He said call.
That's it?
What's going on?
Is there anyone in the room with you?
What?
Is there anyone there with you?

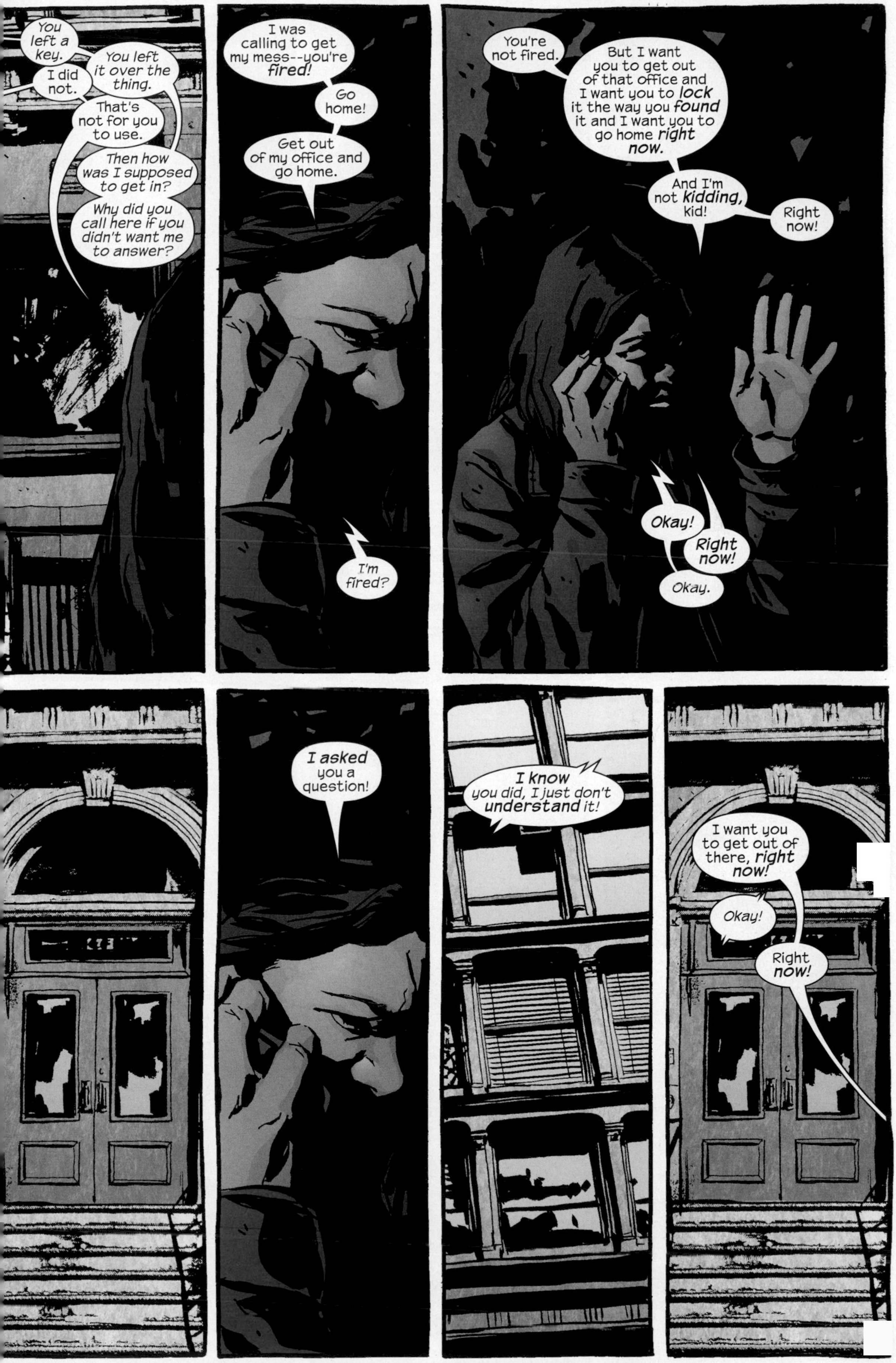
You left a key.
You left it over the thing.
I did not.
That's not for you to use.
Then how was I supposed to get in?
Why did you call here if you didn't want me to answer?
I was calling to get my mess--you're fired!
Go home!
Get out of my office and go home.
I'm fired?
You're not fired.
But I want you to get out of that office and I want you to lock it the way you found it and I want you to go home right now.
And I'm not kidding, kid!
Right now!
Okay!
Right now!
Okay.
I asked you a question!
I know you did, I just don't understand it!
I want you to get out of there, right now!
Okay!
Right now!

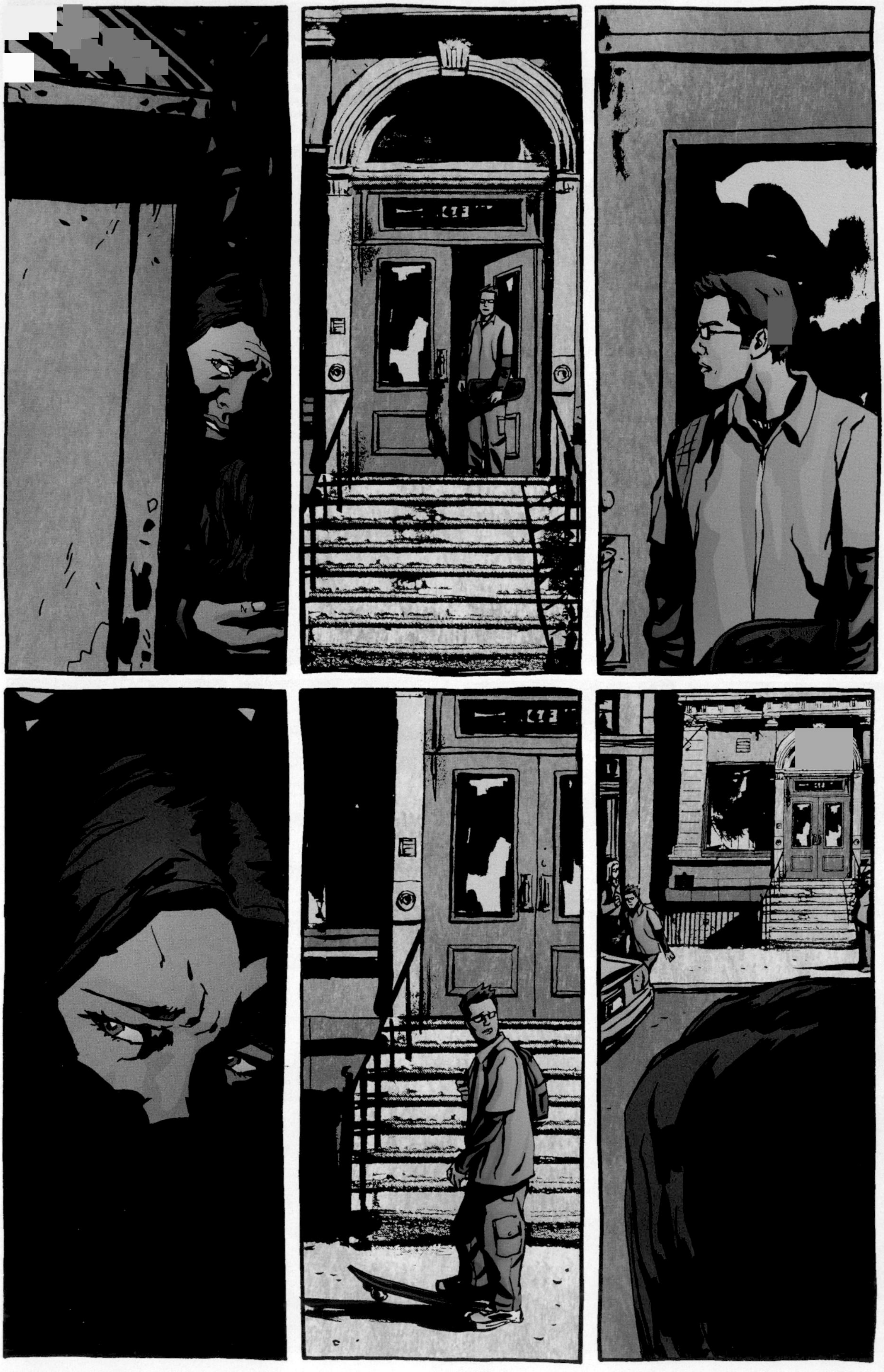

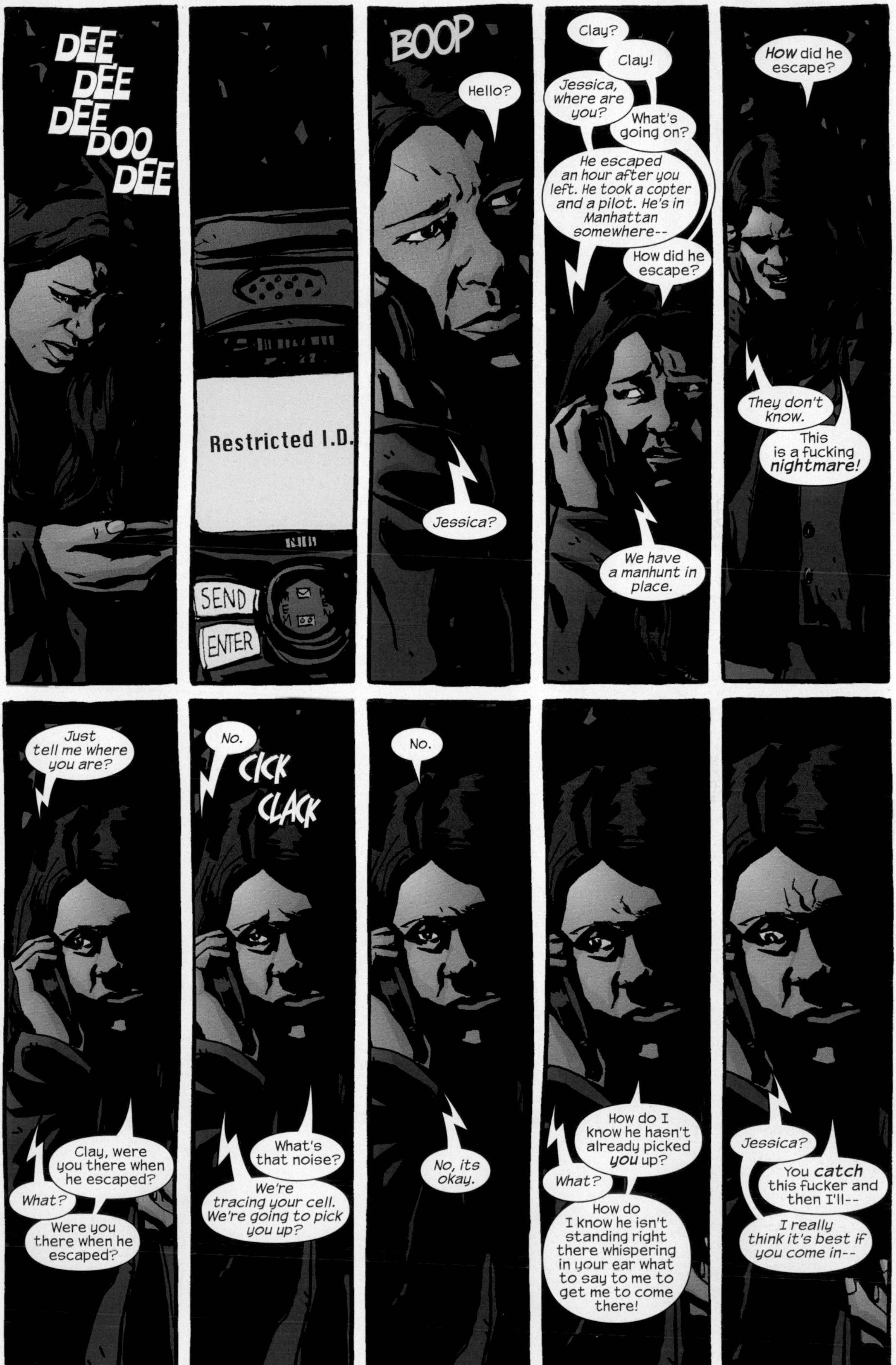
DEE DEE DEE DOO DEE
Restricted I.D.
SEND
ENTER
BOOP
Hello?
Jessica?
Clay?
Clay!
Jessica, where are you?
What's going on?
He escaped an hour after you left. He took a copter and a pilot. He's in Manhattan somewhere--
How did he escape?
We have a manhunt in place.
HOW did he escape?
They don't know.
This is a fucking nightmare!
Just tell me where you are?
Clay, were you there when he escaped?
What?
Were you there when he escaped?
No.
CICK CLACK
What's that noise?
We're tracing your cell. We're going to pick you up?
No.
No, its okay.
How do I know he hasn't already picked YOU up?
What?
How do I know he isn't standing right there whispering in your ear what to say to me to get me to come there!
Jessica?
You catch this fucker and then I'll--
I really think it's best if you come in--

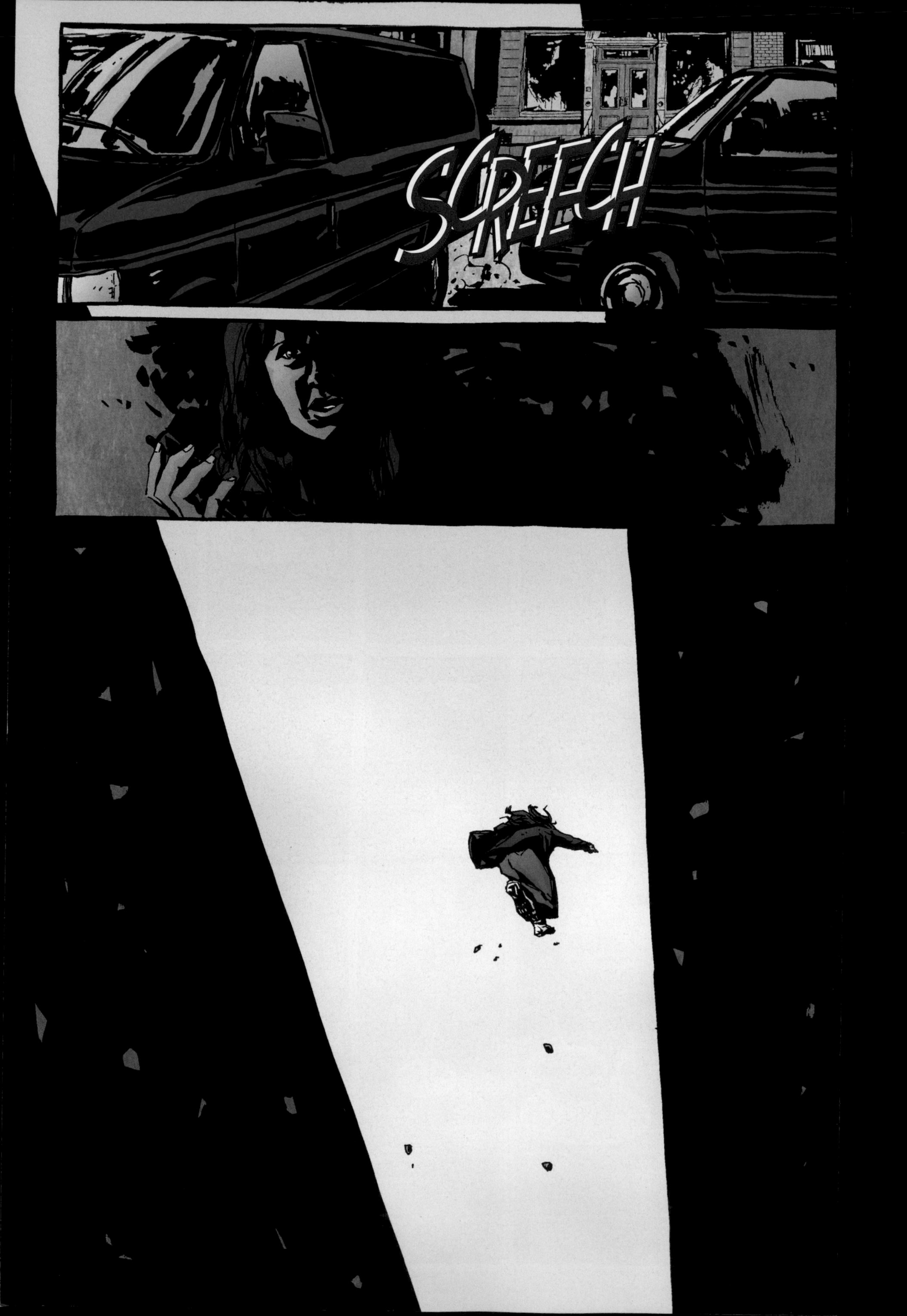
SCREECH

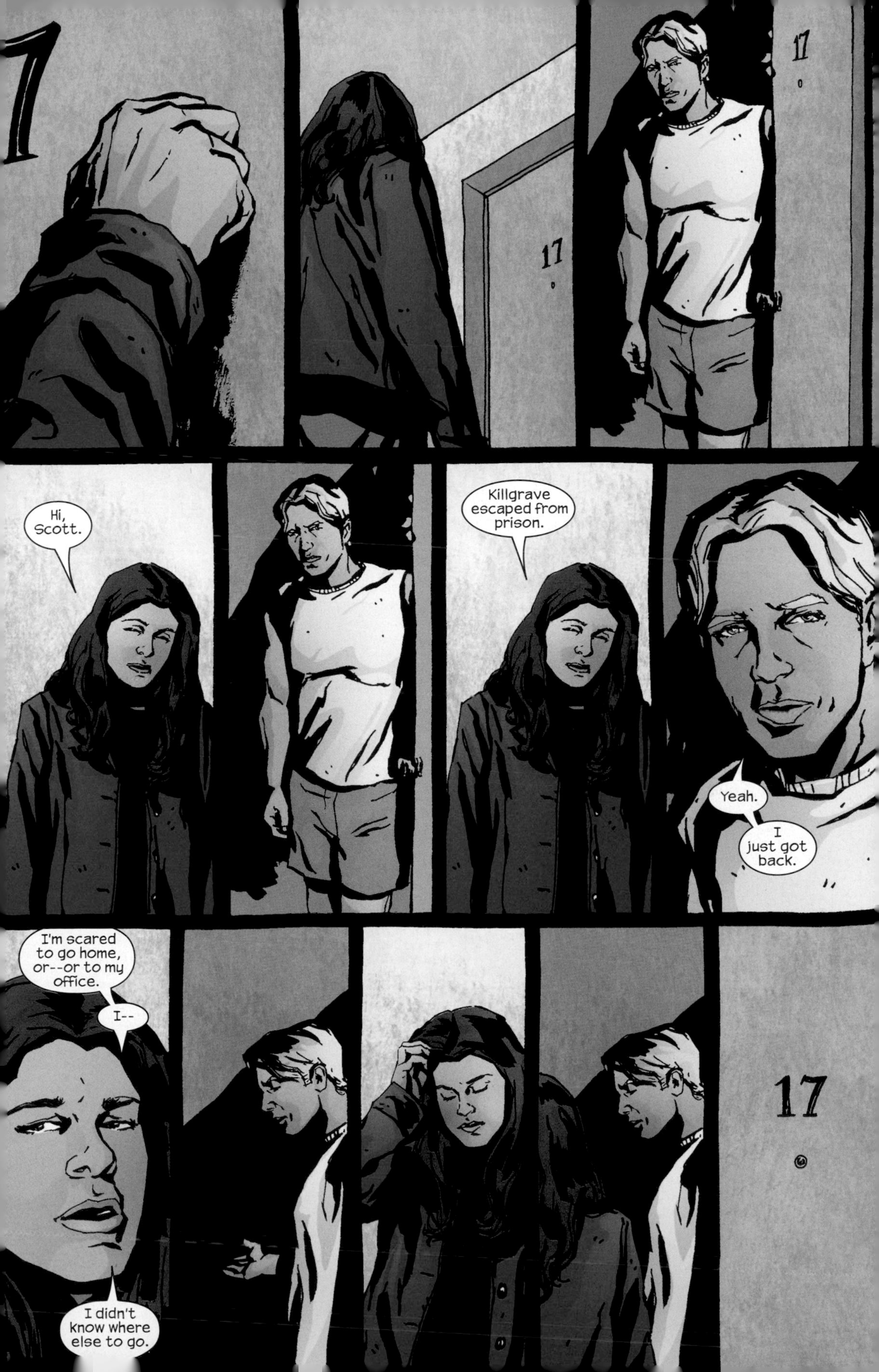
Hi, Scott.
Killgrave escaped from prison.
Yeah.
I just got back.
I'm scared to go home, or--or to my office.
I--
I didn't know where else to go.

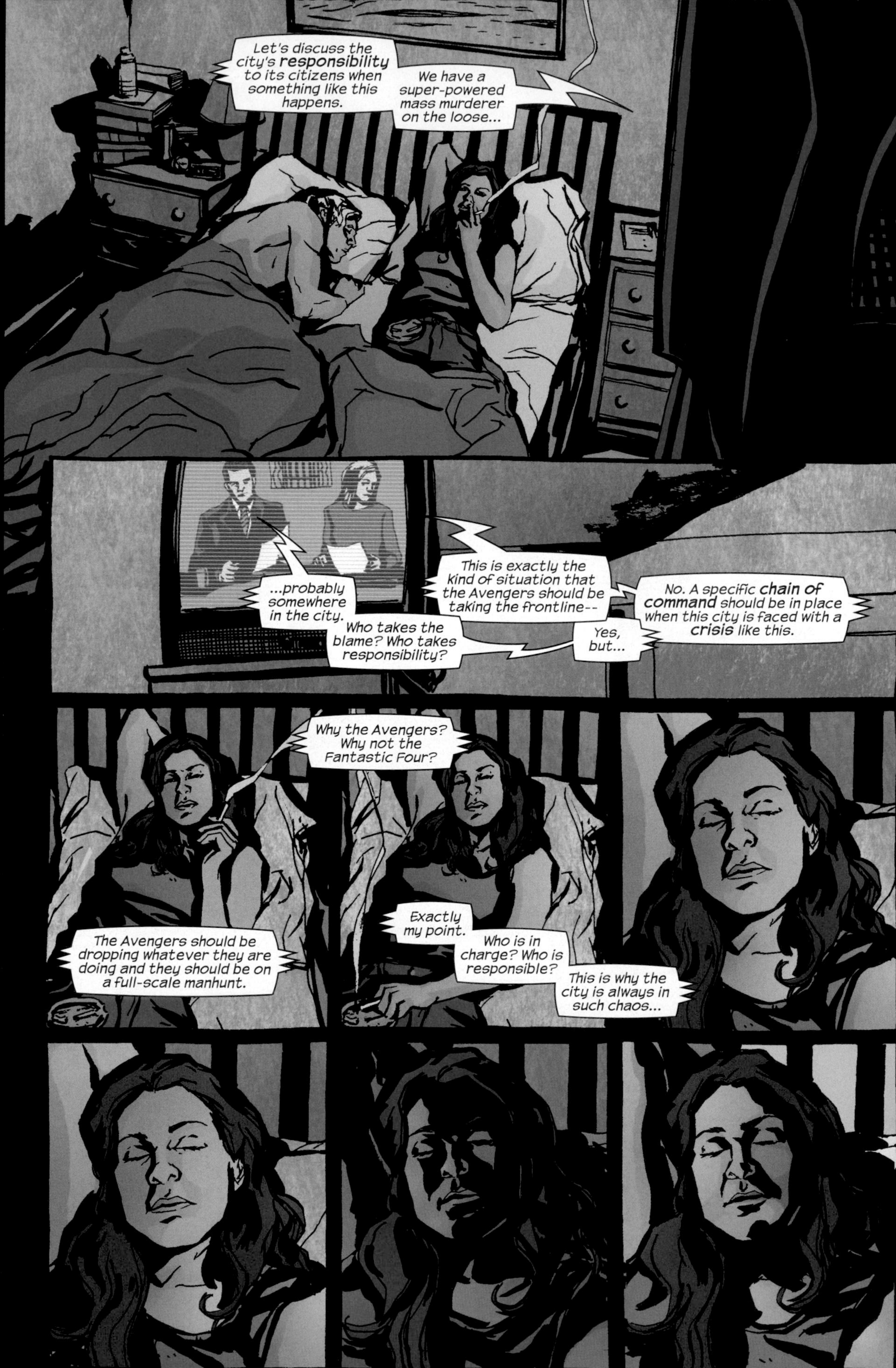
Let's discuss the city's **responsibility** to its citizens when something like this happens.
We have a super-powered mass murderer on the loose...
...probably somewhere in the city.
Who takes the blame? Who takes responsibility?
This is exactly the kind of situation that the Avengers should be taking the frontline--
Yes, but...
No. A specific **chain of command** should be in place when this city is faced with a **crisis** like this.
Why the Avengers? Why not the Fantastic Four?
The Avengers should be dropping whatever they are doing and they should be on a full-scale manhunt.
Exactly my point.
Who is in charge? Who is responsible?
This is why the city is always in such chaos...

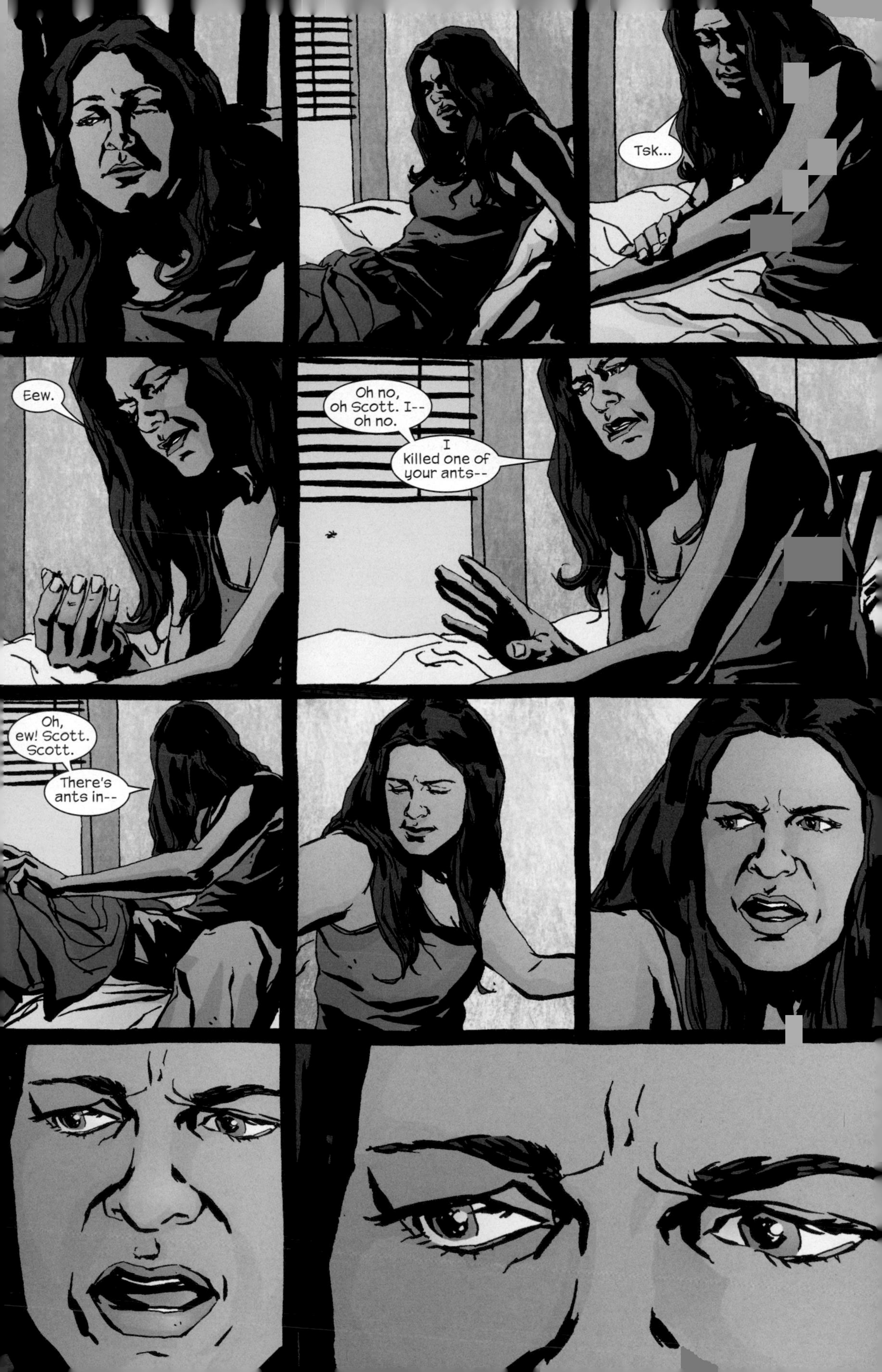
Tsk...
Eew.
Oh no, oh Scott. I-- oh no.
I killed one of your ants--
Oh, ew! Scott. Scott.
There's ants in--

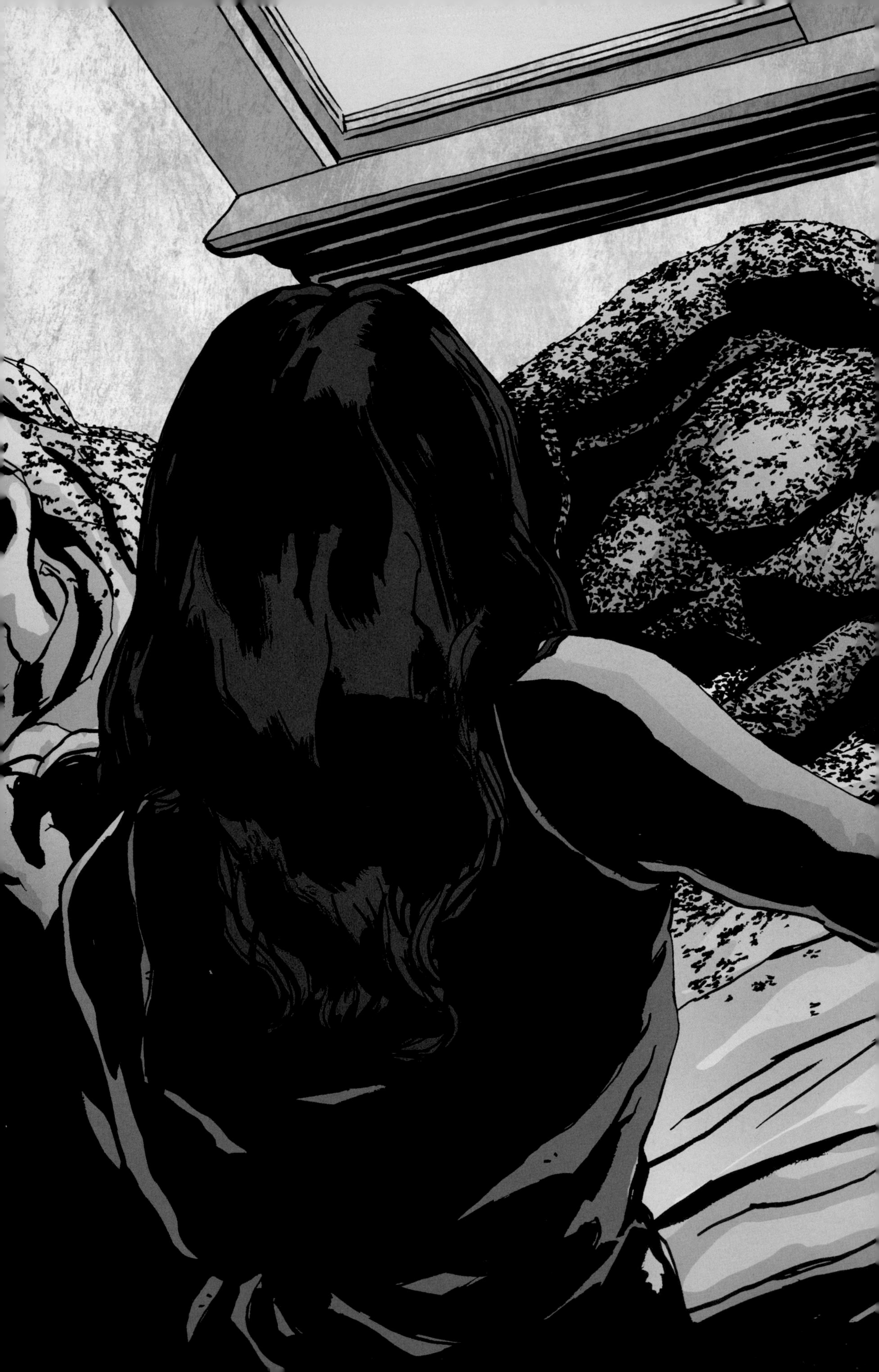

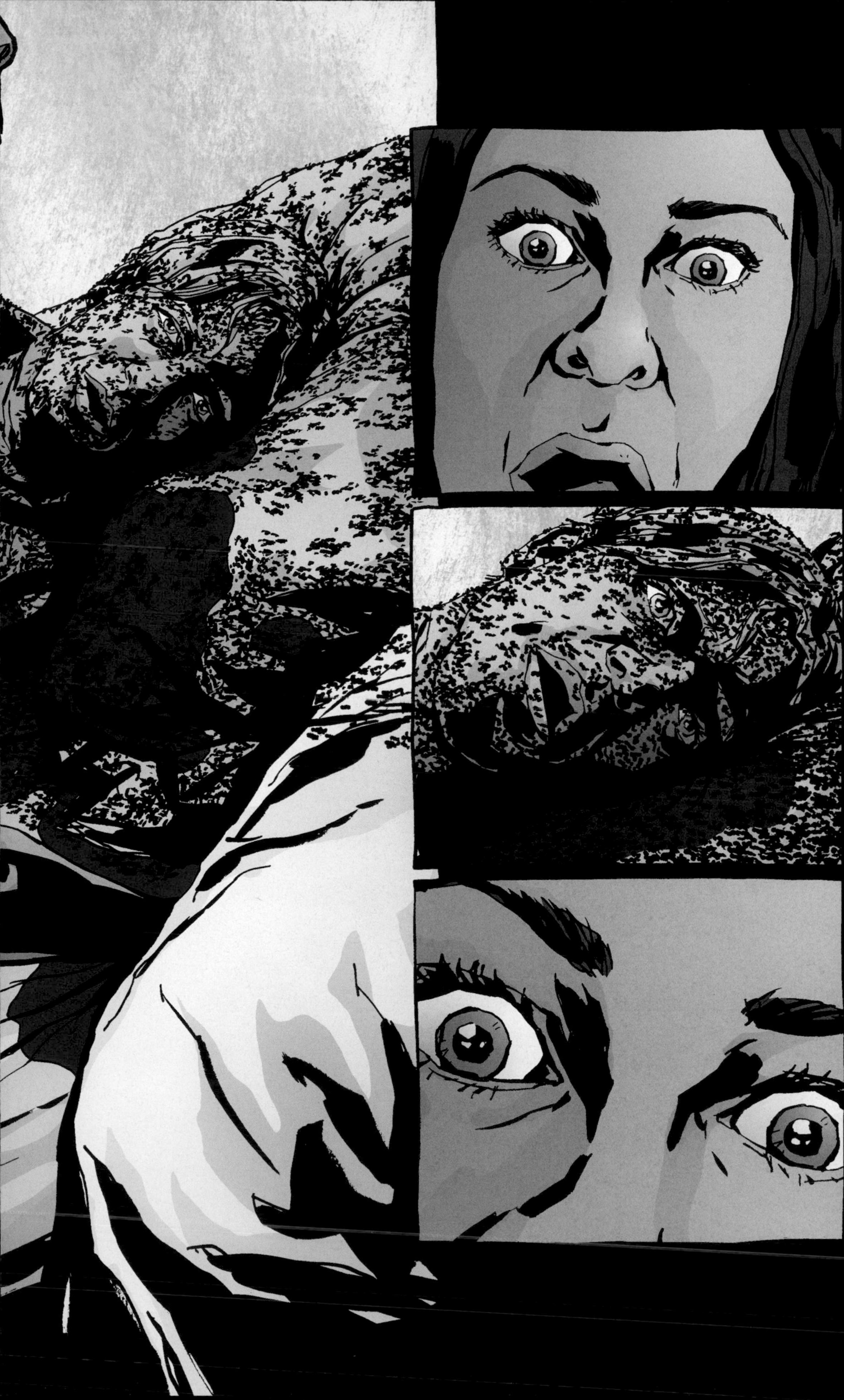

ISSUE #28 KI[redacted]VE

[redacted]2I2

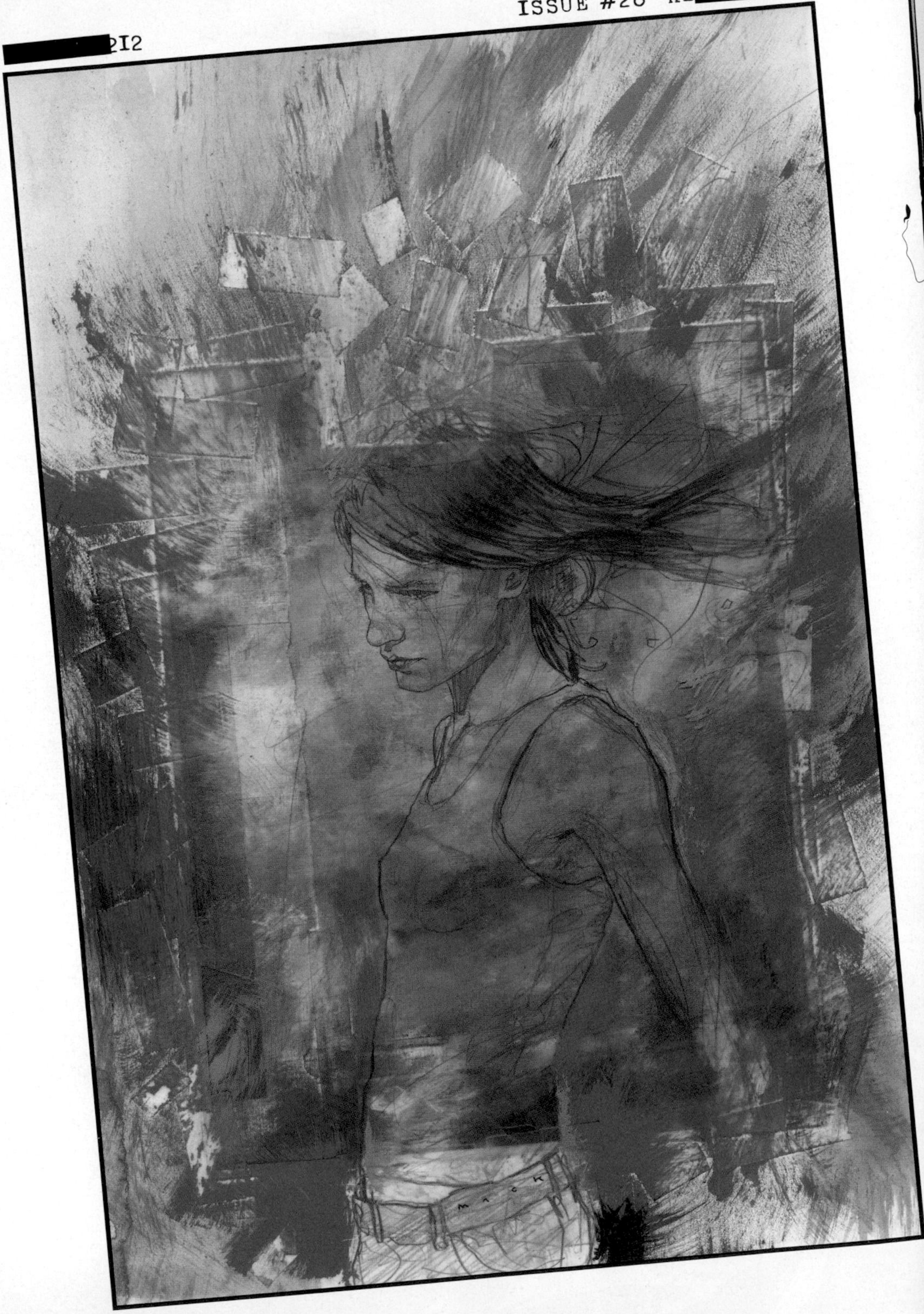

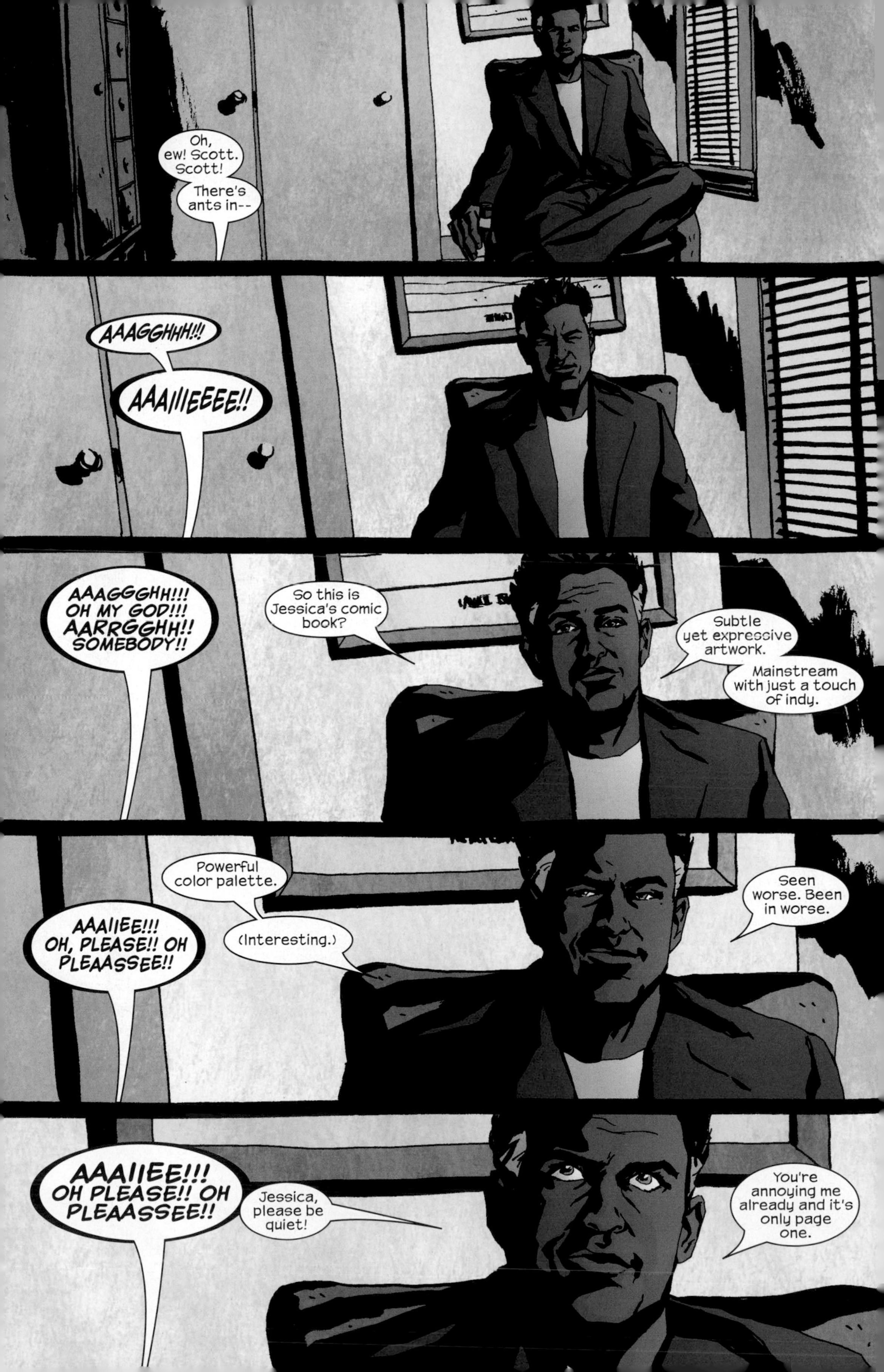

Oh, ew! Scott. Scott!
There's ants in--
AAAGGHHH!!!
AAAIIIEEEE!!
AAAGGGHH!!! OH MY GOD!!! AARRGGHH!! SOMEBODY!!
So this is Jessica's comic book?
Subtle yet expressive artwork.
Mainstream with just a touch of indy.
AAAIIEE!!! OH, PLEASE!! OH PLEAASSEE!!
Powerful color palette.
(Interesting.)
Seen worse. Been in worse.
AAAIIEE!!! OH PLEASE!! OH PLEAASSEE!!
Jessica, please be quiet!
You're annoying me already and it's only page one.

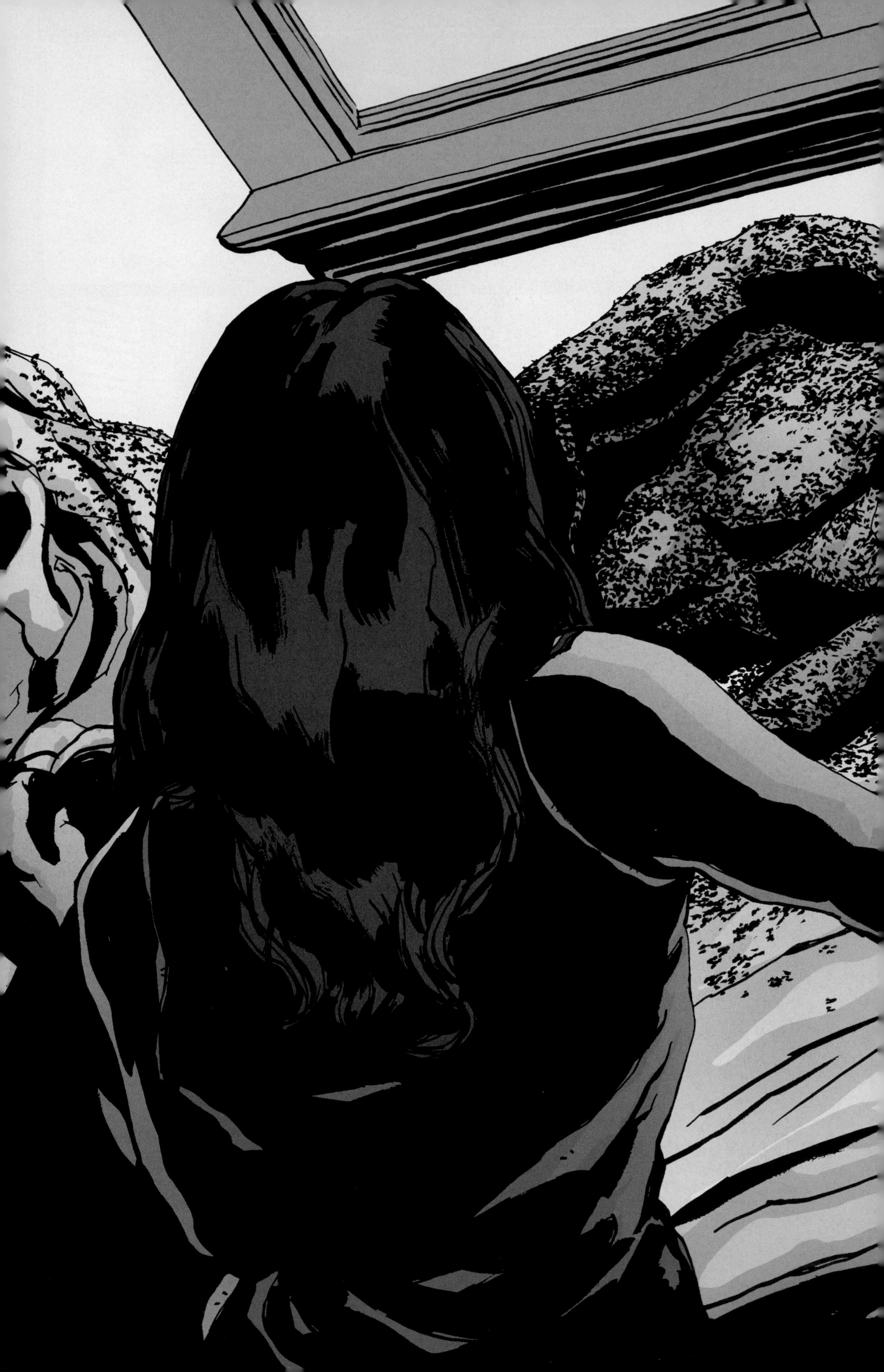

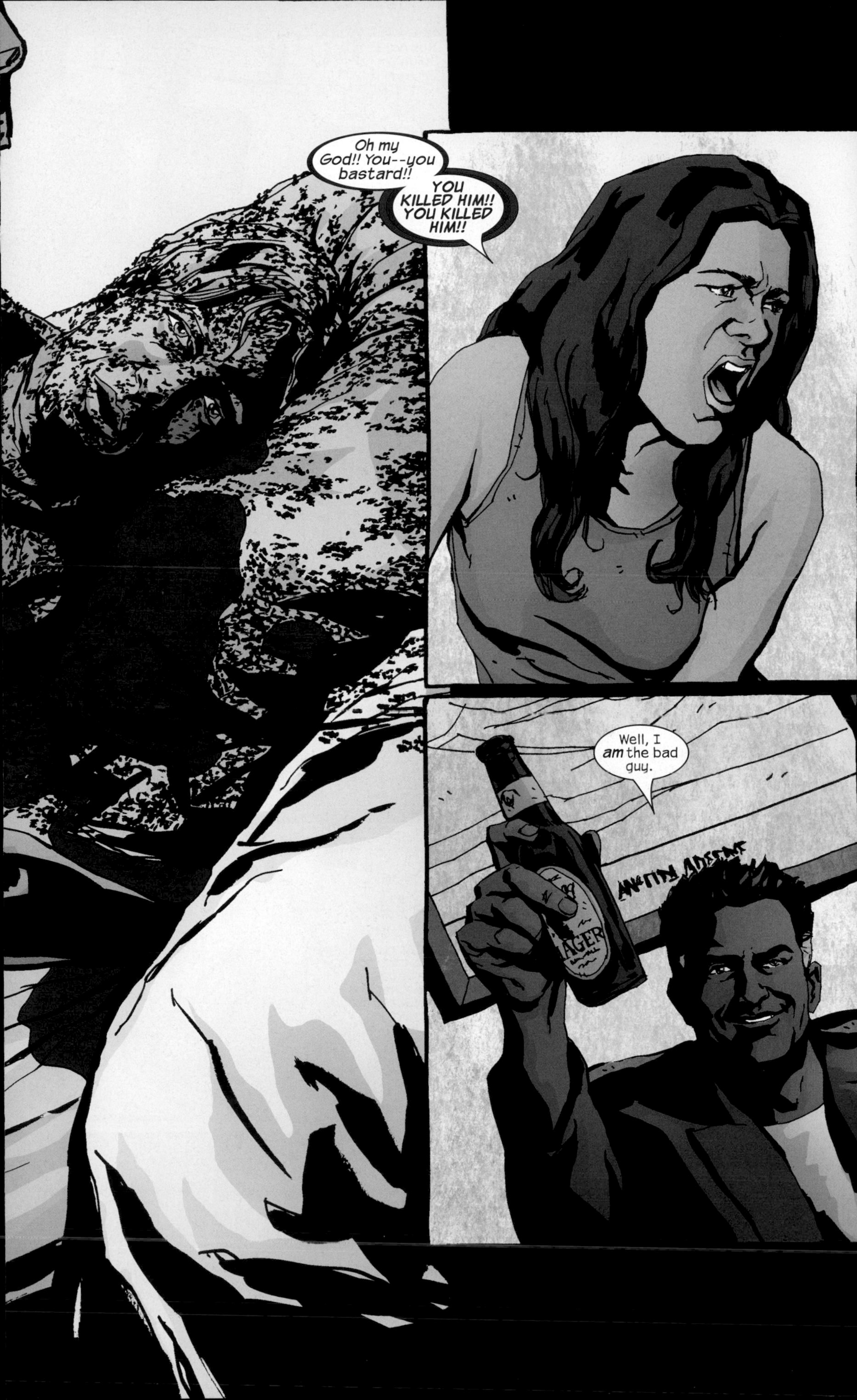
Oh my God!! You--you bastard!!
YOU KILLED HIM!! YOU KILLED HIM!!
Well, I *am* the bad guy.

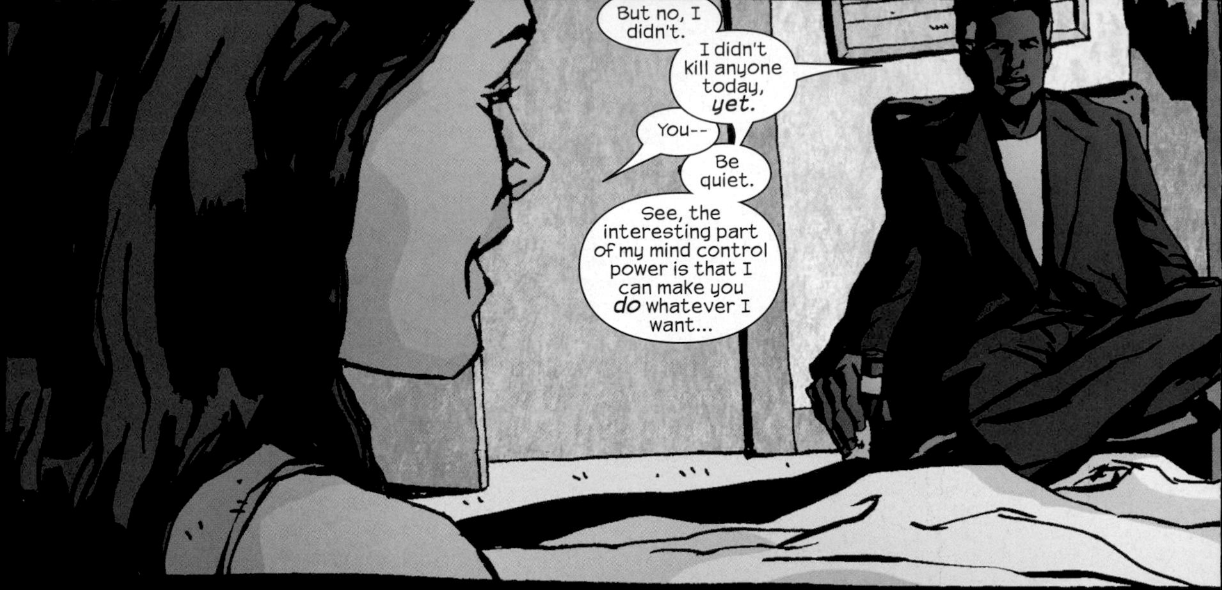
But no, I didn't.
I didn't kill anyone today, *yet.*
You--
Be quiet.
See, the interesting part of my mind control power is that I can make you *do* whatever I want...

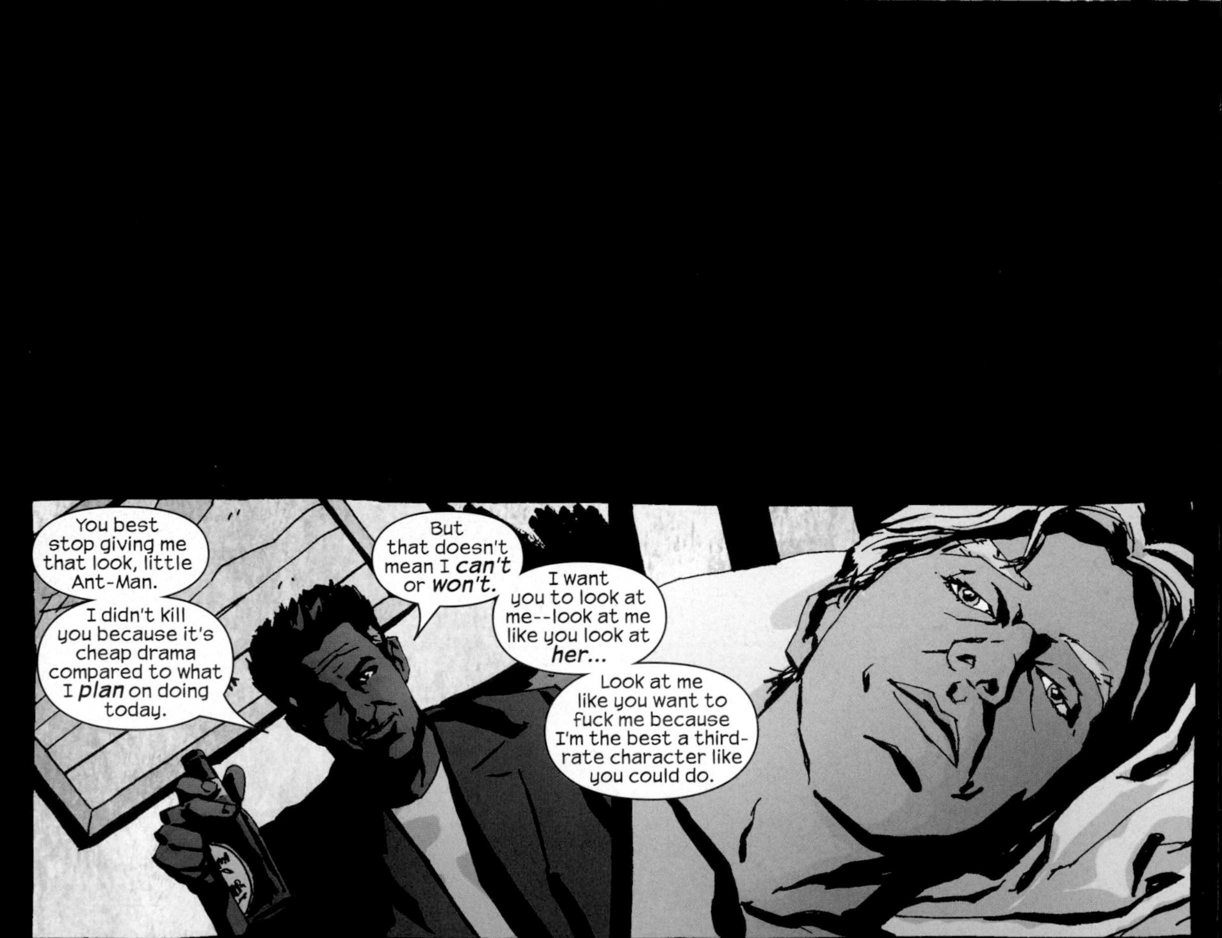
You best stop giving me that look, little Ant-Man.
I didn't kill you because it's cheap drama compared to what I *plan* on doing today.
But that doesn't mean I *can't* or *won't.*
I want you to look at me--look at me like you look at *her...*
Look at me like you want to fuck me because I'm the best a third-rate character like you could do.

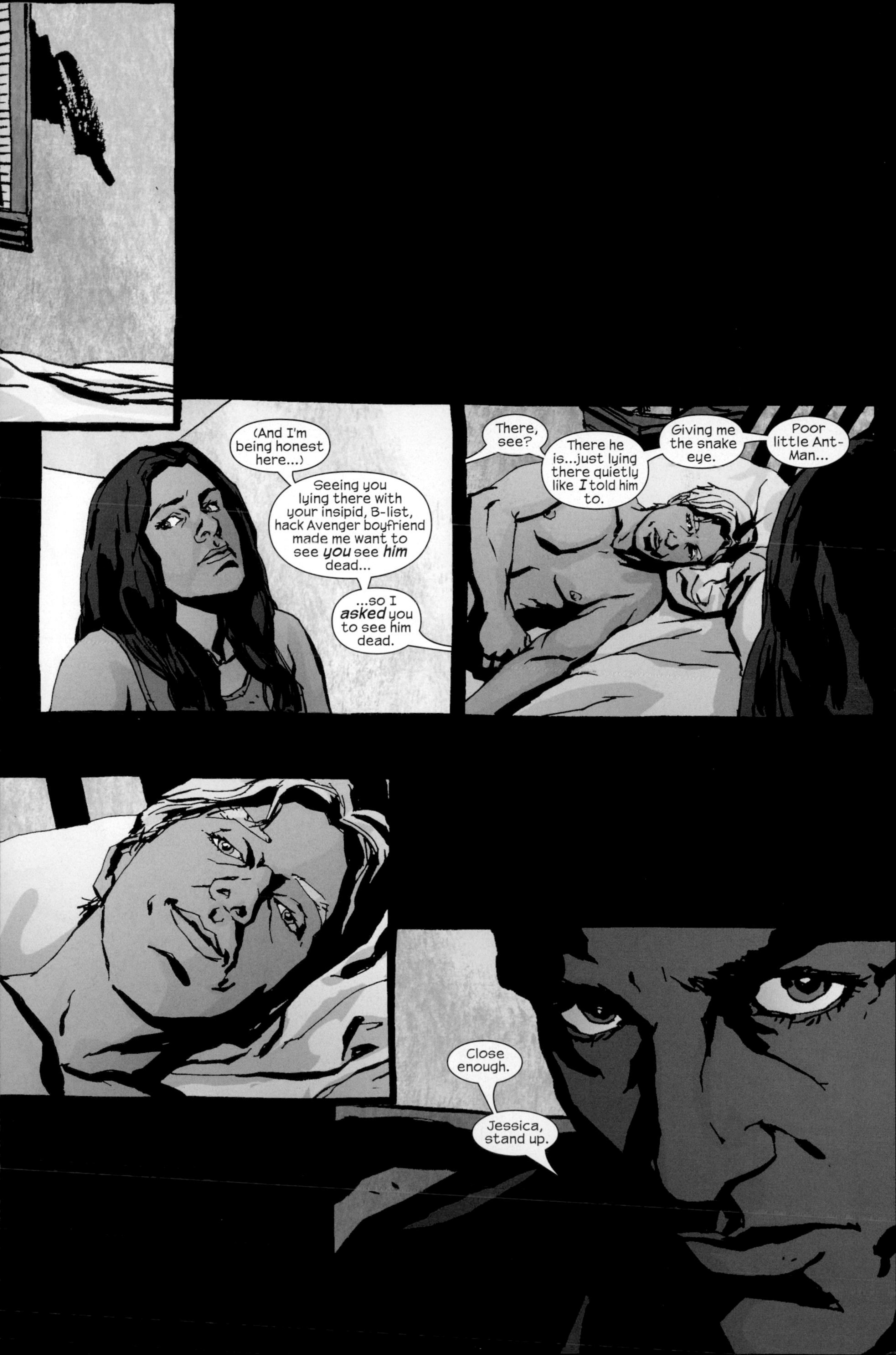

(And I'm being honest here...)
Seeing you lying there with your insipid, B-list, hack Avenger boyfriend made me want to see *you* see *him* dead...
...so I *asked* you to see him dead.
There, see?
There he is...just lying there quietly like *I* told him to.
Giving me the snake eye.
Poor little Ant-Man...
Close enough.
Jessica, stand up.

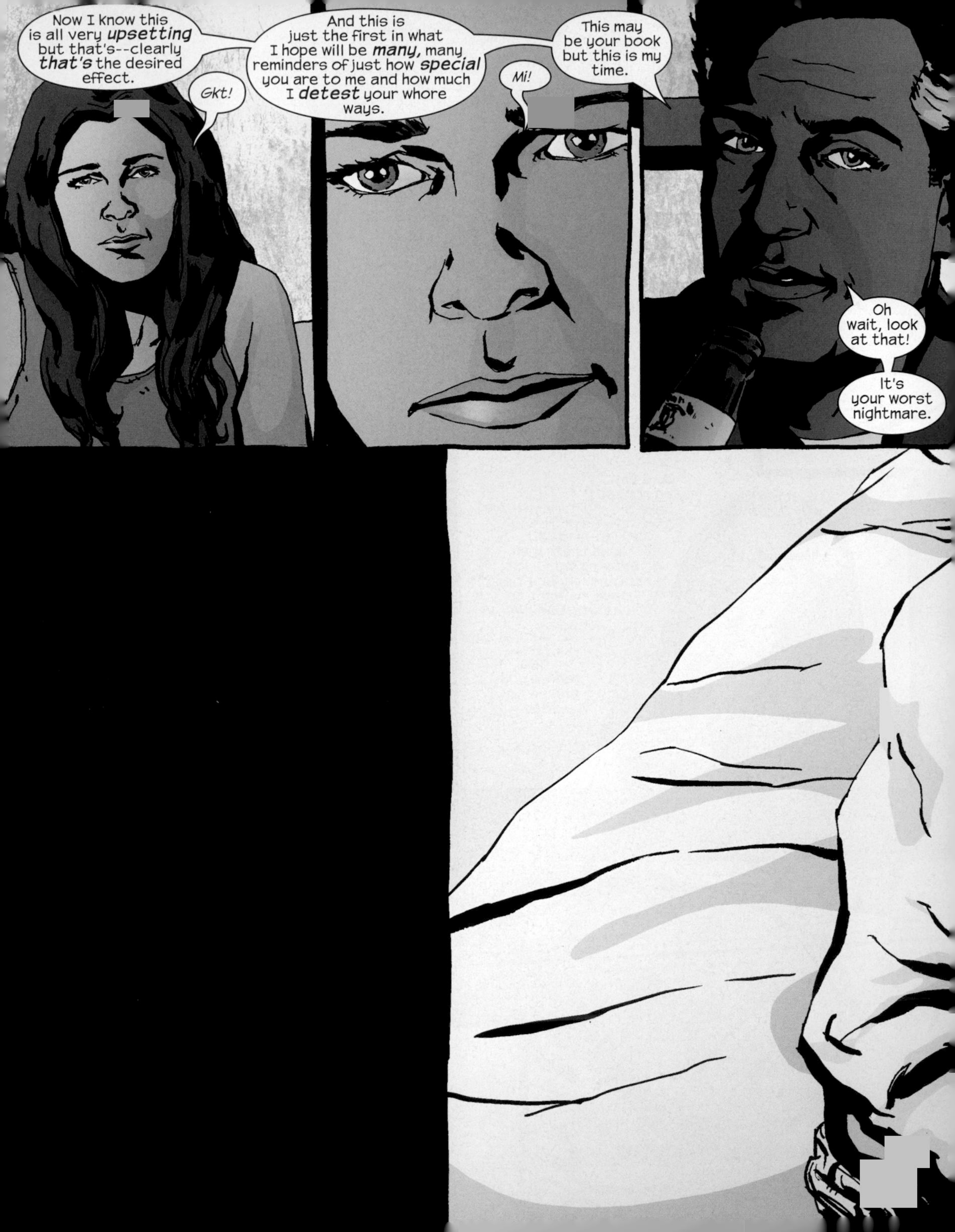
Now I know this is all very *upsetting* but that's--clearly *that's* the desired effect.
Gkt!
And this is just the first in what I hope will be *many,* many reminders of just how *special* you are to me and how much I *detest* your whore ways.
Mi!
This may be your book but this is my time.
Oh wait, look at that!
It's your worst nightmare.

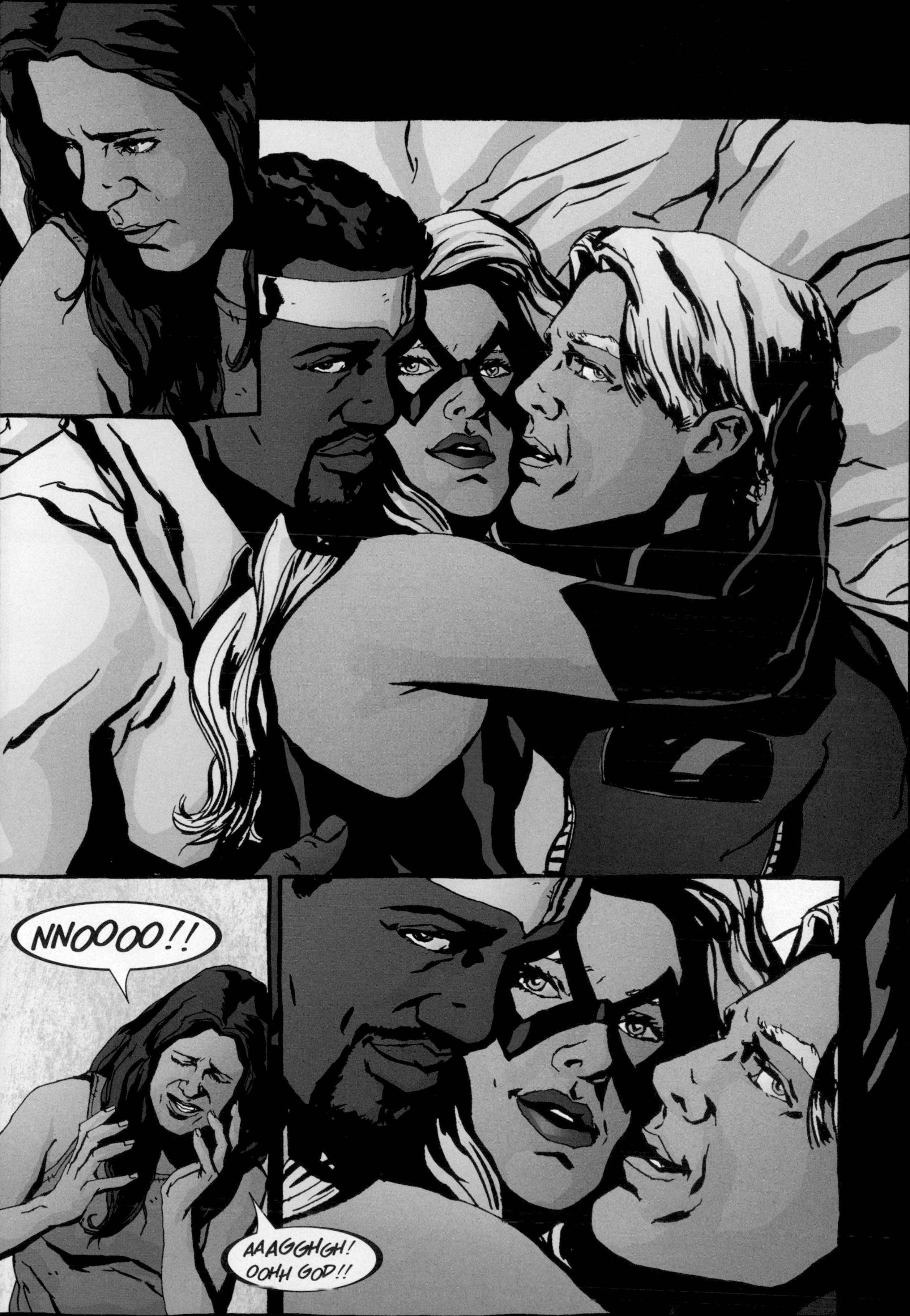
NNOOOO!!
AAAGGHGH! OOHH GOD!!

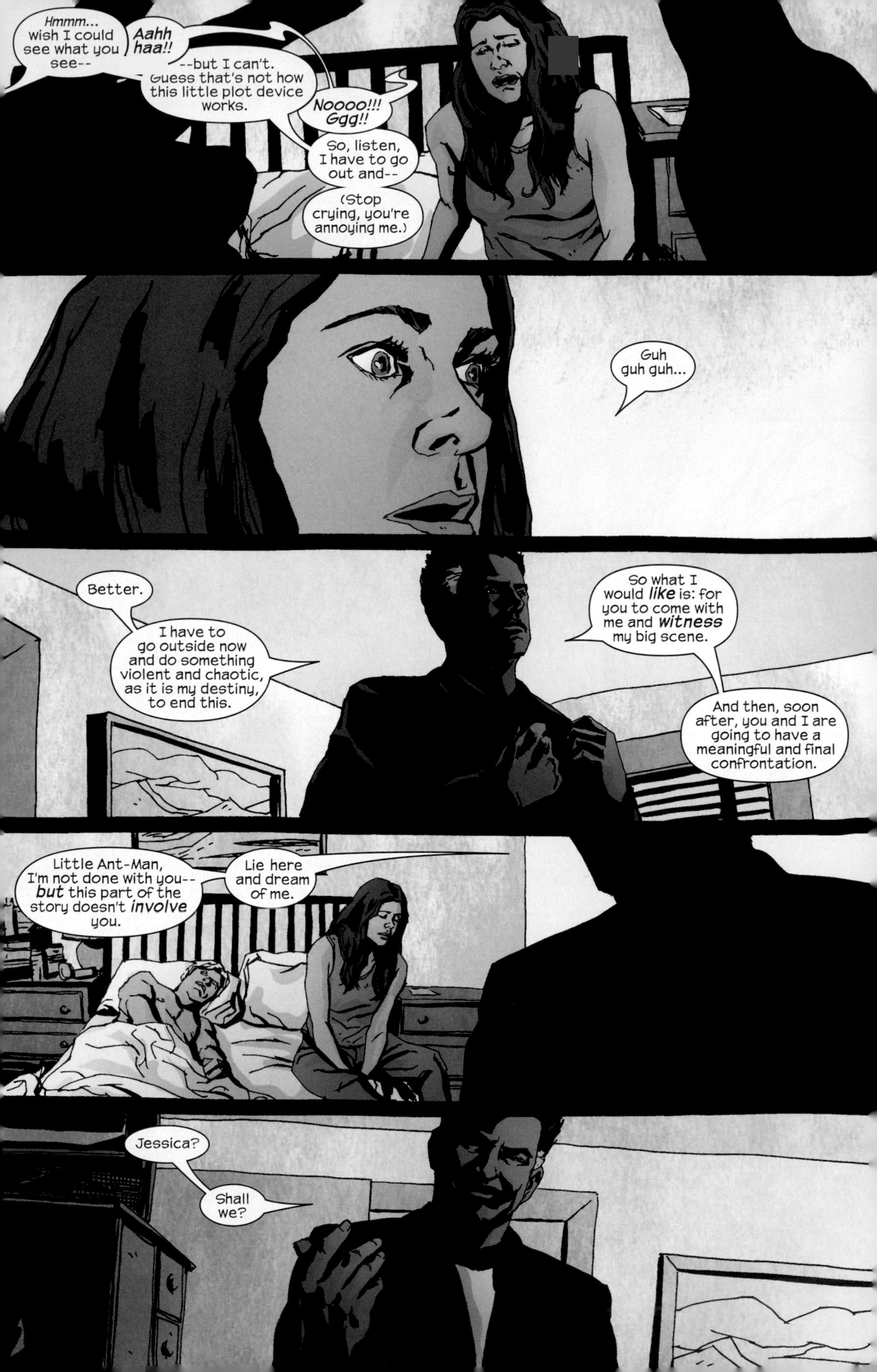
Hmmm... wish I could see what you see--
Aahh haa!!
--but I can't. Guess that's not how this little plot device works.
Noooo!!! Ggg!!
So, listen, I have to go out and--
(Stop crying, you're annoying me.)
Guh guh guh...
Better.
I have to go outside now and do something violent and chaotic, as it is my destiny, to end this.
So what I would *like* is: for you to come with me and *witness* my big scene.
And then, soon after, you and I are going to have a meaningful and final confrontation.
Little Ant-Man, I'm not done with you-- *but* this part of the story doesn't *involve* you.
Lie here and dream of me.
Jessica?
Shall we?

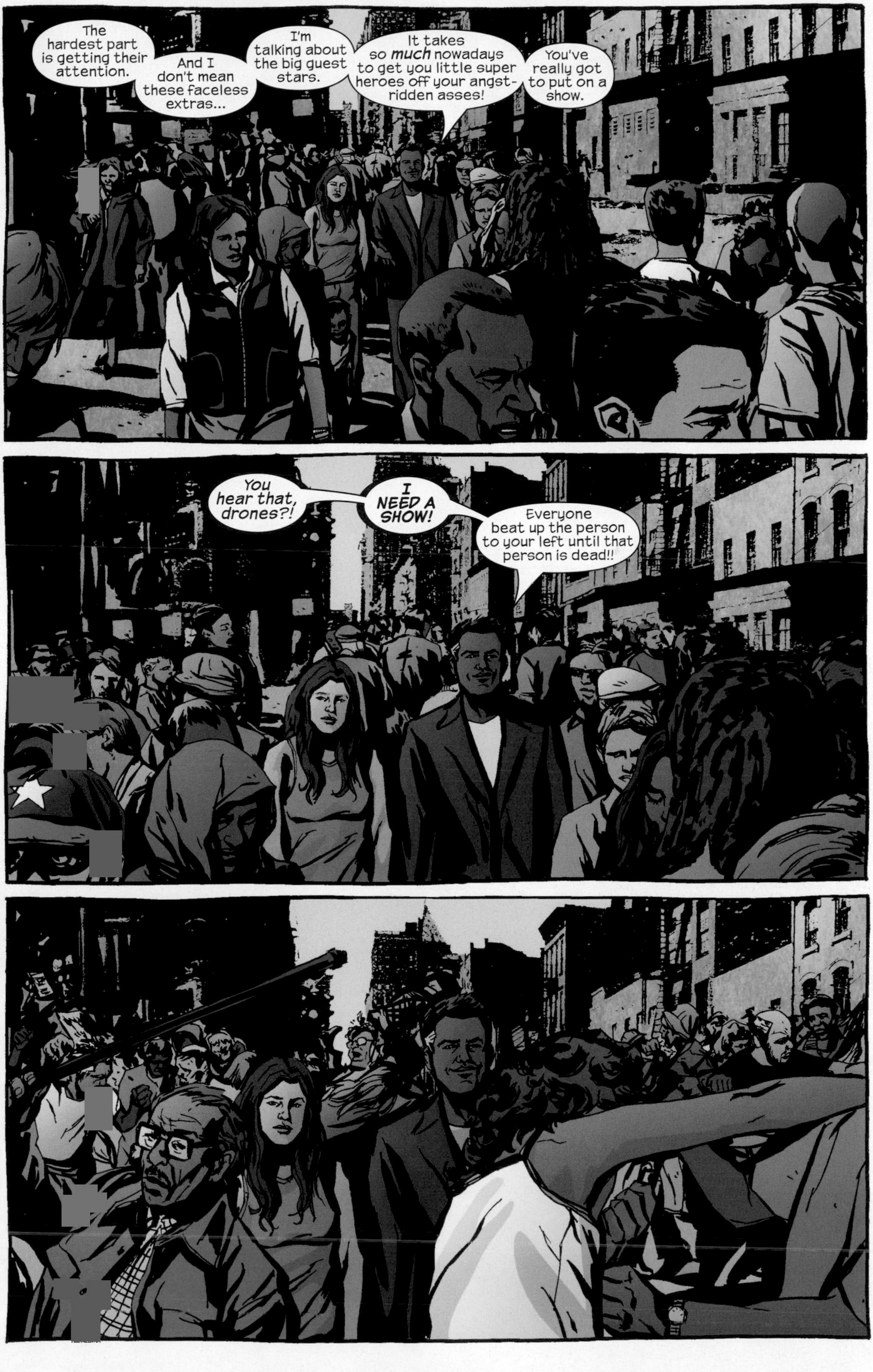
The hardest part is getting their attention.
And I don't mean these faceless extras...
I'm talking about the big guest stars.
It takes so *much* nowadays to get you little super heroes off your angst-ridden asses!
You've really got to put on a show.
You hear that, drones?!
I NEED A SHOW!
Everyone beat up the person to your left until that person is dead!!

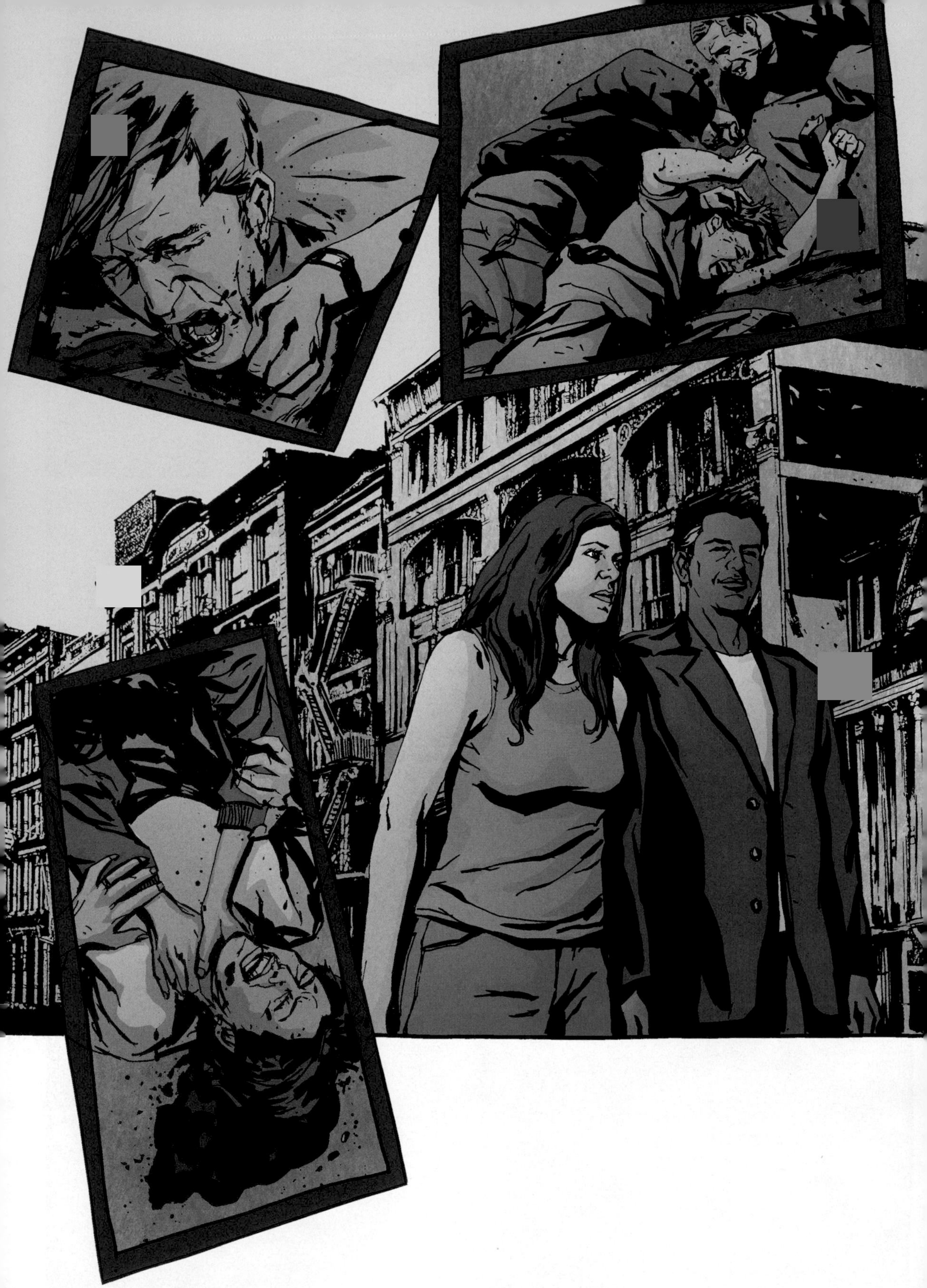

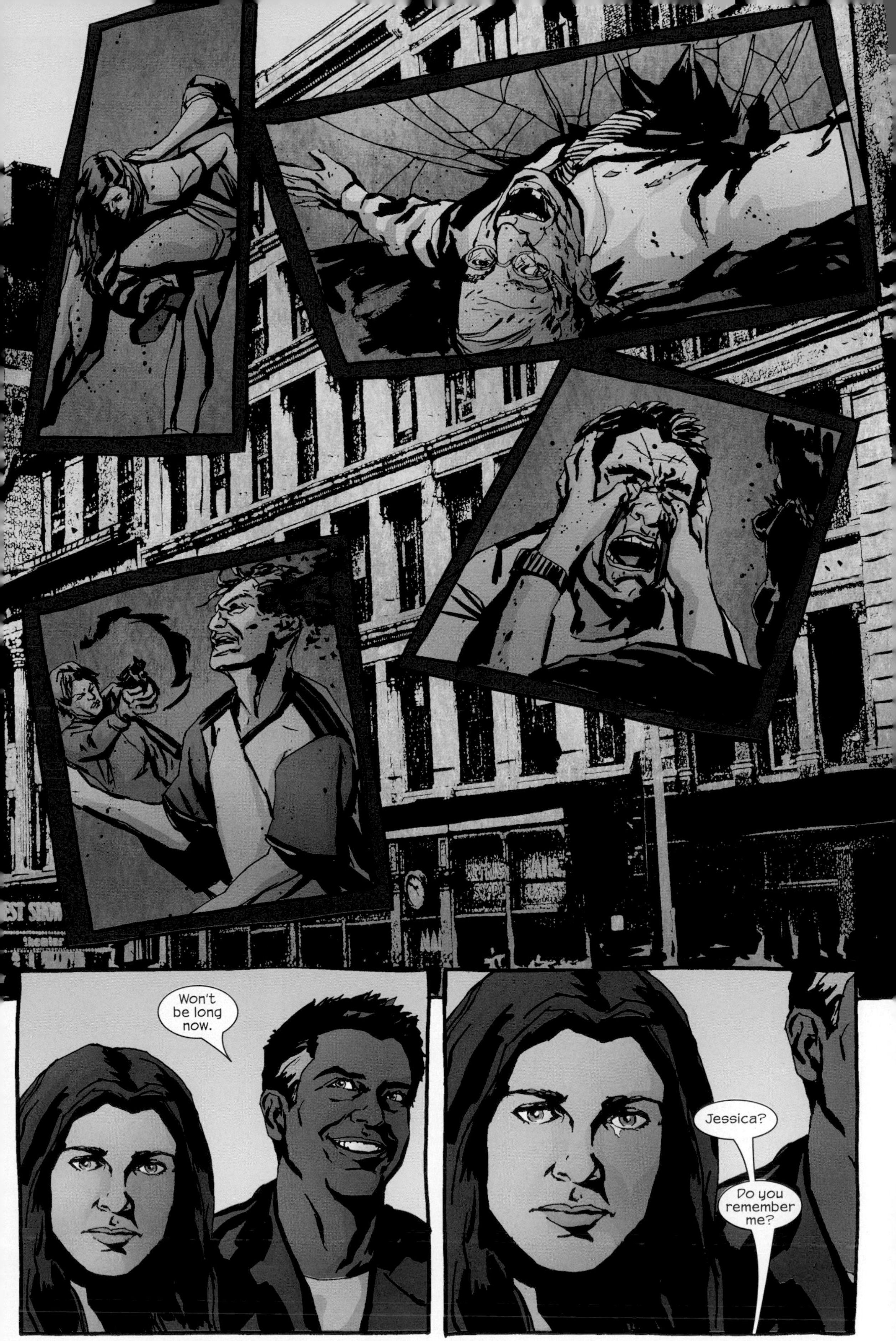
Won't be long now.
Jessica?
Do you remember me?

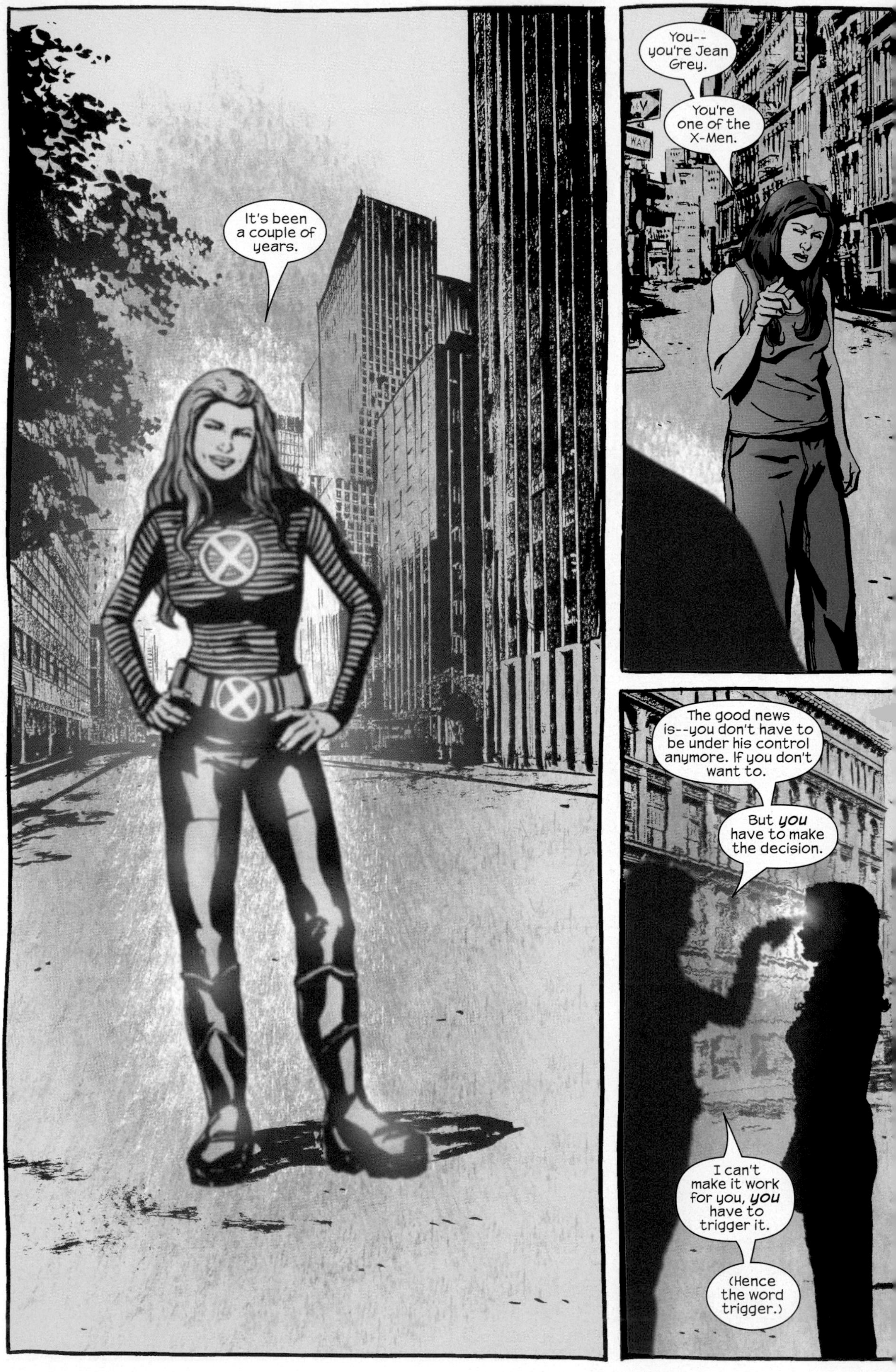
It's been a couple of years.
You-- you're Jean Grey.
You're one of the X-Men.
The good news is--you don't have to be under his control anymore. If you don't want to.
But *you* have to make the decision.
I can't make it work for you, *you* have to trigger it.
(Hence the word trigger.)

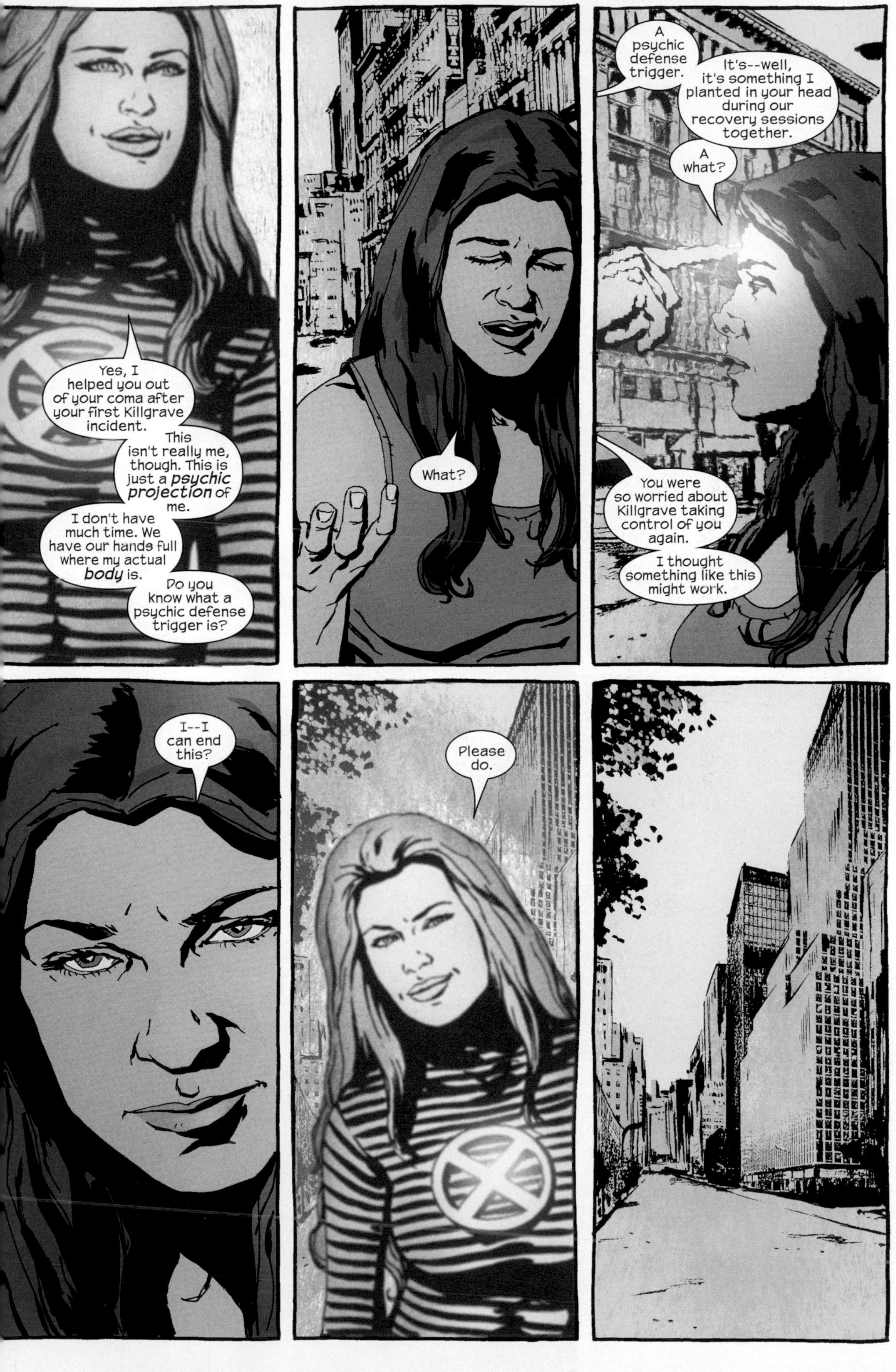
Yes, I helped you out of your coma after your first Killgrave incident.
This isn't really me, though. This is just a *psychic projection* of me.
I don't have much time. We have our hands full where my actual *body* is.
Do you know what a psychic defense trigger is?
What?
A psychic defense trigger.
A what?
It's--well, it's something I planted in your head during our recovery sessions together.
You were so worried about Killgrave taking control of you again.
I thought something like this might work.
I--I can end this?
Please do.

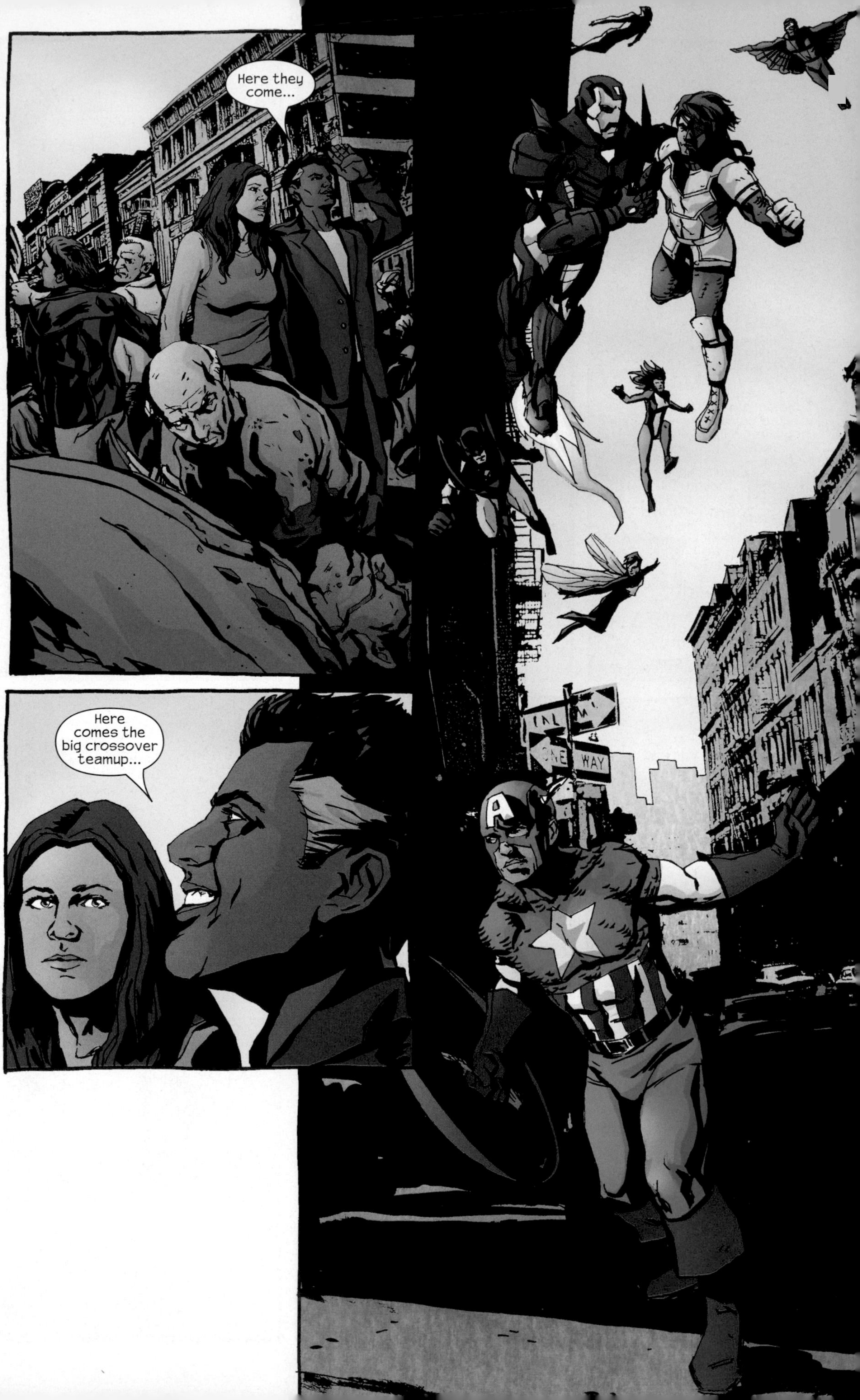
Here they come...
Here comes the big crossover teamup...
ONE WAY

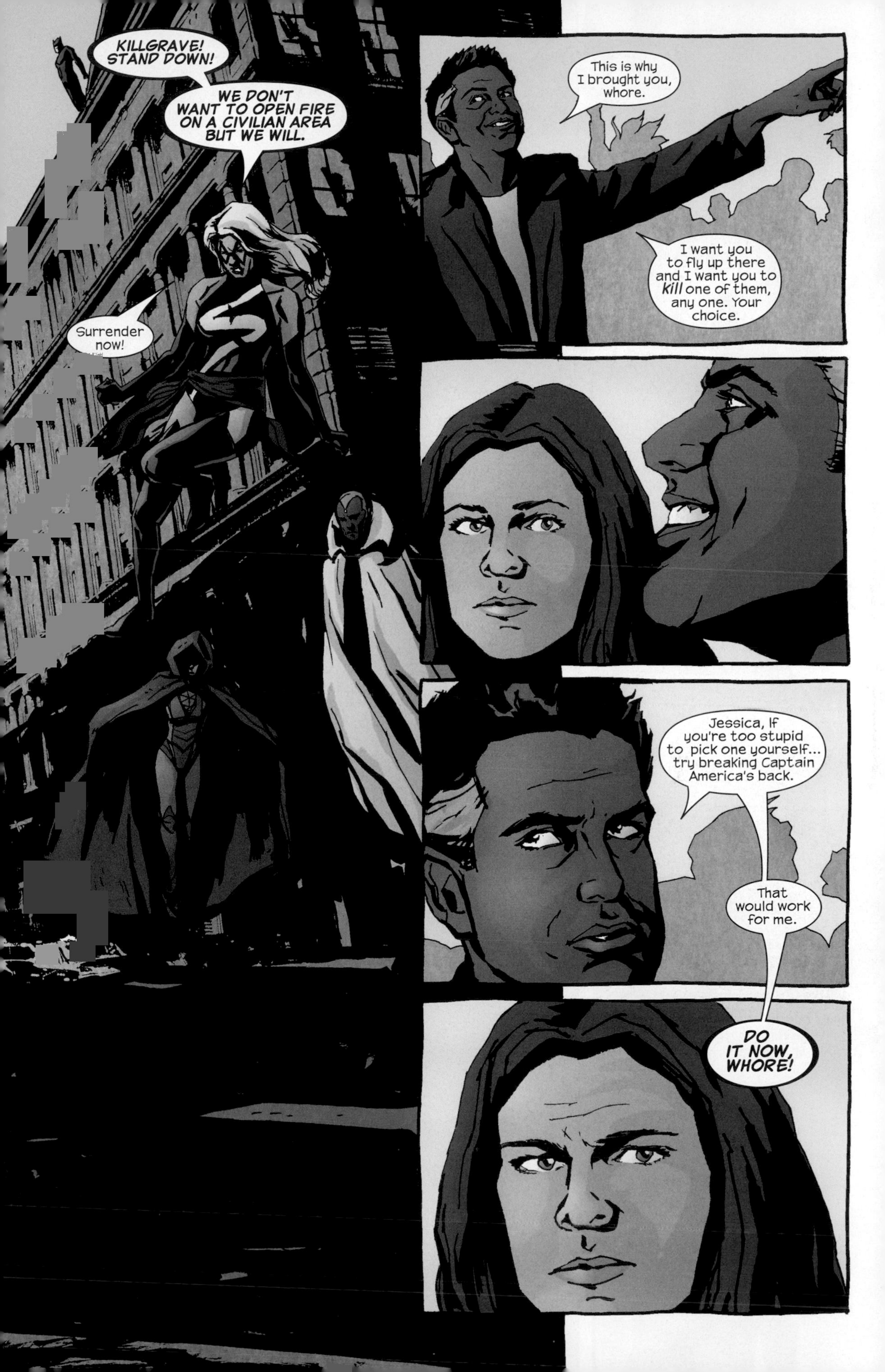
KILLGRAVE! STAND DOWN!
WE DON'T WANT TO OPEN FIRE ON A CIVILIAN AREA BUT WE WILL.
Surrender now!
This is why I brought you, whore.
I want you to fly up there and I want you to kill one of them, any one. Your choice.
Jessica, If you're too stupid to pick one yourself... try breaking Captain America's back.
That would work for me.
DO IT NOW, WHORE!

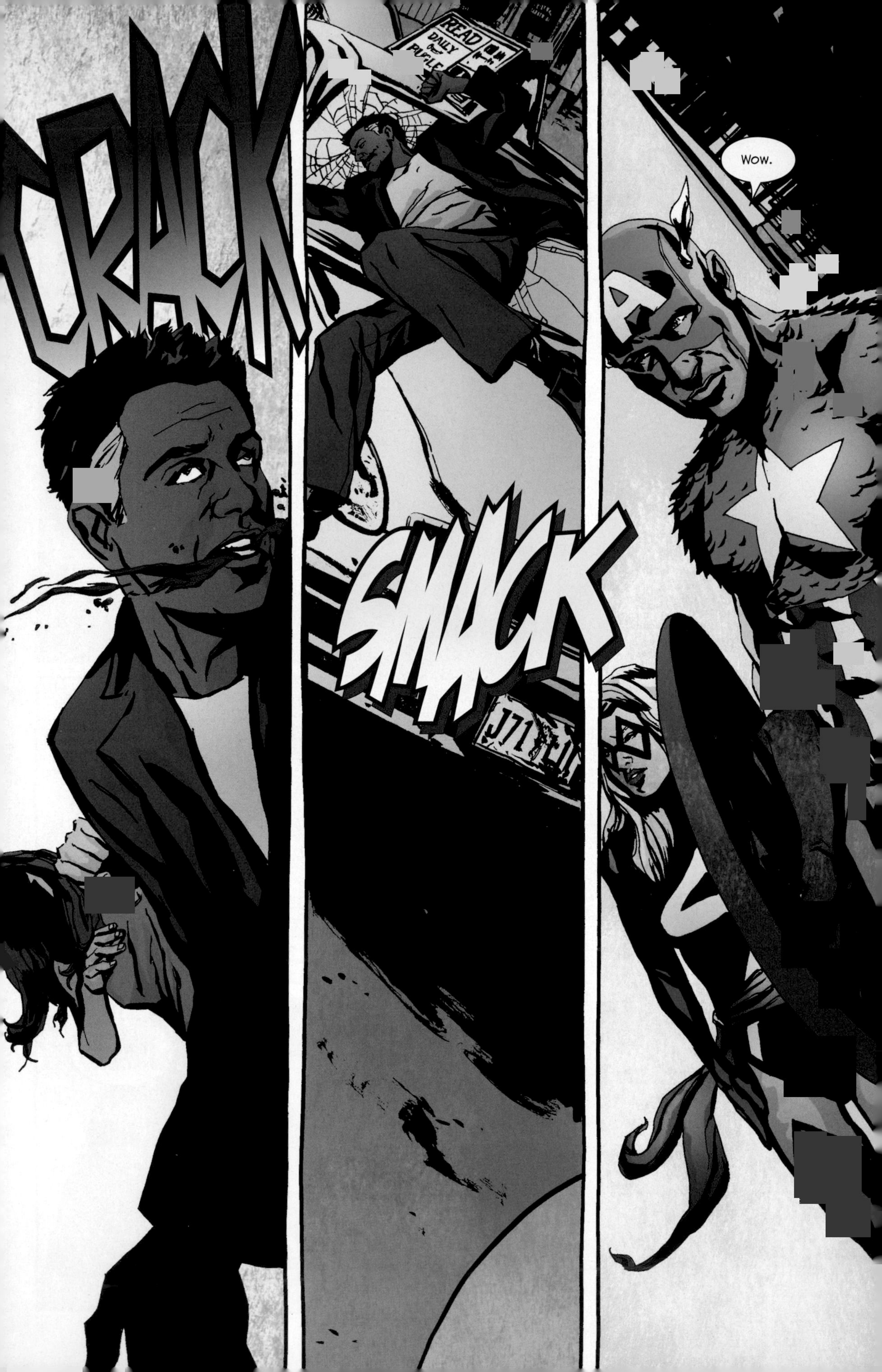
CRACK
READ
DAILY
BUGLE
SMACK
Wow.

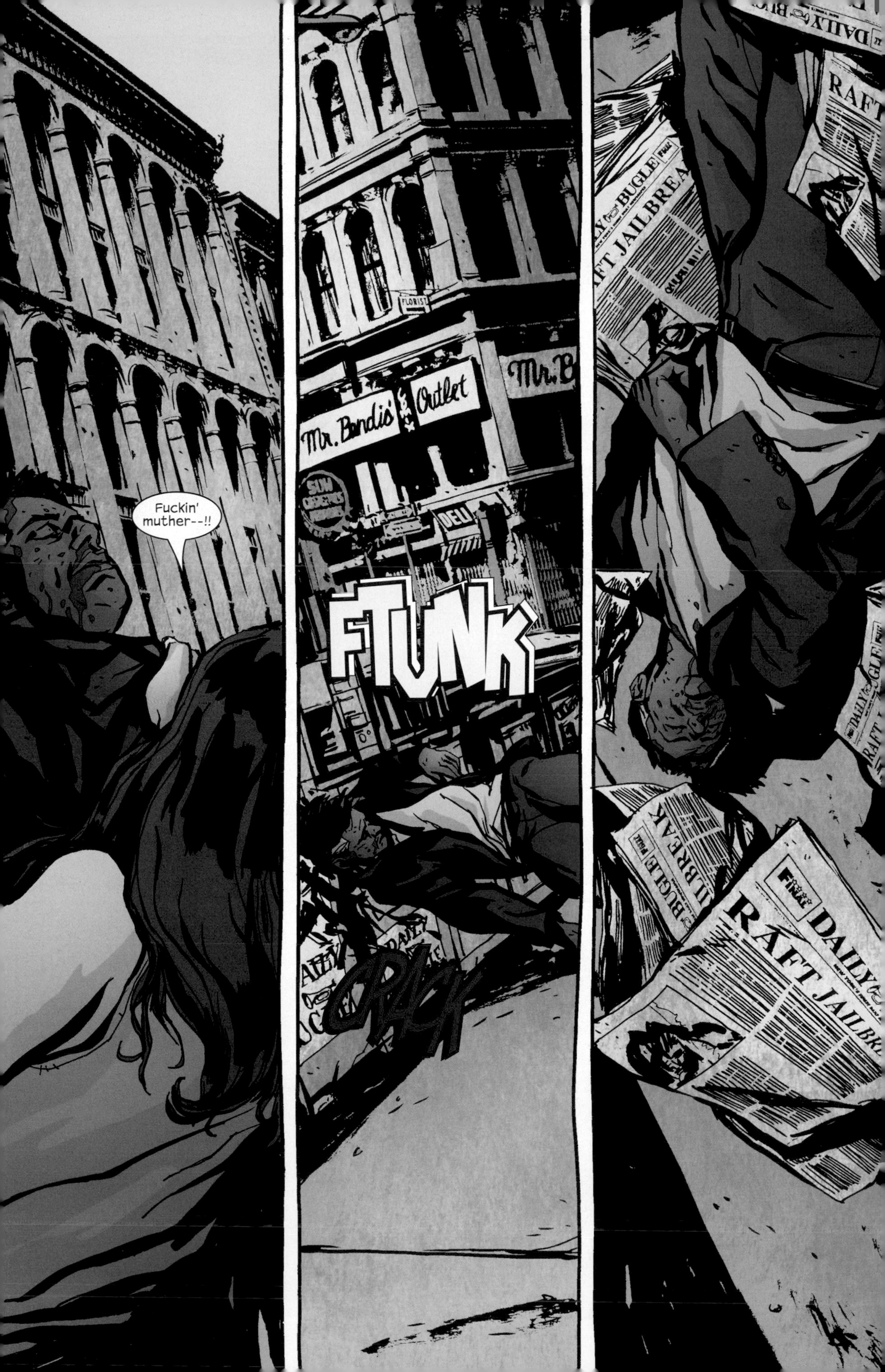
Fuckin' muther--!!
Mr. Bendis' Outlet
FLORIST
DELI
FTUNK
CRACK
DAILY BUGLE
RAFT JAILBREA

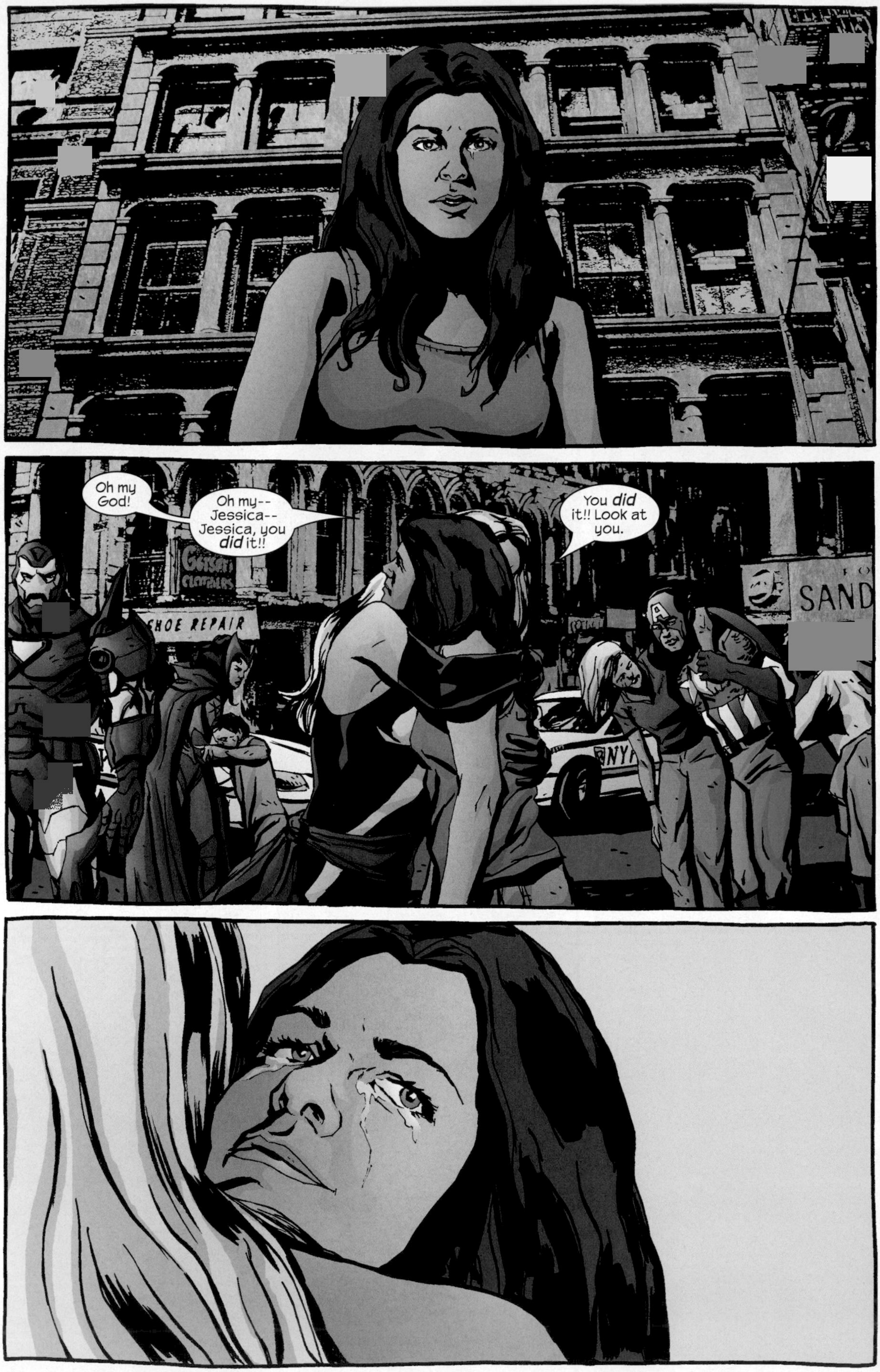
Oh my God!
Oh my-- Jessica-- Jessica, you *did* it!!
You *did* it!! Look at you.

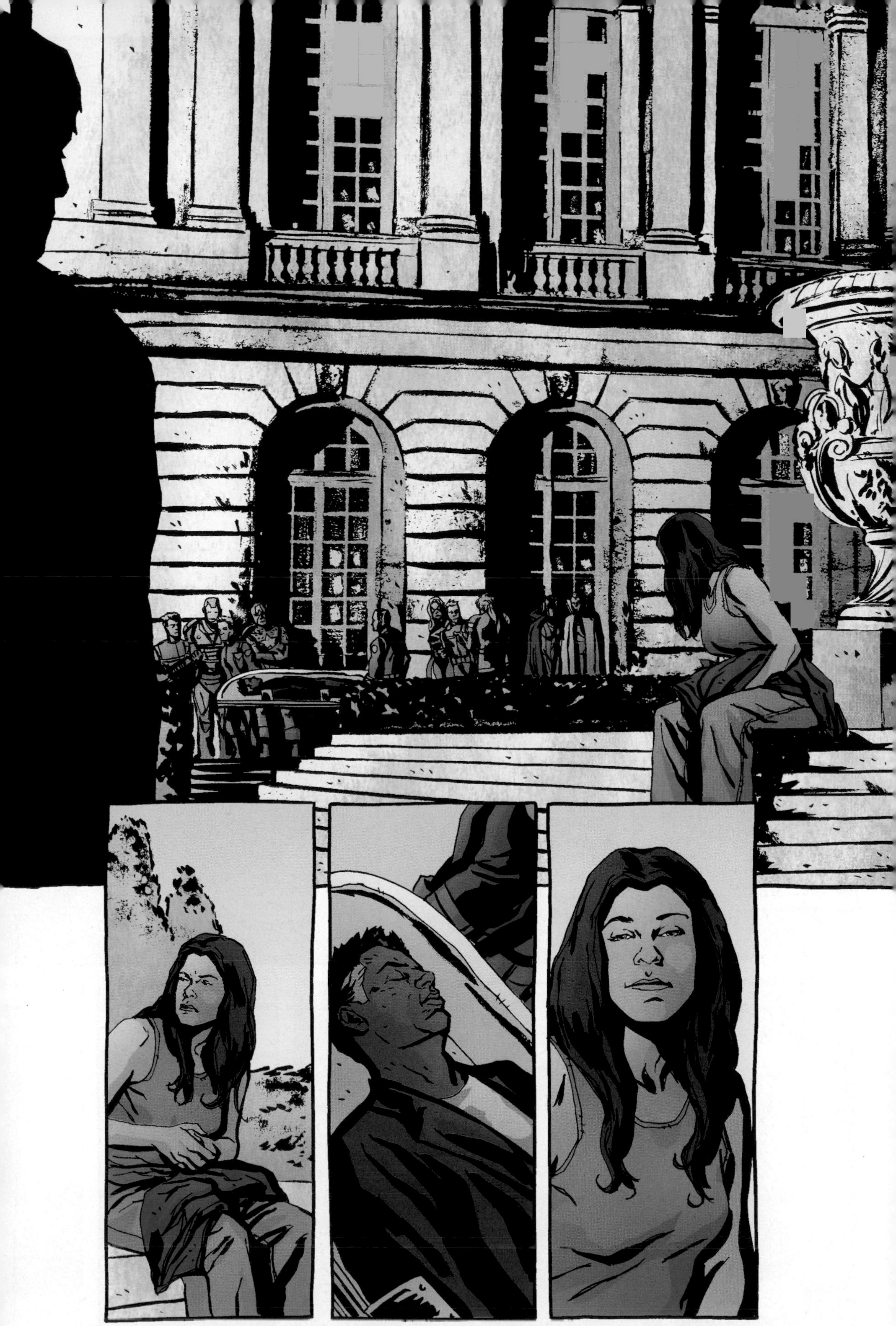

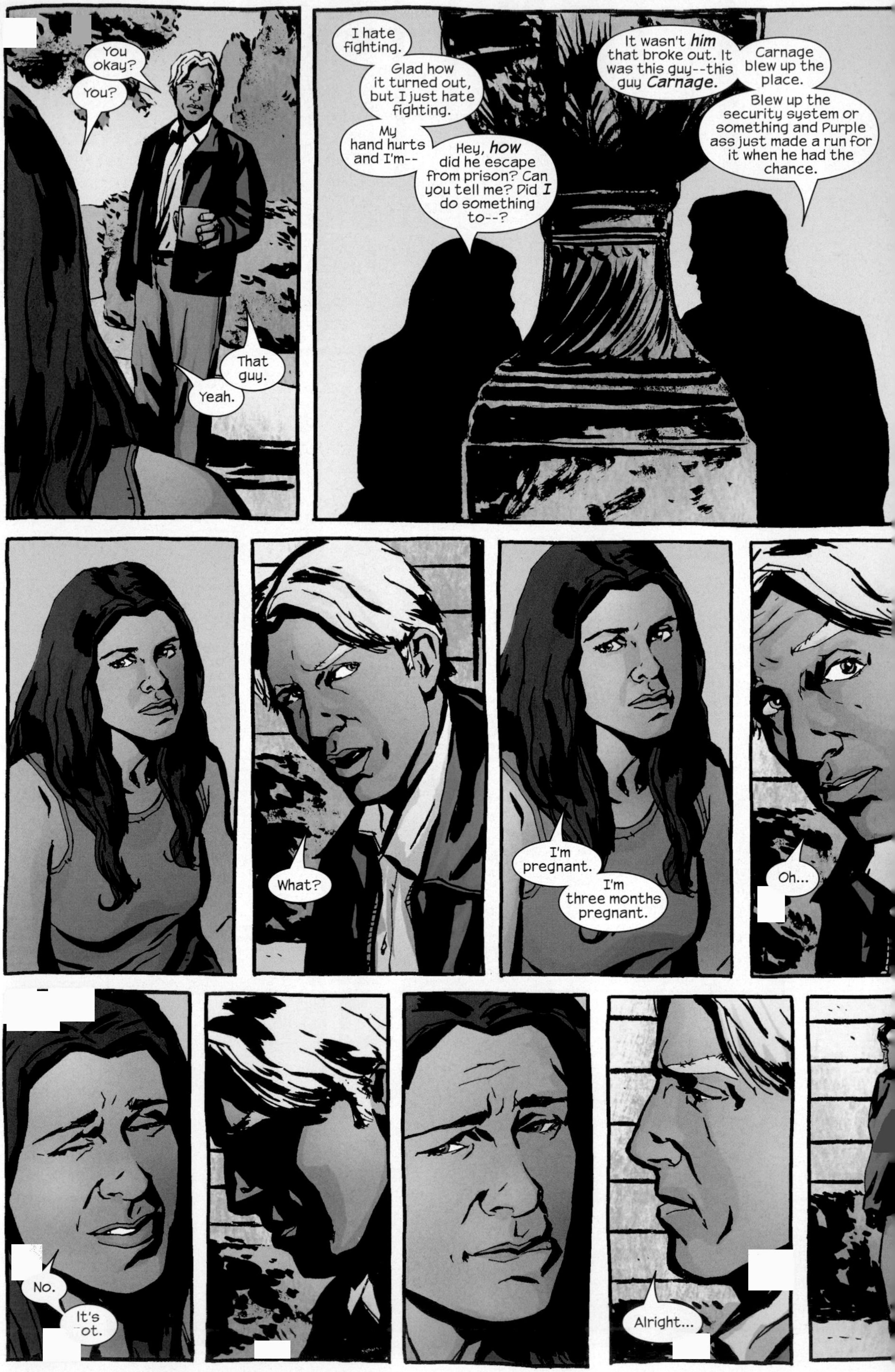
You okay?
You?
That guy.
Yeah.
I hate fighting.
Glad how it turned out, but I just hate fighting.
My hand hurts and I'm--
Hey, how did he escape from prison? Can you tell me? Did I do something to--?
It wasn't him that broke out. It was this guy--this guy Carnage.
Carnage blew up the place.
Blew up the security system or something and Purple ass just made a run for it when he had the chance.
What?
I'm pregnant.
I'm three months pregnant.
Oh...
No.
It's
ot.
Alright...

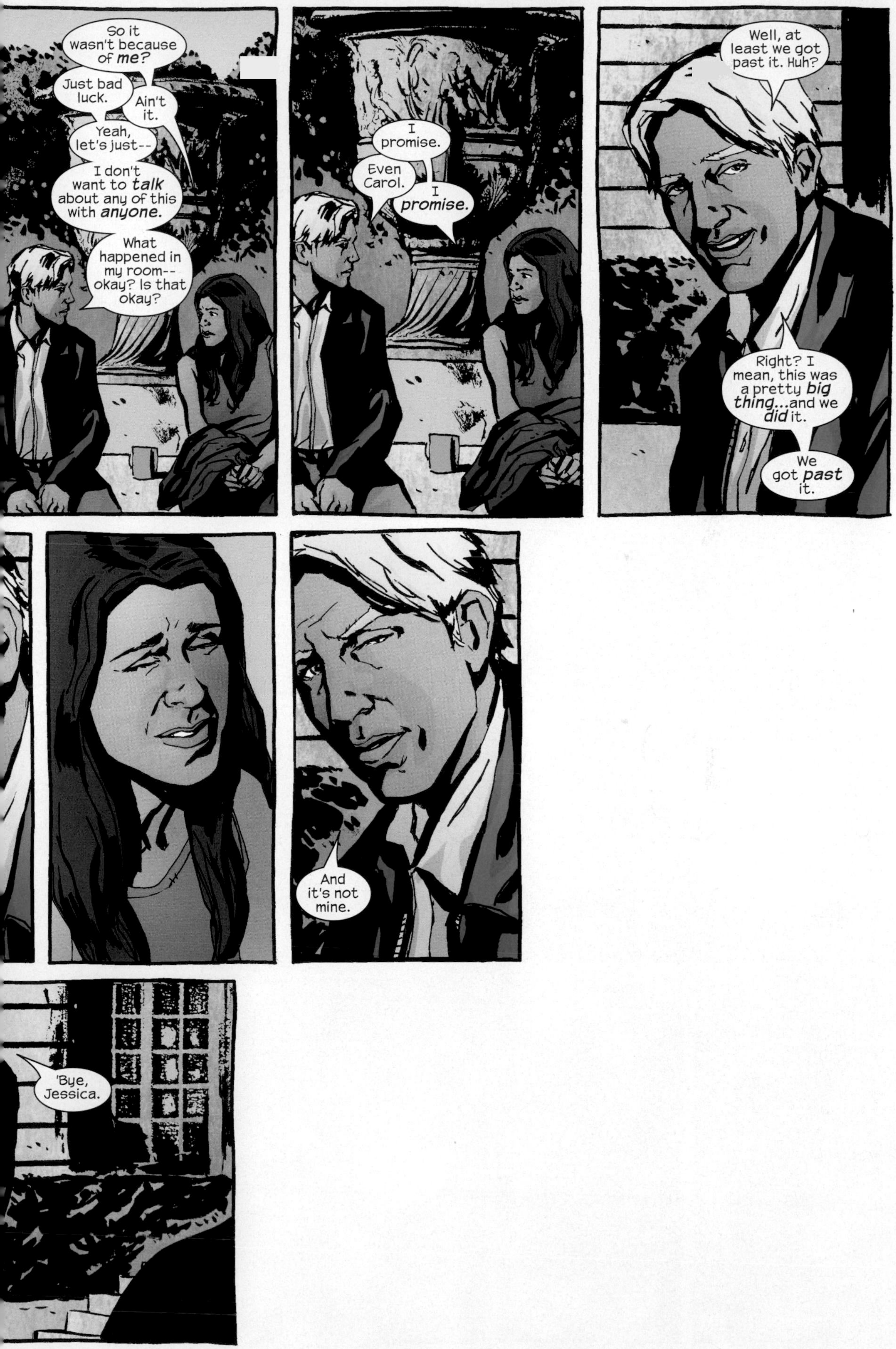
So it wasn't because of *me*?
Just bad luck.
Ain't it.
Yeah, let's just--
I don't want to *talk* about any of this with *anyone*.
What happened in my room--okay? Is that okay?
I promise.
Even Carol.
I *promise.*
Well, at least we got past it. Huh?
Right? I mean, this was a pretty *big thing...*and we *did* it.
We got *past* it.
And it's not mine.
'Bye, Jessica.

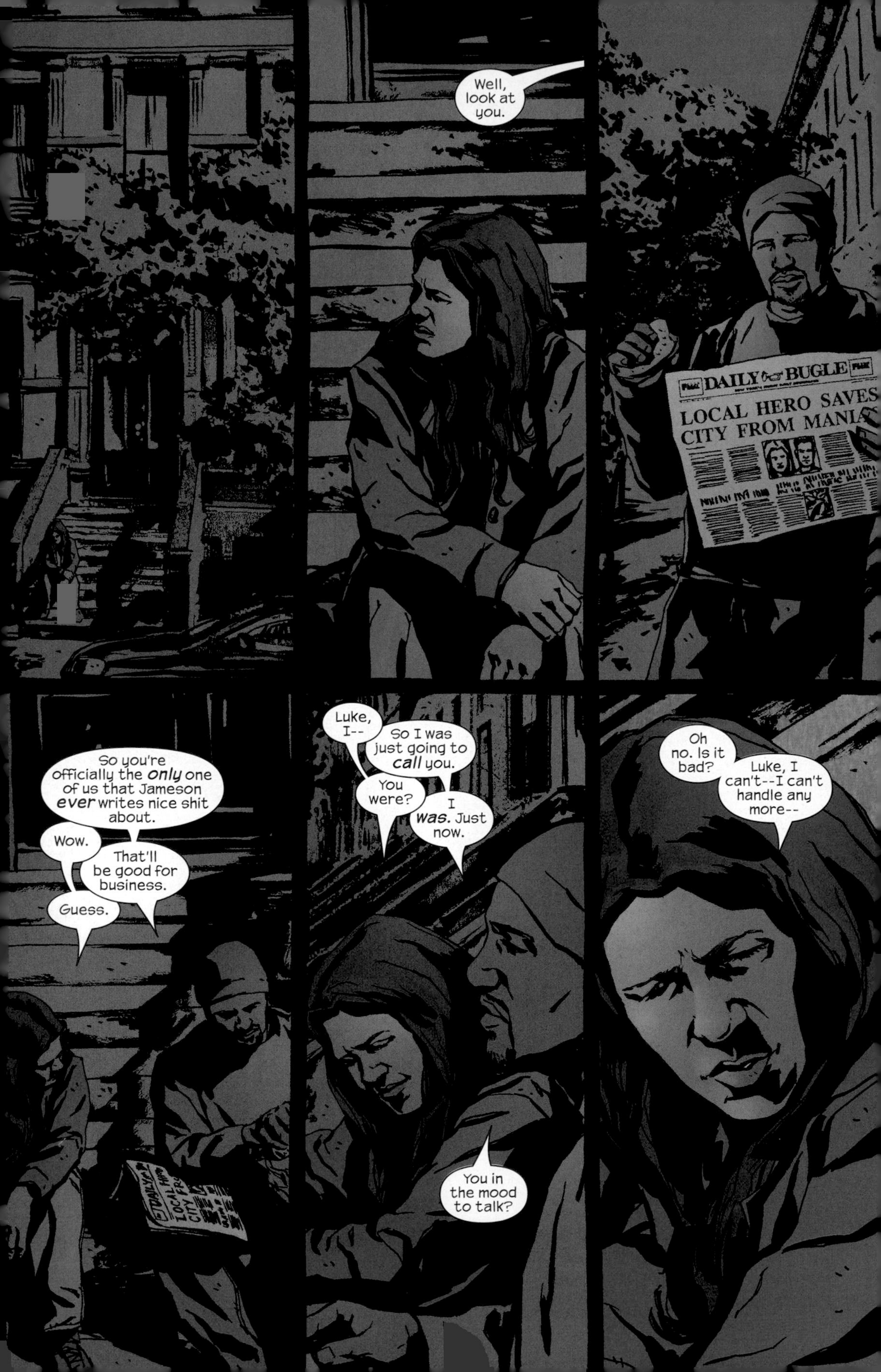
Well, look at you.
DAILY BUGLE
LOCAL HERO SAVES CITY FROM MANIA
So you're officially the only one of us that Jameson ever writes nice shit about.
Wow.
That'll be good for business.
Guess.
Luke, I--
So I was just going to call you.
You were?
I was. Just now.
You in the mood to talk?
Oh no. Is it bad?
Luke, I can't--I can't handle any more--

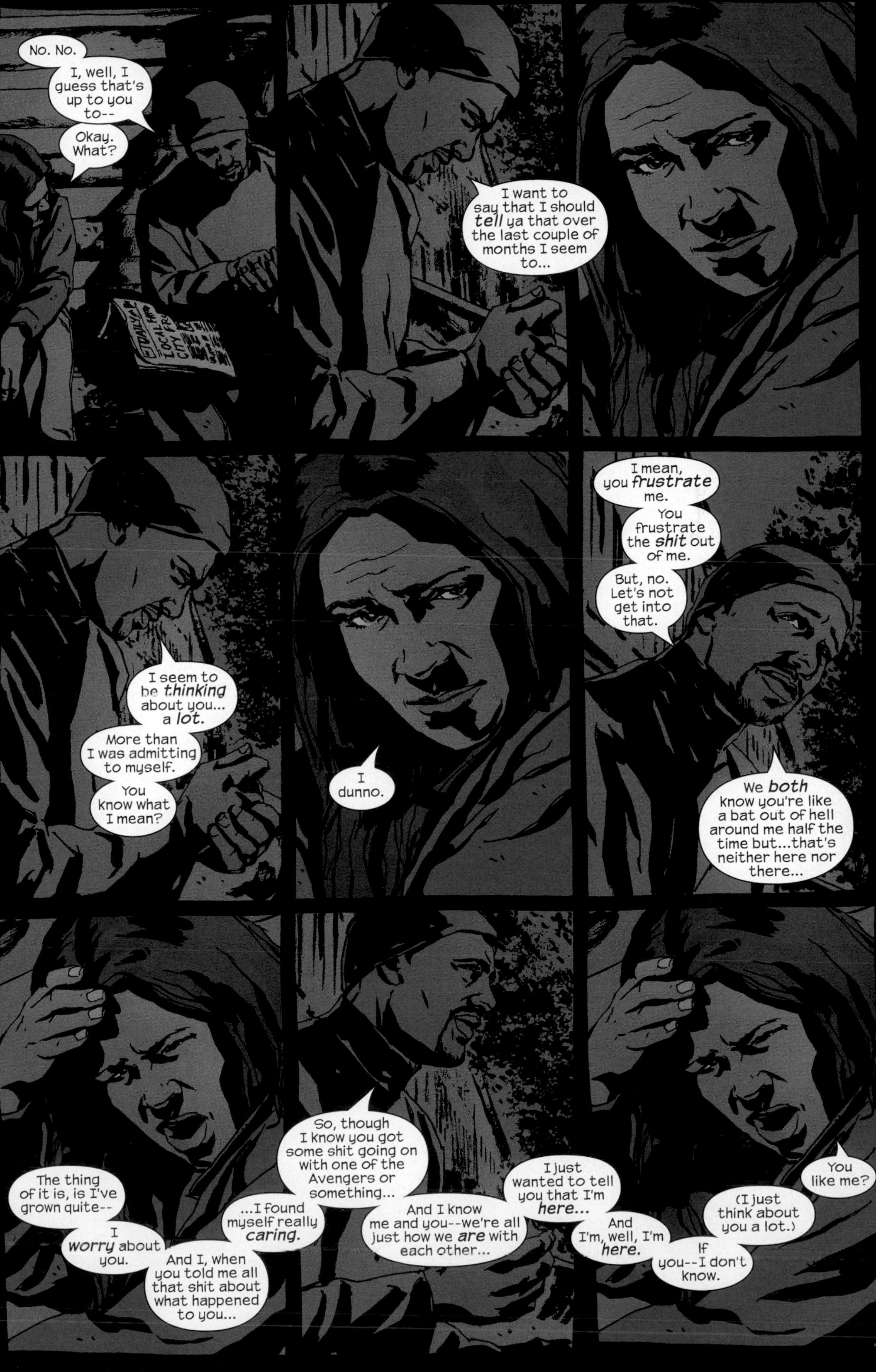
No. No.
I, well, I guess that's up to you to--
Okay. What?
I want to say that I should tell ya that over the last couple of months I seem to...
I seem to be thinking about you... a lot.
More than I was admitting to myself.
You know what I mean?
I dunno.
I mean, you frustrate me.
You frustrate the shit out of me.
But, no. Let's not get into that.
We both know you're like a bat out of hell around me half the time but...that's neither here nor there...
The thing of it is, is I've grown quite--
I worry about you.
And I, when you told me all that shit about what happened to you...
...I found myself really caring.
So, though I know you got some shit going on with one of the Avengers or something...
And I know me and you--we're all just how we are with each other...
I just wanted to tell you that I'm here...
And I'm, well, I'm here.
If you--I don't know.
(I just think about you a lot.)
You like me?

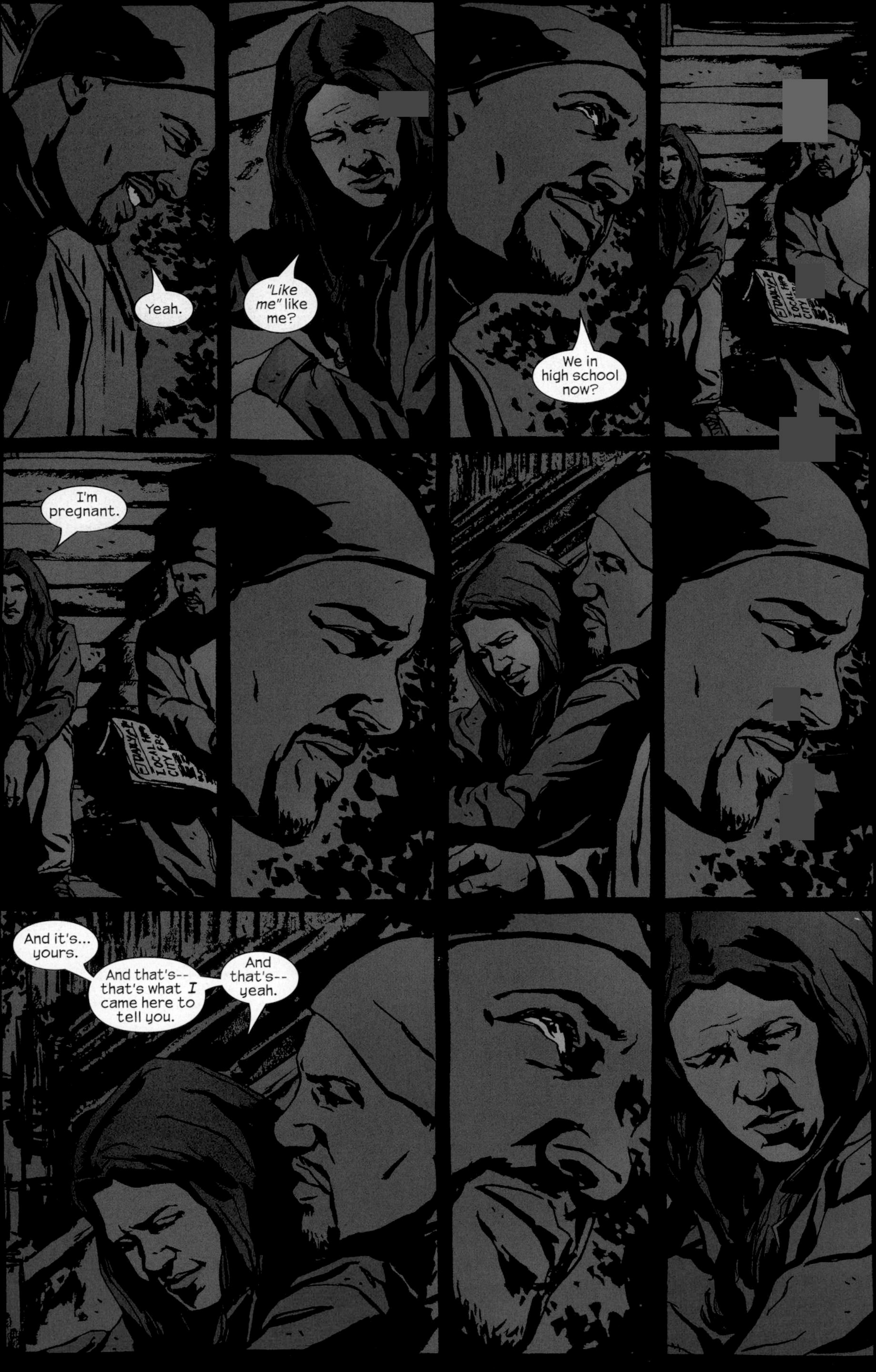
Yeah.
"Like me" like me?
We in high school now?
I'm pregnant.
And it's... yours.
And that's--that's what I came here to tell you.
And that's--yeah.

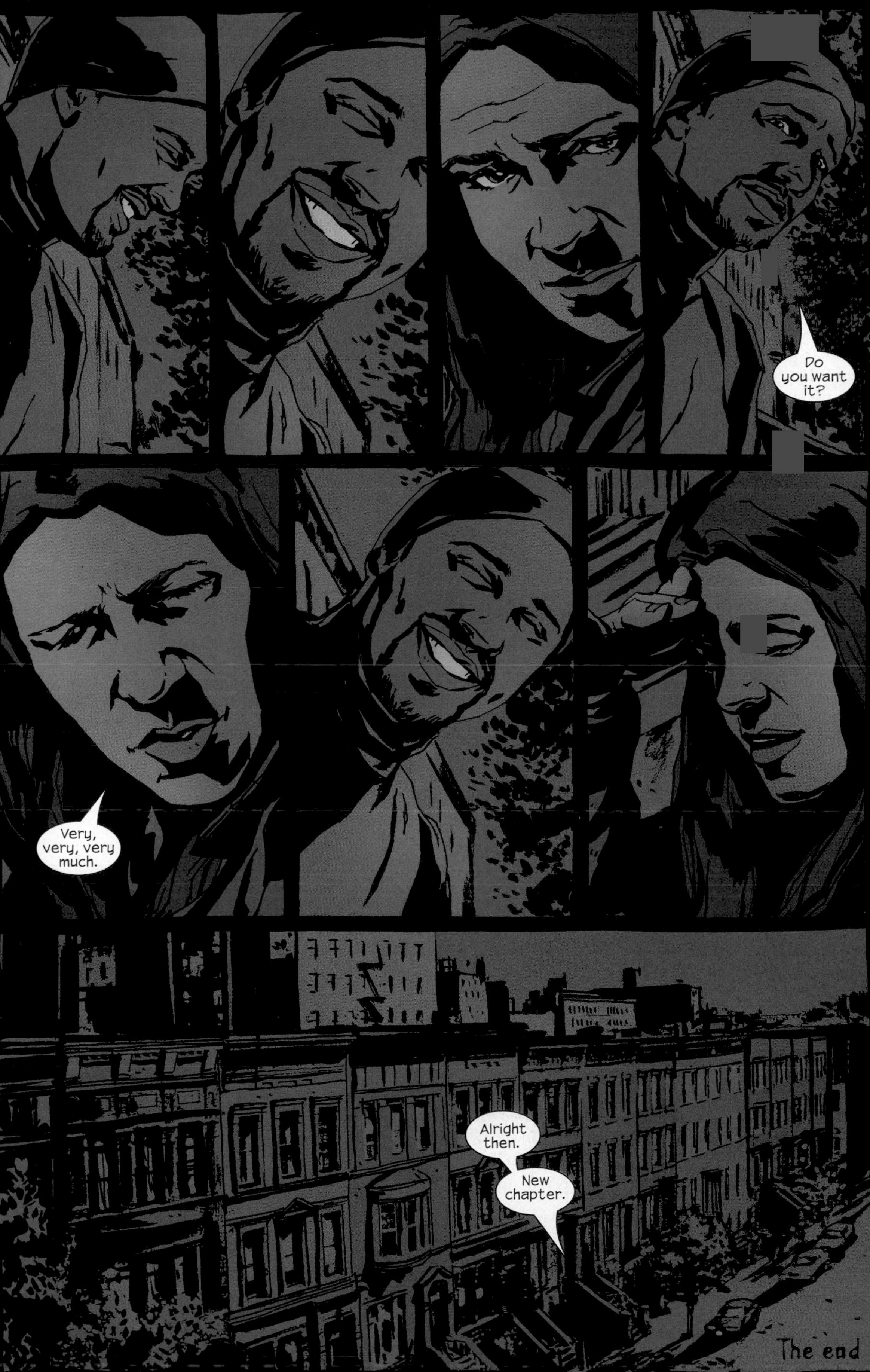

Do you want it?
Very, very, very much.
Alright then.
New chapter.
The end

BRIAN MICHAEL BENDIS'
ORIGINAL CRIME COMIC PITCH

First story arc loose outline.

(Keeping in mind the pages of the crime comic you have already read for mood and voice, here are the bigger plot points for the first arc...)

Jessica is hired by a mysterious woman to find her sister Kira. The woman doesn't want her found, she just wants to see that she is safe and not on drugs. Just proof that she is ok.

Because the woman is paying in cash, Jessica agrees even though she is wary of the vagueness of the job. Jessica calls her client's info to clarify that this is all on the up-and-up. Using the usual investigator sources, Jessica easily finds this woman who doesn't want to be found.

Jessica stakes out Kira's apartment and videotapes Kira coming home with a handsome, hunky blond gentleman. She catches a little hanky-panky on video. All typical stuff.

All of a sudden the blond man is called away. He kisses Kira goodbye. Jessica muses to herself, he's either a doctor or he's cheating on her or with her.

Jessica is surprised to find that the blond man doesn't leave the apartment through the front door that he came in.

Just by happenstance she holds the camera up to the roof of the apartment building and she clearly videotapes Steve Rogers putting on his Captain America costume and leaping to another building.

Jessica shits in her pants. Jessica has videotape of Captain America's secret identity.

End of the first issue.

Jessica doesn't know if it's a coincidence or not. But she knows that the tape is a political nuclear bomb.

Jessica calls the woman who hired her, the phone's disconnected. Jessica goes to the address she gave, it is a Gap store.

Now Jessica feels set up.

She goes straight to Avenger's Mansion. No one answers.
She goes back to the woman Kira's apartment. It's a crime scene, cop cars, ambulances. A crowd of onlookers. The woman has been brutally murdered.

Jessica goes back to her office to get the tape. And NYPD detectives are there.

They had an anonymous tip that Jessica was staking out Kira's house. Jessica lies and says that isn't true. The detectives pull out a crime scene photo. The police photographer always shoots the crowd in case the killer is hanging around. And of course...there is Jessica.

At least Jessica doesn't have to worry if she's been set up.

End of issue two.

Police station. Jessica is interrogated by the police. They have no motive but she has no alibi. Someone strong broke the woman in half with their bare hands. It's an intense interrogation where the cops fill us in on how Jessica got to New York and what's going on with her powers.

Jessica with her ill temper and violent tendencies is looking pretty guilty.

Just as the interrogation is coming to a head...in comes Matt Murdock! He tells the cops to charge her or let her go. They let her go, they have nothing substantial.

Outside Matt tells her that Luke Cage retained his services for her. Matt asks her point blank if she killed the girl. Jessica says no. Matt, of course, believes her because he knows her heartbeat and tells her he will fix this but not to leave town.

Jessica goes after the woman who hired her. She pulls strings. She bribes people. But she finds out that the phone line was paid for by the committee to elect the Republican presidential candidate.

End of the issue.

Washington, DC. Jessica finally finds the woman who set her up.

This leads her on a cat and mouse chase that eventually gives Jessica the answer she was looking for.

Jessica was being used as an unknowing pawn in a conspiracy to not only 'out' Captain America but to embroil him in ugly scandal.

Jessica being down on her luck and not super-hero friendly would either sell the tape or give it up to the cops to save her ass. They used Jessica so it wouldn't seem political. Just a scandal that happened.

Cap is an important part of the President's political good will with the people. A well-timed scandal would shift the power of a new Congress and even the Presidency over to the right. But the saboteur misread Jessica. They did not count of Jessica's surprising amount of quiet selflessness.

The twist is that it is a wash.

Jessica can't rat out the conspirators without outing Captain America, BUT they don't get their scandal. The murder is never solved. Jessica isn't charged.

They don't have any evidence and Matt Murdock's reputation actually gets the DA's office to back down. But Jessica is tainted in the cops' eyes. They think she did it. But Jessica never buckles.

The President is reelected.
The story arc ends with a surprise visit from Steve Rogers!

He has friends in high places and knows he dodged a bullet because of her. Surprisingly, Steve's presence makes Jessica very emotional. The first time we see her with her walls down. She confesses how devastating it is that her powers failed her and that she was never the hero she always hoped she would be. Not like him.

Steve Rogers confesses how empty his life feels when something like this can almost happen to him. But, it's the moments that count. And that she now has one.

She gives him the tape.

(Though the story sounds more political than hard-boiled, it isn't. Don't be fooled. Think of the older noirs. Many had to do with nuclear devices and wartime espoinage. It's always more fascinating when a murder opens a door of huge consequence. Also, we get to examine the idea of Captain America in darker terms, but we never really see him.)

Upcoming.

Next story arc: A missing persons case reveals that a low rent Fantastic Four villain (to be announced) has become a Dr. Swango type serial killer.

A black magic case with a cameo by Dr. Strange.

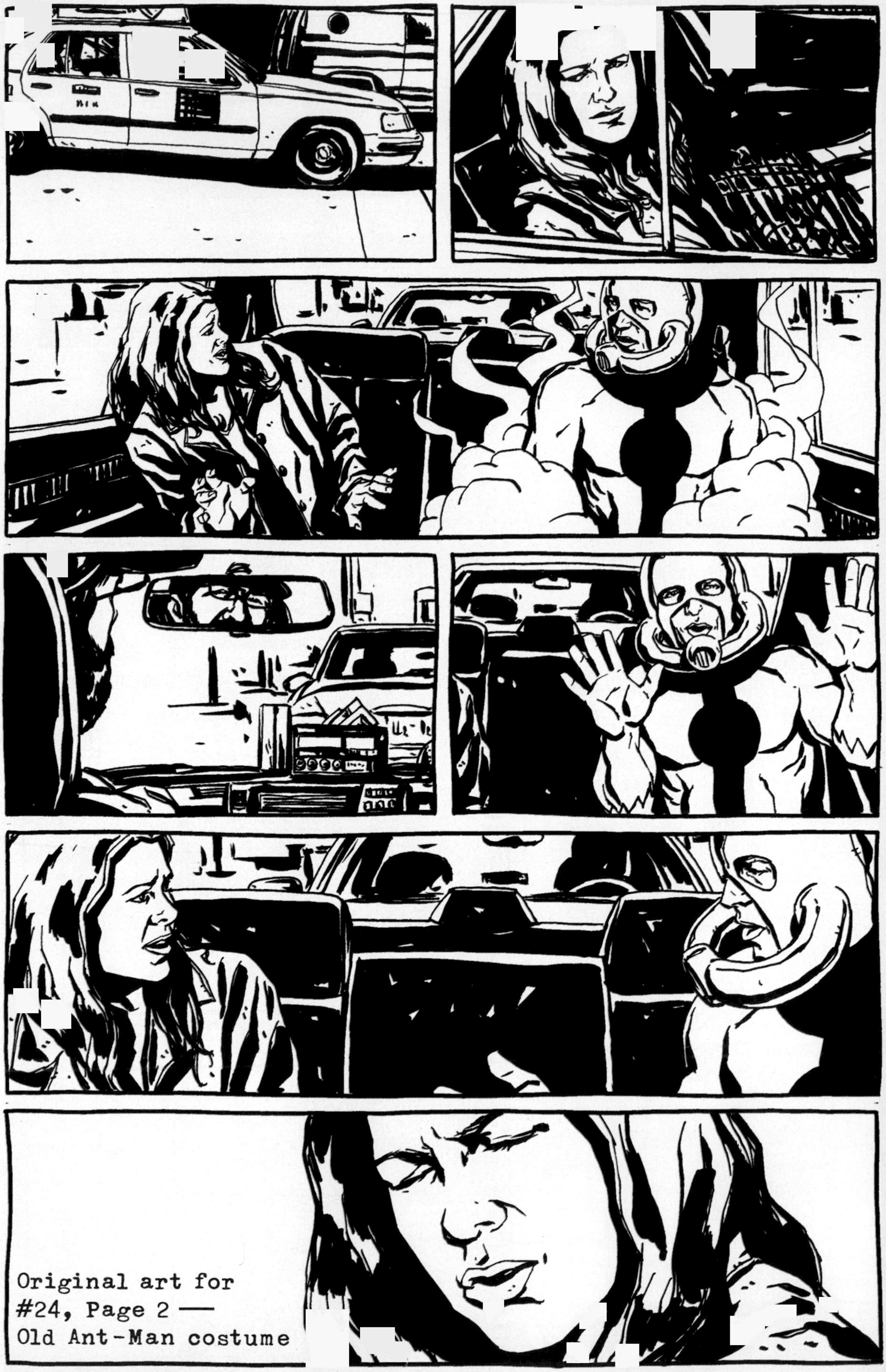

Original art for
#24, Page 2 —
Old Ant-Man costume

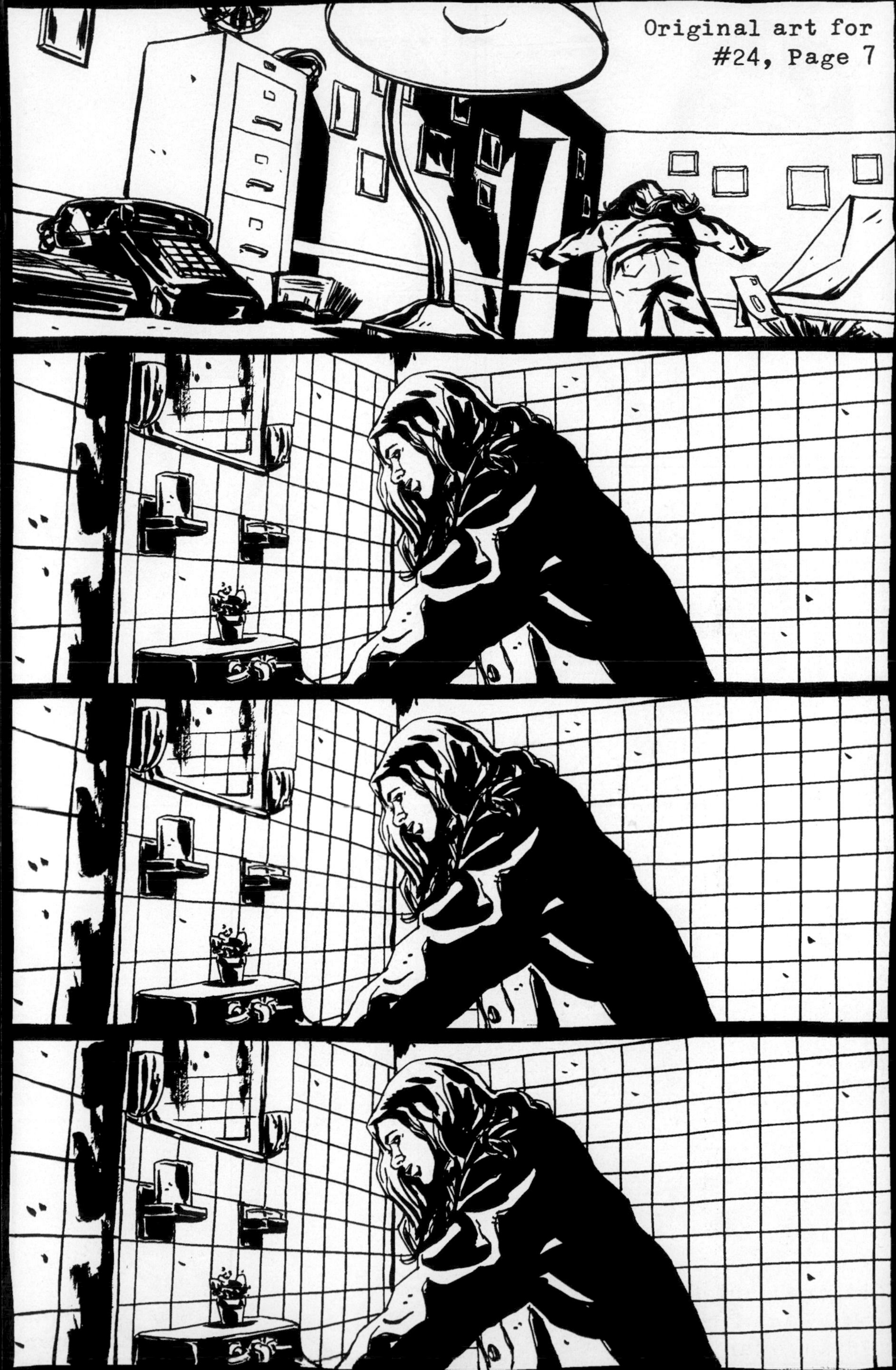
Original art for
#24, Page 7

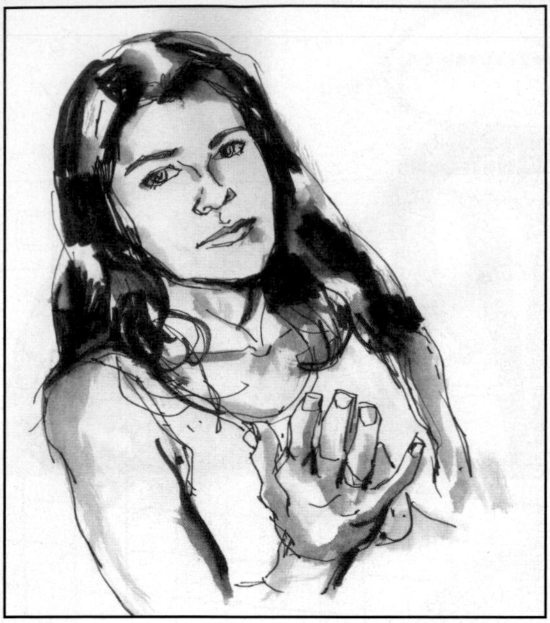
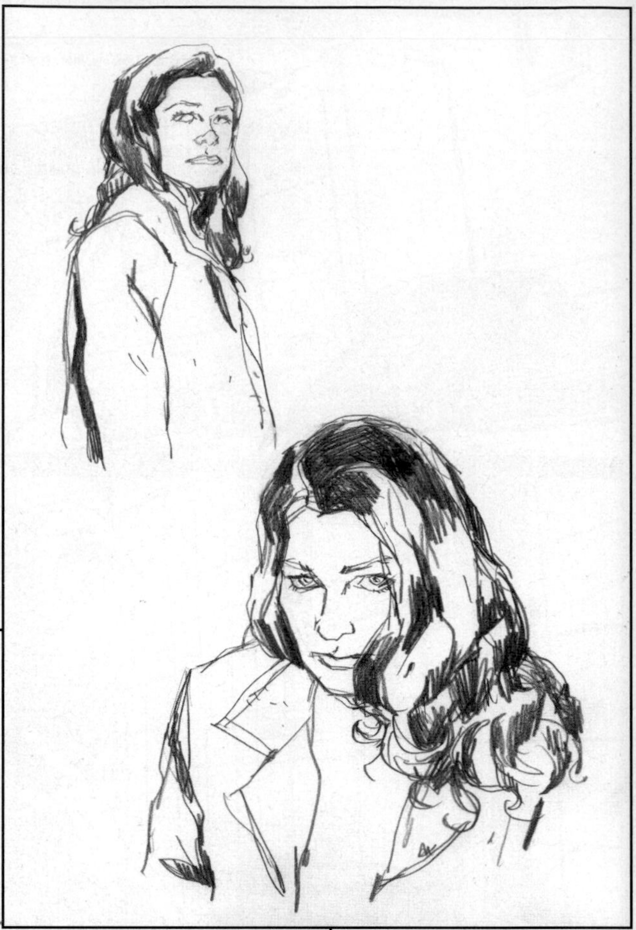
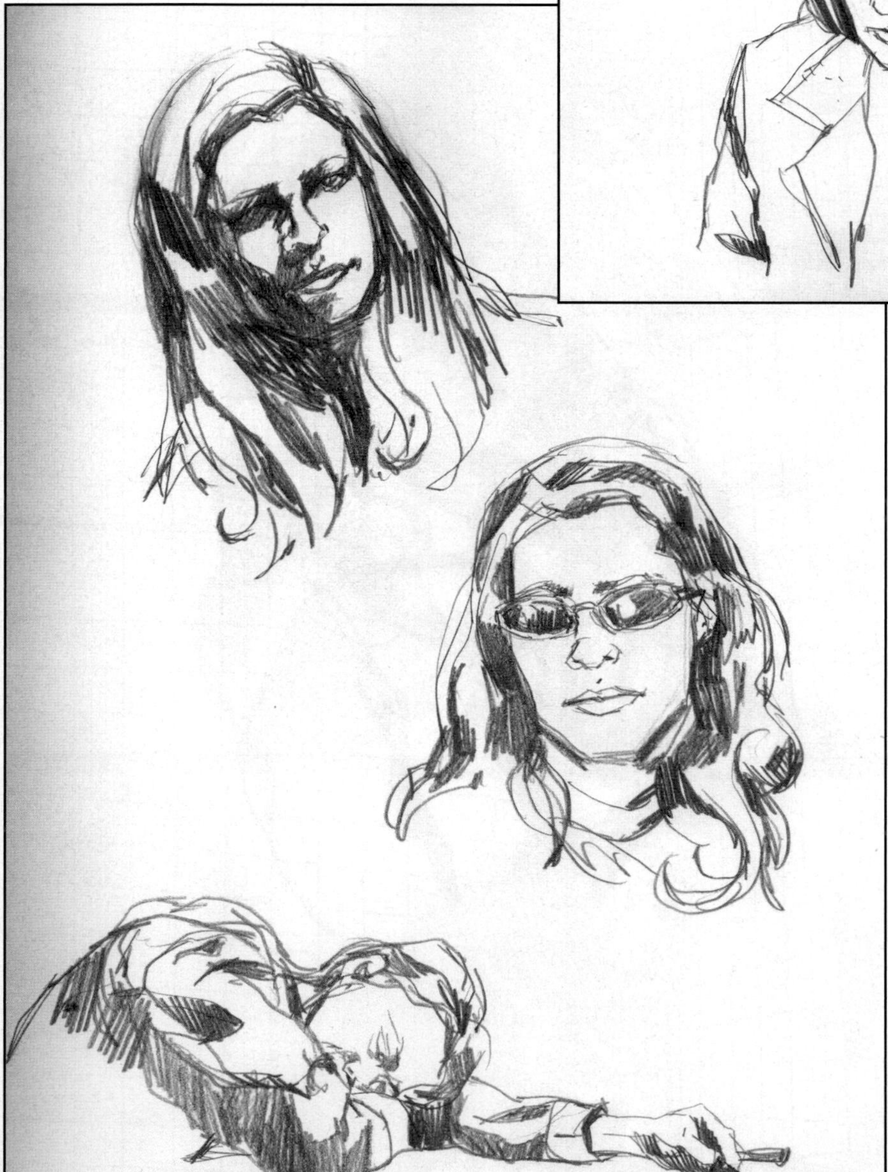

Jessica Jones
sketches by
Michael Gaydos

Brian Michael Bendis' Farewell to Alias
(originally printed in Alias #28)

This is the last issue of Alias? It's over!

That's it? What the fuck?

Yeah, this is the last issue of *Alias*. And it's all my fault.

I wrote #28, which you just read, and I was like, "Uh, I think I just wrapped up the series," but having read it, as you just have, you know that we peaked. The point of the book has been examined, revealed, explained and dealt with in what I would call a satisfactory way. And we never "jumped the shark."

But I, like you, am far from done with Jessica.

What happened was — I let Joe Quesada, the man who keeps the staples from falling out of the books, know that I thought *Alias* might be done. He said Marvel was toying with the idea of a CSI in the Marvel Universe kind of book and that maybe I could take Jessica, who everybody already likes, and create something that worked all these ideas together.

Very inspiring words.

Then, if I did that, it wouldn't need to be Max anymore. Though I like saying 'fuck' a lot, some might say too fucking much, the big eff word was stifling a couple of things I wanted to do with Jessica — like using Spider-man and some other big name Marvel guest stars.

See, we can't have the kids picking up an issue of *Alias* looking for Wolverine and getting a mouth full of my potty, we shouldn't. But still, I have these story ideas. So...

Alias is called *The Pulse* now. *The Pulse.* It's a brand new, ongoing marvel comic starting this February.

The Pulse is a Daily Bugle-focused series. It will center on a section of the paper that will cover superhuman happenings — it's the mysteries of the Marvel universe revealed.

Jonah will hire Jessica Jones in a kind of 'first look' deal. He gets first crack at

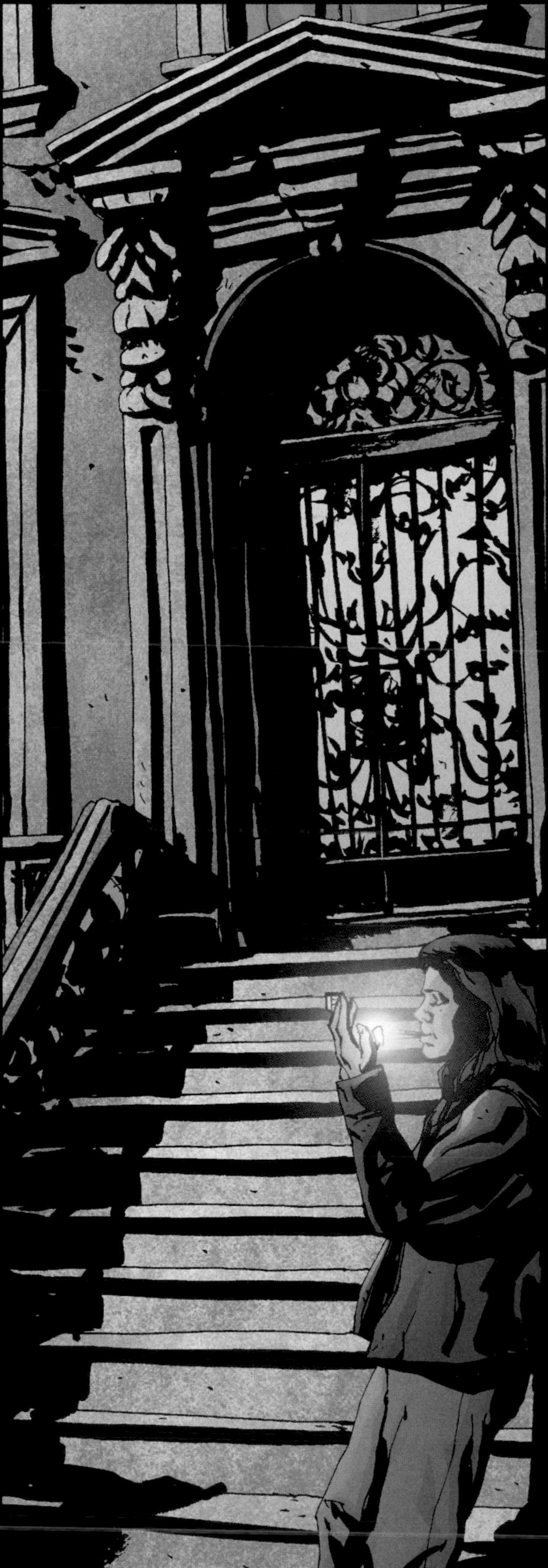

her p.o.v. of the world and Ben Urich, one of my all-time favorite Marvel characters ever, will be her writer.

Plus, Jessica is pregnant now and Luke and Jessica will deal with the complicated aspects of bringing a child into the world of heroes and villains. Jessica's life is different now and the book will reflect that.

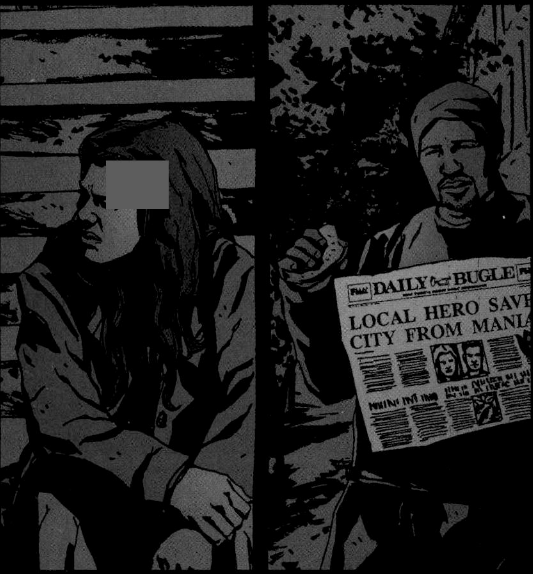
DAILY BUGLE

Worried about the tone of the book now that it is no longer Max? Well don't. Readers of *Daredevil* know that it can be adult and gritty without using the F-word. And sex was never the motivation of Alias; I just wanted to be able to express sex as an adult fully if I wanted to. The stories of this series will be focused on bigger issues but the characters that you love in Alias will be all there in full glory in The Pulse — except Jessica will be happier at least for a couple of pages.

But I tell ya, honest to god, if all I ever got to do in this whacked out business was write Alias for these 28 issues I would have had an amazing fulfilling career. This was an honor and a privilege. I shit you not.

I would like to thank many people for the success of this book. Michael Gaydos is a genius of subtlety and expression and I thank him for his unflinching line work. Not too many people know that Mike and I went to art school together, where he mopped the floor with me every day I went there. But now I have gotten him back by making him draw three years of talking heads.

Matt Hollingsworth was one of my favorite colorists before we started working on *Alias* and *Daredevil*. Working with him and trying to guess how his mind will interpret the scenes has been thrilling.

Thank you to Cory Petit, Nanci Dakesian, Stuart Moore, Tom Brevoort, CB Cebulski, Nick Lowe, Joe Quesada, Rick Mays, Mark Bagley, Bill Sienkiewicz, Howard Chaykin, Ralph Macchio and Andy Schmidt who brought this puppy home.

But most of all I think I want to thank Bill Jemas. Bill Jemas read an eleven page one act play that I wrote that was pretty much the first half of issue one, he read it and literally put the Max line into gear the next day.

His words were: "Why can't we publish this, we should be able to publish this." There's a lot of things Bill will be remembered for in comics, I hope that this is one of them.

But speaking of Mark Bagley, Mike Gaydos couldn't make the schedule to launch *The Pulse* with me because he is finishing up a huge graphic novel called *Heaven's War*, and hopefully he will be back with us as soon as he can. So guess who I wrangled in to draw the first arc of *The Pulse*? Well, it's the award-winning maniac with a pencil, Mark Bagley, my co-conspirator on *Ultimate Spider-Man*.

A lot of people, including myself, think that Bagley and I bring out the best in each other. I am so happy he agreed to try this with me.

So if you liked *Alias* you'll love *The Pulse*, if you like *Ultimate Spider-Man* you'll love *The Pulse*, and if you like ads for Hulk underoos, you will love *The Pulse*. I hope you join us for the next big chapter in Jessica Jones' life and the newest look at what makes the Marvel Universe tick.

And one more time for posterity.... FUCK!

Bendis!